Complexity Leadership

Part I: Conceptual Foundations

a volume in
Leadership Horizons

Series Editor:
Mary Uhl-Bien
University of Nebraska-Lincoln

Leadership Horizons

Mary Uhl-Bien, Series Editor

Complexity Leadership

Part I: Conceptual Foundations

edited by

Mary Uhl-Bien
University of Nebraska-Lincoln

and

Russ Marion
Clemson University

Information Age Publishing, Inc.
Charlotte, North Carolina • www.infoagepub.com

Library of Congress Cataloging-in-Publication Data

Complexity leadership / edited by Mary Uhl-Bien and Russ Marion.
    p. cm. — (Leadership horizons)
  Includes bibliographical references.
  ISBN 978-1-59311-795-5 (pbk.) — ISBN 978-1-59311-796-2 (hardcover)
1. Leadership. 2. Management. 3. Complex organizations. 4. Organizational change.
I. Uhl-Bien, Mary. II. Marion, Russ.
  HD57.7.C652 2008
  658.4'092—dc22

                                                                    2007041242

  ISBN 13: 978-1-59311-795-5 (pbk.)
  ISBN 13: 978-1-59311-796-2 (hardcover)

Cover Art:
Dream 202.85686, by Chris Ursitti, Scott Draves, and the Electric Sheep.

Printed in the United States of America

CONTENTS

VOLUME INTRODUCTION

Mary Uhl-Bien

With this fifth volume in the *Leadership Horizons* series we truly venture into new horizons with the exploration of complexity science and its applications to leadership. Complexity science moves us away from bureaucratic notions of control and predictability to a view of leadership in complex, adaptive, nonlinear feedback networks. It makes us think about leadership not as top-down influence of individuals in managerial roles but, rather, an emergent, interactive process embedded in context and history.

This volume is Part I in a two-part series. The first volume establishes conceptual foundations and tackles the tough issues of considering how complexity science changes the way we think about the study and practice of leadership. It will be followed by a second volume focused on methodological issues and examples of empirical findings and different types of empirical applications appropriate to complexity leadership.

We hope you enjoy this journey into the new world of leadership and complexity!

Complexity Leadership, Part I: Conceptual Foundations
pp. vii

ACKNOWLEDGMENTS

Mary Uhl-Bien and Russ Marion

This book emanates from two workshops on complexity and leadership held in 2005—the first in May at the Center for Creative Leadership in Greensboro, NC, and the second in November at George Washington University. These workshops brought together top scholars from leadership and from the complexity sciences to explore the potential and prospects for incorporating complexity theory into leadership research and practice. The workshops were a critical factor in being able to produce this book, and as such, we are grateful to those who provided financial and intellectual support. In particular, we gratefully acknowledge financial support from the Center for Creative Leadership, George Washington University Executive Leadership Program, University of Central Florida College of Business, Clemson University College of Education, and the Institute for Leadership Research at Texas Tech University. We also acknowledge Ellen Van Velsor (Center Creative Leadership), Margaret Gorman (George Washington University Executive Leadership Program), Dean Thomas Keon (University of Central Florida), Dean Larry Allen (Clemson University), Jerry Hunt (Texas Tech University), and Jim Hazy (Adelphi University), for their support and efforts to make these workshops a reality.

Complexity Leadership, Part I: Conceptual Foundations
pp. ix–x
Copyright © 2008 by Information Age Publishing

We are also indebted to Paul Hanges (University of Maryland) who was involved in the early stages of conception for this book and in the planning of the second leadership and complexity workshop at George Washington University. Paul provided insight into how this book should be designed, as well as coordinated the submission of several of the chapters that appear in this volume.

Finally, we would like to extend our sincere gratitude to all who attended the workshops, with a special thanks to Paul Cilliers (University of Stellenbosch) who made the long trek from South Africa to the United States twice in 1 year to share with us his extensive expertise in complexity science and complex systems. The contributions and combined insights of the many participants tremendously influenced our thinking and helped us see that our vision of a field of complexity leadership was both worthwhile and attainable.

INTRODUCTION

Complexity Leadership—A Framework for Leadership in the Twenty-First Century

Mary Uhl-Bien and Russ Marion

ABSTRACT

In this introductory chapter we set the framework for the book. We begin with a description of swarm theory (a variation of complexity theory) and briefly describe its implications for human systems. We then introduce the chapters included in the book and describe how they relate to the theme.

In a recent article on swarm behavior in *National Geographic*, Peter Miller (2007) described all manner of organized and very smart behavior that occurs in nature without benefit of centralized coordination: no manager/leader, no plan—nothing but individually dumb but collectively intelligent agents acting as if moved by Adam Smith's "hand of God." Birds, fish, gazelles, and water buffaloes swarm, instantaneously moving in sync as if they were a single unit. When threatened by predators, the swarm moves away from the danger even though many individual agents do not

Complexity Leadership, Part I: Conceptual Foundations
pp. xi–xxiv

see the threat and do not know why they are fleeing. The endangered edge of the swarm frays like a torn cloth, making it difficult for prey to choose a target. All this occurs *without* a coordinating manager.

Thousands of ants, Miller continues, can diversify their collective behaviors to best meet the exigencies of the moment (foraging when food is available, maintenance when the nest is damaged, etc.). They do so in response to simple, bottom-up communication behaviors. Bee swarms can quickly and efficiently choose the best nesting site from among several choices using similar mechanisms without a general to make intelligent choices.

These behaviors represent "collective intelligence," a core concept of complexity theory—the study of "the behaviour of large collections of ... simple, interacting units, endowed with the potential to evolve with time" (Coveney, 2003, p. 1058)—and a key underlying theme and driving principle for this book. As described in complexity theory, swarms of ants and bees engage in intelligent acts because agents in the collective act on local conditions and these individual acts interact within a complex, dynamic network of adaptive agents. Agents present a diversity of options to the whole, there is free competition among ideas, and there are effective mechanisms for narrowing choices (Miller, 2007). Individual bees, for example, will find different solutions to collective needs (food, new habitats, etc.) and will represent that solution to the collective; but the best solution attracts scouts more quickly, and those scouts beat others back to the hive where the choice is communicated to others. Inevitably, the best of the options is chosen by the colony, even though no one bee grasps the whole picture. The choice is accomplished because there is free competition among ideas and there are effective mechanisms for narrowing choices. That is, there is collective intelligence because of the actions of *complexity dynamics*.

Complexity dynamics represent a new way of thinking for leadership theory. Swarm theory would seem to suggest that complexity finds leadership unimportant, but human systems are quite a bit different than ant colonies—humans are intelligent, volitional, capable of anticipating, and so on. Leadership offers a competitive advantage to human systems, one that is not needed in ant colonies. The question we pose, then, is: Can human organizations take advantage of the swarm, or complex dynamic, phenomenon? If so, then what does that mean for leadership?

This book explores complexity dynamics in the context of organizations. More specifically, it explores leadership within and of complex adaptive systems (CAS) in the context of organizational hierarchies. A number of scholars have argued that the human equivalent of swarm behavior produces adaptive outcomes. Bonabeau and Meyer (2001), for example, have developed swarm-like strategies for making the package delivery industry more efficient. Plowman et al. (2007) describe how the collective intelligence of church members in a failing inner-city church enabled that church to adapt and survive. Chiles, Meyer, and Hench (2004) used complexity theory to empirically describe how the Branson, Missouri musical industry emerged and expanded over 100 years. Thomas Seely, chair of Cornell University's biology department and swarm researcher, reported in the National Geographic article on swarm theory that he organizes faculty meetings so that participants can (like the bees and ants he studies) freely offer diverse, alternative solutions to problems and vote to narrow choices (Miller, 2007).

LEADERSHIP IN COMPLEX SYSTEMS

So what is the function of leadership relative to complexity dynamics and collective intelligence? Humans systems, of course, differ from bees and ant colonies in that they are capable of intelligent, deliberate decision-making, so the complexity dynamic is more sophisticated in human systems. There are agents within the human swarm that can see larger chunks of the big picture than can agents in an insect swarm. Even so, we believe that swarm technology (or more generally, complexity theory, the umbrella within which swarms are described) can inform effective behavior and leadership in modern organizations.

In fact, we believe that exploring alternatives—such as complexity theory—to traditional thinking dominated by Industrial Age models is imperative for leadership researchers and practitioners: The problems with which human organizations deal are simply too complex to be effectively coordinated by top down managers. Managers and leaders are just as incapable of coordinating the complexities of human environments as queen bees are of bee environments.

Despite this, humans are predisposed (whether by cultural history or genetic structure) to want to suppress this swarm dynamic in their midst, to try to centralize and control the behaviors of the collective. This is most evident in bureaucratic hierarchies—the predominant structures in which leadership theory and practice have been examined in the past. In this book, we propose that we should *enable* collective intelligence and informal dynamics in human organizations rather than suppress them. Complexity dynamics, and their emergent outcomes (e.g., adaptability, innovation, learning), are crucial for success in the highly complex world of the twenty-first century. As described by Dess and Picken (2000):

> The demands of the changing [twenty-first century] environment present a complex set of challenges—and require a shift in focus and emphasis—for

organizational leaders. The traditional tools and techniques of management are designed, in large measure, to ensure organizational stability, operational efficiency, and predictable performance. Formal planning processes, centralized decision-making, hierarchical organization structures, standardized procedures, and numbers-oriented control systems are still the rule in most organizations. As important as these structures and processes are to organizational efficiency, they tend to limit flexibility and create impediments to innovation, creativity, and change. To meet the challenge, organizational leaders must "loosen up" the organization—stimulating innovation, creativity, and responsiveness, and learn to manage continuous adaptation to change—without losing strategic focus or spinning out of control. (p. 19)

But how do we, as Dess and Picken describe, "loosen up" the organization (e.g., enable collective intelligence) without "losing focus" or "spinning out of control"? This is a core question of this book, and is examined in various ways throughout the chapters.

OVERVIEW OF CHAPTERS

The book begins with two chapters that outline the basic premises of complexity theory. These chapters serve to help leadership scholars understand the value of complexity principles for leadership thinking, visualize possibilities for richer research models in leadership studies, and offer improved leadership strategies for organizations.

In the first chapter, Russ Marion provides a primer on complexity theory. He describes what makes complexity theory unique and interesting, briefly overviews the complexity theory paradigm, and then identifies major issues in leadership to which complexity thinking can be profitably applied. Marion proposes that complexity theory is unique in three ways: Complexity dynamics are capable of spontaneously generating new structure without inputs from external agents; they create order by dissipating energy rather than accumulating it; and they generate largely unpredictable outcomes because they are driven by random behaviors and complex interactions. He describes the interactive, dynamic, and adaptive nature of complexity and proposes that behind the "black box" of complexity dynamics lie mechanisms, or "universally available, emergent patterns of behavior that enable a dynamic mix of variables (agents) and causal chains." Marion then offers two roles for leadership: to enable the conditions in which complex mechanisms can emerge, and to prepare organizations to "respond quickly and effectively to unanticipated conditions (both destructive and beneficial)."

In the second chapter, Jeff Goldstein outlines nine major fields that make up complexity theory. These fields and their primary foci of study include systems thinking (boundaries and negative feedback loops), theoretical biology (organizations as organic, evolving, whole systems), nonlinear dynamical systems theory (attractors, bifurcation, chaos), graph theory (connectivity and networks), phase transitions, synergetics, and far-from-equilibrium (emergence of novel order), and complex adaptive systems theory (evolving, adaptive systems of interacting agents). Goldstein does an excellent job of providing a "layman's" view of complexity in a manner that is understandable and accessible to the reader, boiling a large body of scientific work down into a concise and manageable treatment of complexity concepts. For those new to complexity theory, this chapter is an essential foundation for beginning to think about the many concepts involved in complexity theory and how they might be applicable to the study of leadership and organization science.

The third chapter is a fascinating exploration of nonlinear dynamical systems theory in social psychology written by two experts in the field: Robin Vallacher and Andrzej Nowak. We are quite thrilled to have a contribution from Vallacher and Nowak, and believe you will learn why when you read it. The chapter tells a story of the re-emergence of the dynamical perspective in social psychology—a perspective that recognizes and captures the dynamics that lie at the heart of virtually all intrapersonal, interpersonal, and collective phenomena. For this chapter, Vallacher and Nowak adopt a particular focus on interpersonal processes because of the central role of interpersonal dynamics in leadership. They describe these processes relative to intrinsic (interpersonal) dynamics, attractors, and the modeling of social influence and interpersonal synchronization (with cellular automata and mathematical modeling).

In the process they highlight one of the most fascinating and exciting aspects of complexity theory for the study of human science—the concept of *dynamic minimalism*. Dynamical minimalism challenges the assumption in social psychology that the complexity of human thought and behavior must be reflected in the complexity of the model, with many variables and complex interactions among them required to explain the phenomenon of interest. It instead suggests that very simple elements interacting in accordance with simple rules can produce remarkably complex properties at the level of the system. As they describe, the emergence of complexity occurs when the relations among elements are nonlinear and the elements interact over time. Because of this gain in complexity, it may be possible to explain *very complex phenomena with very simple models*. Therefore, the goal of dynamical minimalism is to identify the simplest, yet realistic, set of assumptions capable of producing a phenomenon of interest. The resultant theories provide simple explanations that nonetheless capture the complexity of human thought and behavior—in essence, the approach of dynamical minimalism maximizes parsimony in theory construction but does so without trivializing the phenomenon in question.

This chapter is chock full of fascinating ideas that have strong implications for leadership research. We believe it is a must read for leadership scholars looking for new ways to think about and study the nature of social dynamics relative to leadership processes. It identifies a rich body of literature from which leadership scholars can draw to better theorize and operationalize (in an empirically rigorous way) the emergent and complex nature of human interactions.

In the next four chapters we switch gears from a focus primarily on complexity to a focus on how complexity might inform thinking about leadership and organizational behavior/theory. The first two chapters take a more organizational perspective and explore issues of networks and structuration/social interaction. The second two chapters focus on leadership generally and address the question of how applying complexity principles to leadership theorizing fundamentally changes the way we think about leadership.

In chapter 4, Martin Kilduff, Craig Crossland, and Wenpin Tsai integrate complex adaptive systems approaches with network theory to explore how leadership can be understood in terms of continual opportunity creation in a networked system of emergent complexity. They address the key question: How can leadership arrange for organizational networks to change continuously, providing new opportunities for members, and avoiding the fate of stagnation? To answer this question, they first recognize a problematic omission in network research: the focus on heterogeneous networks. Applying complexity theory concepts, they recognize that network theory has overly emphasized *people* in *homogeneous* nodes whereas what it needs to explore is heterogeneous networks (in which different kinds of nodes and their relationships are studied simultaneously) and the inclusion of cross-level effects of network change and development. They point out the problem of narrowly focusing on "people" as the nodes in the organizational network without considering "technologies" and "projects" (and other entities such as routines, cognitions, ideologies, texts, and machines) as nodes as well. They explore how a new view of heterogeneous networks can be considered relative to leadership and its ability to open new "pathways" for opportunity generation, through means such as adding additional nodes, additional ties, and the rewiring of existing connections.

Overall, their chapter moves network theory away from inertial theories by offering a framework for dynamic opportunity creation in heterogeneous networks. As they say, theories of network behavior that are dynamic, instead of inertial, heterogeneous, instead of homogeneous, and path-creative, instead of path-dependent, will provide researchers with the means to better understand both the characteristics of network systems and the potential influence of individual network leaders.

Dave Schwandt (chapter 5) also takes a complex adaptive systems view, but uses it in his chapter to explore issues of social interaction and emergence in organizational systems. Consistent with Giddens' (1984) structuration theory, Schwandt considers the emergent social structure that arises from interactions and then serves as the context to shape future interactions of the agent. He links social structuring and complexity concepts with leadership behaviors to move us beyond the traditional and narrow person-role centered leadership paradigm. Schwandt provides an ambitious integration of micro- and mesoconcepts to form a strong case for the need to move to a social interaction perspective in leadership. His chapter contributes to complexity theory by bringing in the human element and to leadership theory by bringing in multilevel theorizing about the human dynamics of social interaction and structuration. Schwandts' conclusion is consistent with Vallacher and Nowak's caution to recognize that social reality is quite different from physical reality (humans are not ants, grains of sand, or neurons) and therefore we need to acknowledge the unique elements of human nature as we begin to develop complexity models in the social sciences. He makes a strong step in that direction by showing us how these varied literatures can be merged to provide a basis for actionable theory-building relative to social interaction.

Donde Plowman and Dennis Duchon (chapter 6) step back and take a more philosophical and reflective view of the field of leadership that provides readers with a clear perspective on *why* a new paradigm of complexity leadership is needed. In their chapter, they describe traditional views of leadership from the perspective of cybernetics, with its assumptions of certainty, predictability, control, and the complexity perspective as one of emergence, with a focus on uncertainty, self-organizations, nonlinearity, and the necessity of chaos for growth. They offer a detailed discussion of these two approaches to highlight their differences and basic assumptions. They then use this discussion to dispel "myths" that have predominated leadership research and practice. Overall, their chapter makes a strong "case for change" in leadership research to move to a living systems model grounded in complexity—a view they refer to as *emergent leadership.* They passionately and convincingly explain how and why we must move to an emergent leadership (complexity) perspective of leadership and ultimately change the way we think about conflict, information, teams, change, language, relationships, and fundamentally, control, if we are to seriously advance leadership research to producing more practical and useful models.

Bob Lord's chapter (chapter 7) follows Plowman and Duchon and continues the focus on leadership from the perspective of emergence. Lord identifies emergence as an alternative perspective for leadership that may be equally important to traditional models of transactional and transformational leadership, which focus on the leader as a top-down hierarchical leader. Lord recognizes that a key assumption of a complexity leadership approach is that many aspects of structure have an emergent, bottom-up quality, which means that no one person completely understands or is able to fully predict the outcome of a specific action. But this raises a question that is quite troubling to traditional leadership researchers: If leaders are not in control, how do they lead (or, as he states in his title, can leaders still lead when they don't know what to do?). This is perhaps the biggest hurdle for complexity leadership perspectives—getting leadership researchers and practitioners comfortable with the idea that leaders are *not* really in control (see also Marion & Uhl-Bien, in press; Plowman & Duchon, this volume; Stacey, 1995; Streatfield, 2001).

Lord addresses this question by describing emergence from the standpoint of biasing factors and leaders' roles in influencing these biasing factors (a term borrowed from the literature on neural networks). *Biasing factors* are general properties of the context which influence the nature of the structures that emerge from the interaction of units. As he describes, biasing factors do not directly change outputs of systems; rather, they change the functioning of the entire system by adding or subtracting a little to many interactions. In the process, biasing factors transform the higher level system that emerges. *Biases* can be thought of as changes in the thresholds for activating specific types of neurons when we are focusing on individual level cognitive processes or as changes in the threshold for social behaviors when our concern is with the interaction of people. He describes three types of biasing factors that have particular relevance to leadership: emotions, goal orientations, and identities. For leaders, then, the implication is that complexity leadership involves the creation of biases that can shape the emergence of emotions, goals, and identities. He describes the theoretical and practical implications of this realization, addressing the dynamics of individual level processes as well as interpersonal structures.

The next two chapters, the first by Mary Uhl-Bien, Russ Marion, and Bill McKelvey and the second by McKelvey (chapters 8 and 9) move beyond metaphor to begin to attempt serious theory-building in the area of complexity and leadership. They address the question raised by Dess and Picken (2000) head on: How do we loosen up the organization (foster innovation and adaptation) without letting it spin out of control? Their answer is provided in a framework they call "complexity leadership theory." Complexity leadership theory (chapter 8) is a mesolevel model that integrates complex adaptive systems (CAS) and bureaucracy: CAS provide the innovative and adaptive function ("loosening up") in organizations while *properly structured* bureaucracy keeps it from "spinning out of control" (without stifling or suppressing the adaptive dynamics). They describe these integrated structures with the term *entanglement* to reflect the fully integrated nature of formal (bureaucratic) and informal (complex) dynamics in organizations. This perspective shifts our view of leadership away from a simple view of top-down actions of those in hierarchical positions to a view of leadership as a "complex interplay of many interacting forces" (forces that represent both hierarchical and informal, emergent dynamics).

To elaborate this idea, they present three leadership functions, the first two of which are quite new to leadership research: adaptive leadership, enabling leadership, and administrative leadership. Adaptive leadership is an emergent change dynamic that emerges nonlinearly from interactions between agents. It is a dynamic rather than a person, and is labeled leadership because it is a (and arguably *the*) proximal source of change in organizations. Enabling leadership refers to actions that directly foster and maneuver adaptive leadership. It does this in multiple ways: by fostering complexity mechanisms that produce emergence and by promoting coordination between the adaptive and administrative structures (see Marion & Uhl-Bien, in press, for further discussion of enabling leadership). This concept is consistent with perspectives presented in other chapters in this book (e.g., Hazy; Lord; Plowman & Duchon; Schreiber & Carley) that reflect leadership as fostering rather than directing change. Finally, administrative leadership is the function that occurs in the bureaucracy/hierarchy. It works to plan, coordinate, and organize the structure within which CAS evolve, protect the creative/adaptive dynamic, create strategy that includes adaptive organizational flexibility, and provide resources (among other things; again, see Marion & Uhl-Bien, in press, for further description of the role of administrative leadership in complexity leadership theory). This chapter (a reprint from the August, 2007 issue of *The Leadership Quarterly*) will serve as a basis for further theorizing about how the leadership functions and complex mechanisms interact together to generate productive (or unproductive) outcomes for the firm.

McKelvey (chapter 9) builds on the ideas in chapter 8 but takes a deeper dive into the issue of complexity leadership and collective intelligence. McKelvey focuses on leadership at the top of the organization and its role in fostering "distributed intelligence" throughout the organization. Consistent with the others authors in this book, McKelvey addresses the fundamentally different nature of a complexity approach to leadership, but this time from the standpoint of the need to move beyond our infatuation with "heroic" leadership. McKelvey, a leading scholar on the topic of complexity, draws from his expertise on complexity concepts to provide a detailed discussion of "a microcoevolutionary theory of the firm," addressing topics such as coevolution, distributed intelligence, emergence (versus charismatic leadership), edge of chaos and far-from-equilibrium, attractors, and the essential role of adaptive tension. He uses these concepts to lay out a theoretical and practical framework for how managers at the top of the organization can act to influence (not control) the organization to generate the kind of adaptive dynamics that are essential for fostering distributed intelligence in the firm.

In chapters 10 and 11 we switch gears once again, this time into a focus on research methods and empirical approaches. These chapters developed from the recognition that if we are to advance a theory of complexity leadership, we must find new ways to think about operationalizing studies that reflect the interactive, emergent, dynamic, and systemic nature of complexity theory.

In chapter 10, Dooley and Lichtenstein provide a true service to the field by offering an integrated research methodology for the study of leadership *dynamics*. As they state, given the importance in complexity leadership research of understanding how leadership emerges through specific interchanges—differently in every interaction—we need to develop methodologies for identifying and measuring these complex and temporally based leadership dynamics. Their framework recognizes three differing scales of time—micro, meso, and macro—and how these interact to create what Koehler (2001) has termed, "fractal time ecology." Three specific research methods they present for studying leadership interaction at these three different time scales are:

- Microscale interactions can be studied with real-time observation techniques,
- Mesoscale interactions across days and weeks can be studied using social network analysis, and
- Macroscale interactions across weeks, months, and even longer can be studied using event history analysis.

Using an example from The Software Factory at Arizona State University that helps illustrate the use of these techniques, they show us how we can go beyond the traditional method of collecting data in one-time cross-sectional surveys to methods that capture the subtle dynamics of "leadership-within-interactions." We can do this by (a) conducting studies that are longitudinal and multilevel, (b) collecting data that are rich and multifaceted enough to capture the subtlety of the patterns in the system, and (c) using analyses that are abstract enough to see those patterns above the "trees" and branches and leaves and weeds of data. In such a way, they believe we "will make strong headway in developing a new theory of leadership that goes beyond the myths of the hero or the scapegoat, and instead reflects the dynamic and emergent nature of leadership as it is enacted every day by supervisors, subordinates, and peers across all organizations."

In chapter 11, Craig Schreiber and Kathleen Carley provide a very helpful empirical analysis of complexity leadership theory as proposed by Uhl-Bien et al. in this volume (chapter 8). Dr. Carley and her colleagues at Carnegie Mellon have developed an agent based modeling program called "dynamic network analysis" (DNA), and have used this program (among other things) to analyze the structural dynamics of terrorist networks for the U.S. Department of Defense. Dr. Schreiber is a recent graduate of that program, and his dissertation examined complexity and leadership. DNA is a program in which individual agents interact according to certain rules; the program establishes initial conditions for the system (e.g., level of interdependency, knowledge, etc.) and the system enables simulated agents to interact given these conditions. Such simulations permit "what if" tests and tracks system dynamics over extended periods of time—a capability that is not available or prohibitively resource intensive if attempted with real human systems. After a given number of interactive iterations, DNA produces a final state for that system. Schreiber and Carley use the DNA program in this paper to explore the nature of leadership in complex systems.

The authors propose two types of leadership: leadership of context and leadership of process. Leadership of context "enables organizational processes that allow for adaptable collective action responses to a changing environment." Leadership of process "facilitates learning and adaptation through the emergent interactions and informal dynamics which form collective action." They examine leadership of action (which is analogous to Uhl-Bien et al.'s adaptive leadership) and look at the effect that leadership of context exerts on process outcomes. Schreiber and Carley offer two propositions: enabling leadership (from Uhl-Bien et al., this volume) promotes interactions among heterogeneous agents, and enabling leadership serves to mediate relationships between informal and formal networks thus promoting effective learning in the organization. They examined leadership data from an Army battle command group (the initial conditions) and found, among other things, that learning is maximized when enabling leaders foster relatively loose coupling, strong informal networks, and tension. These findings were consistent with predictions from Uhl-Bien et al.'s, complexity leadership theory.

Finally, with chapters 12-14 we move to practical examples and considerations. In chapter 12, Ellen Van Velsor, from the Center for Creative

Leadership (CCL), draws from her rich experiences working with practitioners to bring our attention to leadership development and how it must shift with our changing focus in leadership. Van Velsor points out that a move toward complexity means that we must shift our perspectives of leadership development from an exclusive focus on individuals in positions of authority to a broader focus on the development of leader*ship* (Day, 2000; Day & O'Connor, 2003; Van Velsor & McCauley, 2003). Interestingly, she points out that making this shift is not so simple as training individual leaders to adopt new "complexity" roles. Instead, to achieve change at a collective level, something more and different is needed: a focus on enhancing interactive dynamics in a system and the development of *connections* between individuals and between groups in an organization—an approach that CCL calls "connected leadership." In her chapter, Van Velsor defines the connected leadership approach and identifies its key components:

- The leadership development initiative is itself seen as a catalyst and a "practice field" for interdependent dynamics, creating a context for further connection and interaction across the organization;
- Senior executives play a key role as sponsors and catalysts for change—acting as "social tags" to encourage interactive dynamics, model "complexity leader" behaviors, and create support for unpredictable outcomes; and
- An action-reflection engagement process that provides multiple opportunities for enhanced interaction between both individuals and groups, demonstrates the value of distributed intelligence, and provides support for learning as an orientation in a performance-oriented culture.

She also describes the experiences they have had in using it to training leaders in accordance with complexity leadership concepts.

Hence, with this chapter, we see complexity leadership concepts already being applied to leadership practice in the context of leadership development. Through their work on connected leadership, CCL has plunged ahead into exploring the practicality of this new approach, and the chapter by Van Velsor helps us to see what we can learn from their experiences.

The final chapters by Jim Hazy offer two case studies providing practical illustrations of how adopting a complexity lens changes the way we see leadership, its nature and its outcomes. The first, an analysis of Intel's shift to microprocessors in the 1970s and 1980s provides an interesting reexamination of the Intel case from a complexity perspective—specifically, from the context of leadership mechanisms. In this chapter, Hazy pursues the question of whether the transformation was due to leadership or to luck, in essence highlighting a key contribution of complexity thinking that change in organizations is emergent (bottom-up) in contrast to traditional thinking that it is a result of top-down strategic directives and initiative. Hazy concludes from his analysis that major transformation in organizations can—and perhaps often does—occur absent strategic initiatives from organizational leaders, instead emerging from nonlinear outcomes of many system dynamics. He does not suggest that this emergent order is anarchical, however; rather, certain conditions must be present to spark productive change in organizations (and he lists what these conditions were in the Intel case). A leadership implication is that for organizations wanting or needing to change, leaders may be able to play a role in creating the conditions that foster mechanisms for adaptive organizational transformation.

In his second paper he continues the theme of how complexity changes the way we think about leadership, but this time from the perspective of how leaders influence complex system dynamics (either intentionally or unintentionally) through their "signaling" behaviors (a concept similar to Bob Lord's chapter on signaling biases). In this paper, Hazy shows how convergent, generative, and unifying leadership interacted with the complex dynamics in influencing how patterns emerged in the organization. Hazy suggests that future leadership research should consider signaling networks and complex dynamics in their analysis of organizational leadership rather than focusing only on isolated actions of individuals. With his case study, he demonstrates how richer research methods can uncover findings both unexpected and unforeseen relative to traditional leadership thinking.

In sum, the chapters in this book reexamine the conceptualization and function of leadership using a complexity frame. The chapters show several strong themes: (1) a need to consider dynamic interactions and coevolutionary forces in leadership research; (2) a movement away from individual, top-down, heroic leadership models and toward collective (distributed) intelligence and leadership emergence; (3) a focus on heterogeneous networks of interacting agents; and (4) new methods that do not rely on one-time cross-sectional surveys but rather rich data that capture the intricacies of complex leadership dynamics. The chapters include work ranging from the physical sciences of complexity to dynamical social psychology to network theory to leadership and organization science. They provide a basis for theory-building as well as empirical investigation. They are ultimately about human swarms and how to lead swarms, or complex, dynamic networks, and they establish a strong basis for the scientific development of a field of leadership called complexity leadership.

REFERENCES

Bonabeau, E., & Meyer, C. (2001). Swarm intelligence: A whole new way to think about business. *Harvard Business Review, 79*(5), 107-114.

Chiles, T., Meyer, A., & Hench, T. (2004). Organizational emergence: The origin and transformation of Branson, Missouri's musical theaters. *Organization Science, 15*(5), 499-519.

Coveney, P. (2003). *Self-organization and complexity: A new age for theory, computation and experiment.* Paper presented at the Nobel symposium on self-organization, Karolinska Institutet, Stockholm.

Day, D. V. (2000). Leadership development: A review in context. *The Leadership Quarterly, 11*(4), 581-613.

Day, D. V., & O'Connor, P. M. G. (2003). Leadership development: Understanding the process. In S. E. Murphy & R. E. Riggio (Eds.), *The future of leadership development* (pp. 11-28). Mahwah, NJ: Erlbaum.

Dess, G. G., & Picken, J. C. (2000). Changing roles: Leadership in the 21st century. *Organizational Dynamics, 28*(3), 18-34.

Giddens, A. (1984). *The constitution of society: Outline of the theory of structuration.* Berkeley: University of California Press.

Koehler, G. (2001). *A framework for visualizing the chronocomplexity.* Sacramento: California Research Bureau, and Time Structures.

Marion, R., & Uhl-Bien, M. (in press). Paradigmatic influence and leadership: The perspectives of complexity theory and bureaucracy theory. In J. K. Hazy, J. Goldstein, & B. Lichtenstein (Eds.), *Complex systems leadership theory.* New York: ISCE.

Miller, P. (2007, July). Swarm theory. *National Geographic, 212,* 126-147.

Plowman, D., Baker, L. T., Beck, T., Kulkarni, M., Solansky, S., & Travis, D. (2007). Radical change accidentally: The emergence and amplification of small change. *Academy of Management Journal, 50*(3), 515-543.

Stacey, R. D. (1995). The science of complexity: An alternative perspective for strategic change processes. *Strategic Management Journal, 16,* 477-495.

Streatfield, P. J. (2001). *The paradox of control in organizations.* London: Routledge.

Van Velsor, E., & McCauley, C. D. (2003). Our view of leadership development. In C. McCauley & E. Van Velsor (Eds.), *The Center for Creative Leadership handbook of leadership development* (pp. 1-22). San Francisco, CA: Jossey-Bass.

CHAPTER 1

COMPLEXITY THEORY FOR ORGANIZATIONS AND ORGANIZATIONAL LEADERSHIP

Russ Marion

ABSTRACT

Complexity theory offers unique perspectives of organizational behavior and of the generation of dynamic adaptability. Those perspectives challenge both reductionist and systems theory assumptions regarding change and importation of energy from the environment; it challenges reductionist-related notions of predictability, planning, and coordination. Complexity theory argues that complex organizational behavior is characterized by non-linear, emergent change; interaction and interdependency; unpredictability; autocatalytic behavior; and dynamic movement. An important role of leadership (what we call, enabling leadership) in complex systems is to enable the conditions in which complex dynamics can emerge.

We begin this book by asking, "Why complexity theory?" What is different about complexity that warrants the interest that it has garnered among

Complexity Leadership, Part I: Conceptual Foundations
pp. 1–16

1

biologists, physicists, economists, and more recently, social scientists. The short answer: It is interesting because complexity science seems to contradict much of what we once took for granted about how systems of things (people, weather patterns, etc.) work. It seemingly contradicts, for example, the science of entropy and challenges Western rationality by arguing that order is free.

So why should we, as leadership theorists, be interested in this science of emergent change? The answer, we propose, is that the organizational environment of the twenty-first century possesses drama and unpredictability, and complexity science is quite comfortable in that world. What is leadership in complex organizations and environments? While this is the subject of most of the chapters in this book, in this chapter I will briefly introduce the reader to some of the major principles of complexity theory and to how they might relate to leadership.

WHY COMPLEXITY?

The challenge in answering the first of the questions posed above (why complexity?) will be to, first, succinctly and clearly define what separates complexity theory from other ways of understanding reality, and, second, to then delve into how complex dynamics operate. However, the significance of the complexity paradigm is neither immediately apparent nor easily communicated. The problem is not that complexity is necessarily dense and impenetrable to those not trained in its intricacies; rather, the problem is that our frames of reference for understanding get in the way. We tend, for example to define our experiences in terms of variables and linear cause and effect, reductionism (or analyzing the specific on the assumption that it will reveal the whole), predictability, equilibrium, and linear evolution (Marion, 1999). We tend to assume that leadership is centered in personalities and based on authority (whether legal or ascribed by those who follow) and that leaders make decisions, solve problems, coordinate, motivate, focus effort, plan, manage conflict, influence, align effort with formal goals, and create change. Complexity theory is not grounded in such common assumptions, thus it may be difficult for some to reorient their thinking to its premises.

Complexity does not deny these realities; rather, it extends them. Just as quantum dynamics provided new lenses by which to understand Newtonian physics, complexity provides different perceptions and tools by which to understand and evaluate organizational behaviors. Like quantum physics, complexity has led to dramatic insights about entropy in physics (Prigogine, 1997) and evolution in biology (Kauffman, 1993); we propose that it holds similar promise for leadership and social dynamics.

The Uniqueness of Complexity Theory

Complexity theory is the study of the dynamic behaviors of complexly interacting, interdependent, and adaptive agents under conditions of internal and external pressure. Complexity theory makes several unique observations about those dynamics, three of which we discuss in this paper.

First, complexity researchers have found that a system of interacting agents does not require coordination or input from sources outside that system in order to create ordered behavior and structure (Goodwin, 1994; Kauffman, 1993; Turing, 1952). Traditional assumptions that outside help is required to create order is evident in biological thought, which has historically presumed that the evolution of structure is explained by inputs of food, air, and so forth, and by the influence of external agents (e.g., the competitive pressures of natural selection). A story that began in the nineteenth century illustrates: Biologists at that time found, inexplicably, that one could cut the embryo of a sea urchin in half and still obtain a full adult (actually two adults)—thus the blueprint for adulthood does not reside exclusively in the seed (remember this was before DNA). So where does the information for order come from? Mid-twentieth century systems theorists "solved" the problem by asserting that the "seed" of life only provides basic information and that the developing embryo draws additional information from its interaction with the environment (von Bertalanffy, 1956). Again, this also was *before* we understood DNA, but the point is that scientists assumed that order is shaped by external forces.

Organization theorists have adopted these premises of evolutionary selection to explain the emergence and development of structure in organizations (Hannan & Freeman, 1977). Leadership theorists, however, have not gravitated toward natural selection, largely because organizational ecology researchers question whether leadership is of much use (Lieberson & O'Connor, 1972; Salancik & Pfeffer, 1977; Weiner & Mahoney, 1981). Leadership theorists assume instead that useful outcomes require top-down coordination and intelligent planning; indeed the root structure of the word, leadership, refers to one who is in front of, showing others the way. That is, top-down leadership, like natural selection, assumes the generative power of external forces that exerts work to shape organizational outcomes.

Complexity theory does not dispute this per se, but does argues that the future of a system lies also in its patterns of internal interactions—its complex behavior. Complexity theory proposes that order is heavily influenced by auto- or self-generative forces, dynamics that are reminiscent of prescientific notions of spontaneous generation. Alan Turing (1952), for example, demonstrated how structural differentiation in living organisms (the emergence of bone and skin from the same embryonic source) can emerge from the interaction of cellular proteins—with no external coordination by chemical stimuli. Marion (1999) similarly argued that the desktop computer emerged from interactions among various technological components. Structuration and elaboration, then, do not necessarily require external help. Kauffman's (1993) notion of autocatalysis (i.e., order catalyzes itself) is based on this assertion.

Second, complexity researchers (several of whom—e.g., Ilya Progogine and Murray Gell-Mann—are Nobel Prize winners) have discovered that order can be created by dissipating—(getting rid of—)energy: by being entropic (see Haken, 1983; Prigogine, 1997)! This flies in the face of traditional assumptions (and the second law of thermodynamics) that order emerges when energy is accumulated (Buckley, 1967). Complexity theorists argue that, when systems become overly tense or destabilized, they will suddenly, and often dramatically, release that energy, and will create new, typically unexpected, order in the process. That is, explosive release can be creative—a mini big bang event. Complexity theory describes this as emergent, nonlinear change, or phase transitions (McKelvey, this volume).

Finally, complexity theory argues that the future is ultimately unknowable and that our sophisticated predictive equations may not be as useful as we think they are. God does play dice with the universe. The reason has to do with the nature of dynamic interactions and interdependency, particularly in social behavior. Relationships among systemic agents—among workers, or between leader and subordinates—are always influenced by complex interactions with other agents in the system. These interactions in turn are influenced by a random substrate that cannot be erased or properly ignored by mathematicians, statisticians, and social scientists (Marion, 1999; Marion & Uhl-Bien, 2001). This substrate is a function of such things as history, random environmental perturbations, and idiosyncratic social decision making (e.g., garbage can decision making; Cohen et al., 1972). The nature of complex interactive influences in combination with this random substrate can have a tremendous, unpredictable effect on the future of a system (e.g., Lorenz's butterfly effect; Lorenz, 1964). Thus, just as quantum science marked the end of certainty at the quantum level (Horgan, 1996), complexity marks the end of certainty in macrolevel dynamics (Prigogine, 1997). Science, therefore, must supplement its predictive equations with methodology that seeks to understand the dynamics by which interactive behavior occurs (Marion & Uhl-Bien, 2007).

Summarizing, complexity dynamics are capable of spontaneously generating new structure without inputs from external agents; they create order by dissipating energy rather than accumulating it; and they generate largely unpredictable outcomes because they are driven by random dynamics and complex interactions. These characteristics challenge common scientific assumptions and elaborate the way we understand organization.

Complexity theory's counterintuitive conclusions enable us to see different ways of knowing and practicing, and it is this lens that the authors in this book use to explore new ways to know and practice leadership.

How Complex Dynamics Operate

We now look a bit closer at the nature of complex systems and then describe the mechanisms by which change occurs in these systems. Regarding its nature, Coveney (2003) defines complexity theory as the "study of the behaviour of large collections of … simple, interacting units, endowed with the potential to evolve with time" (p. 1058). Complexity is in reality far more complex than is captured in this definition (Cilliers, 1998), but this is useful as a starting point because it captures three key characteristics of complex systems: they involve interacting units, they are dynamic (complexity is the study of changing behaviors), and they are adaptive.

Interaction.   Interaction among sentient agents is not a neutral process akin to shaking rocks together in a barrel. Interacting agents change because of interinfluence relationships, interdependent behaviors, and the emergence of subsets of agents acting interdependently with one another (emergent subgroups of all sizes and levels of embeddedness are called, *complex adaptive systems*; Langston, 1986).

Dynamic behaviors and structures that emerge from complex interactive dynamics are unrecognizable as linear combinations of the initial actors in the process. Cilliers (1998), for example, observed that complex (as opposed to complicated) systems cannot be separated into component parts because those components are dynamically changed by their interactions. Complexity theory is also not about describing the networks by which people and other agents relate to one another (i.e., social network theory; Barnes, 1954), although complexity does involve networks. Rather, *complexity theory examines the patterns of dynamic mechanisms that emerge from the adaptive interactions of many agents*.

Interactive behaviors and outcomes feed back on one another in convoluted fashion, with effects becoming causes and with influence often wielded through extended chains of effect. These networks exhibit multiple redundancies, with the same effect receiving input via multiple chains of causation (such that, were one chain interrupted, the others maintain the effect). That is, complex systems are robust. Cilliers (1998) calls this networked process *recurrency*.

Dynamic.   Second, complexity refers to a dynamic process in which things change and emerge over time. Complexity is not about static events, such as atemporal relationships among variables (relationships that are true in the past, present, and future). Complex systems do exhibit global stability and resilience, but that stability is like an outer bank seashore that is recognizable from year to year, yet different every time it is viewed—even dramatically so at times. Change, then, even unpredictable change, is a key characteristic of complex behavior.

Adaptation.   Coveney's description of complexity imposes the ability to adapt, or to make strategic changes that adjust individual or systemic responses to pressures. Adaptation occurs at two levels: individual and aggregate. Individual adaptation is "selfish," as Richard Dawkins (1976) has so eloquently argued. That is, its nature is related to local stimuli and individual preferences. But, whereas biologists argues that adaptive changes which improve an individual's viability will likely improve its ability to pass that gene to future generation, complexity theorists argue that selfish actions interact with, and adapt to, the selfish actions of other individuals. The resulting interactive adaptations and compromises simultaneously serve the locally pertinent, adaptive needs of the individuals involved *and* create adaptive capability for the aggregate as a whole.

In summary, complexity theory is about the dynamics of interaction among multiple, networked agents, and how such interactive dynamics generate emergent events (e.g., creativity, learning, adaptability). The dynamic behaviors in complex systems that accomplish these ends are called mechanisms, and we now turn to that topic.

Inside the Black Box: Mechanisms

A major key to understanding complexity lies in understanding that complex dynamics are driven by certain universal, emergent mechanisms. Mechanisms are defined broadly as processes that generate given outcomes (Hedström & Swedberg, 1998); they are what is going on in complexity's "black box" when change occurs, the dynamics that enable and foster that change. A mechanism can refer to a specific dynamic mix of variables and causal chains that explain some event. For example, medical scientists have explained the molecular mechanisms—the interactions of proteins, molecules, and invasive chemicals—that link cigarette smoking to cancer. Defined in this way, mechanisms are unique to the phenomenon observed.

Complexity theory is, of course, useful for helping understand such outcome-specific mechanisms. Theorists' more immediate interests, however, are mechanisms that are generalizable across phenomena (Uhl-Bien

& Marion, 2007), dynamic types that are likely observed in any given complex behavior. From this perspective, mechanisms are universally available, emergent patterns of behavior that enable a dynamic mix of variables (agents) and causal chains. We label these, complex mechanisms. Note that the first, more specific definition of mechanisms is subsumed within the second, which provides a framework within which particularistic mechanisms can be understood. Complexity theory, then, involves identifying and describing complex mechanisms and patterns of relationships among mechanisms—in addition to more traditional examination of variables and relationships among variables.

One of the more basic mechanisms that emerges in complex interactions is called correlation (Marion & Uhl-Bien, 2001; Poincaré, 1992; Uhl-Bien & Marion, 2007). Correlation occurs when agents interact and share a bit of their resonance (defined loosely but practically as worldviews, assumptions, preferences, etc.; individual resonances fluctuate randomly over time). Correlation fosters bonding and aggregation (a second mechanism), or the clustering of several agents based on the evolution of common or interdependent resonances. Aggregation is readily observed in clusters of cars on a highway. Importantly, aggregation occurs when agents change in part (but never wholly) to conform to a common inter-resonance structure.

Complex dynamics spawn autocatalytic mechanisms, or emergent structures and beliefs that enable certain other mechanisms or that speed their actions (Kauffman, 1993). This phenomenon has been rather widely observed in chemistry and biology. For example, tin deteriorates in cold temperatures and the process, which is called tin pest, accelerates once it begins because the dynamic autocatalyzes further deterioration. In production, the development of technology required for microcomputers was accelerated in the 1970s by the emergence of processor-based toys and calculators (Anderson, 1995; Marion, 1999). Social action is autocatalyzed by the emergence of coordinating structures, and deviant riot behavior (such as looting) is autocatalyzed by (speaking tautologically) rioting behavior.

Nonlinear emergence (a fourth mechanism) is a complexity-generated mechanism in which dynamic states suddenly shift. The sudden demise of the Soviet Union is a rather dramatic example. Nonlinear emergence is based on two causative mechanisms: self-organized criticality (Bak & Chen, 1991; Bak, Tang, & Wiesenfeld, 1989) and far-from-equilibrium dissipation (Prigogine, 1997).

Self-Organized Criticality.   Self-organized criticality refers to sudden, unexpected shifts in structure or behavior in complex, interacting systems of many agents. Agents and clusters of aggregated agents in interacting systems constantly change as they adapt to environmental conditions and to one another. Metaphorically, these changing, adapting systems move around landscapes; these landscapes have numerous pits,[1] or choices, strewn across them, and the systems (or parts of systems) shift unexpectedly when they "fall" into one of these pits. These pits represent strategies/attractors, defined in physics as a realm of behavior to which motion gravitates. The back and forth motion of a pendulum is an (noncomplex) attractor, and motion within its "basin of attraction" will gravitate toward it. Complex attractors describe stable but nonrepetitive behavior (Lorenz, 1993)—their motion is not regular like a pendulum's, but they otherwise exhibit similar characteristics.

No one has yet rigorously defined attractor pits for social systems so any example I provide will be metaphorical. For our purposes, however, we will define it as interresonant behaviors of multiple actors or ideas. A fad—multiple agents acting in concert around a common preference—would be a rather clear example, as would institutional behaviors (DiMaggio & Powell, 1991) or clusters of interacting cars speeding down a highway. Self-organized criticality occurs when an exploring, dynamic system randomly moves within the range of, and suddenly "falls" into, a given complex attractor. The onset of looting in riots, sudden shifts in stock markets, and organizational extinctions (such as the demise of Winn-Dixie food stores in the Southeast United States) all exemplify attractors which draw systems that moved within their basins of attraction. Such emergent shifts are not "caused" in the traditional sense of the word; rather, they occur because of the dynamic, random movements of complex systems.

Emergence expressed as self-organized criticality, then, is a function of adaptive exploration and complex attractors. Emergence is naturally occurring change and stabilization and does not require external work or energy to occur. This order is free (Kauffman, 1993).

Dissipative Structures.   Dissipation traditionally refers to the release of energy and resultant entropy. Entropy is associated with deterioration of order while increasing energy is associated with the creation of order. General systems theory, for example, postulates that social and biological order is based on negentropic absorption of energy from the environment (Buckley, 1967; von Bertalanffy, 1956). Prigogine (1997), however, found mechanisms by which order can actually emerge, rather than deteriorate, from the dissipation of energy. He refers to the results as *dissipative structures*. Heated oil, for example, absorbs energy from a stove but will exhibit little change (new order) until its energy builds to an unstable level—what Prigogine called, "far-from-equilibrium"; at that point, the interacting oil molecules suddenly dissipate energy—they "break" the built-up tension. This nonlinear release allows them to move into an ordered, gently rolling, lower energy state (Haken, 1983); that is, they increase order by dissipating energy. Unlike criticality, external agents (e.g., leaders, environmental pressures: any agent that controls energy) can influence dissipative structures. Put differently, external agents can control the knobs on Haken's stove.

Complex Dynamics and Emergence

Emergence is a sudden, unpredictable change event produced by the actions of mechanisms. Emergence occurs at all levels of intensity with most changes being of low intensity and an occasional few, of high intensity (plotting intensity by frequency yields a power law curve; Bak, 1996; Schroeder, 1991). That is, a complex system is a dynamic soup of interactive agents and mechanisms that continually spawn multi- but mostly low-intensity, emergent changes (with occasional high intensity changes). Emergent outcomes are differentiated from steady growth outcomes that build steadily, step by step, from known beginnings and with predictable trajectories (the "stuff" of traditional science).

Importantly, emergence is generated by interaction and energic pressure rather than by individuals acting alone; it is produced by the dynamic actions of mechanisms rather than by variables that exert constant, predictable effect. There are numerous interactive dynamics (mechanisms) going on in Haken's oil prior to phase transition that influence the system's trajectory and the nature of phase transition. Similarly, there are important interactive dynamics (mechanisms) happening on criticality's surfaces that influence trajectories across surfaces and influence the likelihood of jumping out of a given attractor pit. The dynamic interactions that generate change (i.e., the mechanisms described earlier) are both the source of complexity's unpredictability and are the proximal cause of the outcomes that make complex dynamics so valuable to organizations.

Complex Outcomes

Creative change is an important emergent outcome of complexity dynamics. This can manifest as (for example) innovative ideas, breakthrough solutions to problems, new insights, or revised ways of understanding issues. For example, new products that represent the "collapsing together" of various, seemingly unrelated technologies in the same (or related) attractor are emergent outcomes of complex dynamics; the emergence, in 1975, of the microcomputer illustrates (Marion, 1999). Unique adaptive strategies can emerge from complex dynamics, as can learning surges, differentiated structuring, and sudden structural collapses (e.g., organizational extinction).

The goal of the complexity leader is to create such outcomes within an environment in which it would be difficult to anticipate that you even need them. Such environments are rapidly changing and highly interconnected. Complexity allows systems to "adapt on the fly," so to speak, to effectively adjust to exigencies as they arrive.

LEADERSHIP IN COMPLEX SYSTEMS

The introduction to this chapter asked three questions: What is uniquely different about complexity theory, why should leadership theorists be interested in this science, and what is leadership in complex environments? We have answered the first question and turn now to the next two (but only briefly—the subsequent authors in this book will flesh out these questions).

The introduction proposed a condensed answer to the "why" question for leadership: Complexity theory is a comfortable fit for today's complex organizational environment. Uhl-Bien, Marion, and McKelvey have addresses this question in their article in this book (Uhl-Bien, Marion, & McKelvey, this volume). The problems with which organizations deal are highly complex and cannot be solved by top-down planning alone (Marion & Uhl-Bien, 2007). These problems often appear quickly and unexpectedly, as 9/11, Katrina, the collapse of Enron, the precipitous emergence of new technology demonstrate. The modern organizational environment is hyperturbulent and rapidly changing (Hitt, 1998). It is global and highly interconnected. These (and other) issues pose significant challenges for leadership, particularly as it is traditional conceptualized (appropriate for a more stable, commodity-based economy; Uhl-Bien et al., this volume). A leadership approach based on complexity theory, one that is tailored for complex organizations and complex environments, is better suited for dealing with this knowledge-based environment. We refer to this approach as complexity leadership.

Complexity Leadership

Among other things, complexity leadership provides a framework in which certain leader behaviors work to foster complex mechanisms and generate conditions in which agents can respond quickly and effectively to unanticipated conditions (both destructive and beneficial). Mechanisms, as defined earlier, are the dynamic processes that emerge within complex systems. Mechanisms enable emergent creativity, learning, and adaptability (Uhl-Bien et al., this volume).

In complexity leadership, *enabling leaders* work to catalyze mechanisms by creating conditions in which those mechanisms can thrive (see Uhl-Bien et al., this volume). This is a different sort of role for leadership than is typically presented in the literature: enabling leaders allow things to occur over which they have relatively little direct control. They create the structures, rules, interactions, interdependencies, tension, and culture in which complex mechanisms can thrive and unanticipated outcomes can occur—and, they create mechanisms that weed out poorly adaptive outcomes.

Second, in complexity leadership enabling leaders foster conditions that allow the system to respond effectively and rapidly to catastrophic or opportunistic changes. Effective leadership during catastrophic events is, of course, critical. But what constitutes effective leadership under such conditions? Events during the week following Katrina are, perhaps, instructive. Structured, preplanned, and top down leadership such as that provided by Federal Emergency Management Agency appeared impotent during that crucial week. Conditions were simply too overwhelming, complex, and fast moving for the agency. The most effective responses to the Katrina crisis were more bottom-up in nature. Cajun boatmen, for example, coordinated their efforts via two-way radios and helped evacuate many stranded citizens. No bureaucrat in Washington, DC worked the red tape or planned their efforts: rather the boatmen responded adaptively and spontaneously to the needs of the moment (see Stephenson & Bonabeau, 2007 for further discussion and other examples).

Complexity leadership theory proposes that effective leadership creates conditions in which localized instances of adaptive behavior (Uhl-Bien et al., this volume) can emerge and adapt to situations such as Katrina. It enables agents to take initiatives, it enables communication/interaction, and it builds interdependencies. That is, a complexity leadership framework allows us to see ways to enable the emergence of what Bonabeau and Meyer (2001) call, swarm behavior. Such behavior emerges in crisis conditions when enabling leadership fosters bottom-up action and adaptive (emergent) leadership. Agents can similarly respond to unanticipated, fast-paced opportunities in business, nongovernmental organizations, schools, and elsewhere when leaders work to foster complex structures in their organizations.

DISCUSSION

Earlier in this chapter, I suggested (somewhat implicitly) that traditional approaches to leadership may not be sufficient for dealing with complex environments. Traditional strategies for leadership have been quite successful in the commodity-oriented organizations that characterized the twentieth century. However, these strategies exhibit basic characteristics that limit their applicability in situations requiring dynamic creativity, adaptability, and learning (Uhl-Bien et al., this volume).

The issues that shape—and limit—traditional leadership thought were articulated many decades ago by Chester Barnard (1938). He proposed that the role of leadership is to align unstructured organizational forces (individual preferences, goals, and strategies, work habits, social behaviors, activities, etc.) with formal organizational goals. The legacy of this premise is readily observed in transformational leadership, LMX theory, and other current approaches to leadership study and practice (Marion, 2006).

Traditional theories have implemented Barnard's notions with top-down control; planning, structuring, and evaluation; centralized vision and focus; and rationalized structures. While such strategies have been powerful in commodity oriented environments, they are a weak fit for tasks requiring adaptability, creativity, and rapid response—the conditions that we proposed in this paper characterize twenty-first century organizational environments. For example, top-down approaches to leadership do not adequately address the demands of creative enterprises (such as R&D or scholarly research), highly complex tasks (such as sophisticated software production), or conditions that require rapid change and adaptability (e.g., modern battlefield conditions that deal with guerrilla tactics; Schreiber & Carley, this volume). Scholars who study creativity in organizations have recognized the importance of creative autonomy within a broader context of top-down planning and structuring (e.g., Mumford, Bedell-Avers, & Hunter, in press); other leadership theorists have struggled with challenges of fast-paced environments (creativity, flexibility, rapid response; e.g., Fletcher, 2004; Pearce & Conger, 2003). However, complexity theory deals with these environments directly, thoroughly, and systematically.

Complexity theory makes the rather unique assertion that Barnard's uncontrolled activities can be useful for the organization and that leadership under conditions of knowledge production should develop strategies for taking advantage of this resource. This chapter has begun to describe the nature of these uncontrolled activities (i.e., complex dynamics) and to describe how leaders and leadership might enable and utilize these forces.

Complex dynamics produce surprise and flexibility—surprise in the form of creative solutions to problems, and flexibility in the form of rapid adaptation to complex environmental conditions. Complexity theory underscores the significant importance of internal dynamics in the production of new structures and ideas. Complexity uniquely describes change processes as nonlinear emergent events and it identifies an unpredictable substrate within complex systems that complicates planning and top-down leadership. It proposes that we should appreciate the importance of interactive dynamics in organizational processes and it challenges the dyadic relationship as the primary unit of analysis in organizational studies.

Complexity theory may be unsettling because it challenges "givens" in our Western mindset—the Newtonian-inspired assumptions of predictable outcomes, logical relationships, and linear cause and effect. But the extreme complexity of organizational activities in the twenty-first century are likewise "unsettling," unpredictable, and nonlinear. Complexity theory addresses these thorny problems facing twenty-first century organizations, problems brought on by globalization, rapid change, the unpredictable behaviors of technological advances, the tremendous complexity of many of the tasks we undertake, and the shifting organizational focus on knowledge rather than commodities (Boisot, 1998; Hitt, 1998; Meyer, Gaba, & Colwell, 2005).

So complexity turns things upside down and looks at events differently. Complexity leadership redefines Barnard's maxim, stating that leadership mines the resources of the "irrational" forces that Barnard sought to suppress. It recognizes the importance of many critical minds struggling autonomously but interdependently over problems that a system faces. Complexity theory seeks to understand organization with paradigmatically different lenses than have been used in the past and to derive lessons from those lenses about how to deal with unpredictability and rapidly changing organizations and environments.

NOTE

1. Actually, a surface with pits may be misleading to some because of its association with the potential energy surface in physics. In potential energy surfaces, pits are low energy states—the deeper the pit, the lower the energy. In complexity, these pits represent fitness strategies: the deeper the pit, the more useful the strategy (Kauffman, 1993).

REFERENCES

Anderson, P. (1995). Microcomputer manufacturers. In G. R. Carroll & M. T. Hannan (Eds.), *Organizations in industry* (pp. 37-58). New York: Oxford University Press.

Bak, P. (1996). *How nature works*. New York: Copernicus.

Bak, P., & Chen, K. (1991). Self-organized criticality. *Scientific American*, 46-53.

Bak, P., Tang, C., & Wiesenfeld, K. (1989). Self organized criticality: An explanation of 1/ƒ noise. *Physical Review Letters, 59*, 381-384.

Barnard, C. I. (1938). *The functions of the executive*. Cambridge, MA: Harvard University Press.

Barnes, J. A. (1954). Class and committees in a Norwegian island parish. *Human Relations, 7*(1), 39-58.

Boisot, M. (1998). *Knowledge assets: Securing competitive advantage in the information economy*. Oxford, England: Oxford University Press.

Bonabeau, E., & Meyer, C. (2001). Swarm intelligence: A whole new way to think about business. *Harvard Business Review, 79*(5), 107-114.

Buckley, W. (1967). *Sociology and modern systems theory*. Englewood Cliffs, N.: Prentice Hall.

Cilliers, P. (1998). *Complexity and postmodernism: Understanding complex systems*. London: Routledge.

Cohen, M. D., March, J. G., & Olsen, J. P. (1972). A garbage can model of organizational choice. *Administrative Science Quarterly, 17*, 1-25.

Coveney, P. (2003). *Self-organization and complexity: A new age for theory, computation and experiment*. Paper presented at the Nobel symposium on self-organization, Karolinska Institutet, Stockholm.

Dawkins, R. (1976). *The selfish gene*. New York: Oxford University Press.

DiMaggio, P. J., & Powell, W. W. (1991). The iron cage revisited: Institutional isomorphism and collective rationality in organizational fields. In W. W. Powell & P. J. DiMaggio (Eds.), *The new institutionalism in organizational analysis* (pp. 63-82). Chicago: University of Chicago Press.

Fletcher, J. K. (2004). The paradox of postheroic leadership: An essay on gender, power, and transformational change. *The Leadership Quarterly, 15*(5), 647-661.

Goodwin, B. (1994). *How the leopard changed its spots: The evolution of complexity*. New York: Charles Scribner's Sons.

Haken, H. (1983). *Synergetics, an introduction* (Vol. 3). Berlin: Springer-Verlag.

Hannan, M. T., & Freeman, J. (1977). The population ecology of organizations. *American Journal of Sociology, 82*, 929-964.

Hedström, P., & Swedberg, R. (1998). *Social mechanisms: An analytical approach to social theory*. Cambridge, England: Cambridge University Press.

Hitt, M. A. (1998). Presidential address: Twenty-first century organizations: Business firms, business schools, and the academy. *The Academy of Management Review, 23*, 218-224.

Horgan, J. (1996). *The end of science: Facing the limits of knowledge in the twilight of the scientific era*. New York: Broadway Books.

Kauffman, S. A. (1993). *The origins of order*. New York: Oxford University Press.

Langston, C. G. (1986). Studying artificial life with cellular automata. *Physica, 22D*, 120-149.

Lieberson, S., & O'Connor, J. F. (1972). Leadership and organizational performance: A study of large corporations. *American Sociological Review, 37*, 117-130.

Lorenz, E. (1964). The problem of deducing the climate from the governing equations. *Tellus, 16*, 1-11.

Lorenz, E. (1993). *The essence of chaos*. Seattle: University of Washington Press.

Marion, R. (1999). *The edge of organization: Chaos and complexity theories of formal social organizations.* Newbury Park, CA: Sage.

Marion, R. (2006). Complexity in organizations: A paradigm shift. In A. Sengupta (Ed.), *Chaos, nonlinearity, complexity: The dynamical paradigm of nature* (Vol. 206, pp. 248-270). Berlin: Springer-Verlag.

Marion, R., & Uhl-Bien, M. (2001). Leadership in complex organizations. *The Leadership Quarterly, 12*, 389-418.

Marion, R., & Uhl-Bien, M. (2007). Paradigmatic influence and leadership: The perspectives of complexity theory and bureaucracy theory. In J. K. Hazy, J. Goldstein & B. Lichtenstein (Eds.), *Complex systems leadership theory* (pp. 141-158). Mansfield, MA: ISCE.

Meyer, A. D., Gaba, V., & Colwell, K. A. (2005). Organizing far from equilibrium: Nonlinear change in organizational fields. *Organization Science, 16*(5), 456-473.

Mumford, M., Bedell-Avers, K. E., & Hunter, S. T. (in press). Planning for innovation: A multi-level perspective. In M. D. Mumford, S. T. Hunter & K. E. Bedell (Eds.), *Research in multi-level issues.* Oxford, England: Elsevier.

Pearce, C. L., & Conger, J. A. (2003). *Shared leadership: Reframing the hows and whys of leadership.* Thousand Oaks: Sage.

Poincaré, H. (Ed.). (1992). *New methods of celestial mechanics* (Vol. 13). New York: Springer-Verlag.

Prigogine, I. (1997). *The end of certainty.* New York: The Free Press.

Salancik, G. R., & Pfeffer, J. (1977). Constraints on administrator discretion: The limited influence of mayors on city budgets. *Urban Affairs Quarterly, 12*, 475-498.

Schroeder, M. (1991). *Fractals, chaos, power laws.* New York: W.H. Freeman.

Stephenson, W. D., & Bonabeau, E. (2007). Expecting the unexpected: The need for a networked terrorism and disaster response strategy [Electronic Version]. *Homeland Security Affairs, 3* from http://www.hsaj.org/?article=3.1.3

Turing, A. M. (1952). The chemical basis of morphogenesis. *Philos Trans Royal Society of London B, 237*(37).

Uhl-Bien, M., & Marion, R. (2007). *The mechanisms of emergence in complexity leadership theory: A meso-model of adaptive dynamics in organizations.* Manuscript submitted for publication.

von Bertalanffy, L. (1956). General systems theory. In L. von Bertalanffy & A. Rapoport (Eds.), *General systems: Yearbook of the society for the advancement of general systems theory* (Vol. 1, pp. 1-10). New York: George Braziller.

Weiner, N., & Mahoney, T. A. (1981). A model of corporate performance as a function of environmental, organizational, and leadership influences. *Academy of Management Journal, 24*, 453-470.

CHAPTER 2

CONCEPTUAL FOUNDATIONS OF COMPLEXITY SCIENCE

Development and Main Constructs

Jeffrey Goldstein

ABSTRACT

This chapter offers a descriptive survey of 9 major fields making-up contemporary complexity theory as well as the main constructs being developed in these fields. The emphasis is on uncovering enough about the nature and development of these ideas so as to inform readers to their potential utility in their research. Connections among these fields are explored and the reader is provided literature for further exploration.

INTRODUCTION

It is certainly no accident that the study of complex systems, a field of inquiry known generally under the term "complexity theory," has arisen during our current historical period. The theoretical emphases of the

Complexity Leadership, Part I: Conceptual Foundations
pp. 17–48
Copyright © 2008 by Information Age Publishing

former no doubt reflect the dominant features of the latter, namely, inter-connectedness, interdependencies, and unprecedented rates of change. It was for these reasons that no less a scientific luminary than Stephen W. Hawking declared the twenty-first to be *the* century of complexity.

Complexity theory obviously did not emerge en masse but instead represents a confluence of many ideas across from many fields in the sciences and mathematics that have been developing in many exciting new ways. In fact, in an important respect, there is no one unified discipline to which the term "complexity theory" actually refers. Because of the many diverse types of complex systems which have been studied plus the wide-range of mathematical and scientific methods and constructs which have been spawned from these studies, it's been hard put to arrive at a general consensus on the definitions of "complex" and "complexity." Neverthe-less, nine major interrelated research traditions and their main notions have been selected according to some agreement among complexity theo-rists at least regarding a set of shared ideas, these core traditions and notions to be described in the second part of this chapter.

To be sure, because of the wide extent and richness of the multifarious complexity constructs and methods, justice can not be done to an exposi-tion of all or even most them here. Instead, this chapter focuses on just a small selection of core ideas used across the varied studies of complex sys-tems. Hopefully, then, what can be accomplished here is an appreciation of how such constructs have been developed and appropriated from dif-ferent but related conceptual traditions. Such an exposition also aims at piquing interest as to their potential utility in the organizational and lead-ership fields of interest to the readers.

Such caveats also imply that certain important complexity-based ideas will not be covered here. There is always a selection of what to cover, whether this selection is explicit or implicit. Although other complexity thinkers would probably supplement what is covered here with additional concepts, this author holds that the set of core ideas discussed below would most likely find their way into most discussions of complexity the-ory in general. If the reader is at least inspired to inquire further into these other complexity notions, so much the better, and he/she can find some of these additional complexity constructs mentioned in Figure 2.1.

One of the criteria used for the selection process here is the basis of a concept in science, mathematics, or both. There are of course complexity-related conceptions that have arisen outside of science and math, such as in philosophy, literature, the arts, and even theology, which may indeed prove in the long run to be just as significant as the ones included here and perhaps even to have more staying power for the study of complex systems. This author, however, doesn't have the means to evaluate the importance or endurance of such ideas and therefore is content, for the purposes of this book, to concentrate on just those complexity-based ideas which have already an established track record in diverse scientific and mathematical communities of practice. This should not be taken as a value judgment concerning the worth of complexity ideas emerging outside of the stated communities. Scientific and mathematical regions of study are themselves, of course, circumscribed by all sorts of sociological and anthropological facts. So be it, but that is not what this chapter is about.

A final note is in order for this introduction to the chapter: I will not be going over current or recent organizational/leadership applications of the core complexity notions discussed in this chapter since the literature making up such investigations will without doubt be cited throughout the rest of the book. This chapter instead aims at an understanding of the core complexity notions in order to set a stage for their use in the study of leadership and organizations.

NINE MAIN RESEARCH TRADITIONS
AND THEIR CORE CONSTRUCTS

Although the scientific and mathematical disciplines making up contemporary complexity theory formed out of a confluence of variegated sources, many of which can be traced back to the World War II and its aftermath, nine main interrelated strands can be discerned. A brief exposition of each can shed light on the central themes and issues of complexity theory. These nine influences are highlighted with underlines in Figure 2.1. This figure also displays some of the minor influences which for brevity are mostly side-stepped in this short review of the origins of the sciences of complex systems.

Compiled from Figure 2.1 is this list of nine major complexity fields and the core constructs that will be described below:

- *Systems thinking:* boundaries and positive and negative feedback loops;
- *Theoretical biology:* organizations as organic, evolving, whole systems;
- *Nonlinear dynamical systems theory (NDS):* attractors, bifurcation, chaos;
- *Graph theory:* connectivity and networks;
- *Phase transitions, Turing's morphogenetic model, synergetics, and far-from-equilibrium thermodynamics:* emergence of novel order; and

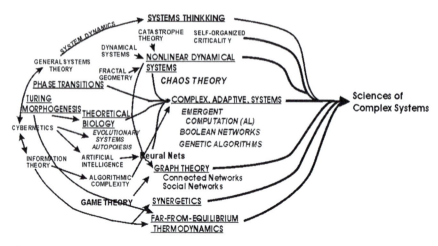

Figure 2.1.   Mathematical and scientific roots of the sciences of complex systems.

- *Complex adaptive systems theory:* evolving, adapting systems of inter-acting agents.

The nine major fields have been included in only six sections because of overlap and deep connections between some of them. It should also be pointed out that these nine fields include two which are purely mathematical, NDS and graph theory, although the other fields both utilize these two or have generated their own mathematical innovations.

Organizations as Constituted by Positive and Negative Feedback Loops—Systems Thinking

The very idea of a system being that sort of entity which is somehow coordinated across its part and existing within a boundary separating it from the environment can be made out as far back as ancient Western as well as Eastern philosophy. However, this rather vague conception really started to come of modern age riding on the tail of the great and revolutionary scientific achievements of Galileo, Descartes, Newton, and Leibniz in the seventeenth century. The next two centuries found an even greater emphasis on expostulating on the idea of a system in general, reaching its apotheosis during the arising of *Naturphilosophie* with such luminaries as Kant, Blumenbach, Goethe, Schelling, and Hegel (Lenoir, 1982). However exciting and intriguing and inspirational these early ideas of a system may have been, they did not achieve the status of workable scientific and mathematical constructs until the mid-twentieth century. Much of this was due to the arrival of powerful computers and communicational networks during World War II and used afterwards for more peaceful pursuits. Computation allowed vast ensembles of information about systems to be analyzed and for patterns to be detected that was simply not possible before. The recognition and probing of these patterns was aided by concomitant developments in mathematics, some of which we will explore below.

All too often one hears some complexity aficionado enthusiastically praise a complexity idea as if it were just now hatched out of some contemporary scientist's or mathematician's brain. Yet many of these same ideas turn out, upon more careful scrutiny, to be derived from earlier systems thinking which had already worked through many of the constructs' problems and potential applications. This author finds it surprising how little many contemporary researchers actually know about the development of the very systems ideas they use in their research and theorizing. This ignorance can result in going over ground that was already conceptually tilled, sometimes with much greater facility, many years ago. That is one reason we are starting off this chapter with a discussion of earlier systems approaches. Not only do many contemporary complexity notions have their roots in earlier traditions in math and science, a comparison of some of what's being done now with what was worked out earlier can sometimes reveal a deficit in the current idea with respect to the one in the past.

As can be seen from the left portion of the "whale diagram" of Figure 2.1, systems thinking evolved out of cybernetics, information theory, and related fields which, although initiated under the impetus of WWII, developed speedily thereafter. Also, even though many of these early systems thinkers came out of technical fields where a major objective was improving the efficiency of a host of actual machines, the conceptual understanding of systems that was developing at that time had them posited as more than mere inert mechanisms passively acted upon by external circumstances. On the contrary, these pioneers conceived systems as inherently dynamic in the sense of alternating rhythms of change and stability. This dynamic property of systems was made possible by their being constituted out of positive and negative feedback interactions among the components of the system, an essentially nonlinear perspective that we'll come back to later. Whereas positive feedback refers to the amplification of one component's effects on another (or itself), negative feedback refers to an opposite dampening of such effects.

Although systems were conceived as the interweaving of such positive and negative feedback resulting in the possibility of both change and stability, what dominated early systems thinking was negative feedback, in the sense that systems were understood as essentially equilibrium seeking, that is, would seek to restore an earlier stable state when disturbed by external perturbations or internal fluctuations. This conception most likely derived from the cybernetic origins of systems thinking and the work done on guidance systems, which had as a major objective the devising of mechanisms for bringing systems back on track after disturbances, as in a guided missile.

The interweaving of feedback loops was considered the central feature by which systems were conceived as wholes, allowing for an intactness of the system in relation to its outer environments. Indeed, it was partly because of understanding systems as being essentially made-up of interlocking feedback loops that the term "complexity" was applied to such systems. As early as 1948, in an article in *American Scientist*, the mathematician Warren Weaver (1948) was referring to feedback looped systems when he defined the "organized complexity" of systems, "a sizable number of factors which are interrelated into an organic whole" (p. 437).

A major player in applying the cybernetics idea of positive and negative feedback loops to organizations was J. W. Forrester (1961) and his group at MIT. This was done both for the theoretical purpose of operations research as well as providing insight to managers as to the underlying factors in organizational functioning. Forrester's work was popularized in the 1990s by Peter Senge (1990), who dealt with so-called system "archetypes" or common patterns in organizations determined in large measure by positive and negative feedback. A related employment of early cybernetically inspired systems concepts to organizations and management was provided by the brilliant British scientist and consultant Stafford Beer (1972).

Around the end of World War II, another idea, that of "self-organization," was starting to find its way into the burgeoning field of cybernetics where it primarily meant a kind of self-regulatory effect of feedback loops. The actual origin of the idea, even the term itself, although in a nascent form, could be found in the work of Descartes and then Kant (Shalizi, n.d.). In terms of cybernetics, the eminent British neurologist and systems theorist W. Ross Ashby (1962) used the idea of self-organization to indicate goal-oriented systems capable of pursuing their objectives without the need for external imposition or guidance. In contrast to Kant, Ashby held that a cybernetic machine, that is, a *system* according to the new understanding of systems then developing, could actually be self-organizing by undergoing spontaneous changes in its internal order or organization. However, Ashby tempered his views of self-organization by demonstrating that, strictly speaking, self-organization should not be thought of as an innate systemic propensity but was more accurately conceived as a mechanical-like, randomization process (Dupuy, 2000).

Recognizing the lack of reference to earlier systems models on the part of some recent complexity researchers, the condensed matter physicist and complexity researcher Kurt Richardson (2005, 2006) has identified a set of principles which are commonly presumed in complexity theory but whose origin can be traced to earlier systems approaches, a few of which include:

- Complementary law: Any two or more perspectives or models may reveal truths about the system that are neither entirely independent nor entirely compatible. Although this principle appears to be anachronistically postmodern in its sensibility, Richardson is actually hinting at the idea of multirealizability, that is, the way that system goals and eventual properties may be reached by different pathways and configurations of internal elements.
- Darkness principle: No system can be known completely and therefore there is an implication of unpredictability. This topic will be returned to in later sections but for now it needs to be stressed that unpredictability does not necessarily imply a lack of determinative causes or laws, but rather how the very complexity of such systems may hinder attempts to precisely deduce future states.
- Law of requisite variety: Formulated most strongly by Ashby, the idea here was that the control of systems could only be effectuated "if the variety of the controller is at least as great as the variety of the situation to be controlled" (Ashby quoted in Richardson, 2006, Part 2, p. 499).

To be sure, more general principles of early systems thinking could be adumbrated but neither space nor purpose would allow such an undertaking here. Instead, we end this section by pointing out an essential feature lacking in systems thinking per se, namely, the idea of *emergence* or the coming into being of radically novel structures and properties in systems. The ideology of earlier systems thinking does not seem to have been ready for this idea, although there were even earlier expositions of the idea in philosophy and even theology (Goldstein, 1999). Because of this deficiency, it is hard to find in systems thinking allowance for the kind of innovation that would become essential to later complexity theory. For the most part, systems thinking has retained an equilibrium-seeking model of organizations and in such a model ultimately there can be no place for emergence, an issue that has been superceded in complexity theory by a switch, as we'll see below, to *far-from-equilibrium* systems.

Organizations as Organic, Evolving, and Whole Systems— Theoretical Biology

The significant conceptual shift in complexity theory by which complex systems are increasingly understood as more like organisms than machines, more like evolutionary systems than static entities, and more like ecologies of coevolving subsystems than rigidly designed superstructures, owes much of its potency to that aspect of the sciences of complex systems derived from advances in theoretical biology during the twentieth century. Of particular importance in this respect have been advances in evolutionary biology, the rise of ecology, and the rise of new ways of understanding morphogenesis or the changes in shape of organisms during their embryological development. At the heart of these conceptual shifts is a growing sense that reductionistic approaches can only be of partial value in explanations of organic life. In so far as the complexity theory view of systems has taken-up these perspectives from theoretical biology, it also has been emphasizing the need to go beyond a strict adherence to reductionist constructs and methods. This does not imply a wholesale rejection of reductionism but instead a supplementation of it in the direction of giving more attention to the *whole* of systems, and not just their components.

Antireductionism and "Delving Downwards"

The Nobel laureate and trailblazer in the study of complex systems, Herbert Simon (1981) once made a suggestion that has became something of a working principle among complexity theorists, "in the face of complexity, an *in-principle* reductionist may be at the same time a *pragmatic* holist" (p. 86; emphasis added). One field where such a perspective had indeed been developing was theoretical biology, especially that aspect of the field under the influence of the organicist philosophy of the British mathematician and philosopher Alfred North Whitehead. The main progenitors in this direction were members of the "Theoretical Biology Club" at Cambridge University: J. H. Woodger, Joseph Needham, and C. H. Waddington (Depew & Weber, 1996). These theoretical biologists interpreted Whitehead's approach as a way to bulwark their realm of inquiry, that of biology, from the encroachment of reductionist/mechanist physicists and chemists.

Needham, for example, explicitly traced the appeal of Whitehead's work to the manner by which it shifted the focus of biology toward the *organizing relations* making up biological wholes, phenomena which could be dealt with in a scientific, yet nonreductionist manner (Jones, 2002). Waddington, who went on to become one of the premier embryologists of his generation, took Whitehead's metaphysics as providing the theoretical foundation for a method Waddington termed *delving downwards*. Unlike the reductionist strategy of building-up a complex phenomenon from a given set of simpler entities, delving downward instead searches downwards from a given, whole complex phenomena to the simpler entities which proved adequate to explain the whole (Waddington, 1977). An example is the deficiency of classical laws of organic chemistry in accounting for changes in the overall shape of protein molecules—once a more global change of shape was discovered, insight could then be obtained about the properties of atoms as they were exhibited in molecular groupings.

Such a perspective has deep repercussions for understanding organizations as systems, since it puts the onus of understanding on three facts about systems typically ignored in traditional organizational theory and leadership practice based on that theory. First, there is the need to keep the whole system in mind whenever attempting to influence change or design of its parts. Second, there is the requirement to realize that new levels of complexity imply new principles of regularities and laws of behavior at work on that new level, a principle we will come back to below in the discussion on Anderson's constructionist hypothesis. It suggests that each new emergent level requires understanding and action that may be quite different than that found on other levels, a realization that no doubt many skilled executives operate on intuitively if not intentionally. Third, there is the often overlooked fact that optimization effects may be quite different for the whole and for its parts, a finding that is exploited in complex, adaptive systems (which is discussed in the last section of the chapter).

Feedback Loops and Systemic Closure

Early systems ideas of feedback were also of great importance in theoretical biology, indeed they developed in tandem with it. Thus, the title of the first meeting in 1946 of the Macy Foundation Conferences on cybernetics was "Feedback Mechanisms and Circular Causal Systems in Biological and Social Systems," a theme which remained in effect for the duration of the conferences until the last one in 1953 (Dupuy, 2000). Feedback in this sense was reciprocal, and thus implied a kind of *circular causality* quite similar, in fact, to the much earlier notions of Kant in his differentiation of organisms from machines. Circularly causal feedback cycles in biological systems became central in the development of general systems theory (GST) by the German (and then American) embryologist Ludwig von Bertalanffy (1951). The manner in which webs of feedback loops interlocked resulted in what Bertalanffy termed the *steady state* of organic systems, characterized by a capacity for the whole to restore itself after being disturbed, another example of the idea of an equilibrium seeking. However, for Bertalanffy, the steady state required a system open enough to its environment in order to be replenished from exchanges with that environment.

Paul Weiss, another embryologist who emigrated to the United States from Germany (and coincidentally had Whitehead himself on his dissertation committee at Harvard), did not believe there was a cogent story of how wholes could pass continuously from the mechanism of parts to the "integrated overall systemic order" of the whole, comparing it to the enigma of how a railroad on tracks could keep making progress toward its destination beyond a wasteland if the tracks suddenly came to an end in the wasteland (Dupuy, 2000). Instead, he speculated that the system as an integrated whole gave "guiding cues" in the form of a "dynamic field structure of the total complex" (quoted in Dupuy, 2000, p. 131). Weiss referred to systemic wholes as "self-contained," "self-perpetuating," and "self-sustaining"—the latter term almost certainly derived from Whitehead's much earlier descriptions of organic wholes.

Perhaps, the apotheosis of this holistic tendency in theoretical biology, one which went on to make its mark in the development of complexity theory, was the theory of *autopoiesis* put forward by the Chilean biologists Humberto Maturana and Francisco Varela (1980). Maturana, who had earlier tie-ins to cybernetics through his seminal research on certain animal nervous systems, joined with Varela to define the unique character of a living form: "autopoeisis" coming from "poiesis," a Greek term meaning "production," and "auto-" for "self," so that "autopoiesis" means "self-production." The correspondence with the phrase "self-organization" can be seen in the usual form of the latter term in many non-English languages as "auto-organization." Their concept of self-referential circularity acted to create a self-contained identity, a boundary which Varela and Goguen (1977) later termed *closure*, a counter to the earlier viewpoint of Bertalanffy and others, that living organisms were open systems in constant information and energy exchanges with their environment (for a similar notion see Rosen, 1996). Maturana and Varela (1987) offered an analogy to illustrate what closure entailed: a pilot flying blind in conditions of very poor visibility relying only on the instrumentation in the cockpit where any environmental inputs are mere blips on the radar screen. This seems, however, to place autopoesis squarely in the equilibrium-seeking camp, since, as being essentially removed from its environment, there doesn't appear to be any possible way for real change to occur—that is, emergence of genuinely innovative adaptations.

Nonlinear Dynamical Systems Theory

Nonlinear dynamical systems theory (NDS), known more popularly in recent years under the more provocative phrase "chaos theory," forms the greater part of the mathematical superstructure of contemporary complexity theory. NDS has bequeathed such key conceptual constructs and mathematical methods as attractors, phase or state space, bifurcation, nonlinearity, iterative and recursive functions, deterministic chaos, and fractals (to name just a few). Originally developing out of the prescient mathematical research of Henri Poincaré a century ago, NDS has undergone significant expansion and supplementation through the work of many esteemed mathematicians including Liapunov, Andronov, Birkhoff, Cartwright, Peixoto, Smale, Arnol'd, May, Feigenbaum, Yorke, Li, and many others (see Abraham & Shaw, 1984). The "nonlinear" of NDS refers to those equations, functions, or "maps" (functions involving discrete changes in the values of variables) which exhibit curvilinearity when graphed (literally: *not* lines). For example, the nonlinear equation, $y = x^2$ graphs as a curve since when x is 3, y equals 9, but when x is increased by only one unit (when $x = 4$), y jumps to 16, a disproportionality which continues ad infinitum.

Nonlinearity in mathematics has of course been around in one form or another since ancient times. What NDS has added to the mix are the fascinating phenomena revealed when nonlinear functions are also "dynamical," that is, when they and the systems they represent undergo a kind of evolution passing through different dynamical regimes called "attractors," each of which circumscribes only that type of behavior consonant with the particular attractor regime at sway. This *dynamical* nature of nonlinear dynamical systems can be appreciated in a prototypical example of a nonlinear equation that has become something of an emblem for complexity theory, namely, the so-called "logistic map" which evolves in discrete steps or "tics" of time, often employed in calculating discrete changes in populations from year to year. It is not pertinent for our purposes to go into the details of this particular function but what is relevant is to recognize how the evolution of these kinds of functions can show "bifurcations," or shifts to new attractor regimes under certain conditions.

It is necessary, though, to keep in mind that an attractor is the mathematical description of a certain possibility of system behavior, that is, a certain range of the values of variables at a certain phase of the system, and that a bifurcation refers to seemingly discontinuous jumps from one attractor(s) to another. As such the constructs of attractors and bifurcations refer to what is happening in an abstract mathematical space termed space or state space, and not in actual physical or social spaces. Unlike more traditional graphs which plot changes in the values of variables on the vertical axis against time on the horizontal one (e.g., NASDAQ indices over time periods), in phase space, coordinate axes represent the variables plotted *against each other* with time functioning only as an implicit factor. This means that each point in phase space represents the intersection of the values of each of the variables at each instance of time (hence the phase or state of the system at each instant of time). The evolution of a system over time can be discerned in the pattern made up of such phase points as the system changes, that is, the phase trajectory and the phase portrait. From this, scientists and mathematicians have made impressive inroads into aspects of the dynamics of evolving systems that would not previously have been accessible. For example, Figure 2.2 shows a phase portrait for a prey/predator model of an ecosystem in which the predators increase when there are enough prey to keep their hunger abated but then die off when the population of the prey becomes too small because too many have been eaten. Attractors are considered *stable* phase portraits since such a pattern depicts where the system mathematically settles to in the longer run.

NDS has introduced striking examples of unpredictability even in deterministic systems. Usually associated with the feature of chaos in such systems, this type of unpredictability was intuited by Poincarè himself, "it may happen that small differences in the initial conditions produce very great ones in the final phenomena. A small error in the former will pro-

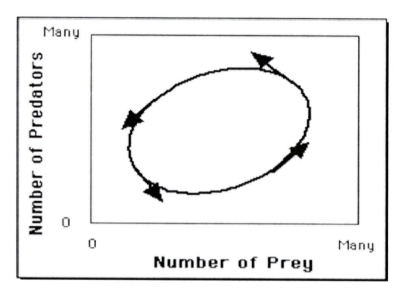

Figure 2.2.   Phase space portrait of predator/prey model (Chaos/workshop A and B, n.d.).

duce an enormous error in the latter. Prediction becomes impossible, and we have the fortuitous phenomenon" (Poincarè quoted in Peterson, 1995, p. 167). What Poincarè intuited was later termed *sensitivity to initial conditions* since in such a system, slight changes in the values of variables representing a particular condition could be tremendously amplified. The phase portraits of chaotic nonlinear dynamical systems reveals their unusual properties, as seen in Figure 2.3, the famous Lorenz chaotic attractor after the meteorologist Edward Lorenz (1996) who first discovered the "signature" of chaos in his computationally based meteorological research in the early 1960s. Notice that although the trajectory making up the phase portrait moves around somewhat unpredictably in phase space, the phase trajectory never actually returns to the same exact point, yet manages to stay within a certain limited region of the phase space. This means the chaotic system is not periodic yet also not random, a strange melange not previously considered in science or mathematics.

Because of its unprecedented utility in exposing mathematical structure where it was not seen before, the concepts of phase space, attractor,

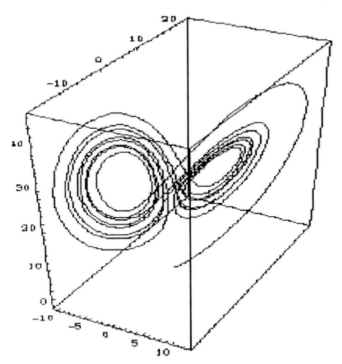

Figure 2.3. Chaotic Lorenz attractor in three dimensions (Chaos/workshop A and B, n.d.)

and so forth have found a plethora of applications in many disciplines (see, e.g., Diacu & Holmes, 1996, p. 199; Weiss, 1987). Of particular interest in this regard for the study of leadership is the so-called "qualitative" dynamics of NDS phase portraits, referring to investigations into the geometrical, graph theoretical, set theoretical, and topological properties of phase portraits. These qualitative dynamics give insight into the general behavior allowed in such systems and how this behavior may be changed.

It must be admitted that the use of NDS constructs in organizational theory has been mostly metaphoric. But this need not count against their utility in prodding thinking in new directions. A case in point is to understand an attractor in a social system as a way of talking about a "meta-level" perspective. In this metaphoric sense, an attractor is a figurative manner of speaking about patterns of behavior occurring during particular times or places in an organization. Leaders then can operate on the "level" of the organizational attractors, for unless the attractor is changed, behavior under its sway cannot really shift. This may include investigating what is driving the stability of an attractor, how can this be changed through what interventions, and so forth. No doubt, as we learn more about complexity applied to leadership, much of this initial, intuitive work will be more amenable to quantification and we will see a shift of direction of influence from social system theory and practice to the so-called hard sciences.

Connectivity and Networks—Graph Theory

We've seen how the conceptual framework of NDS underlies the mathematical representations of both how a complex system's dynamics may be circumscribed by particular attractor regimes as well as the manner in which such systems can change, that is, bifucations. Another mathematical field, graph theory, focuses on the mathematics of the networks constituting complex systems, both the internal connectivities among the system's multifarious components and the connectivities between these internal networks and external networks in the system's environment. Graph theory can also provide insight into change since innovations in system functioning may arise through the establishment of new linkages of connectivity.

Perhaps the best example of such a networked system is the internet which consists of connections built on connections built on connections built on connections and on and on. A Web site links users to itself and other users; email service providers link people all over the globe in an almost instantaneous fashion; and varied configurations like chat rooms,

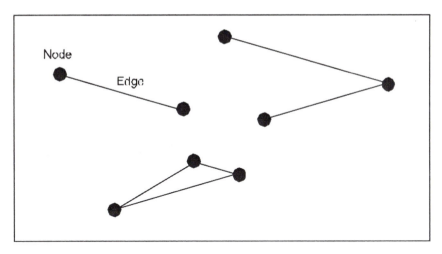

Figure 2.4.   The nodes and edges of graphs.

online education, and meeting places link groups of people simultaneously. After all, Web sites like Google, YouTube, and Wikipedia are all
about connectivities, and graph theory is a mathematical way of formulating such connectivities. Other examples of connectivity-constituted complex systems include social networks (Kilduff & Tsai, 2003), hub networks
(so crucial to such fields as telecommunications and transportation; see,
e.g., Skorin-Kapov, 1998), and sundry species of artificial life and agent-
based modeling which will be described in more depth in later section of
the chapter. It should be added that the graph theoretical portrayal of a
network can also show how network-based complex systems grow and
become adaptable to changing situations through the establishment of
new linkages.

In its simplest form, the structure of a graph is exactly what one would
expect in a formalism for connectivity, namely, a set of nodes (or vertices)
connected by edges (linkages) as in Figure 2.4.

Nodes and edges can be multiplied without limit, and the specific way
these connectivities take place determine the dynamics of a system at a
particular instant in time as well as how the system may change, even suddenly.

An example of the application of graph structures is in explaining the
so-called *small world* phenomena (Watts, 2003). In the popularized idea of
"six degrees of separation" people all over the earth are viewed as connected like vertices by edges. The most notorious example is the tongue-
in-cheek Kevin Bacon number: the actor Kevin Bacon (a hub-like node) is
shown to be linked (by edges) to every other actor in Hollywood by no

more than six intervening actors (nodes) since Kevin has worked with a bunch of actors and they in turn have worked with a bunch of the same as well as other actors, some of which are not known by Kevin, and so on and on.

One of most far-reaching findings of graph theory was developed out of the work of the brilliant English logician, mathematician, and economist Frank Ramsey (who sadly died tragically young) (Lesser, 2001). Ramsey's theorem was then extended through the so-called *random graph* theory devised by the great Hungarian mathematicians Paul Erdos and Alfred Renyi (Barabási, 2002). Ramsey proved a famous theorem which can be translated (from its highly technical status) as addressing the question: How large a structure (e.g., a graph) need we have to be certain that it contains a certain orderly substructure? Ramsey's theorem demonstrated that complete *dis*order turns out to be impossible in a large enough randomly composed graph, the ramifications of which have proved significant way beyond Ramsey's delimited focus.

To see why, first it must be recognized that a randomly composed graph is one in which edges are laid down by a random procedure. Following Ramsey's theorem, random graph theory has it that if nodes are connected in an ongoing, random fashion, eventually a structured organized network will be formed, the implication seeming to be that randomness by itself can lead to organization, at least in regards to graphs.

An example of the formation of order out of randomly produced graphs can be adapted from one given by the Hungarian born physicist Albert-László Barabási (2002) now working at the University of Notre Dame. First, imagine a cocktail party where none of the guests know each other. A graph of such an event would consist merely of nodes and no edges because no one is linked. Next, suppose the host comes up with a scheme to randomly introduce the guests one to the other by first choosing any two guests (i.e., two nodes) and tossing a die so that if the result is a six, the two guests are introduced (an edge is formed between two nodes) but if any other number besides a six comes up, there is no introduction but instead two other guests are selected and the procedure is repeated. Following this method, if only some links are added, the result will merely be the accumulation of linkages as found in Figure 2.5.

If the linkage making protocol continues in this fashion, eventually some of the established pairs (two nodes and an edge) will themselves be linked to other pairs resulting in the formation of clusters of several nodes shown in Figure 2.6:

If this process continues long enough, even if each node has just an average of one link, a "giant cluster" can emerge, that is, a cluster linking most nodes into a large connected network where, starting from any

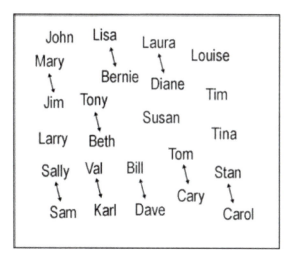

Figure 2.5.   Random linkages (edges) between guests (nodes).

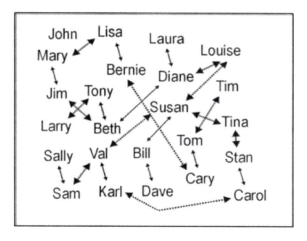

Figure 2.6.   Linkages between linkages.

node, any other node can be gotten to through navigating along the links (the heavy dotted curve in Figure 2.7):

According to Barabási, the emergence of the giant component is a type of phase transition, what physicists call percolation and sociologists a community. What is going on then is that through the random establishment of many linkages on a local level, that is, the level of individual pair-

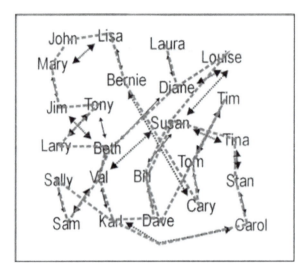

Figure 2.7.   Emergence of giant cluster (emergent order).

ings, a global-level connectivity gets established. This shift from local to global is an indication of the emergence of novel order in the system.

We can liken this adding of edges in a graph to the role of leadership in establishing connectivities among the parts and agents of the organization and between the internal system and its multifarious environments. This is to ensure enough connections to insures an optimal flow of information across the whole system

Organizations as Exhibiting the Emergence of New Order—Emergence

One of the most important features of complex systems that have been researched in recent years is that of emergence, or the arising of new structures with new properties out of the interactions taking place inside the system and between the system and its environment (Goldstein, 1999; Crutchfield, 1993). In respect to organizations and leadership this research into emergence is proving to have great importance, since it is shedding light on how social innovations can come about. As mentioned earlier in this chapter, emergence was not something discussed in early systems theorizing, mainly because the early models of systems were equilibrium seeking and thus did not allow for radically novel innovations that could render systems more adaptable. That is, the positing of negative feedback around these systems meant that any significant departure from the norm would be dampened whereas emergence is all about the amplification of deviations from the norm.

Emergence of Novel Coherent Order at Criticalization—
Phase Transitions

Although emergence as a philosophical notion can be traced back to the late nineteenth century (Blitz, 1992), an actual science of emergence can be said to have begun with inauguration of research into phase transitions in condensed matter physics (although the specific "term" emergence was not yet in use) because phase transitions exhibit the striking onset of new structures with new properties at critical thresholds of control parameters. Interest in such phenomena is, of course, nothing new given the age old fascination with the apparently sudden emergence of ice crystals forming out of the amorphous quality of liquid water when temperature is lowered to a critical threshold (32° F. for H_2O). Another common instance of a phase transition is the arising of ferro-magnetism at a low threshold temperatures. Two more exotic varieties are the onset of superconductivity and superfluidity taking place when certain metals, ceramics, and gases are cooled to low threshold temperatures.

As these examples show, the phase transitional emergence of new order follows a course of criticalization in that the new order emerges at *critical* thresholds of such key control parameters such as temperature, pressure, make-up of the materials involved, and so forth (Anderson & Stein, 1987). In the case of water turning to ice, the very fact that the number of molecules remains the same in ice as it was in the liquid H_2O before criticalization implies that at the critical temperature ice must be about a new kind of *organization* of the molecules. Indeed, whereas in the gaseous state of water vapor molecules move about randomly and in the liquid phase they are subject to forces of attraction, in the crystalline phase of ice the molecules are configured in a periodic lattice. It is the commencement of this latter mode of organization that is responsible for the very different macro-properties ice possesses, e.g., its rigidity. Figure 8 illustrates the change of organization occurring at a threshold during a phase transition.

The top square represents the state of the system before the critical phase transition, for example, a non-magnetized state depicted by the "magnetic spin" arrows going in all sorts of different directions (a state that physicists say has greater symmetry for mathematical reasons). The bottom square is the magnetized state once the ferromagnet has gone through a phase transition. Note that the "spin" arrows are now all lined up in the same direction, signifying the emergence of new order or coher-

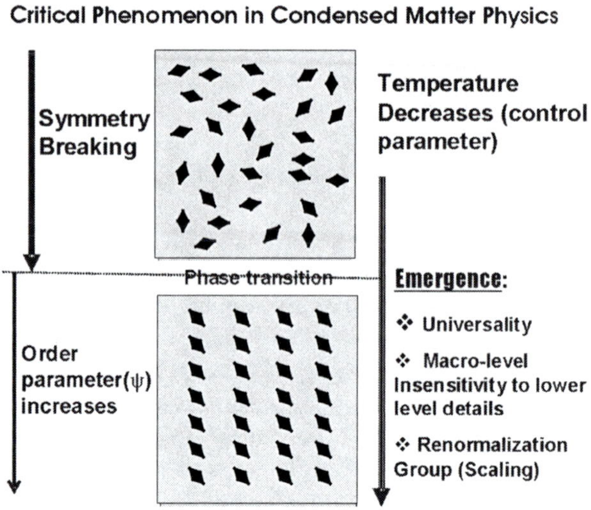

Critical Phenomenon in Condensed Matter Physics

Figure 2.8.   Onset of coherent order in phase transitions.

ence in the system which, from an explanatory perspective, shifts attention away from control parameters (e.g., temperature, pressure, composition of material, and so on) to *order parameters*, an idea emanating from the celebrated Russian physicist Lev Landau in the 1930s (Anderson, 1997).

In effect, the order parameter gauges the degree of new *coherence* in the system, clearly illustrated in the crystalline structure of ice, the unidirectional alignment of spins in ferromagnetism, and the synchronized orientation of electron spin pairs found in superconductivity. The emergence of coherence at phase transitions at criticalization is considered an instance of *universality* since it takes place in nearly the same way in all systems undergoing this kind of emergence, no matter that such systems can be quite different from one another, e.g., water and iron and helium. This universal feature implies, according to Robert Batterman (2001), a certain kind of *in*-sensitivity of the emergent, macro-order to its microlevel properties.

The coherence measured by the increase in an order parameter is the result of an amplifications of fluctuations in the correlation lengths connecting the parts of the system to one another. Indeed, such fluctuations grow to infinite magnitudes, leading to coherence across the system. The presence of infinities in the mathematics has led to a search for new ways of mathematically formalizing such systems, the most significant being what is known as the renormalization group, the technicalities of which are not pertinent here except to mention they involve understanding the fluctuations as happening at all different levels of scale, that is, a sort of "scale invariance" which will be encountered later in the chapter with the idea of power law distributions.

The Nobel Prize winning solid-state physicist Philip Anderson (1972) postulated a strongly antireductionist interpretation of science in general in what he called his "constructionist hypothesis." It argues that the ability to reduce everything to simple fundamental laws did not then imply the ability to start from those laws and reconstruct the universe from them since we discover, at each new level of complexity, novel phenomena with novel properties which then help us understand lower-level behavior even better. In an important respect, Anderson's hypothesis is another version of Waddington's delving downward strategy for theoretical biology discussed above. In both cases, it is the emergent level where the wholeness of the system is manifest and from which new laws must be derived. Another Nobel laureate in solid state physics, Robert Laughlin (2005) has recently gone even further by declaring that science in general is leaving the age of reductionism and now entering the age of emergence.

It also needs mentioning that because the emergence of novel order in systems undergoing phase transitions is associated with a lowering of temperature, there need be no conflict between this emergence and the second law of thermodynamics, that is, a lowering of temperature is associated with a lowering of entropy and lowered entropy is associated with increased orderliness. However, as we'll see in the kind of emergence in self-organizing physical systems, if new order emerges when temperature is raised, then we are up against a dilemma arising from the way increasing order is not traditionally consonant with increasing entropy.

Turing's Morphogenetic Model of Self-Organizing Emergence

Two closely connected approaches to the study of self-organization are described in the next subsection. But as a prelude to them, it is useful at this juncture to go over earlier work which established a foundation for how self-organization might occur in nature, namely, mathematical research conducted by the English mathematician Alan Turing to explain the onset of biological morphogenesis. Turing was renowned not only for his seminal theorems in mathematical logic associated with the work of Kurt Gödel, his pioneering work in the development of the computer, but, perhaps more significant from a world historical perspective sense, his work in cryptography during World War II which led to the breaking of the famous German Enigma code (Hodges, 1992).

After the war, Turing became quite interested in the question of how new biological forms could arise in embryological development without the need to call on some external explanation. Specifically, Turing

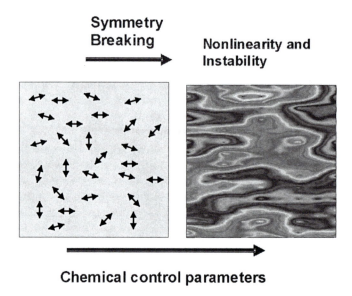

Chemical control parameters

Figure 2.9.   Onset of morphogenetic forms in Turing's model.

devised a mathematical formulation to represent how a mixture of chemicals, diffusing and reacting with each other, could generate a pattern of chemical concentrations encompassing and organizing millions of cells, that is, a self-organizing process of new form generation (Goodwin, 1994; Turing, 1952).

In this scheme, a "stew" of chemicals (represented by mathematical elements) originally without form as such (depicted in Figure 2.9 in the box on the left containing a random distributions of arrows going in different directions), develops novel patterns (the wave forms in the right box) due to the dynamics of the nonlinear equations used and the instabilities which are then generated, thereby bringing about novel order in the system. Such instabilities are cognate to both the nonlinearity-induced bifurcations of NDS and the phase transition critical points where the systems in question fail to dampen fluctuations. The presence of instability as a way whereby emergence of new order comes about has now become a cornerstone of complexity theory.

Emergence of Novel Order in Self-Organizing Systems— Synergetics and Far-From-Equilibrium Thermodynamics

The emphasis on processes of self-organization as the key to the emergence of novel order was taken up after Turing by the respective schools of Haken and Prigogine in their laboratory research. Haken has

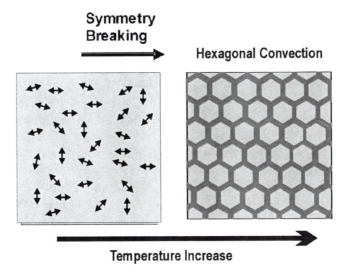

Figure 2.10.   Emergence of new order in self-organizing systems (Haken and Prigogine)

emphasized the coherence of macrolevel order, formulating it in the phase transitional terms order parameters (Haken, 1981, 1987). In particular, Haken has resorted to laser light as an exemplar of self-organizing coherence. Yet the author of this chapter has questioned the plausibility of laser light as an example of a self-organizing system since so many external constraints are needed to produce it (Goldstein, 2005). Nevertheless, the Haken school has also explored many other systems exhibiting the startling emergence of spatial and temporal order such as that paragon of self-organization, the Benard liquid which exhibits striking hexagonal convection cells when heated as shown in its stylized form in Figure 2.10.

The organized Benard convection cells on the right correspond to the "chemical" patterns Turing found in his mathematical representation of morphogenesis, and in both cases the onset of novel order has been interpreted as the *self-organization of new order* out of the internal dynamisms of the system. As mentioned, a key difference in phase transitions and the kinds of self-organization studied by Haken and Prigogine is that while in the former, temperature must decrease in order for there to be emergence, in the latter, temperature increases—a discrepancy that, as we'll say more about below, has had profound implications for the idea of entropy increase associated with the second law of thermodynamics.

Whereas Haken termed the novel coherent structures he observed "partly structured" to indicate the constant flux of energy and matter passing through them, Prigogine instead called emergent order "dissipative structures," cleverly juxtaposing two terms usually kept apart in thermodynamics circles: "dissipative" and "structure" (Nicolis, 1989; Prigogine & Stengers, 1984). "Dissipative" customarily refers to the loss of energy during a transmutation of one kind of energy to another, for example, the loss of heat seen in steam engines, a phenomena quite crucial in the early formulations of the second law and its emphasis on increasing entropy. Since an increase of entropy was customarily understood as a disintegrating tendency, "dissipative" then should carry connotations diametrically opposite to those of the building-up of "structure." Dissipative structures are often described as steady states (in this way paralleling the similar concept of Bertalanffy discussed earlier), thus connoting something that is in a dynamic, rather than static equilibrium. An analogy would be a vortex whose shape remains intact although the water molecules constituting it are are in constant flux. By bringing these contrary terms together, Prigogine was calling attention to how, in a dissipative structure," heat transfer is not correlated with the dissolution of order but can actually be a prompt for new order! We can thus appreciate how far thermodynamical based theory has come from the traditional days equating entropy increase with increased disorder (see Baranger, n.d.; Swenson, 1989). This means that the emergence of novel order in complex systems is not barred by thermodynamic considerations, but under certain circumstances, can instead be ensured.

Despite their superficial differences, the Haken and Prigogine schools rely on a similar conceptualization of the emerging order being the result of the amplification of fluctuations in the systems. In both cases, fluctuations in correlations across the system grow until they form the nucleus of a new way the system is organized after criticalization. On the one hand, it is in part the random quality of these fluctuations that accounts for much of the unpredictability (and by implication the novelty) in the outcomes of self-organizing processes (see, e.g., Allen & McGlade, 1987). On the other hand, some of the orderliness of what emerges can be traced to the orderliness of the *containers* in which self-organization takes place. Thus, Berge, Pomeau, and Vidal (1984) found that in the Benard convection, the distance separating two neighboring currents is on the order of the vertical height of the container and Weiss (1987) found that instabilities in the thermal boundaries of liquid systems similar to the Benard system lead to more complicated kinds of convection.

Organizations as Evolving, Adapting Systems of Interacting Agents: Complex Adaptive Systems Theory

We are now reaching the finale of our tour of the major schools and constructs making up the contemporary study of complex systems, that of complex, adaptive systems theory (CAS). We've waited for this juncture for an important reason: It can be plausibly asserted that CAS has assimilated most of the preceding material on complexity, not just in the sense of a grand synthesis, but, more to the point, as prompting many innovative research initiatives out of this very synthesis. Associated in the beginning with the Santa Fe Institute in Santa Fe, New Mexico, complex, adaptive systems theory is an amalgamation of research unified by a search for general features of complex systems cutting across many different fields of inquiry. The Santa Fe Institute was fashioned together in the 1980s by a group of preeminent scientists and mathematicians, including many Nobel laureates, in order to hasten the cross-fertilization of what was then being increasingly learned about the nature of complex systems. The Santa Fe Institute has, through both public and private funding, focused its energies on understanding how complex, nonlinear, interactive systems can possess and augment a capability for adapting to a changing environment. And it has gone about this daunting task through putting together into one geographical location theorists and researchers from what might previously have been thought incompatible fields: particle physicists, solid state physicists, theoretical biologists, chemists, economists, meteorologists, nonlinear dynamical systems theorists, graph theorists, computer scientists, geologists, anthropologists, writers, artists, and a host of others.

Perhaps the primary concern and uniqueness of CAS is the computational basis of much of its research. This began with "cellular automata" originally conceived by the eminent mathematician John von Neumann (von Neumann & Burks, 1966) and others (see Dyson, 1998) and later realized in the phenomenally widespread "Game of Life" invented by the mathematician John Conway (Berlekamp, Conway, & Guy, 2001). These are computer programs composed of a grid of "cells" connected to their neighboring cells according to certain simple "rules" of being "on" or "off," rules relating to the "on/off" status of neighboring cells, for example, one rule might have it that a cell be "on" if its four neighbor cells (east, west, north, and south) are also on. The striking discovery made by Conway and the literally hundreds of thousands of players since the Game of Life was invented is that the entire array can self-organize into global patterns that appear to move around the screen, some examples of which can be observed in Figure 2.11. These emergent patterns can be

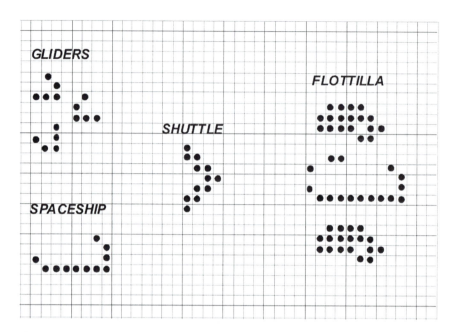

Figure 2.11.   Emergent structures in the Game of Life (from Poundstone, 1985).

quite complex although they emerge from very simple rules governing the connections among the cells.

Even more pertinent is that the strength, number, and quality of connectivities among people or groups can be modeled by these kinds of computational simulations with their cells, and rules among cells, and connections among the cells. Experimenters can change the rules, that is, qualities of connectivity, and then observe how these changes influence the emergence of new patterns which themselves can then be investigated. Thus, we get a glimpse of the huge potential such simulations have for further investigations into emergence.

The study of cellular automata has evolved under the name "artificial life" because the exploration of cellular automata and their patterns has led to insights into the way structure is built up in biological and other complex systems (e.g., see Adami, 1998; Fontana & Buss, 1996; Langton, 1996; Reitman, 1993). Artificial life evolves through various forms of recombination and randomization strategies, here copying methods used by evolution to bring about novelty (Holland, 1994, 1998). Related electronic arrays are the N/K models with "N" standing for number of nodes and "K" for number of connections, terminology which betrays the graph theoretical nature of much of this research as discussed above. Out of his research into N/K networks, the theoretical biologist turned complexity guru Stuart Kauffman (1993) has extended the use of a method called a "fitness landscape" from earlier work by Waddington and Sewall Wright. A fitness landscape amounts to a graphical way to measure and explore the adaptive value or "fitness" of different configurations of some elements in a system, such as genes in determining new traits. Each configuration and its neighbor configurations (i.e., slight modifications of it) are graphed as lower or higher peaks on a landscapelike surface. Thus, high fitness is portrayed as mountainouslike peaks, and low fitness is depicted as lower peaks or valleys. Such a display provides an indication of the degree to which various combinations add or detract from the system's survivability or sustainability. An important implication that there may be "local" peaks or "okay" solutions instead of one, perfect, optimal solution. Moreover, studies of N/K models using fitness landscapes demonstrates that there is a decreasing rate of finding fitter adaptable configurations as one travels uphill on a fitness landscape, which makes sense given that the trek is now stuck within one vertically circumscribed region of possibilities.

The complex systems finding expression in artificial life and similar computational/electronic networks are characterized by a potential for self-organization, evolving through combinatorial methods and random mutation, as well as a capacity for transforming their internal models to become more adaptable to changing environments. Examples of CAS besides artificial life include living organisms, the nervous system, the immune system, the economy, corporations, societies, and so on. In a CAS, semiautonomous agents interact according to rules of interaction and evolve by way of suboptimizing some fitness measures. The linked agents can be both diverse in form and capability and can adapt by changing their rules and, hence, their behavior, as they gain experience. Furthermore, unanticipated, emergent structures can play a determining role in the evolution of such systems. CAS's can also *coevolve*, meaning a coordinated and interdependent evolution of two or more systems within a larger ecological system, with feedback among the systems in terms of competition or cooperation and different utilizations of the same limited resources (Kauffman & Macready, 1995).

Finally, we cannot leave our description of complexity methods without mentioning a crucial construct often allied with that of a CAS, namely, *self-organized criticality* developed for the most part by the late Danish physicist Per Bak (1996), another way to understand sudden changes in organization. Central to the formulation of self-organized criticality has been that of *power law* distributions (related to the scaling method of reconciling the presence of infinities in phase transitional formulations). Power law distributions are a statistical notion standing in contrast to our customary idea of normal distributions, an example being Richter's law of earthquakes in which the magnitude of shocks is inversely proportional to their frequency, meaning that small earthquakes happen with the highest frequency, mid-level strength earthquakes take place at midrange frequency, and large earthquakes with the least frequency. If earthquakes were normally distributed, we would instead find that both the smallest and largest earthquakes would take place with less frequency than that of midrange strength earthquakes. Similar power law distributions have been found in such wide-ranging phenomena as heart beat intervals, brain activity, stock market price changes, income distribution, even in Hollywood revenues as a film's rank declines, and winners of sports tournaments.

According to Per Bak, the problem of explaining statistical features of complex systems could be phrased mathematically as the problem of explaining the underlying power laws, in particular the value of the exponents. Actually, way before Per Bak, George Kingsley Zipf (1949) discovered what he called Zipf's law which found power law distributions in many aspects of human culture, such as, the numbers of cities plotted against their populations as well as word usages in literature as well as newspapers, for example, the tenth most frequently used word in Joyce's *Ulysses* appeared 2,653 times, the twentieth 1,113 times, and the 20,000th most frequent was used only once. Bak stressed that simple systems based on equilibrium were not capable of producing phenomena with power law distributions. Even the systems studied in phase transitions, according to Bak are not complex enough except very near the critical transition point. The exact way self-organized criticality works is still under investigation and will no doubt prove to possess a great deal of context dependence.

CONCLUSION

For some readers, no doubt many of the ideas described above are new and will require some conceptual digestion. The references below can be perused and followed, or perhaps a more direct way is Wikipedia which has a great many entries on various aspects of complexity theory and is expanding these daily.

The sciences making up the study of complex systems are really in their infancy, one feature of which can be seen in the way many key complexity ideas are phrased beginning with a "negative" prefix, such as, *un*predictability, *non*linear, *non*equilibrium, and so on. This indicates two things: First, that it has been a development fueled in large part as a revolt against received wisdom; and second, that it speaks to Richardson's "darkness principle" mentioned above, that is, a recognition of our ignorance concerning complex systems. As the field matures, no doubt, there will be a filling-in of these early insights with greater differentiations, perhaps types of nonlinearities, limitations on unpredictability, and so forth.

Finally, although there's a general impression around that science has proceeded by way of a transfer of concepts and methods from the so-called "hard" sciences and mathematics to that of the "soft" sciences like sociology or organizational research, the historical record shows that many times the influence was more in the reverse direction, the development of statistics being a case in point. A similar reversal of the directionality of influence may also arise in the study of organizations as complex systems because the latter are directly accessible, do not require elaborate or expensive instruments to measure, and data can be checked and rechecked. What does seem required, however, is a change in our perspectives about what organizations essentially are and then what we should measure and how.

REFERENCES

Abraham, R., & Shaw, C. (1984). *Dynamics: The geometry of behavior* (4 parts). Santa Cruz, CA: The Visual Mathematics Library/Aerial Press.

Adami, C. (1998). *An introduction to artificial life*. New York: Springer-Verlag.

Allen, P., & McGlade, J. (1987). Evolutionary drive: The effect of microscopic diversity, error making, and noise. *Foundations of Physics, 17*, 723-738.

Anderson, P. (1972). More is different: Broken symmetry and the nature of the hierarchical structure of science. *Science, 177*(4047), 393-396.

Anderson, P. W. (1997). *Basic notions of condensed matter physics*. Boston: Perseus.

Anderson, P., & Stein, D. (1987). Broken symmetry, emergent properties, dissipative structures, life: Are they related? In F. E. Yates, A. Garfinkel, D. Walter, & G. Yates (Ed.), *Self-organizing systems: The emergence of order* (pp. 445-457). New York: Plenum Press.

Ashby, R. (1962). Principles of the self-organizing system. In H. Von Foerster & G. Zopf (Eds.), *Principles of self-organization: Transactions of the University of Illinois symposium* (pp. 255-278). London: Pergamon Press.

Bak, P. (1996). *How nature works: The science of self-organized criticality*. New York: Springer.

Barabási, A. (2002). *Linked: The new science of networks*. Cambridge, MA: Perseus Books.

Baranger, M. (n.d.) *Chaos, complexity, and entropy*. Retrieved October 1, 2006, from http://www.necsi.org/projects/baranger/cce.pdf

Batterman, R. W. (2001). *The devil in the details: Asymptotic reasoning in explanation, reduction, and emergence*. New York: Oxford University Press.

Beer, S. (1972). *Brain of the firm: The managerial cybernetics of organization*. New York: Penguin Press.

Berlekamp, E., Conway, J., & Guy, R. (2001). *Winning ways for your mathematical plays* (Vol. 1). New York: A. K. Peters.

Berge, P., Pomeau, V., & Vidal, C. (1984). *Order within chaos: Towards a deterministic approach to turbulence* (L. Tuckerman, Trans.). New York: Wiley.

Blitz, D. (1992) *Emergent evolution: Qualitative novelty and the levels of reality.* Dordrecht, Netherlands: Kluwer.

Chaos/workshop A and B. (n.d.). Retrieved August 5, 2006 from http://www.vanderbilt.edu/AnS/psychology/cogsci/chaos/workshop/WorkshopF.html

Crutchfield, J. (1993). *The calculi of emergence: Computation, dynamics, and induction* (Santa Fe Institute working paper # 94-03-016). Santa Fe, NM: Santa Fe Institute.

Diacu, F., & Holmes, P. (1996). *Celestial encounters: The origins of chaos and stability.* Princeton: Princeton University Press.

Depew, D., & Weber, B. (1996). *Darwinism evolving: Systems dynamics and the genealogy of natural selection*. Cambridge, MA: MIT Press.

Dupuy, J. (2000). *The mechanization of mind* (M. Debevoise, Trans.). Princeton, NJ: Princeton University Press.

Dyson, G. (1998). *Darwin among the machines: The evolution of global intelligence*. Boston: Perseus Books.

Fontana, W., & Buss, L. (1996). The barrier of objects: From dynamical systems to bounded organizations. In J. Casti & A. Karlqvist (Eds.), *Boundaries and barriers: On the limits to scientific knowledge* (pp. 55-115). Reading, MA: Perseus Books.

Forrester, J. W. (1961). *Industrial dynamics*. Cambridge, MA: Productivity Press.

Goldstein, J. (1999). Emergence as a construct: History and issues. *Emergence: A Journal of Complexity Issues in Organization and Management, 1*(1), 49-62.

Goldstein, J. (2003). The construction of emergence order, or how to resist the temptation of hylozoism. *Nonlinear Dynamics, Psychology, and Life sciences, 7*(4), 295-314.

Goldstein, J. (2005). Flirting with paradox: Emergence, creative process, and self-transcending constructions. *Capital Science 2004*. Washington, DC: Washington Academy of Science.

Goodwin, B. (1994). *How the leopard changed its spots: The evolution of complexity.* New York: Charles Scribner's Sons.

Haken, H. (1981). *The science of structure: Synergetics*. New York: Van Nostrand Reinhold.

Haken, H. (1987). Synergetics. In F. E. Yates, A. Garfinkel, D. Walter, & G. Yates (Eds.), *Self-organizing systems: The emergence of order* (pp. 599-613). New York: Plenum Press.

Holland, J. (1994). *Hidden order: How adaptation builds complexity.* Reading, MA: Addison-Wesley.

Holland, J. (1998). *Emergence: From chaos to order*. Reading, MA: Addison-Wesley.

Hodges, A. (1992). *Alan Turing: The enigma*. New York: Vintage.

Jones, P. (2003). Organizing relations and emergence. In R. Standish, H. Abbass, & M. Bedau (Eds.), *Artificial life VIII* (pp. 418-422). Cambridge, MA: MIT Press.

Kauffman, S. (1993). *The origins of order: Self-organization and selection in evolution.* New York: Oxford University Press.

Kauffman, S., & Macready, W. (1995). Search strategies for applied molecular evolution. *Journal of Theoretical Biology, 173,* 427-440.

Kilduff, M. & Tsai, W. (2003). *Social networks and organizations.* Thousand Oaks, CA: Sage.

Langton, C. (1996). Artificial life. In M. Boden (Ed.), *The philosophy of artificial life* (pp. 39-94). Oxford, England: Oxford University Press.

Laughlin, R. (2005). *A different universe: Reinventing physics from the bottom down.* New York: Basic Books.

Lenoir, T. (1982). *The strategy of life: Teleology and mechanics in nineteenth century German biology.* Dordrecht, Netherlands: Reidel.

Lesser, A. (2001). *Theoretical and computational aspects of Ramsey theory.* Retrieved September 9, 2006, from www.math.su.se/~x01ale/sciramsey.ams.pdf

Lorenz, E. (1996). *The essence of chaos.* Seattle, WA: University of Washington Press.

Maturana, H., & Varela, F. (1980). *Autopoeisis and cognition: The realization of the living.* Boston: Reidel.

Maturana, H., & Varela, F. (1987). *The tree of knowledge: A new look at the biological roots of human understanding.* Boston: Shambhala/New Science Library.

Nicolis, G. (1989). Physics of far-from-equilibrium systems and self-organisation. In P. Davies (Ed.), *The new physics* (pp. 316-347). Cambridge, England: Cambridge University Press.

Nicolis, G., & Prigogine, I. (1989). *Exploring complexity: An introduction.* New York: W. H. Freeman.

Petersen, I. (1995). *Newton's clock: Chaos in the solar system.* New York: W. H. Freeman.

Poundstone, W. (1985). *The recursive universe: Cosmic complexity and the limits of scientific knowledge.* Chicago: Contemporary Books.

Prigogine, I., & Stengers, I. (1984). *Order out of chaos.* New York: Bantam Books.

Reitman, E. (1993). *Creating artificial life: Self-organization.* New York: McGraw-Hill.

Richardson, K. (2005). Systems theory and complexity: Parts 1 and 2. In K. Richardson, J. Goldstein, P. Allen & D. Snowden (Eds.), *Emergence: Complexity and organization 2005 Annual, Volume 6* (pp. 490-508). Mansfield, MA: ISCE.

Rosen, R. (1996). On the limitations of scientific knowledge. In J. Casti & A. Karlqvist (Eds.), *Boundaries and barriers: On the limits to scientific knowledge* (pp. 199-214). Reading, MA: Perseus Books.

Senge, P. (1990). *The fifth discipline: The art and practice of the learning organization.* New York: Doubleday.

Shalizi, C. R. (n.d.). *Notebooks.* Retrieved October 3, 2006 from, http://www.cscs.umich.edu/~crshalizi/notebooks/

Simon, H. A. (Ed.). (1981), The architecture of complexity. In *The sciences of the artificial* (pp. 192-229). Cambridge, MA: MIT Press.

Skorin-Kapov, D. (1998). Hub network games. *Networks, 31,* 293-302).

Swenson, R. (1989). Emergent attractors and the law of maximum entropy production. *Systems Research, 6*(3), 187-198.

Turing, A. (1952). The chemical basis of morphogenesis. *Philosophical Transactions of the Royal Society,* Series B 237 (641), 37-72.

Varela, F., & Goguen, J. (1977). The arithmetic of closure. In R. Trappl (Ed.), *Progress in cybernetics and systems research* (Vol. 3, pp. 48-63). New York: Wiley Hemisphere.

Von Bertalanffy, L. (1951). *General systems theory. A new approach to unity of science*. Baltimore: Johns Hopkins University Press.

Von Neumann, J., & Burks, A. (1966). *Theory of self-reproducing automata*. Urbana: University of Illinois Press.

Waddington, C. H. (1977) Whitehead and modern science. In J. Cobb & D. Griffin (Eds.), *Mind in nature: The interface of science and philosophy*. Washington, DC: University Press of America.

Watts, D. (2003). *Small worlds: The dynamics of networks between order and randomness*. Princeton, NJ: Princeton University Press.

Weaver, W. (1948). Science and complexity. *American Scientist, 36*, 536-544.

Weiss, N. (1987). Dynamics of convection. In M. Berry, I. Percival, & N. Weiss (Eds.), *Dynamical chaos: Proceedings of the Royal Society of London* (pp. 71-85). Princeton: Princeton University Press.

Zipf, G. K. (1949). *Human behavior and the principle of least effort*. Cambridge, MA: Addison-Wesley.

CHAPTER 3

DYNAMICAL SOCIAL PSYCHOLOGY

On Complexity and Coordination in Human Experience

Robin R. Vallacher and Andrzej Nowak

ABSTRACT

Human experience reflects the interplay of myriad forces operating on various time scales to promote constantly evolving patterns of thought, emotion, and behavior. Yet people's mental states, actions, and social relations are also characterized by coherence and stability. The simultaneous dynamism and coherence of human experience represents a serious challenge for traditional theories and research paradigms in social psychology, but it reflects the essence of dynamical systems. Recent years have witnessed the emergence of a new paradigm—dynamical social psychology—that develops the implications of dynamical systems for a wide range of personal and interpersonal phenomena. We outline the essential concepts and principles of this perspective and illustrate its utility by describing its recent application to 2 perennial issues: social influence and the coordination of behavior and internal states in social relationships.

Complexity Leadership, Part I: Conceptual Foundations
pp. 49–81

49

With the dawn of the twenty-first century, social psychology shows signs of coming full circle, returning to roots established in the first half of last century. During that seminal period, several psychologists, philosophers, and sociologists provided a foundation for the fledgling discipline that was firmly anchored in the dynamic nature of human social experience. Such pioneers as James (1890), Cooley (1902), Mead (1934), Lewin (1936), and Asch (1946) all emphasized the multiplicity of interacting forces operating in individual minds and in social groups and the potential for sustained patterns of change resulting from such complexity. They also recognized the converse of dynamism and complexity: a desire for stability and simplicity, mirrored in the individual's press for mental coherence and in the tendency for groups to strive for coordination in members' thoughts, feelings, and actions. These foundational features of personal and social life—complexity and dynamism, coherence and stability—never fully disappeared from social psychology, but neither were they fully exploited in theory and research as the field moved beyond the insights of its founding fathers to stake its claim as a legitimate area of scientific inquiry. Only with the relatively recent advent of nonlinear dynamical systems theory has social psychology spawned paradigms designed to capture the dynamics that lie at the heart of virtually all intrapersonal, interpersonal, and collective phenomena.

Our aim in this chapter is to characterize the re-emergence of the dynamical perspective in social psychology. We will not attempt to describe every manifestation of this perspective. Such an attempt may have been realizable in the 1990s (see, e.g., Vallacher & Nowak, 1994a) when dynamical social psychology was just beginning to achieve momentum. Since that time, there has been a proliferation of innovative research strategies—some forwarding formal models implemented in computer simulations, others offering empirical means for capturing the dynamics of personal, interpersonal, and societal processes—each warranting a lengthy treatment in its own right. Rather, we will highlight what we feel to be the essential elements that find expression in otherwise distinct theories and research strategies, with special emphasis on those that center on interpersonal processes.[1]

We begin with an overview of basic concepts from the study of nonlinear dynamical systems that are directly relevant to the subject matter of social psychology. These concepts, despite their intuitive appeal, are difficult to identify and investigate within traditional approaches to social psychology. These difficulties in effect provide a rationale for the implicit de-emphasis of complexity and dynamism in much of mainstream social psychology. We then offer a perspective—dynamical minimalism—that provides a workable entrée into the nature and expression of dynamic processes at different levels of social reality. This approach is exemplified in the context of two lines of research concerning interpersonal dynamics—one emphasizing the emergence of group-level properties from the self-organization of individual agents, the other exploring factors that enable individuals to coordinate their respective behavioral and mental dynamics in service of forming dyads and social groups. In a concluding section, we consider the trajectory of dynamical social psychology thus far and offer caveats regarding applications of this approach to the unique features of human experience.

DYNAMICAL ESSENTIALS

Intrinsic Dynamics

People's internal states, overt actions, and social relations evolve and change in the absence of external influence. Although this observation was central to the early formulations of social psychology, and despite its clear, almost self-evident intuitive appeal, contemporary social psychological theory and research rarely focuses on the "intrinsic dynamics" of personal and interpersonal phenomena (cf. McGrath & Kelley, 1986; Nowak & Vallacher, 1998). Instead, canonical research typically concentrates on the prediction of some outcome variables (operationalized as dependent measures) from the knowledge of other factors (independent variables). External causation is obviously relevant to social processes, and the focus on outside forces has generated a wealth of insight into interpersonal, group, and societal phenomena. External factors, though, do not act on an empty or passive system, but rather interact with the intrinsic dynamics associated with the process in question.

The importance of intrinsic dynamics can be observed at different levels of social reality, from basic intrapersonal processes to macrolevel societal phenomena. At the intrapersonal level, the temporal pattern of cognitive and affective elements in the stream of thought (James, 1890) often provides a better characterization of a person's mental make-up than does the summary aspects of his or her thoughts (e.g., overall attitude, final decision) that are more commonly the focus of investigation (cf. Vallacher & Nowak, 1994b). The research on thought-induced attitude polarization, for example, has shown that when people simply think about an attitude object (e.g., another person) in the absence of external influence or new information, their evaluation of the object tends to become more extreme over time (e.g., Tesser, 1978). Research on social judgment, meanwhile, has shown that internally generated thoughts and feelings about a target person often reflect rich and elaborate patterns of change that convey important information about the person's judgment.

A judgment of someone that is neutral when collapsed over time, for instance, can have quite different meanings and implications, depending on the intrinsic dynamics of the judgment process (Vallacher, Nowak, & Kaufman, 1994). If neutrality reflects relatively little variation in evaluation occurring on a relatively slow time-scale, the summary judgment might indeed reflect a truly neutral sentiment (or detachment). If, however, neutrality reflects oscillation on a rapid timescale between highly positive and highly negative judgments, the summary judgment is indicative of heightened involvement and ambivalence rather than neutrality per se.

Personal action can also be characterized with respect to intrinsic dynamics. Actions typically have a hierarchical structure. This means that the performance of an action entails the coordinated interplay of more basic actions or subacts. The simple act of "getting to work," for example, may involve getting dressed, leaving the house, driving, and entering a building. Each of these lower-level acts, in turn, can be decomposed into yet more basic lower-level elements. Thus, "driving" consists of starting the car, turning the steering wheel, braking, making turns, and so on. Each level in an action hierarchy is associated with a different time scale, with the implementation of lower-level acts taking place in correspondingly shorter intervals of time (cf. Newtson, 1994). "Getting to work" operates on a longer time scale than does "driving," for example, and the time scale for "driving" is longer than that for each instance of "turning the steering wheel." The intrinsic dynamics of action can thus span the levels of action in an overall action hierarchy. A person's behavior may look like a continual succession of momentary movements when defined in low-level, mechanistic terms, but take on the appearance of switching between qualitatively different actions, each occurring on a longer time scale, when defined in higher-level terms. Interestingly, there is reason to believe that the embedded time scales in an action hierarchy may have a fractal structure (Newtson, 1994). The level at which an action is identified and regulated is influenced by a variety of factors (cf. Vallacher & Wegner, 1987). Research has also shown that people reliably differ in their default level of action identification across a wide variety of action domains (Vallacher & Wegner, 1989).

Social interaction involves the temporal coordination of individuals' behavior and thus can be investigated with respect to intrinsic dynamics. Research on this topic has largely centered on the interpersonal coordination of relatively low-level actions, such as speaking (e.g., Condon & Ogston, 1967; Dittman & Llewellyn, 1969) and limb movement (e.g., Beek & Hopkins, 1992; Kelso, 1995; Newtson, 1994; Turvey, 1990). Two individuals, for example, might simply be asked to swing their legs while sitting down across from one another (Beek & Hopkins, 1992). One person swings his or her legs in time to a metronome and the other person tries to match those movements. This research reveals two forms of coordination: in-phase, with the individuals swinging their legs in unison, and antiphase, with the individuals swinging their legs with the same frequency but in the opposite direction. Hysteresis is also commonly observed. When participants are instructed to synchronize antiphase, they are able to do so only up to a certain frequency of movement, at which they switch to in-phase synchronization. When the tempo decreases, at some value they are able to coordinate antiphase again, but this tempo is significantly lower than the point at which they originally started to synchronize in-phase. The appearance of hysteresis shows that movement coordination can be analyzed as a nonlinear dynamical system (Kelso, 1995). Yet more complex modes of coordination have been captured in this line of research (cf. Baron, Amazeen, & Beek, 1994; Rosenblum & Turvey, 1988; Turvey, 1990; Turvey & Carello, 1995).

Interpersonal dynamics go beyond the coordination of speech and motor movements to include the temporal coordination of higher-level actions (e.g., plans, goals) and internal states (moods, judgments, etc.). Research on this form of interpersonal dynamics is somewhat sparse, although there is reason to believe that the quality of a social relationship is reflected in the ability of partners to coordinate in-phase with respect to their respective higher-level actions, feelings, and opinions (e.g., Baron et al., 1994; McGrath & Kelly, 1986; Nowak, Vallacher, & Zochowski, 2002; Tickle-Degnen & Rosenthal, 1987). Dynamically speaking, the ebb and flow of sentiment, information exchange, and action may be more informative about the nature of a relationship than are global indices such as the average sentiment, the amount of information exchanged, or the summary action tendencies. In everyday parlance, people who like one another are said to "be in synch" or "on the same wavelength" with respect to their internal states. In a subsequent section (Interpersonal Synchronization), we present a formal model of social coordination that has been implemented in computer simulations, and we develop the implications of this approach for classic and contemporary issues in interpersonal relations.

At a societal level, tracking the temporal trajectory associated with the emergence of norms and public opinion may provide greater insight into the society's future makeup and likely response to external threat than simply knowing what the norms and public sentiments are (cf. Nowak, Szamrej, & Latané, 1990). When norms and opinions develop slowly and incrementally, for example, the society is likely to display resistance to external threats or even to new information that might promote better economic conditions. Societal change in political and economic ideology, however, can also occur in a rapid, nonlinear manner (e.g., Nowak &

Vallacher, 2001; Nowak, Vallacher, Kus, & Urbaniak, 2005), with a trajectory that resembles phase transitions in physical systems (Lewenstein, Nowak, & Latané, 1993). Such nonlinear societal transitions can render the society vulnerable to subsequent rebounds of the earlier ideologies and highly responsive to threats and new information, and they can promote a period of sustained oscillation between conflicting worldviews (Nowak & Vallacher, 2001).

Attractors

Psychological systems display intrinsic dynamics, but as noted by the founding fathers of social psychology (James, Lewin, Asch, etc.), they also demonstrate stability and remarkable resistance to change. Each day provides vast amounts of information relevant to social judgment and social relations, much of it mutually contradictory, yet people nonetheless manage to forge and maintain coherent patterns of thought and behavior in their social lives. Individuals in a close relationship, for example, may experience a wide variety of thoughts and feelings about one another, but over time each person's mental state is likely to converge on positive sentiment toward the other. Despite the dynamic nature of personal and interpersonal experience, then, the trajectory of people's mental, affective, and behavioral states tends to converge on relatively narrow sets of specific states or on patterns of change between specific states. These states or patterns of change are referred to as *attractors*.

The presence of an attractor for a dynamical system implies not only convergence of intrinsic dynamics on a small set of states or a pattern of change between states, but also resistance of the system to external perturbation. When a system is at its attractor, it tends to maintain that state despite forces and information that hold potential for destabilizing that state. Although external influences can in principle move the system to almost any state, the system will relatively quickly return to one of its attractors. From a dynamical perspective, many important and well-documented psychological processes imply the existence of an attractor. Self-regulation, for example, involves resistance to temptations and distractions, impulse control, and the maintenance of states corresponding to standards of regulation (cf. Carver & Scheier, 1999, 2002; Vallacher & Nowak, 1999). In similar fashion, psychological reactance (Brehm & Brehm, 1966), self-esteem maintenance (Tesser, Martin, & Cornell, 1996), and self-verification (Swann, 1990) all reflect a tendency of the cognitive system to converge on a particular mental state and to resist outside forces that threaten to dislodge the person's opinions and beliefs from that state.

Three basic types of attractors have been identified in different domains of science: fixed-point attractors, periodic (including multiperiodic) attractors, and deterministic chaos (cf. Eckmann & Ruelle, 1985; Nowak & Lewenstein, 1994; Schuster, 1984). Each type may have particular relevance for interpersonal processes, although this relevance has yet to be demonstrated for many central phenomena in social psychology.

Fixed-Point Attractors. A *fixed-point attractor* is similar to the notion of equilibrium or homeostasis (cf. Cannon, 1932; Miller, 1944). It describes the case in which the state of the system converges to a stable value. In psychological systems, a fixed-point attractor may correspond to a desired end state or goal (cf. Carver & Scheier, 1999, 2002; Vallacher & Nowak, 1997). Thus, a person might display a tendency to maintain a belief, an evaluation of someone, or an action tendency, despite forces or sources of information that challenge these tendencies. Attractors, however, are not limited to goals, intentions, or desired states. Indeed, a person might display a pattern of hostile behavior in his or her social relations, despite efforts to avoid behaving in this manner. In similar fashion, an individual with low self-esteem may initially embrace positive feedback from someone, but over time he or she may discount such feedback, displaying instead a pattern of self-evaluative thought that converges on a negative state (Swann, Hixon, Stein-Seroussi, & Gilbert, 1990). In an intergroup context, warring factions may exhibit conciliatory gestures when prompted to do so, but revert to a pattern of antagonistic thought and behavior when outside interventions are relaxed. A system governed by a fixed-point attractor, in short, will consistently evolve to a particular state, even if this state is not hedonically pleasant, and will return to this state despite being perturbed by forces that might promote a more pleasant state.

A system may have multiple attractors, each corresponding to a distinct stable state. The attractor that is salient in a particular instance depends on the initial states or starting values of the system's evolution. The set of initial states leading to each attractor constitutes the *basin of attraction* for that attractor. In a person or a group characterized by multiple fixed-point attractors, then, the process in question can display different equilibrium tendencies, each associated with a distinct basin of attraction. Within each basin, even quite different initial states will follow a trajectory that eventually converges on the same stable value. By the same token, however, even a slight deviation in the system's initial state may promote a dramatic change in the system's trajectory if this deviation represents a state that falls just outside the original basin of attraction and within a basin for a different attractor. In a conflict situation, for example, there may be two dominant responses, corresponding to aggression and conciliation. Very slight differences in the circumstances associated with the conflict will thus lead to dramatically different behaviors, with no option for a response that integrates the two tendencies (e.g., Coleman, Vallacher, Nowak, & Bui-Wrzosinska, 2007).

A simple metaphor conveys the essence of the attractor concept and its relevance for personal and social processes. Imagine a ball on a hilly land-scape, as in Figure 3.1, with the ball representing the current state of the system and the valleys (A and B) representing different fixed-point attrac-tors for the system. The state of the system evolves toward an attractor, much like the ball rolls down a hill and comes to rest at the bottom of a valley. Each attractor is associated with a set of states that will evolve toward the attractor—that is, it has a particular basin attraction. The basin of attraction for Attractor A in Figure 3.1 is somewhat wider than the basin for Attractor B, which means that a wider variety of states will evolve toward Attractor A than toward Attractor B. Attractors can also vary in their respective strength, corresponding to the relative depth of the two valleys in Figure 3.1. Attractor B, then, is stronger than Attractor A. When the current state of the system is within the basin of attraction for Attractor B, it is more difficult for it to be dislodged by external influ-ence than if it were within the basin of attraction for Attractor A.

The potential for multiple fixed-point attractors conveys the intuition captures that people often have different (perhaps conflicting) goals, val-ues, self-views, and patterns of interpersonal behavior. Someone may have more than one standard for self-regulation, for example, with each providing for action guidance and self-control under different sets of con-ditions. The person's action may conform to an achievement standard under a range of conditions that promote this tendency, but reflect affilia-tion standards under a different set of conditions. Likewise, a person may have multiple self-views (e.g., Markus & Nurius, 1986), each representing a coherent and stable way of thinking about him or herself that comes to

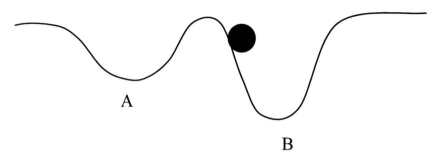

Source: Vallacher & Nowak (in press).

Figure 3.1.   A dynamical system with two fixed-point attractors (A and B).

the fore when a specific set of self-relevant information is primed or made salient by virtue of context or role expectations. Apparent inconsistency or conflict in personality, too, can be viewed as the existence of multiple attractors, each associated with a different basin of attraction for thought and action (cf. Nowak et al., 2002). One set of conditions and initial states might promote a trajectory that evolves toward compassion and warmth, while another might promote instead dominance and competition.

Because the strength of an attractor and the size of its basin of attraction are independent (at least in principle), different combinations of these properties may have distinct implications for psychological processes.[2] Consider Attractors A and B in Figure 3.1. Attractor A is relatively weak but has a wide basin of attraction. This means that a relatively small force may be sufficient to change the state of the system (i.e., move the ball up the gradual slope), but even if these changes are relatively large, the system is likely to return to the attractor (i.e., it will roll back into the valley). Attractor B, in contrast, is relatively strong but has a narrower basin of attraction. Thus, considerable influence is necessary to have even a slight impact on the system (i.e., move the ball up the steep slope), but if this effect is achieved, the system will lose its ability to return to the attractor (i.e., it will escape the valley).

To illustrate the implications of this difference, imagine a romantic couple that has a strong attractor associated with positive feelings, but also a weak attractor associated with negative feelings. The couple are likely to evolve toward positive feelings if the partners begin an interaction within a broad range of affective states (e.g., neutral to very positive), but they may just as consistently end up feeling negative about one another if they begin an interaction within a different (more restricted) range of affective states (e.g., mildly to highly negative). Because the couple has a wider basin of attraction for positive feelings than for negative feelings, a broader range of initial states are likely to promote a communication trajectory that results in an exchange of warm sentiments. But if the couple routinely starts out with negative feelings, the negative attractor, although relatively narrow, may dictate the predominant trajectory for feelings expressed in the couple's interactions. Conceivably, of course, the couple could have a wider basin of attraction for negative feelings, so that anything short of a highly positive initial state could dissolve into a negatively toned exchange.

Latent Attractors. A system may be characterized by multiple attractors, but when the system is at one of them, the others may not be visible to observers (perhaps not even to the actors themselves). The existence of these potential states of the system might not even be suspected. These *latent attractors* may be highly important in the long run, however, because they determine which states are possible for the system when conditions change. By specifying possibilities for a system that have yet to be observed or experienced, the concept of latent attractor goes beyond the traditional notion of equilibrium. Critical changes in a system might not be reflected in the observable state of the system, but rather in the creation or destruction of a latent attractor representing a potential state that is currently invisible to all concerned.

The implications of latent attractors have recently been explored in the context of social relations characterized by seemingly intractable conflict (Coleman et al., 2007; Nowak, Vallacher, Bui-Wrzosinska, & Coleman, in press). Consider intergroup relations, for example. Although factors such as objectification, dehumanization, and stereotyping of outgroup members are preconditions for the development of intractable conflict (Coleman, 2003; Deutsch, 1973), their immediate impact may not be apparent. Instead, these factors may gradually create a latent attractor to which the system can abruptly switch in response to a provocation that seems relatively minor, even trivial. But by the same token, efforts at conflict resolution that seem fruitless in the short run may have the effect of creating a latent positive attractor for inter-group relations, thereby establishing a potential relationship to which the groups can switch if other conditions permit. The existence of a latent positive attractor can promote a rapid de-escalation of conflict, even between groups with a long history of and seemingly intractable conflict.

Periodic Attractors. Rather than converging on a stable value over time, some systems display sustained rhythmic or oscillatory behavior. A temporal pattern conforming to this tendency is referred to as a periodic or limit-cycle attractor. Periodicity is clearly associated with many biological phenomena, such as circadian rhythms and menstrual cycles (cf. Glass & Mackey, 1988), but this dynamic tendency may also underlie important psychological phenomena (Gottman, 1979). Moods, for example, have been shown to have a periodic structure, often corresponding to a weekly cycle (e.g., Brown & Moskowitz, 1998; Larsen, 1987; Larsen & Kasimatis, 1990). Investigation of the intrinsic dynamics associated with both social judgment (Vallacher et al., 1994) and self-evaluation (Vallacher, Nowak, Froehlich, & Rockloff, 2002), meanwhile, has demonstrated that the stream of thought often oscillates between positive and negative assessments, sometimes in accordance with remarkably fast time scales. Periodic structure has also been shown to characterize human action (Newtson, 1994) and is a feature of social interaction as well (e.g., Beek & Hopkins, 1992; Gottman, 1979; Nezlek, 1993).

It may be difficult to distinguish a periodic attractor from the existence of multiple fixed-point attractors. In both cases, the system displays movement between different states over time. The distinction centers on the regularity of the movement between states and the role of external factors in producing such movement. A periodic attractor represents a repetitive temporal pattern, with the values of the dynamical variable repeating after a time T, $x_i(t) = (t + T)$, where T is the period of motion. Even in the absence of noise or external influence, the state of the system undergoes constant change. For a pattern of change to qualify as a periodic attractor, then, it must represent a pattern on which the system converges, and to which it returns after small perturbations. In a daily cycle of activity, for example, a sleepless night might temporarily disrupt the pattern (e.g., oversleeping the next few days), but eventually the pattern will be restored.

A system characterized by fixed-point attractors, in contrast, displays a tendency to stabilize on a particular state or set of states. Because such attractors capture all trajectories within their respective basins, a disturbance, noise, or an external influence operating on the system is necessary to move the system from one stable state to another. A person with self-regulatory standards for both confrontation and compromise, for example, will display one of these tendencies as long as the context surrounding the person is within the basin of attraction for that tendency. If the two attractors differ in the size of their respective basins, and if contexts are avoided that attract the person's mental, emotional, or behavioral state toward the smaller basin, the person may operate for long periods of time in line with the stronger attractor. Likewise, a romantic couple may have fixed-point attractors for both positive and negative affective states, but whether they display periodic movement between them will depend on the starting conditions associated with their interactions. Thus, even if the couple seems to oscillate between positive and negative states, each of these states provides at least temporary stability. In periodic evolution, stability is not afforded by any particular state, but rather by the pattern of changes between states.

The distinction between periodic and fixed-point attractor dynamics was observed in a study investigating the temporal trajectories of affective states on the part of bipolar depressive individuals (Johnson & Nowak, 2002). Time-series analysis of mood and other symptoms revealed that many of these patients seemed to oscillate between a normal and a depressed state. The results showed, however, that patients whose temporal dynamics did not reflect fixed-point attractor tendencies were at highest risk for suicide and were hospitalized more often for their depression. These risks were equally low for individuals whose moods oscillated around a single attractor, even one corresponding to a depressed state, and those whose moods switched between two distinct attractors reflecting a normal state and a depressed state. These results suggest an interesting connection between attractor dynamics and self-regulatory tendencies. Self-regulation implies approach and stabilization with respect to some states and avoidance and destabilization of other states. The stable states represent fixed-point attractors for a person's mental and emotional dynamics. From this perspective, the lack of fixed-point attractors for one's internal state signals a breakdown in the capacity for self-regulation.

Deterministic Chaos. The best known, and arguably the most popular insight concerning nonlinear dynamical systems centers on *deterministic chaos* (cf. Schuster, 1984). Indeed, many researchers and scholars—especially those from fields other than mathematics and physics—commonly discuss the primary insights from the work on nonlinear dynamics as chaos theory (cf. Gleick, 1987). When investigating a chaotic system, anything short of infinite precision in the knowledge of a system at one point in time can undermine knowledge of the system's future states. This decoupling between determinism and practical predictability occurs because all initial inaccuracies are amplified by the system's intrinsic dynamics, so that the inaccuracies grow exponentially over time. After some finite (often quite short) time, exponential growth assures that the size of the error will exceed the possible range of states of the system's behavior.

Chaos represents an ever-present possibility in nonlinear dynamical systems (cf. Goldstein, 1996; Nowak & Lewenstein, 1994). In fact, chaos has been demonstrated in many biological and physical phenomena. One cannot rule out the possibility, then, that human thought and behavior may sometimes follow a chaotic trajectory. After all, social psychology is replete with nonlinear phenomena, such as threshold functions, inverted-U relations, and complex interactions among causal variables (Nowak & Vallacher, 1998; Vallacher & Nowak, 1997). But despite this potential, unequivocal evidence for deterministic chaos in human thought and behavior remains to be documented. Human dynamics invariably contain some degree of randomness and human behavior is often unpredictable. However, it can be quite difficult to determine the degree to which such unpredictability reflects deterministic chaos, the stochastic nature of the laws governing human nature, or the multitude of influences unaccounted for by measurement that can be treated as noise.

Attractor Dynamics in Perspective. Attractor dynamics are highly relevant to personal and interpersonal processes. Beyond capturing basic intuitions underlying many social psychological phenomena, framing such phenomena in terms of attractors may allow for a significant simplification in the description of a system's dynamics. Instead of describing moment-to-moment changes in a system's state, one can describe the structure of attractors in the system and the patterns of transition between the attractors. Short-lived reversible changes of the state of the system correspond to transitions between attractors. Deep and lasting changes, on the other hand, usually correspond to changes in the structure of attractors.

DYNAMICAL MINIMALISM

The traditional approach to theory construction assumes that the complexity of human thought and behavior must be reflected in the complexity of the model, with many variables and complex interactions among them required to explain the phenomenon of interest. The approach of *dynamical minimalism* (Nowak, 2004) challenges this assumption. Basic to this approach is the observation that very simple elements interacting in accordance with simple rules can produce remarkably complex properties at the level of the system. The emergence of complexity occurs when the relations among elements are nonlinear and the elements interact over time. For example, in a simple network of binary elements, where each element reacts to the input it receives from other elements, one can observe complex cognitive phenomena, such as learning on the basis of examples, pattern recognition, error correction, and generalization (e.g., Hopfield, 1982).

The complexity of the system can greatly surpass the complexity of its elements and the rules of their interaction. Because of this gain in complexity, it may be possible to explain very complex phenomena with very simple models. The goal of dynamical minimalism is to identify the simplest, yet realistic, set of assumptions capable of producing a phenomenon of interest. The resultant theories thus provide simple explanations that nonetheless capture the complexity of human thought and behavior. Indeed, many of the more interesting relationships in social psychology—such as inverted-U relations, threshold phenomena, and statistical interactions—reflect nonlinearity and thus have the potential for self-organization and emergence if the variables are embedded in a larger system that evolves over time (cf. Nowak & Vallacher, 1998; Vallacher & Nowak, 1997). In effect, the approach of dynamical minimalism maximizes parsimony in theory construction, but does so without trivializing the phenomenon in question.

Dynamical minimalism offers a new perspective on the relation between micro- and macro-levels of description. In models assuming reductionism, the rules observed at one level of description directly correspond to the rules observed at another level. The properties at higher levels of description, in other words, can be directly reduced to the properties of lower-level elements. A reductionist account, for example, would suggest that the relation between poverty and crime on the social level can be reduced to the relation between frustration and aggression at the level of individuals.

Such isomorphism is not assumed in dynamical models. To the contrary, the rules operating at one level are likely to generate wholly different rules at a higher level. In our *society of self* model of self-structure, for instance, we implemented very simple rules concerning the integration of self-relevant information (Nowak, Vallacher, Tesser, & Borkowski, 2000). We assumed only that each element of information concerning the self assumed the prevailing valence (i.e., positivity or negativity) of related elements. Repeated iterations of this simple rule of influence generated several interesting but largely unanticipated consequences at the global level of self-concept, including the differentiation of self-structure into locally coherent regions (e.g., social roles) of contrasting valence, resistance to discrepant incoming information (e.g., negative social feedback), and the emergence of self-esteem and self-certainty.

Emergence refers to properties on the system level that cannot be derived from properties of the elements comprising the system. This represents somewhat of a paradox for theory construction. In a system characterized by emergence, how can knowledge of lower-level elements serve as an explanation of higher-level properties? This question can be resolved by highlighting the centrality of computer simulations to dynamical minimalism. With computer models, one can specify the properties of system elements and the rules of interaction among these elements. When the elements interact over time according to the specified rules, one observes dynamics at the system level that were not assumed or programmed for the individual elements. In this sense, computer simulations allow for a theory constructed at one level of psychological reality to be tested at a different level of psychological reality.

Computer simulations are essential to the minimalist approach for another reason. The properties of individual elements are often uninteresting, even trivial, and the interactions among such elements with these properties may have minor impact on the properties at the system level. Some properties of individual elements, however, may have profound impact on the system's higher-order properties when the elements interact over time. It may not be obvious in advance which properties are trivial and which are crucial to emergence. The goal of dynamical minimalism is make this distinction and build a model that incorporates only the variables that are critical for the emergence of macro level properties. Computer simulations allow one to systematically vary the assumptions concerning different properties of elements and their interactions, and observe which assumptions result in noteworthy and meaningful changes at the macro level. The properties of elements that do not have consequences at the system level can be omitted from the model. In effect, computer simulations distill the minimal set of components necessary to capture the essence of the phenomenon of interest.

Computer simulations clearly play a pivotal role in dynamical minimalism, but they cannot substitute for empirical verification of a theory's assumptions. Rather, computer simulations should be viewed as a means of identifying the crucial assumptions of a theoretical model and thereby providing guidance for empirical efforts. Thus, computer simulations of processes assumed to operate at lower level are used to investigate the consequences of these processes at a higher level. These consequences, in turn, can be used as hypotheses to be tested in empirical research. Computer simulations, for example, were used to derive predictions from dynamic social impact theory (Nowak et al., 1990) concerning spatial-temporal patterns of social change processes. These hypothesized patterns were subsequently assessed by means of archival data concerning patterns of entrepreneurship and voting patterns in Poland following the fall of Communism in the 1990s (Nowak et al., 2005). The relationship between computer simulations and empirical research can take the opposite pattern as well. Thus, rather than testing a model's assumptions, empirical tests can be used to refine the model. The refined model can then be implemented in computer simulations, the results of which can provide further hypotheses to be tested in empirical research. This reciprocal loop between theory, computer simulation, and empirical research is central to dynamical social psychology.

SOCIAL INFLUENCE: BINDING INDIVIDUALS INTO GROUPS

A social group is clearly different from a collection of individuals. A throng of people may stand shoulder to shoulder on a street corner, for example, but they are unlikely to think about themselves as constituting a meaningful group. Two different processes assemble individuals into groups. First, social interdependence, as described by game theoretic approaches (cf. Thibaut & Kelley, 1959), captures the realization that the decisions and actions of one individual have consequences for the decisions and actions of others. The Prisoner's Dilemma Game (PDG) epitomizes social interdependence and has been the subject of intense dynamical modeling (e.g., Axelrod, 1984; Messick & Liebrand, 1995).

The other assembly process is social influence, considered by many to be the core process of social psychology (cf. Vallacher, Nowak, & Miller, 2003). Broadly defined, social influence refers to any change in an individual's thoughts, feelings, or behavior that occurs as the result of the real or imagined presence of others (cf. Allport, 1968). Although social influence encompasses a wide assortment of specific phenomena (e.g., conformity, obedience, stage fright, social loafing, bystander intervention, imitation), at some level of abstraction its magnitude can be described with respect to three basic factors: the number, strength, and immediacy of the sources of influence (Latané, 1981). Many empirical studies have shown that social influence can be described as a multiplicative function of these sources.

Modeling the Dynamics of Social Influence

Nowak et al. (1990) modeled the dynamics of social influence with cellular automata. In the model, each individual is characterized by three factors: his or her opinion on a topic, persuasive strength, and position in a social space. For simplicity sake, individuals are usually assumed to have one of two opinions on an issue (e.g., pro vs. con). The social group consists of n individuals located on a two-dimensional grid, as portrayed in Figure 3.2, with each cell corresponding to an individual. The color of the box indicates the individual's current opinion (light gray denotes pro, dark gray denotes con), and the height of the box represents the individual's strength (e.g., confidence, expertise). Each individual discusses the issue with other group members to assess the degree of support for each position. In the process of social interaction, each individual adopts the opinion that is most prevalent. The strength of influence of each opinion is expressed as follows:

$$I_i = \left(\sum_{1}^{N} \left(\frac{s_j}{d_{ij}^2} \right)^2 \right)^{1/2},$$

where I_i denotes total influence, s_j corresponds to the strength of each individual, and d_{ij} corresponds to the distance between individuals i and j. The opinions of those who are closest and have the greatest strength are weighted most heavily. An individual's own position is also taken into consideration and is weighted most heavily by virtue of immediacy (0 distance). Influence also grows with the square root of the number of people exerting influence.

In computer simulations, one individual is chosen (usually at random), and influence is computed for each opinion in the group. The updating rule is simple: if the resultant strength for an opinion position is greater than the strength of the individual's current position, he or she changes his or her opinion to match the prevailing position. This process is performed for each individual. This procedure is repeated until there are no further changes. This typically requires several rounds of simulation, because a person who had previously changed his or her position to match that of his or her neighbors may revert to the original position if the neighbors change their opinions. Figure 3.2 illustrates representative results of the computer simulations. In Figure 3.2a, there is a majority of 60% (light gray) and a minority of 40% (dark gray). The majority and minority members are randomly distributed, and each group has the same relative proportions of strong and weak members (tall vs. short boxes). After six rounds of simulated discussion, an equilibrium is reached, which is depicted in Figure 3.2b. The majority (now 99%) has grown at the expense of the minority (now 10%). The minority opinion has survived by forming clusters of like-minded people and these clusters are largely formed around strong individuals.

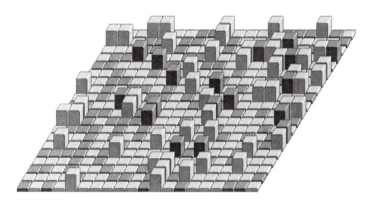

Source: Vallacher & Nowak (in press).

Figure 3.2b.   Initial distribution of opinions in the simulated group.

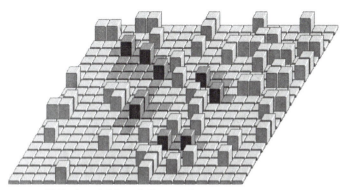

Source: Vallacher & Nowak (in press).

Figure 3.2b.   Final equilibrium of opinions in the simulated group.

These two group-level outcomes, referred to as *polarization* and *clustering,* are routinely observed in computer simulations (cf. Latané, Nowak, & Liu, 1994). They are reminiscent of well-documented social processes. As demonstrated in empirical research on group dynamics (e.g., Myers & Lamm, 1976), the average attitude in a group becomes polarized in the direction of the prevailing attitude as a result of group discussion. This process reflects the greater influence of the majority opinion. In the initial (random) configuration (Figure 3.2a), the average proportion of neighbors holding a given opinion (pro or con) reflects the proportion of this opinion in the total group. The average group member, in other words, is surrounded by more majority than minority members, which results in more minority members being converted to the majority position than vice versa. Of course, some majority members are converted to the minority position because they happen to be located close to an especially influential minority member or because more minority members happen to be at this location.

Clustering is also a pervasive feature of social life. Attitudes, for example, have been shown to cluster in residential neighborhoods (Festinger, Schachter, & Back, 1950). Clustering has been observed for political beliefs, religions, clothing fashions, and farming techniques. The tendency for opinions to cluster in the simulations is due to the relatively strong influence exerted by an individual's neighbors. When opinions are distributed randomly, the sampling of opinions through social interaction provides a reasonably accurate portrait of the distribution of opinions in the larger society. But when opinions are clustered, the same sampling process will produce a highly biased result because the opinions of those in the nearby vicinity are weighted the most heavily. The prevalence of one's own opinion, in other words, is likely to be overestimated. This means that opinions that are in the minority in global terms can form a local majority, thereby enabling individuals who hold a minority opinion to maintain this opinion in the belief that it represents a majority position.

Three basic factors distinguish this scenario from unification of the group around the majority opinion (Latané & Nowak, 1997; Lewenstein et al., 1993; Nowak, Lewenstein, & Frejlak, 1996). Minority clusters survive, first of all, because of individual differences in strength. Strong leaders stop minority clusters from decaying by counteracting the sheer number of majority opinions. Because of social influence, moreover, individual differences in strength tend to become correlated with opinions. This occurs because the weakest minority members will most likely adopt the majority position, so that the average strength of the remaining minority members will grow over time at the expense of the majority. This scenario may explain why individuals who advocate minority positions are commonly more influential than those who advocate majority positions (cf. Moscovici, Lage, & Naffrechoux, 1969).

The second factor serving to preserve minority clusters is nonlinearity in attitude change. Abelson (1979) demonstrated that when individuals move incrementally toward the opinions of their interaction partners, groups become unified in their support of the majority opinion. In the Nowak et al. (1990) model, however, attitudes change nonlinearly in accordance with a threshold function. This means that individuals maintain their current opinion until social influence reaches a critical level, at which point they switch from one categorical position (e.g., pro) to the other (con). A linear change rule implies a normal distribution of opinions and promotes unification of opinions. In contrast, a nonlinear change rule implies a bimodal distribution and can prevent complete unification and enable minority opinion to survive in clusters. Latané and Nowak (1994) demonstrated that a normal distribution tends to develop for relatively unimportant attitudes, but that a bimodal distribution tends to be observed when the attitudes at issue have high personal importance. This implies that to achieve consensus in a group may require temporarily decreasing the subjective importance of the topic.

The third factor relevant to the survival of minority clusters concerns the geometry of the space in which individuals interact (Nowak, Latané, & Lewenstein, 1994). People clearly do not communicate equally with all members of a group, nor are their interactions often random. Different communication patterns can be approximated in the cellular automata model with various geometries of social space. When geometry is lacking altogether and interactions occur randomly between people, minority opinion decays rapidly and the group converges on the majority position. Other geometries, representing different communication patterns, have been found to have predictable consequences for the fate of minority opinions. Of course, in real social settings several different geometries are likely to coexist and determine the emergence of opinion structure. The ready availability of telephones, e-mail, shopping malls, and common areas for recreation add many dimensions to the effective geometry in which interactions take place. The combined geometries in real life undoubtedly play important roles in shaping the distribution of public opinion.

Social Influence in Perspective

People clearly attempt to influence one another and such attempts sometimes represent only a concern with forwarding one's agenda. But social influence has a nobler role to play as well in social life. It provides the mechanism that binds separate individuals into a social group with a common psychological state and platform for action. In interacting with one another, individuals adjust their opinions, mood, or behavior to promote consensus. Even if the individuals have diverse opinions and initially disagree with one another, uniform opinions tend to form over time during the course of sustained social interaction. However, the group-level product of local social interactions does not simply reflect the central tendency of members' individual initial opinions. Rather, social interaction promotes the emergence of an opinion that is typically more extreme than the average of group members' opinions (e.g., Myers & Lamm, 1976). And assuming that there are individual differences in persuasiveness, minority opinions are likely to be preserved, albeit at a lower proportion, particularly if the issue being discussed has high subjective importance for group members.

The adoption of a common psychological state through social interaction is largely adaptive. It provides the social coordination and consensus necessary for social life and group action. At the same time, though, there are noteworthy downsides associated with the tendency for groups to achieve uniformity. Classic research in social psychology, for example, has shown how social influence in groups can promote mindless conformity to inaccurate assessments of reality (cf. Asch 1955; Sherif, 1936). The emphasis on like-mindedness in groups can also produce decisions and recommendations for action that are guided more by a concern for reaching consensus than for developing the best policy. People under the spell of "groupthink" (Janis, 1982), for example, expend considerable mental energy on achieving and maintaining group solidarity and opinion unanimity. And once a group has achieved a common psychological state, anyone who expresses a contrary view is likely to experience enormous pressure to change. Those who do not cave in to such pressure run the risk of being rejected (Schachter, 1951). The rejection of deviates has clear implications for various social phenomena, from peer pressure among adolescents to jury deliberations in cases where a guilty verdict carries the death sentence (e.g., Hastie, Penrod, & Pennington, 1983).

INTERPERSONAL SYNCHRONIZATION

The dynamical theory of social influence portrays how the state (e.g., attitude) of a single individual depends on the state of other individuals. As noted earlier, however, many psychological processes are defined in terms of intrinsic dynamics. This implies that individuals cannot be adequately described as a set of states but rather are best conceptualized as displaying patterns of change. Since the influence process is ongoing as individuals interact with one another, social influence is manifest as the coordination over time of individual dynamics. Building on this observation, Nowak, Vallacher, and Zochowski (2002, 2005) recently suggested that social influence can be understood in terms of *synchronization*, a phenomenon that characterizes coupled dynamical systems (Kaneko, 1993; Shinbrot, 1994). The central idea is that individuals in an interaction or a relationship are not static or passive entities, but instead represent separate systems capable of displaying rich dynamics, and that the synchronization of their respective dynamics produces a higher order system with its own dynamic properties. To achieve synchronization, each individual adjusts his or her internal state or overt behavior in response to the state or behavior of the other individual. Thus, the individuals modify their respective thoughts, feelings, or action tendencies to promote coordination over time in these features of experience.

The most basic form of synchronization is positive correlation or in-phase relation. This simply means that the overt behaviors, attitudes, or emotions of one person induce similar behaviors or states in the other person at the same time. Imitation and empathy provide common instances of this form of synchronization. Other forms of synchronization are clearly possible, however, and these may be manifest in different contexts for social interaction (Newtson, 1994). Turn-taking in conversation, for example, is a clear instance of negative correlation (antiphase relation) between individuals in their respective talking and listening (i.e., when one person speaks, the other is silent). Negative correlation can also characterize antagonistic relationships, with the sadness or despair of one person inducing satisfaction or happiness in the other and vice versa. Synchronization can also be manifest in more complex forms that reflect nonlinear relationships and higher-order interactions between the partners' respective behaviors and internal states (cf. Nowak & Vallacher, 1998; Nowak et al., 2002). However, because positive correlation represents the most fundamental and arguably the most common form of coordination, we focus on this form in our model of interpersonal dynamics.

A Formal Model of Synchronization

We use coupled dynamical systems as a formal model of interpersonal synchronization. Each system is defined in terms of a set of *dynamical variables* (x) that change in time, and one or more *control parameters* (r) that play a decisive role in influencing the dynamical variables. The simplest dynamical system capable of complex (e.g., chaotic) behavior is the logistic map (Feigenbaum, 1978; Schuster, 1984). The logistic map involves repeated iteration, such that the output value of the dynamical variable

(x) at one step (n) is used as the input value at the next step ($n + 1$). The current value of the dynamical variable (which varies between 0 and 1), in other words, depends on the variable's previous value—that is, $x_{n+1} = f(x_n)$.

This dependency is represented in two opposing ways. The higher the previous value, first of all, the higher the current value—specifically, x_{n+1} equals x_n multiplied by the value of r. Second, the higher the previous value, the *lower* the current value—specifically, x_{n+1} equals $(1 - x_n)$ multiplied by the value of r. The combined effect of these two opposing forces is represented in the logistic map as $x_{n+1} = rx_n(1 - x_n)$, where x_{n+1} is the value of a dynamical variable at one time, x_n is the value of the same variable at the preceding time, and r is the control parameter (the crucial variable influencing temporal changes of x). With changes in the value of r, the logistic equation displays qualitatively different patterns of behavior (i.e., patterns of changes in x), including convergence on a single value, oscillatory (periodic) changes between two or more values, and very complex patterns of evolution resembling randomness (i.e., deterministic chaos).

In modeling human dynamics, the dynamical variable (x) can be interpreted as intensity of behavior. The control parameter, r, may be interpreted as corresponding to internal states, such as personality traits, moods, and values, that shape the person's pattern of behavior (i.e., changes in x over time). Because the logistic equation is generic in form, it is intended to reflect basic processes involving the conjunction of conflicting forces, and thus does not depend on specific identities of x and r. In principle, x can refer to behavior at any level of identification, from simple movements to broad action categories, each of which may be associated with a correspondingly different time scale (e.g., seconds vs. days). The central point of the logistic map is that a person can display a pattern of changes in behavior in the absence of external influences. External factors clearly have a role to play, but they exert their influence by modifying the person's intrinsic dynamics—his or her internally generated patterns of behavior.

We have used coupled logistic maps to model the synchronization of people in social interaction (Nowak & Vallacher, 1998; Nowak, Vallacher, & Borkowski, 2000; Nowak et al., 2002, 2005). The dynamics of each individual are represented by a logistic equation. To capture interpersonal synchronization, the behavior of each person not only depends on his or her preceding state but also to a certain extent on the preceding state of the other person. The coupling of individuals' dynamics is achieved according to the following equation:

$$x_1(t+1) = \frac{r_1 x_1(t)(1 - x_1(t)) + \alpha r_2 x_2(t)(1 - x_2(t))}{1 + \alpha}$$

$$x_2(t+1) = \frac{r_2 x_2(t)(1 - x_2(t)) + \alpha r_1 x_1(t)(1 - x_1(t))}{1 + \alpha}$$

To the value of the dynamical variable representing one person's behavior (x_1), one adds a fraction, denoted by α, of the value of the dynamical variable representing the behavior of the other person (x_2). The size of this fraction (α) represents the strength of coupling and can be viewed as reflecting mutual influence, which in social interaction can be interpreted as the intensity of communication. When the fraction is 0, there is no coupling (e.g., influence or communication) on the behavior level. When the fraction is 1, each person's behavior is determined equally by his or her preceding behavior and the influence of the other person. Intermediate values of this fraction represent moderate values of coupling.

Modeling the Synchronization of Behavior

When individuals interact, their respective control parameters are rarely, if ever, identical. Nor are all interactions and relationships characterized by the same degree of influence and interdependence. Hence, in our computer simulations (Nowak & Vallacher, 1998) we systematically varied the similarity of partners' control parameters (r), representing their internal states, and their degree of coupling (α), representing their mutual influence (e.g., intensity of communication). For each simulation, we started from a random value of x for each person, drawn from a uniform distribution that varied from 0 to 1. We let the simulations run for 300 steps, so that each system had a chance to come close to its pattern of intrinsic dynamics and both systems had a chance to synchronize. For the subsequent 500 simulation steps, we recorded the values of x for each system and measured the degree of synchronization.

The results revealed that, in general, the degree of synchronization between partners' behaviors increased both with α and similarity in r. For a given level of coupling, the more similar the internal states, the greater the synchronization. Likewise, for a given level of similarity in internal states, the stronger the coupling, the greater the synchronization. For two people to achieve a high degree of synchronization, then, relatively little coupling is necessary if they have similar control parameters. Conversely, if the partners have different internal states, high mutual influence (mutual reinforcement, constant monitoring, communication, etc.) is necessary to maintain the same level of synchronization. If we interpret the strength of coupling as the intensity of communication, it follows that if two (or more) individuals have similar internal parameters, a relatively low level of communication is necessary to maintain coordination. In contrast, for two dissimilar individuals the maintenance of coordination requires high level of intensity of communication. This suggests, somewhat paradoxically, that constant and intense communication in a work team may be a sign that the members of the team are not well coordinated with respect to relevant internal states (e.g., goals, interest). In effect, the group's time and effort is devoted mainly to communication. In effective work teams, however, the efforts of team members can be devoted to the task rather than to constant clarification and monitoring.

Modeling the Synchronization of Internal States

Some internal variables, such as emotions, clearly vary across time and contexts. Synchronization will obviously be easier to obtain in a group that is experiencing a common mood or sentiment. Other internal parameters, however, may be more stable, representing habits, personality traits, attitudes, and so forth. In principle, however, even stable internal parameters are subject to modification, and this potential can be understood in terms of synchronization dynamics (see Nowak, Vallacher, & Zochowski, 2005). The basic assumption of the model is that individuals, in an effort to achieve synchronization, may vary their internal parameters in a direction that leads to increasing synchronization. A value that results in synchronization will be engraved as an attractor for that internal state.

To model the synchronization of control parameters, we assume that on each simulation step, the value of each person's control parameter drifts somewhat in the direction of the value of the other person's control parameter. The size of the initial discrepancy between the values of the respective control parameters and the rate of this drift determine how quickly the control parameters begin to match. The exact value of the other person's control parameter may be invisible and difficult to infer, but each person remembers the other person's most recent set of behaviors (i.e., the most recent values of x) as well as his or her own most recent behaviors. The person compares his or her own behavior with that of the other person, and adjusts his or her control parameter in the direction of increased similarity with the other person's behavior pattern, until there is a match (cf. Zochowski & Liebovitch, 1997, 1999). For example, if the other person's behavior is more complex than the person's own pattern of behavior, the person slightly increases the value of his or her own control parameter. By the same token, if the other person's behavior is less complex than one's own behavior, the person slightly decreases the value of his or her own control parameter. In short, the individuals can estimate one another's internal state by monitoring the evolution of each other's behavior.

We simulated the convergence of behavior and internal states under both relatively weak and relatively strong coupling (α = .25 and .7, respectively). The results of these simulations are displayed in Figure 3.3. The y-axis corresponds to the magnitude of difference in behavior or internal states between the two respective systems, and the x-axis corresponds to time, as reflected in the number of iterations. Figure 3.3a shows that under weak coupling, the convergence of behavior is relatively slow and nonlinear. However, the control parameters show a clear tendency towards convergence as well, and when a match is achieved in internal states, full synchronization of behavior is obtained. In marked contrast, Figure 3.3b shows that under strong coupling there is immediate synchronization of behavior, but the control parameters fail to synchronize, even after 1,000 iterations.

These results have interesting implications for interpersonal relations. Even for systems with very different control parameters, strong coupling promotes full synchronization of behavior. Once full synchrony is achieved, the two systems may be totally unaware that their control parameters are different. Hence, if the coupling were to be removed, the dynamics of the two respective systems would immediately diverge. This suggests that using very strong influence to obtain coordination of behavior may hinder synchronization of internal parameters. More generally,

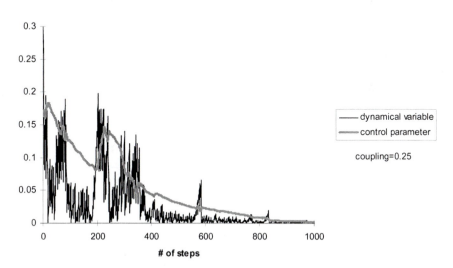

Source: Nowak, Vallacher, and Zochowki (2002). Copyright © 2002 by Guilford Publications. Reprinted by permission.

Figure 3.3a. Convergence of behavior and internal states under weak coupling.

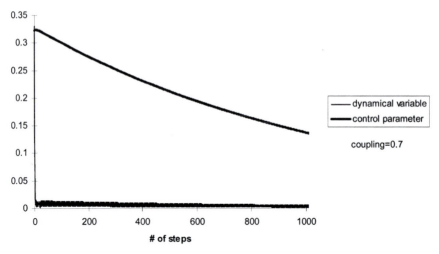

Source: Nowak, Vallacher, & Zochowki (2002). Copyright © 2002 by Guilford Publications. Reprinted by permission.

Figure 3.3b.   Convergence of behavior and internal states under strong coupling.

there may be an optimal level of influence and control over behavior in interpersonal relations (cf. Vallacher, Nowak, & Miller, 2003). Synchronization may fail to develop when influence is too weak, but when it is very strong it can prevent the development of a relationship based on mutual understanding and empathy. For synchronization on a deep level to occur, intermediate levels of mutual influence would seem to be most effective. The most advantageous degree of coupling, from this perspective, is the minimal amount necessary to achieve synchronization.

This reasoning is consistent with considerable research suggesting that behavior attributed to external causes is less likely to promote psychological change than is behavior attributed to internal causes. In particular, people have been shown to resist changing their attitudes and other internal states if they believe that their behavior was in response to direct orders, rewards, threats, and other external influences (cf. Bem, 1967; Brehm & Brehm, 1981; Lepper & Greene, 1978). Ironically, in fact, salient external influences may activate mechanisms to counter the influences, creating an internal state that is opposite of the intended effect of the influence.

DYNAMICAL SOCIAL PSYCHOLOGY IN PERSPECTIVE

Dynamical social psychology, by returning to the roots of the field, captures and brings into focus the central features of human experience. But it does so with a degree of scientific rigor that simply was not available until very recently. The advent of nonlinear dynamical systems in mathematics and the physical sciences has proven to be a rich source of methods and formalisms that has essentially enabled social psychology to have its cake and eat it, too. Computer simulations enable us to capture the complexity of social processes and document the emergence of higher-order properties from the interaction of basic elements in a mental or social system. Methods of time-series data collection and analysis provide rigorous yet deep insight into the intrinsic dynamics of mental, affective, and behavioral processes. And formal models allow us to identify the critical parameters necessary for understanding the nature and emergence of psychological and social processes. The approach of dynamical minimalism employs each of these means and consequently provides a means by which social psychology can advance as a precise science while preserving (and refining) the basic insights that set the field in motion last century.

It is somewhat ironic that an approach ideally suited to capture the dynamics of human experience is grounded in concepts and methods that provide broad and meaningful integration with the natural sciences. Once these disciplines came to appreciate intrinsic dynamics, nonlinear phenomena, self-organization, and the significance of complexity, it became clear to many in psychology that these features of systems in nature had counterparts in mental, interpersonal, and collective experience. Today it would be odd indeed for a psychologist to discount the potential for emergence or to ignore the role of computer simulations and time series in illuminating how minds, groups, and societies work.

A word of caution is in order, however. Social reality is not the same as physical reality. People are not atoms, sand grains, or neurons. Unlike these elements of physical systems, people have goals and plans, moments of self-reflection and sudden impulse, common concerns and idiosyncratic tendencies. One of the basic rules of human operation is that people can reflect on these rules and even attempt to override them. People do not respond in a reflexive way to the objective features of the world around them, but rather to their symbolic construction of reality. These unique yet defining features of human psychology go beyond the recognition that people are dynamic and complex, making the task of dynamical social psychology all the more daunting. A straightforward application of dynamical models developed in the natural sciences may be a good first approximation, but ultimately the properties that separate us from other systems in the world must be incorporated into theory and research. It is only fitting that a coherent theory of social psychology should be assembled from elements that are both universal and unique to human experience.

NOTES

1. Our focus is not organizational or leadership dynamics per se, as these topics are not areas in which we have an established track record. Nonetheless, the dynamical approach to interpersonal processes would seem to have fairly clear implications for how people function in organizational settings, whether as leaders or as team members. Considerable work in recent years has focused explicitly on organizations from a dynamical systems perspective, however, and the interested reader is encouraged to explore this excellent body of work (e.g., Axelrod & Cohen, 1999; Guastello, 1995, 2002; Losada, 1999; Losada & Heaphy, 2004; Marion & Uhl-Bien, 2001).

2. See Nowak et al. (2002) for a detailed discussion of the properties of fixed-point attractors.

REFERENCES

Abelson, R. P. (1979). Social clusters and opinion clusters. In P. W. Holland & S. Leinhardt (Eds.), *Perspectives in social network research* (pp. 239-256). New York: Academic Press.

Allport, G. W. (1968). The historical background of modern social psychology. In G. A. Lindzey & E. Aronson (Eds.), *The handbook of social psychology* (Vol. 1, pp. 1-80). Reading, MA: Addison-Wesley.

Asch, S. E. (1946). Forming impressions of personalities. *Journal of Abnormal and Social Psychology, 41,* 258-290.

Asch, S. E. (1955). Opinions and social pressure. *Scientific American, 19,* 31-35.

Axelrod, R. (1984). *The evolution of cooperation.* New York: Basic Books.

Axelrod, R., & Cohen, M. D. (1999). *Harnessing complexity: Organizational implications of a scientific frontier.* New York: The Free Press.

Baron, R. M., Amazeen, P. M., & Beek, P. J. (1994). Local and global dynamics of social relations. In R. R. Vallacher & A. Nowak (Eds.), *Dynamical systems in social psychology* (pp. 111-138). San Diego, CA: Academic Press.

Beek, P. J., & Hopkins, B. (1992). Four requirements for a dynamical systems approach to the development of social coordination. *Human Movement Science, 11,* 425-442.

Bem, D. J. (1967). Self-perception: An alternative interpretation of cognitive dissonance phenomena. *Psychological Review, 74,* 183-200.

Brehm, S. S., & Brehm, J. W. (1981). *Psychological reactance: A theory of freedom and control.* New York: Academic Press.

Brown, K. W., & Moskowitz, D. S. (1998). Dynamic stability of behavior: The rhythms of our interpersonal lives. *Journal of Personality, 66*(1), 105-134.

Cannon, W. B. (1932). *The wisdom of the body.* New York: Norton.

Carver, C. S., & Scheier, M. F. (1999). Themes and issues in the self-regulation of behavior. In R. S. Wyer, Jr. (Ed.), *Advances in social cognition* (Vol. 12, pp. 1-105). Mahwah, NJ: Erlbaum.

Carver, C. S., & Scheier, M. F. (2002). Control processes and self-organization as complementary principles underlying behavior. *Personality and Social Psychology Review, 6*, 304-315.

Coleman, P. T. (2003). Characteristics of protracted, intractable conflict: Towards the development of a meta-framework—I. First paper in a three-paper series. *Peace and Conflict: Journal of Peace Psychology, 9*, 1-37.

Coleman, P. T., Vallacher, R. R., Nowak, A., & Bui-Wrzosinska, L. (2007). Intractable conflict as an attractor: Presenting a model of conflict, escalation, and intractability. *American Behavioral Scientist, 50*, 1454-1475.

Condon, W. S., & Ogston, W. D. (1967). A segmentation of behavior. *Journal of Psychiatric Research, 5*, 221-235.

Cooley, C. H. (1902). *Human nature and the social order*. New York: Scribner.

Deutsch, M. (1973). *The resolution of conflict: Constructive and destructive processes*. New Haven: Yale University Press.

Dittman, A. T., & Llewellyn, L. G. (1969). Body movement and speech rhythm in social conversation. *Journal of Personality and Social Psychology, 11*, 98-106.

Eckmann, J. P., & Ruelle, D. (1985). Ergodic theory of chaos and strange attractors. *Review of Modern Physics, 57*, 617-656.

Feigenbaum, M. J. (1978). Quantitative universality for a class of nonlinear transformations. *Journal of Statistical Physics, 19*, 25-52.

Festinger, L., Schachter, S., & Back, K. (1950). *Social pressures in informal groups*. Stanford, CA: Stanford University Press.

Glass, L., & Mackey, M. C. (1988). *From clocks to chaos: The rhythms of life*. Princeton, NJ: Princeton University Press.

Gleick, J. (1987). *Chaos: The making of a new science*. New York: Viking-Penguin.

Goldstein, J. (1996). Causality and emergence in chaos and complexity theories. In W. Sulis & A. Combs (Eds.), *Nonlinear dynamics and human behavior* (pp. 161-190). Singapore: World Scientific.

Gottman, J. M. (1979). Detecting cyclicity in social interaction. *Psychological Bulletin, 86*, 338-348.

Guastello, S. J. (1995). *Chaos, catastrophe, and human affairs: Applications of nonlinear dynamics to work, organizations, and social evolution*. Mahwah, NJ: Erlbaum.

Guastello, S. J. (2002). *Managing emergent phenomena: Nonlinear dynamics in work organizations*. Mahwar, NJ: Erlbaum.

Hastie, R., Penrod, S. D., & Pennington, N. (1983). *Inside the jury*. Cambridge, MA: Harvard University Press.

Hopfield, J. J. (1982). Neural networks and physical systems with emergent collective computational abilities. *Proceedings of the National Academy of Sciences, 79*, 2554-2558.

James, W. (1890). *Principles of psychology*. New York: Holt.

Janis, I. L. (1982). *Victims of groupthink* (2nd ed.). Boston: Houghton Mifflin.

Johnson, S. L., & Nowak, A. (2002). Dynamical patterns in bipolar depression. *Personality and Social Psychology Review, 6*, 380-387.

Kaneko, K. (Ed.). (1993). *Theory and applications of coupled map lattices*. Singapore: World Scientific.

Kelso, J. A. S. (1995). *Dynamic patterns: The self-organization of brain and behavior*. Cambridge, MA: The MIT Press.

Larsen, R. J. (1987). The stability of mood variability: A spectral analytic approach to daily mood assessments. *Journal of Personality and Social Psychology, 52,* 1195-1204.

Larsen, R. J., & Kasimatis, M. (1990). Individual differences in entrainment of mood to the weekly calendar. *Journal of Personality and Social Psychology, 58,* 164-171.

Latané, B. (1981). The psychology of social impact. *American Psychologist, 36,* 343-356.

Latané, B., & Nowak, A. (1994). Attitudes as catastrophes: From dimensions to categories with increasing involvement. In R. R. Vallacher & A. Nowak (Eds.), *Dynamical systems in social psychology* (pp. 219-249). San Diego, CA: Academic Press.

Latané, B., & Nowak, A. (1997). The causes of polarization and clustering in social groups. *Progress in Communication Sciences, 13,* 43-75.

Latané, B., Nowak, A., & Liu, J. (1994). Measuring emergent social phenomena: dynamism, polarization and clustering as order parameters of social systems. *Behavioral Science, 39,* 1-24.

Lepper, M. R., & Greene, D. (Eds.) (1978). *The hidden costs of reward.* Hillsdale, NJ: Erlbaum.

Lewenstein, M., Nowak, A., & Latané, B. (1993). Statistical mechanics of social impact. *Physics Review A, 45,* 703-716.

Lewin, K. (1936). *Principles of topological psychology.* New York: McGraw-Hill.

Losada, M. F. (1999). The complex dynamics of high performance teams. *Mathematical and computer modeling, 30,* 179-192.

Losada, M. F., & Heaphy, E. (2004). The role of positivity and connectivity in the performance of business teams: A nonlinear dynamics model. *American Behavioral Scientist, 47,* 740-765.

Marion, R., & Uhl-Bien, M. (2001). Leadership in complex organizations. *The Leadership Quarterly, 12,* 389-418.

Markus, H., & Nurius, P. (1986). Possible selves. *American Psychologist, 41,* 954-969.

McGrath, J. E., & Kelley, J. R. (1986). *Time and human interaction: Toward a psychology of time.* New York: Guilford.

Mead, G. H. (1934). *Mind, self, and society.* Chicago: University of Chicago Press.

Messick, D. M., & Liebrand, V. B. G. (1995). Individual heuristics and the dynamics of cooperation in large groups. *Psychological Review, 102,* 131-145.

Miller, N. E. (1944). Experimental studies of conflict. In J. M. Hunt (Ed.), *Personality and the behavior disorders.* New York: Ronald.

Moscovici, S., Lage, E., & Naffrechoux, M. (1969). Influence of a consistent minority on responses of a majority in a color perception task. *Sociometry, 32,* 365-379.

Myers, D. G., & Lamm, H. (1976). The group polarization phenomenon. *Psychological Bulletin, 83,* 602-627.

Newtson, D. (1994). The perception and coupling of behavior waves. In R. R. Vallacher & A. Nowak (Eds.), *Dynamical systems in social psychology* (pp. 139-167). San Diego, CA: Academic Press.

Nezlek, J. B. (1993). The stability of social interaction. *Journal of Personality and Social Psychology, 65,* 930-941.

Dynamical Social Psychology 79

Nowak, A. (2004). Dynamical minimalism: Why less is more in psychology. *Personality and Social Psychology Review, 8,* 183-192.

Nowak, A., Latané, B., & Lewenstein, M. (1994). Social dilemmas exist in space. In U. Schulz, W. Albers, & U. Mueller (Eds.), *Social dilemmas and cooperation* (pp. 114-131). Heidelberg, Germany: Springer-Verlag.

Nowak, A., & Lewenstein, M. (1994). Dynamical systems: A tool for social psychology? In R. R. Vallacher & A. Nowak (Eds.), *Dynamical systems in social psychology* (pp. 17-53). San Diego, CA: Academic Press.

Nowak, A., Lewenstein, M., & Frejlak, P. (1996). Dynamics of public opinion and social change. In R. Hegselman & H. O. Pietgen (Eds.), *Modeling social dynamics: Order, chaos, and complexity* (pp. 54-78). Vienna, Austria: Helbin.

Nowak, A., Szamrej, J., & Latané, B. (1990). From private attitude to public opinion: A dynamic theory of social impact. *Psychological Review, 97,* 362-376.

Nowak, A., & Vallacher, R. R. (1998). *Dynamical social psychology.* New York: Guilford.

Nowak, A., & Vallacher, R. R. (2001). Societal transition: Toward a dynamical model of social change. In W. Wosinska, R. B. Cialdini, D. W. Barrett, & J. Reykowski (Eds.), *The practice of social influence in multiple cultures* (pp. 151-171). Mahwah, NJ: Erlbaum.

Nowak, A., Vallacher, R. R., & Borkowski, W. (2000). Modeling the temporal coordination of behavior and internal states. In G. Ballot & G. Weisbuch (Eds.), *Applications of simulation to the social sciences* (pp. 67-86). Oxford, England: Hermes Science Publications.

Nowak, A., Vallacher, R. R., Bui-Wrzosinska, L., & Coleman, P. T. (in press). Attracted to conflict: A dynamical perspective on malignant social relations. In A. Golec & K. Skarzynska (Eds.), *Understanding social change: Political psychology in Poland.* Haauppague, NY: Nova Science.

Nowak, A., Vallacher, R. R., Kus, M., & Urbaniak, J. (2005). The dynamics of societal transition: Modeling nonlinear change in the Polish economic system. *International Journal of Sociology, 35,* 65-88.

Nowak, A., Vallacher, R. R., Tesser, A., & Borkowski, W. (2000). Society of self: The emergence of collective properties in self-structure. *Psychological Review, 107,* 39-61.

Nowak, A., Vallacher, R. R., & Zochowski, M. (2002). The emergence of personality: Personal stability through interpersonal synchronization. In D. Cervone & W. Mischel (Eds.), *Advances in personality science* (pp. 292-331). New York: Guilford Press.

Nowak, A., Vallacher, R. R., & Zochowski, M. (2005). The emergence of personality: Dynamic foundations of individual variation. *Developmental Review, 25,* 351-385.

Rosenblum, L. D., & Turvey, M. T. (1988). Maintenance tendency in coordinated rhythmic movements: Relative fluctuations and phase. *Neuroscience, 27,* 289-300.

Schachter, S. (1951). Deviation, rejection and communication. *Journal of Abnormal and Social Psychology, 46,* 1990-207.

Schuster, H. G. (1984). *Deterministic chaos.* Vienna, Austria: Physik Verlag.

Sherif, M. (1936). *The psychology of social norms.* New York: Harper.

Shinbrot, T. (1994). Synchronization of coupled maps and stable windows. *Physics Review E, 50,* 3230-3233.

Swann, W. B., Jr. (1990). To be adored or to be known? The interplay of self-enhancement and self-verification. In E. T. Higgins & R. M. Sorrentino (Eds.), *Handbook of motivation and cognition: Foundations of social behavior* (Vol. 2, pp. 408-448). New York: Guilford.

Swann, W. B., Hixon, J. G., Stein-Seroussi, A., & Gilbert, D. (1990). The fleeting gleam of praise: Cognitive processes underlying behavioral reactions to self-relevant feedback. *Journal of Personality and Social Psychology, 59,* 17-26.

Tesser, A. (1978). Self-generated attitude change. In L. Berkowitz (Ed.), *Advances in experimental social psychology* (Vol. 11, pp. 85-117). New York: Academic Press.

Tesser, A., Martin, L., & Cornell, D. (1996). On the substitutability of self-protective mechanisms. In P. M. Gollwitzer & J. A. Bargh (Eds.), *The psychology of action* (pp. 48-68). New York: Guilford.

Tickle-Degnen, L., & Rosenthal, R. (1987). Group rapport and nonverbal behavior. *Review of Personality and Social Psychology, 9,* 113-136.

Thibaut, J. W., & Kelley, H. H. (1959). *The social psychology of groups.* New York: Wiley.

Turvey, M. T. (1990). Coordination. *American Psychologist, 4,* 938-953.

Turvey, M. T., & Carello, J. (1995). Some dynamical themes in perception and action. In R. F. Port & T. van Gelder (Eds.), *Mind as motion: Explorations in the dynamics of cognition* (pp. 373-402). Cambridge, MA: MIT Press.

Vallacher, R. R., & Nowak, A. (Eds.) (1994a). *Dynamical systems in social psychology.* San Diego, CA: Academic Press.

Vallacher, R. R., & Nowak, A. (Eds.). (1994b). The stream of social judgment. In *Dynamical systems in social psychology* (pp. 251-277). San Diego, CA: Academic Press.

Vallacher, R. R., & Nowak, A. (1997). The emergence of dynamical social psychology. *Psychological Inquiry, 8,* 73-99.

Vallacher, R. R., & Nowak, A. (1999). The dynamics of self-regulation. In R. S. Wyer Jr. (Ed.), *Advances in self-regulation* (Vol. 12, pp. 241-259). Mahwah, NJ: Erlbaum.

Vallacher, R. R., & A. Nowak, (in press). Dynamical social psychology: Finding order in the flow of human experience. In A. W. Kruglanski & E. T. Higgins (Eds.), *Social psychology: Handbook of basic principles* (2nd ed.). New York: Guilford.

Vallacher, R. R., Nowak, A., Froehlich, M., & Rockloff, M. (2002). The dynamics of self-evaluation. *Personality and Social Psychology Review, 6,* 370-379.

Vallacher, R. R., Nowak, A., & Kaufman, J. (1994). Intrinsic dynamics of social judgment. *Journal of Personality and Social Psychology, 66,* 20-34.

Vallacher, R. R., Nowak, A., & Miller, M. E. (2003). Social influence and group dynamics. In I. Weiner (Series Ed.) & T. Millon & M. J. Lerner (Vol. Eds.), *Handbook of psychology: Vol. 5. Personality and social psychology* (pp. 383-417). New York: Wiley.

Vallacher, R. R., & Wegner, D. M. (1987). What do people think they're doing? Action identification and human behavior. *Psychological Review, 94,* 1-15.

Vallacher, R. R., & Wegner, D. M. (1989). Levels of personal agency: Individual variation in action identification. *Journal of Personality and Social Psychology, 57*, 660-671.

Zochowski, M., & Liebovitch, L. S. (1997). Synchronization of the trajectory as a way to control the dynamics of the coupled system. *Physical Review E, 56*, 3701.

Zochowski, M., & Liebovitch, L. S. (1999). Self-organizing dynamics of coupled map systems. *Physical Review E, 59*, 2830.

CHAPTER 4

PATHWAYS OF OPPORTUNITY IN DYNAMIC ORGANIZATIONAL NETWORKS

Martin Kilduff, Craig Crossland, and Wenpin Tsai

ABSTRACT

How do organizational networks change continuously to provide new opportunities for members? We view organizations as complex adaptive systems embedded in heterogeneous networks consisting of different kinds of nodes (such as people, machines, projects, and heterogeneous components of the modern technological environment), and consider new opportunities to reside in the creation of new pathways linking previously unconnected nodes. We identify 2 broad classes of ideology relevant to opportunity creation in organizational networks: serendipity and goal directedness. These ideologies operate as explicit and tacit theories of networking, affecting the addition of new nodes as well as the creation and rearrangement of ties.

Organizations can be understood as networks of procedures, puzzles, interpretations, and behaviors that provide opportunities for sensemaking (Weick, 1979, p. 4). These fluid and shifting networks are at least in part constituted in terms of tacit or explicit theories concerning what peo-

Complexity Leadership, Part I: Conceptual Foundations
pp. 83–99
Copyright © 2008 by Information Age Publishing
All rights of reproduction in any form reserved.

ple expect to experience. Managers and other occupants of formal leadership positions who expect the world to be stable and routine may well help confirm this expectation for themselves and others by structuring experience as a series of habitual routines. Theories about organizations—concerning their design and their operation—may have even more powerful self-fulfilling prophecies (cf. Ferraro, Pfeffer, & Sutton, 2005). To the extent that organizational theories emphasize stability rather than change, routines rather than serendipity, and control rather than self organization, organizations themselves may not only appear to be inertial, but may also be constituted according to taken-for-granted theoretical prescriptions. Thus, organizational research that posits the importance of routines and inertial processes (cf. Hannan & Freeman, 1977) is likely to both see and experience the world of organizations in terms of stability of organizational forms.

Organizations as complex adaptive systems embedded in environments both internal and external are often described in terms of bundles of routines that store the cumulative results of learning (e.g., Kilduff, 1992). This emphasis on the recursiveness by which systems self-learn and self-organize is a starting point for understanding the process of opportunity creation within dynamic, open-system organizational networks. Complexity theory seeks to understand how system level self-organization emerges from interactions among nodes in the system (Anderson, 1999; Eisenhardt & Bhatia, 2002; Kauffman, 1993). In drawing from complexity theory, we propose a view of organizational systems that includes the following characteristics associated with complex systems (cf. Cilliers, 1998, pp. 3-5). (1) The organization contains a large number of interacting nodes (cf. McKelvey, 1999), such nodes comprising both individual people as well as other heterogenous elements such as technologies (cf. Carley, 2002). (2) Small investments of effort (such as efforts to establish new connections between nodes) are capable of nonlinear yields (such as dramatically increased connectivity across the organizational system). (c) Opportunity creation and destruction are recursive processes in that activities initiated by particular nodes are likely to cycle back into the vicinity of these nodes. (4) The organization, to the extent that it is understood as a complex network system, operates far from equilibrium, requiring a constant flow of energy: "equilibrium is another word for death" (Cilliers, 1998, p. 4). (5) The historical memory of the system (embedded in routines) undergoes constant change. (6) Each node has only local knowledge—no godlike purview of the whole system is possible.

Thus, complexity emerges from the interactions of heterogeneous nodes—it cannot be imposed by an omniscient organizational designer. We draw from these complexity ideas throughout the chapter to explore how leadership can be understood in terms of continual opportunity creation in a system of emergent complexity. From this perspective, opportunity creation can be facilitated or hindered by those in formal leadership positions. Not all organizations exhibit the dynamic properties of continual opportunity creation—indeed, we think that network stagnation is the more likely outcome for most organizations most of the time, given the well-known human aversion to constant change. But, just as at the individual level, people are interested in the extent to which exceptional states of "flow" can be attained in the production of work (Csikszentmihalyi, 1991) so, at the organizational level, organizational leaders are likely to be interested in the extent to which exceptional states of dynamic opportunity creation can be attained.

We consider organizations as transformational engines that generate opportunities for members to learn from each other and from organizational resources such as data bases, procedures, and goals. Given that an organization functions in part as a dedicated arrangement of specialized resources (Lawrence & Lorsch, 1967) we consider how the arrangement of specialized resources leads to the emergence of opportunity generation. Specifically, given the self-organizing, emergent characteristics of complex systems, our research question is: How can leadership arrange for organizational networks to change continuously, providing new opportunities for members, and avoiding the fate of stagnation? In order to answer this question we first must define what we mean by an organizational network in this complexity context.

HETEROGENEOUS NETWORKS

A network can be defined as a set of nodes and the relations that connect them. The nodes in any specific network are often assumed to be of the same kind. Thus, we have studies of interpersonal networks in which the nodes are people (e.g., Mehra, Kilduff, & Brass, 2001) and interorganizational networks in which the nodes are organizations or organizational units (e.g., Tsai, 2002). But we have almost no studies of heterogeneous networks in which different kinds of nodes and their relationships are studied simultaneously. In fact, a key assumption in previous network studies is that nodes are homogeneous or, at least, at the same level (Wasserman & Faust, 1994). This assumption simplifies the job of conceptualizing or defining the boundary of a network but ignores the possibility of interactions among different kinds of nodes or across different levels. As a result, previous studies tend to find that networks are stable or relatively inert over time because the way nodes are defined in these studies excludes cross-level effects of network change and development. To more meaningfully observe change and new opportunities in networks, we need to consider a broader set of nodes. For example, in an organization where employees utilize different technologies and work on different projects, we should not narrowly focus on "people" as the nodes in the organizational network without considering "technologies" and "projects" as nodes as well.

Although research in the actor-network theory (A-NT) tradition (Law & Hassard, 1999) has described the importance of studying connections between people, machines, texts, projects, and other heterogeneous components of the modern technological environment, this research tradition appears to have had almost no influence on social network research. Whereas A-NT research is deliberately qualitative in its pursuit of connections that are considered important from the point of view of the participant-observer, and eschews the use of quantitative methods (Law & Hassard, 1999), social network research is relentlessly quantitative in its use of mathematical algorithms to detect network structure. Without abandoning the advantages of quantitative modeling, it may be possible to incorporate more heterogeneous components within standard social network analyses. (Indeed, in pursuit of optimal organizational design considerations, computational modeling approaches have incorporated diverse network elements within what is termed the "metamatrix"—see Carley, 2002, for a review. And the discussion of heterogeneous agents in interaction with each other and with artifacts in Axelrod & Cohen, 1999 explores organizational implications of a complexity perspective.)

We know from A-NT research that large-scale technological projects can produce self-organization among human actors whose relations with each other are subservient to relations with the many dynamic aspects of project management (Knorr-Cetina, 1981). In such circumstances, there appears to be no need for conventional leadership initiatives. We also know that people have intense relationships with texts and machines of all kinds (Latour, 1996). Thus, in considering what entities to include in an organizational network, the analyst is faced with a boundary choice that differs from the usual dilemma omnipresent in social network research. Whereas social network researchers are usually concerned at the beginning of a research project with the question of which nodes of the same kind to include (Wasserman & Faust, 1994, p. 31), in organizational research the analyst is less concerned with the boundary of the population, because the formal boundary of the organization can be taken to contain the relevant set of internal entities. However, within that formal boundary there is a potentially unlimited set of heterogeneous nodes that could include entities such as people, routines, cognitions, ideologies, texts, and machines.

Network Regions

Heterogeneity refers not only to the different types of nodes but also encompasses different network regions within the overall organizational network. Figure 4.1 illustrates the typical topography of a complex organizational network. The outer belt—labeled the Disconnected Component—consists of isolated clusters that have few or no connections to other parts of the network. Moving inwards, we reach the region labeled the Weakly Connected Component in which all nodes are mutually reachable if direction of ties is ignored, the assumption being that "the mere presence of a relationship, regardless of its direction, allows some possibility for communication" (Scott, 2000, 104). At the center of the network, within the Weakly Connected Component, is the Strongly Connected Component, within which all nodes are mutually reachable and all paths "are aligned in a continuous chain without any change of direction" (Scott, 2000, p. 103). Thus, communication and other resources flow along paths "without interruption" (Scott, 2000, p. 104). The In Component contains all the nodes from which the Strongly Connected component is approachable, whereas the Out Component contains all the nodes

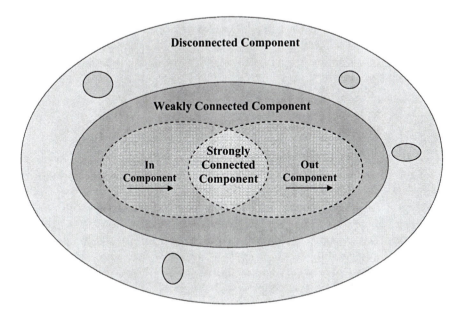

Source: Adapted from Dorogovtsev and Mendes (2003, p. 20).

Figure 4.1.   The structure of organizational networks.

that are approachable from the Strongly Connected component by directed paths (Dorogovtsev & Mendes, 2003, p. 21). The relative size of these regions is likely to vary from one organizational network to another, and is also likely to vary over time as weak and strong components wax and wane.

The topological structure illustrated in Figure 4.1 is likely to emerge as a result not of deliberate ordering by leaders but through self-organizing processes, the most important of which is the process of preferential linking: popular nodes will tend to attract more connections than unpopular nodes (see Simon, 1957, for an early development of this idea). By default, therefore, growing networks will tend to produce a surprisingly robust topology, with distinct regions. Such self-organized networks may prove highly resilient to disruption, and highly efficient in the transmission of information across large distances. The resiliency and efficiency are directly related to the emergence of network hubs (i.e., highly popular nodes) within the strongly connected component and elsewhere. These hubs direct traffic within the network and tend to keep even rapidly-growing networks compact in terms of short average distances between nodes. One of the keys, therefore, to understanding how heterogeneous networks self-organize in the absence of control by formally appointed leaders is the emergence of network hubs.

Organizational networks may be subject to other organizing processes, however, in addition to the default process of preferential linking characteristic of other complex networks. Specifically, goal-directedness and serendipity may facilitate the structuring of growing networks in ways we discuss in the next section.

NETWORK IDEOLOGIES

Under what circumstances are opportunity-generating processes likely to emerge in organizational networks? Our speculation is that the emergence of opportunity-producing processes are less likely to derive from the efforts of organizational leaders than from the sensitivity of the organizational system to a range of initial ideological conditions that include organizational culture, standard operating procedures, and taken for granted assumptions. As we suggested earlier, organizations—and the networks within them—exhibit self-fulfilling prophecies with respect to their dominant ideologies. Two broad classes of ideologies relevant to opportunity creation in organizational networks are goal-directedness and serendipity (Kilduff & Tsai, 2003). These ideologies operate as explicit and tacit theories of networking, affecting the addition of new nodes as well as the creation and rearrangement of ties.

From a goal-directedness perspective, relationships develop around specific group-level or network-level goals. This process exhibits purposive and adaptive movement towards an envisioned end state (Van de Ven & Poole, 1995). Individual nodes are attracted to the network by the promise of goal-fulfillment. It is the collective goal rather than preferential linking that drives the development of relationships. Thus, the goal itself acts as a substitute for a formal leader in attracting resources, promoting relationship building, and directing energies toward a valued end state.

In contrast, from a serendipity perspective, relationships develop haphazardly based on opportunistic encounters. There is no group-level or network level goal in this process. Individual nodes interact without guidance from any leader or leader substitute concerning goals. To the extent that a formally appointed leader promotes serendipity, this is likely to be exhibited in the randomization of ties between nodes. For example, a manager may attempt to promote diverse linkages among staff by placing people from different disciplinary backgrounds or functional areas next to each other. By discouraging the powerful pressures toward homophilous networking, the leader may be targeted for strong criticism by individuals whose cliques are disrupted.

Regions of organizational networks that are strongly goal-oriented may incorporate mechanisms that trigger corrective action whenever "deviant" processes emerge. Such network regions may minimize the emergence of self-organizing systems in favor of opportunity generation around shared goals. Thus, formal or informal leaders may play a role in policing adherence to all-important goals. By contrast, regions in which ambiguous ideologies encourage serendipitous changes to procedures, unexpected interactions between members and technologies, and the articulation of heretical thoughts, may witness the emergence of opportunity generating systems that span across conventional boundaries. Projects may be nurtured until they reach into hitherto isolated corners of the organization, providing previously unconnected members with opportunities to connect to forms of thinking, novel routines, and collaboration possibilities with established cliques. Formal or informal leaders in these settings may work to prevent the tendency for closed networks to monopolize knowledge.

Goal-directedness and serendipity orientations can coexist in different regions of the same extensive network even though the two ideologies represent dramatically different organizing principles. But both of these organizing principles may require generating mechanisms to prevent entropy from dissipating the production and reproduction of structure. Goal-directedness may require goal iteration and extensive monitoring to maintain network relations focused on consensually accepted end states.

Either a human node—such as a local leader skilled in focusing attention—or a nonhuman node—such as a dominant technology or an attractive project—can provide the center around which ancillary nodes can cluster. The central node can thus play the role of a goal-generating device, helping to prevent the network cluster from dissipating into the surrounding space.

Serendipity also requires an active generative presence if network relations are to be organized to maximize surprise and knowledge flow. As discussed above, networks, by default, tend to operate according to the principle of preferential linking: new nodes attach themselves to nodes that are already popular (Barabasi & Albert, 1999). To counter this strong inertial tendency may require the creation of specific policies to allocate resources—such as coffee bars, technology labs, and exercise facilities—to different network regions rather than allowing them to congregate collectively. Leaders, in this context, are the facilitators of network emergence. Serendipity generators may take the form of particular individuals who systematically attempt to bring together disparate nodes that otherwise would have little chance of connecting. Serendipity generators can also take the form of organizational procedures such as random lotteries to determine such important aspects of networking as office allocation. If goal-directedness dominates the whole network, then a core-periphery structure is likely to emerge with tight coupling and few structural holes. In contrast, when serendipity is dominant, a network tends to have a decentralized structure with a diffuse boundary and many structural holes.

Dynamic networks may exhibit both the rigid discipline of goal directedness and the spontaneity of serendipity either serially (over time) with fluctuations from one state to the other; or simultaneously in the sense that some parts of the network may be goal directed whereas other parts may exhibit serendipity. Indeed, the dynamic production of pathways of opportunity (in terms of new structural holes and brokerage to span across these structural holes—Burt, 2005) may require the network to maintain a balance between the two organizing principles of goal-directedness and serendipity. For a network to stay in this edge-of-chaos region (Kauffman, 1993) requires a great deal of energy that can be supplied by the generative mechanisms we have mentioned as well as by the strategic management of the throughput of new cognitions or new network members (March, 1991). To the extent that these new ideas of members are significantly different from those currently passing through or comprising the network system, the network can continue to exploit new knowledge and transform its relationship with the environment.

THE EMERGENCE OF OPPORTUNITIES IN NETWORKS

What do we mean by "opportunity"? In the context of a network perspective on opportunity creation, an opportunity is defined as the possibility of new pathways of connections among nodes in the network. Leadership, from this perspective, involves a sophisticated understanding of the ways in which new knowledge emerges from the interstices between nodes whereas existing, relatively mundane knowledge in one part of the network may offer new ideas to nodes in a distant part of the network.

Thus, we focus on pathways in networks because of the overwhelming importance of connectivity in the production and diffusion of knowledge within organizations (Hansen, 1999; Powell, Kogut, & Smith-Doerr, 1996). There are three possible types of connectivity pathways we consider—walks, paths, and trails (Wassermann & Faust, 1994, pp. 105-107), as Figure 4.2 illustrates. These different types of pathways have different implications for opportunity creation. The most general type of connectivity is a walk, defined as a sequence of nodes and ties between these nodes. In a walk, nodes and the ties that connect them can be included more than once. Thus, a walk provides for the possibility for reciprocal flows of knowledge and resources within an egalitarian network structure. A trail, by contrast, is more restrictive in that each tie occurs only once but

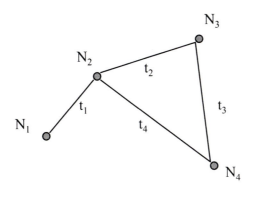

$$Walk = N_1 \ t_1 \ N_2 \ t_2 \ N_3 \ t_2 \ N_2$$

$$Path = N_1 \ t_1 \ N_2 \ t_2 \ N_3 \ t_3 \ N_4$$

$$Trail = N_1 \ t_1 \ N_2 \ t_2 \ N_3 \ t_3 \ N_4 \ t_4 \ N_2$$

Figure 4.2.   How walks, paths, and trails differ.

each node may occur more than once. The identification of trails, therefore, allows the analyst to determine which nodes serve as the hubs of local activity in opportunity provision. Paths are the most restrictive of all three types of connectivity—in a path, each node and each tie occur only once. Thus, paths allow only for linear flows of knowledge and other resources—for example, from peripheral nodes to the center. Adding new nodes, adding new ties, or rewiring ties to different nodes in the existing network can open up these pathway possibilities.

New Nodes

The addition of new nodes (such as new projects, new thinking, new members, random variations in established routines, and ambiguous mandates) increases network interaction capacity. For example, a mandate from the top leadership of the organization concerning the importance of "convergence" can represent a new node that organizes activity and members. The arrival of this new node may lead to the development of cross-departmental procedures and interactions that take on a life of their own unrelated to the minimal requirements of interactivity between different groups

Nodes may be added to a network randomly (through serendipitous processes) or purposively by leaders (through goal-directed processes). In a network region dominated by serendipity, nodes will be added in a deliberately randomized fashion. There may be high variation in terms of the type of nodes that are considered, with less concern given to whether or not nodes and the connections they bring with them survive competitive selection procedures. There may be an acceptance of the likelihood of high mortality in terms of nodes—such as projects—balanced by an expectation of continual new knowledge production given unexpected opportunity creation through novel pathways of resource flow. This contrasts with network regions governed by goal-directedness, where variation in potential node addition will tend to be lower and selection criteria more strict. To the extent that new nodes are deliberately attached to existing centralized and goal-oriented networks, there will be much greater concern to nurture the survival of nodes and to protect node activity from predations of neighboring network regions. Nodes are likely to be seen as belonging to centralized clusters rather than being available for opportunistic exchange. The rate at which new nodes are added will depend on the extent to which the network can find goal-oriented nodes or convert nodes to the prevailing ideology.

The addition of new nodes to the system creates new opportunities for network members. A new node changes the pathways of network interaction from the perspective of network agents. For example, consider a goal-directed research network where pathways consist of interaction between researchers and data. The introduction of a new statistics package will create a new pathway between researcher and data and thus a new opportunity to interact with such data. Thinking of networks in terms of heterogeneous mixtures involving people, units, technology, and projects provides organizational leaders with many possibilities for encouraging pathways of opportunity.

In a goal-directed network, the goal itself may emerge as the central node, and its influence may help prohibit divergent path creation to the extent that new nodes are efficiently socialized into the existing ideology. A new node recruited into such a network is likely to be immediately imbued with the nature and dimensions of the network goal. Slow learning nodes (those that resist adaptation to the prevailing norms, values and routines) are likely to provoke conflict within such network regions, and may offer novel pathways such as walks in an environment dominated by paths (cf. March, 1991). Thus one leadership initiative to promote new opportunity to existing network members may involve the judicious recruitment of slow learners of organizational cultural norms.

A slow learning node could, for example, consist of a new technology discrepant with established procedures that throws into confusion networks of exchange comprising people and machines (e.g., Barley, 1986). The recruitment of certain nodes can, of course, change the whole pattern of future node recruitment. For example, when the Oakland A's baseball team recruited new general manager Billy Beane in 1999, he brought to the organization a new system of statistical analysis based on past player performance (in high school and college) that led the organization to target players largely overlooked by rival teams (Lewis, 2003).

As networks increase in size, the average number of connections per node decreases (Bossard, 1945). Therefore, new nodes (and the new ties that they bring with them) in a goal-directed network may eventually result in a polarized network—as the network core becomes denser, the periphery may become isolated. The principle of serendipity, therefore, may be more important in large growing networks than in smaller networks. It is in the larger networks that a leader's systematic encouragement of random ties between nodes is likely to considerably reduce average path length, as we discuss in the next section.

New Ties

The World Wide Web is one example of a self-organizing network in which new ties, and thereby network opportunities, are created every minute—in chat rooms and online gaming sites, via financial transactions, or through simple information transfer. No leader controls access or distribution. Through the principle of preferential linking network ties tend to pull the edges of the vast network closer together in a striking demonstration of the small world effect (Albert, Jeong, & Barabasi, 1999). Even though no person or organization can be said to dominate the Web, there are leadership activities going on all the time in terms of the promotion of network links by organizations that include the major search engines (Google etc.) and the growing number of interpersonal networking services that provide opportunities for strangers to connect to similar others.

The addition of new ties between strangers may have a disproportionately greater influence on opportunity creation in serendipitous, compared to goal-directed, networking. In network regions reflecting goal-directedness, new ties are likely to occur near the center of the network, whereas, in a serendipitous network region, ties may be allocated randomly, often linking previously unconnected parts of the network. The opportunities for knowledge creation and for organizing activities are thus expanded beyond the domain of goal-directed organizational boundaries by the increase in serendipitous encounters in Web-space controlled by networking sites and search engines.

Rewiring

This refers to the cutting of existing connections and their replacement by new connections. There is no net increase in the number of nodes or number of ties in the network, and thus time and other resource constraints are observed. Through the process of rewiring, new pathways are created without burdening nodes with increases in the number of connections.

Rewiring can occur through serendipitous or goal-directed processes. Consider a network describing whose office is next to whom in an organization following the opening of a new building (that in itself represents a new node, of course). This network can be rewired by a manager randomly reassigning individual employees to different offices or by purposively arranging proximate relationships between preselected employees (to preserve departmental boundaries, for example). In the case of random rewiring, the network experiences serendipitous variation that may open up pathways of opportunity hitherto not available. In the case of purposive rewiring, preferential linkages are maintained in pursuit of organizational preselected goals.

Product architecture can also be rewired in ways that may prove difficult or impossible for competitors to understand (Henderson & Clark, 1990). To the extent that workflow networks within organizations provide for knowledge flow to move in certain directions and not others, the rewiring of relationships within products may well mirror the rewiring of relationships between the humans and technologies that produce those products (Kilduff, Funk, & Mehra, 1997). Thus, technological decisions taken by engineers interested only in product efficiency can have indirect effects on the rewiring of social relationships in workgroups.

The idea of rewiring can be applied at the level of an ego network. Ego may serendipitously rewire its connections due to a haphazard change in the environment or location. Ego can also purposively rewire its connections to maximize its contact efficiency and its ability to span across structural holes (Burt, 1992). To the extent that opportunities to span across structural holes decay rapidly in organizational settings (Burt, 2002) those who wish to become the network leaders of their interpersonal connections must engage in constant monitoring and rewiring of those connections.

DISCUSSION

Opportunity creation in the heterogeneous networks characteristic of organizations can be understood in terms of new pathways triggered by additional nodes, additional ties, and the rewiring of existing connections. Organizational networks exhibit complex and multifaceted features that research has only begun to explore in terms of different regions, different entities, and dynamic properties. Leadership from the perspective of pathways of opportunity involves discerning and managing heterogeneous collections of nodes in the service of explicit goals or more serendipitously desired outcomes.

A focus on dynamic heterogeneous networks opens up many important research initiatives. First, we draw attention to the extent to which opportunity generation may depend on the dynamic configuration of the organizational network—the changing size and shape of different regions. An interesting question is the extent to which new pathways within the strongly connected component affect overall network activity relative to new pathways in the weak and disconnected components.

Second, the issue of rewiring of existing pathways is itself worthy of much greater attention. As organizations attempt to restructure the flow of opportunities (because of new leaders, new technologies, or changing environments) there may be attempts to deliberately destroy old pathways. But research suggests that some network configurations may be highly resilient to flow disruption (see the extensive discussion in Dorogovtsev & Mendes, 2003). In order to completely disrupt the existing flow of resources and communication it would be necessary to destroy the strong and weak components. This would require the removal of most of the connected nodes in the network. Although it is not uncommon for new organizational regimes to remove and replace many existing nodes—including people, organizational units, technologies, and procedures—in pursuit of systemwide culture change, it may be that the compensatory tendencies of complex heterogeneous networks are capable of reconfiguring prior resource flows along new pathways. Specifically, to the extent that the weakly connected component survives relatively intact, organizational networks may exhibit resistance to attempted change. It is this weakly connected region within which relatively disordered connectivity may preserve possibilities of resource rerouting to preserve the status quo. The pathways of connectivity may be longer, and new nodes may emerge as brokers, but even the most deliberate attempt at network rewiring may experience puzzling difficulties in establishing the viability of new pathways of opportunity given the resiliency and the importance of the belt of weak connectivity surrounding the epicenter of the network.

We have said little concerning how research on these complex and fascinating topics could be undertaken. Clearly, simulations allow an expedient analysis of widely disparate initial system conditions and system adjustments. For example, building on prior explorations of the impact of slow learners on organizational learning (March, 1991), one could simulate the extent to which diffusion of organizational culture varied under conditions of goal-directedness or serendipity. It might be that goal-directed networks would be more vulnerable to disruption and replacement given their relative efficiency and the absence of redundancy in terms of network pathways compared to self-organized networks that tend to exhibit surprising resiliency. Further, organizational learning might proceed at a faster rate given goal-directedness rather than serendipity, but organizational adaptation (defined as culture change that matches organizational change) might be more effective under conditions of serendipity.

We also see possibilities for the selective application of complexity approaches to organizational network research. The application of complexity theory to organizational science has been stymied by the small sample sizes characteristic of human populations in organizations. The theoretical move to heterogeneous networks results in a vast number of potential nodes and connections available for analysis in any organizational system. These networks can be studied using complexity techniques, such as NK modeling (Kauffman, 1993) and cellular automata (Wolfram, 2002). Already research on the World Wide Web has demonstrated how issues of network evolution and disruption can be investigated from the perspective of self-organization (Dorogovtsev & Mendes, 2003).

Complexity research suggests that dissipative forces tend to pull a network into less complex states (Eisenhardt & Bhatia, 2002). A potential area of future research concerns those networks that are able to overcome this tendency and actually increase network complexity levels. Although complexity theory typically suggests that (in natural systems) there is no lead agent controlling the configuration of a network, we have drawn attention to the possibility that (for organizational systems) goal-generators and serendipity-generators may act to reconfigure the network by adding nodes, adding ties, and rewiring.

A final implication of our research relates to network node and tie survival from the perspective of opportunity generation. It may be that network nodes and ties survive based on their ability to provide new pathways of opportunity. Opportunity generation may in fact be integral to the life cycle of network nodes and ties. Rates of structural hole bridge decay (Burt, 2002) would thus be related to diminishing opportunity generation provided by these bridges over time.

CONCLUSION

Organizational network research has been colonized by a wide range of inertial theories, focusing on path-dependent member behavior in homogeneous networks. Although dissipative forces do indeed push organizational systems toward stability and equilibrium, network research remains deficient while it continues to neglect the means by which networks avoid such a fate. We offer a first step in redressing this neglect by developing a framework to illustrate dynamic opportunity creation in heterogeneous networks. Theories of network behavior that are dynamic, instead of inertial, heterogeneous, instead of homogeneous, and path-creative, instead of path-dependent, will provide researchers with the means to better understand both the characteristics of network systems and the potential influence of individual network leaders.

REFERENCES

Albert, R., Jeong, H., & Barabasi, A. (1999). Internet: Diameter of the World Wide Web. *Nature, 401,* 130-131.

Anderson, P. (1999). Complexity theory and organization science. *Organization Science, 10,* 216-232.

Axelrod, R., & Cohen, M. (2000). *Harnessing complexity: Organizational implications of a scientific frontier.* New York: The Free Press.

Barabasi, A., & Albert, R. (1999). Emergence of scaling in random networks. *Science, 286,* 509-512.

Barley, S. (1986). Technology as an occasion for structuring: Evidence from observations of CT scanners and the social order of radiology departments. *Administrative Science Quarterly, 31,* 78-108.

Bossard, J. (1945). The law of family of interaction. *American Journal of Sociology, 50,* 292-294.

Burt, R. (1992). *Structural holes: The social structure of competition.* Cambridge, MA: Harvard University Press.

Burt, R. (2002). Bridge decay. *Social Networks, 24,* 333-363.

Burt, R. (2005). *Brokerage and closure: An introduction to social capital.* New York: Oxford University Press.

Carley, K. M. (2002). Computation organization science: A new frontier. *Proceedings of the National Academy of Sciences, 99,* 7257-7262.

Cilliers, P. (1998). *Complexity and postmodernism: Understanding complex systems.* New York: Routledge.

Csikszentmihalyi, M. (1991). *Flow: The psychology of optimal experience.* New York: Harper Collins.

Dorogovtsev, S., & Mendes, J. (2003). *Evolution of networks: From biological nets to the Internet and WWW.* New York: Oxford University Press.

Eisenhardt, K., & Bhatia, M. (2002). Organizational complexity and computation. In J. Baum (Ed.), *The Blackwell companion to organizations* (pp. 442-466). Malden, MA: Blackwell.

Ferraro, F., Pfeffer, J., & Sutton, R. (2005). Economics language and assumptions: How theories can become self-fulfilling. *Academy of Management Review, 30,* 8-24.

Hannan, M., & Freeman, J. (1977). The population ecology of organizations. *American Journal of Sociology, 82,* 929-964.

Hansen, M. (1999). The search-transfer problem: the role of weak ties in sharing knowledge across organizational subunits. *Administrative Science Quarterly, 44,* 82-111.

Henderson, R., & Clark, K. (1990). Architectural innovation: The reconfiguration of existing product technologies and the failure of established firms. *Administrative Science Quarterly, 35,* 9-30.

Kauffman, S. (1993). *The origins of order: Self-organization and selection in evolution.* New York: Oxford University Press.

Kilduff, M. (1992). The friendship network as a decision-making resource: Dispositional moderators of social influences on organizational choice. *Journal of Personality and Social Psychology, 62,* 168-180.

Kilduff, M., Funk, J., & Mehra, A. (1997). Engineering identity in a Japanese factory. *Organization Science, 8,* 579-592.

Kilduff, M., & Tsai, W. (2003). *Social networks and organizations.* London: Sage.

Knorr-Cetina, K. (1981). *The manufacture of knowledge.* Oxford, England: Pergamon.

Latour, B. (1996). *ARAMIS, or the love of technology* (C. Porter, Trans.). Cambridge, MA: Harvard University Press.

Law, J., & Hassard, J. (Eds.). (1999). *Actor network theory and after*. Malden, MA: Blackwell.

Lawrence, P., & Lorsch, J. (1967). Differentiation and integration in complex organizations. *Administrative Science Quarterly, 12,* 1-47.

Lewis, M. (2003). *Moneyball: The art of winning an unfair game*. New York: W. W. Norton & Company.

March, J. (1991). Exploration and exploitation in organizational learning. *Organization Science, 2,* 71-87.

McKelvey, B. (1999). Avoiding complexity catastrophe in coevolutionary pockets: Strategies for rugged landscapes. *Organization Science*, 10: 294-321.

Mehra, A., Kilduff, M., & Brass, D. J. (2001). The social networks of high and low self-monitors: Implications for workplace performance. *Administrative Science Quarterly, 46,* 121-146.

Powell, W., Kogut, K., & Smith-Doerr, L. (1996). Interorganizational collaboration and the locus of innovation: Networks of learning in biotechnology. *Administrative Science Quarterly, 41,* 116-145.

Scott, J. (2000). *Social network analysis: A handbook* (2nd ed.). Newbury Park, CA: Sage.

Simon, H. (1957). *Models of man*. New York: Wiley.

Tsai, W. (2002). Social structure of "coopetition" within a multiunit organization: Coordination, competition, and intraorganizational knowledge sharing. *Organization Science, 13,* 179-190.

Van de Ven, A., & Poole, M. (1995). Explaining development and change in organizations. *Academy of Management Review, 20,* 510-540.

Wasserman, S., & Faust, K. (1994). *Social network analysis: Methods and applications*. New York: Cambridge University Press.

Weick, K. (1979). *The social psychology of organizing* (2nd ed.). Reading, MA: Addison-Wesley.

Wolfram, S. (2002). *A new kind of science*. Champaign, IL: Wolfram Media.

CHAPTER 5

INDIVIDUAL AND COLLECTIVE COEVOLUTION

Leadership as Emergent Social Structuring

David R. Schwandt

ABSTRACT

This chapter addresses the interactive and coevolutionary nature of human structuring actions and interactions as leadership in and across 2 levels of analysis: the organization (mesolevel) and the individual person (microlevel). It suggests that an "action theory" approach can provide a more robust understanding of the dynamics of structuring actions as bridging mechanisms across levels of analysis while maintaining the invariance of the properties of complex adaptive systems. It incorporates social cognitive theory to explain microactions, such as personality development, mastery, and sensemaking, and uses Gidden's (1984) modalities of structuration to characterize the meso level and its coevolution with the micro level. This multilevel theory building approach (Morgeson & Hofmann, 1999) focuses on the functional (outcomes) invariance of human dynamics in the context of a complex adaptive systems. This chapter is not about a new "type" of leadership behavior, it is about recognizing the emergent structuring that is inherent in all social interaction.

Complexity Leadership, Part I: Conceptual Foundations
pp. 101–127

If we are trying to understand anything about human society, past or present, or about individual actions, we must go to a finer level of analysis and consider human natures as actually formed in the world. (Ehrlich, 2000, p. 13)

Biologist Paul R. Ehrlich's observation exemplifies the increasing acknowledgement by diverse scientific communities (biology, sociology, psychology, economics, physics, and management to mention a few) of the complex and evolutionary nature of human social systems. With this acknowledgement have come attempts to apply the concepts of complex adaptive systems (Anderson, 1999; Axelrod, 1997) to social interaction and the emergence of social phenomena. These applications of the "new" science have resulted in the "complexifying" all sorts of human organizational phenomena, including leadership (Maguire, McKelvey, Mirabeau, & Oztas, 2006). Although these efforts have forced social scientist to reconsider their basic assumptions concerning the rational and linear basis of social theory, they have remained at the systems level of analysis, resulting in a neglect of the specification of the dynamics associated with human interactions (Lewin, Long, & Carroll, 1999).

This "systems" orientation has resulted in organizational theorists (Morel & Ramanujam, 1999) using the concepts of complexity science to deal almost exclusively with meso/macro level organizational issues. They are concerned primarily with the coevolution of the organization with its environment and assume (or ignore) the dynamic adaptive developmental nature of the individual agent.[1] Preoccupation with macro level theory has diminished efforts to understand the invariance of the features of complex adaptive systems across the interface of individual-collective interactions (Klein, Tosi, & Cannella, 1999), and has emphasized the metaphoric stage of paradigm formulation over realism (Maguire et al., 2006) or normal science (Kuhn, 1970). The purpose of this chapter is to address these two underdeveloped areas by concentrating on the dynamics of the human interactions that constitute the human system and provide an argument for the invariance of complex adaptive system's properties and outcomes across the individual-collective interface.

COMPLEX ADAPTIVE SYSTEMS

Complex adaptive systems (CAS) theory "asks how changes in the agent's decision rules, the interconnections among agents, or the fitness function that agents employ produce different aggregate outcomes" (Anderson, 1999, p. 220). One of the outcomes of human interactions is a continuing emergent social structure that defines future interactions of the agent.

Social structure is any enduring pattern of social arrangements within a particular collective (the term "collective" represents social configurations that include groups, teams, units, and organizations). These patterns can emanate from visible mechanisms such as rules and language, or they can be less visible and emanate from cultural values, norms, and relationships among the agents. Because these patterns of structure are always in flux, I will use the term *structuring* (the verb form of structure) to connote the "active" and "variable" nature of the structural patterns and their dependence on human interactions.

Social structuring includes what has been traditionally called leadership behaviors. The application of complexity concepts to human interactions is challenging this traditional and quite narrow person-role centered leadership paradigm. For example, Uhl-Bien, Marion, and McKelvey (2007) propose a multifaceted leadership model that includes entangled roles of administrative, adaptive, and enabling actions. Their model focuses on human actions and interactions as the basis for the emergence of these leadership roles. This conceptualization provides us with a broader definition of leadership in the context of complex adaptive social systems. It moves beyond other treatments of the phenomena of leadership by the complexity sciences that have remained grounded in the person-role orientations (Griffin, 2000; Guastello, 1998) resulting in additions to the list of "leadership types." If we are to take full advantage of the convergence of multi-disciplinary thought and further our understanding of the nature of complex social change we must pursue paths of inquiry that challenge the single focus of the person-role, or leadership types, and broaden our perspectives to include a more distributed concept of human structuring interactions.

The convergence of leadership theory with the concepts of complex adaptive systems must account for the dynamic nature of human interactions. McKelvey (2003) draws our attention to this point by simply saying, "it doesn't make sense to talk about emergence in organizations without worrying about: Emergence from what?" (p. 119). This chapter addresses the "Emergent from what?" question by examining the interactive and coevolutionary nature of human structuring interactions in and across two levels of analysis: the collective (mesolevel) and the individual person (microlevel). It uses an action theory approach (Giddens, 1984; Habermas, 1987; Parsons & Shils, 1952) to provide a more robust understanding of the dynamics of structuring interactions as "bridging" mechanisms (Davis, 2005; Morgeson & Hofmann, 1999) across the micro- and meso-levels of analysis while maintaining the invariance of the properties of complex adaptive systems. It incorporates social cognitive theory (Bandura, 1999; Weick, 1995) to explain microindividual actions, such as personality development, mastery, self-efficacy, and sensemaking. At the mesocollective level, Giddens' (1984) modalities of structuration characterize the social structuring patterns as they coevolve with the micro interactions. This multi level theory building approach (Morgeson & Hofmann, 1999) focuses on the functional (outcomes) invariance of human dynamics in the context of complex adaptive systems. I am not arguing for a new "type" of leadership behavior, rather I want to recognize and describe the emergent structuring that is inherent in all social interactions. It is this emergent structuring that we may choose to either centralize as positional traits and behaviors, or allow for a wider distributed structuring across the collective as they deal with ever increasing complex environments.

The chapter is presented in five sections. The first defines social action and presents a coevolutionary model of micro-meso structuring actions. The second and third sections discuss the microindividual and mesocollective levels independently with respect to structuring interactions. The fourth section provides a discussion of the invariance of the properties and outcomes of complex adaptive systems across and within the two levels of analysis. The final section suggests three areas requiring empirical/simulation research with implications for practice.

COEVOLVING HUMAN ACTIONS AS STRUCTURING

Human structuring interactions are composed of agents' explicit actions (e.g., setting boundaries, physical interaction, organization of work, social status, rules, leadership) and implicit guiding social patterns (e.g., norms, values, traditions, culture). When individual agents interact with each other, or with objects in their environment each action potentially alters both the context and nature of the proceeding actions. These interactions, over time, create collective structural patterns. It is important to set forth a definition of "human action" that contains an inherent structuring orientation and mechanisms so as to fully represent this dynamic nature of interactions in their evolution. This section defines human action and presents a model of coevolving interactions.

Definition of Human Action

The sociological perspective of a general theory of action[2] defines a social system as, "a set of categories for the analysis of the relations of one or more actors to, and in, a situation" (Parsons & Shils, 1952, p. 61). This definition is primarily concerned with the structure and processes involved in the agent's relationship to the contextual nature of the situation, which includes other agents as persons and as members of the collective. Action[3] is conceptualized as normatively expended energy in a situation that is goal oriented. It requires a *situation* that includes the means and conditions that enable the act to occur. These include the resources to act, the signal to act, the information needed to act, and the time and space to act. It requires an *end or goal*, which is a future state of affairs to which action is oriented by virtue of the fact that it is deemed desirable by the agent(s) but which differs in important respects from the state they would expect to occur by merely allowing the predictable trends of the situation to take their course without active intervention. And finally, it requires a set of *norms or values,* both collective and individual, which provide the agent with meaning that relates the *ends* to the *situation.* This is the essence of "structuring," because the norms and values provide a framework for the agent to interpret and select appropriate actions for the situation (Rocher, 1975).

An example of an action meeting this definition would be a person standing when the national flag passes during a parade. The *Situation* is characterized by the presences of the flag and the *means* include the ability of the individual to physically stand. The *End* is the expression of allegiance and commitment to the country. The *Norm* is a social expectation that an individual shows this commitment in a public forum when the flag is presented (other norms exist with respect to the flag's presences in differing situations such as flying on a flag pole in front of a building). The *Values* associated with the action may have the meaning of patriotism and pride in belonging to the nation. Of course, withholding of the gesture provides a much different meaning—but this constitutes a different act. From this example, it can be seen that the definition of human actions is comprehensive in that it relates the latent normative character of the social system (value of country) to its structuring processes such as acts of allegiance (standing of the individual). It illustrates the interdependent and coevolutionary relation between an individual agent's actions and the social structure of the collective.

An Action-Based Model of Micro-Meso Coevolution

Although there are some variations in terminology, sociologist classify actions and interactions within and among three levels of the social system: (1) the microsociological level of analysis dealing with the individual person and personal interactions; (2) the mesosociological level dealing with groups or collectives, formal organizations, social movements, and some aspects of institutions; and (3) the macrosociological level dealing with social structure and societies overall (Smelser, 1995). Each of these levels of the human system contributes to structuring interactions through influencing values, norms and goals of actions; however, for the purposes of these discussions, the model presented in this section will be limited to the microindividual and mesocollective levels.

The model portrayed in Figure 5.1 consists of both the reciprocating actions of microindividuals and the emerging mesocollective structures (Graen & Uhl-Bien, 1995). It represents a social system comprised of two coevolving complex adaptive systems—the individual and the collective (this assertion is further developed later in the chapter). It illustrates how structuring interactions provide the bridge between the two levels of analysis, simultaneously (Hedstrom & Swedberg, 1998). These interactions fulfill both the individual's and collective's need for structure in reducing equivocality. The word equivocality is used to represent a sensemaking state in which all alternative interpretations are equally valid. Reduction in this state of equivocality is accomplished through the application of discriminatory structures, categories, mental schema, and so forth, to

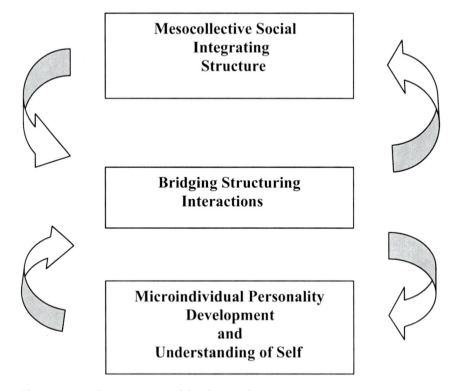

**Mesocollective Social
Integrating
Structure**

**Bridging Structuring
Interactions**

**Microindividual Personality
Development
and
Understanding of Self**

Figure 5.1.   Micro-meso coevolving interactions.

achieve human meaning (Weick, 1995). They also fulfill the collective's need to integrate multiple actions toward organizational goal attainment while fulfilling the individual's need for understanding of the "self."

For the human system to remain viable these structuring interactions must provide for continuous integration of the system's elements as they differentiate, grow, or expend energy (Katz & Kahn, 1978; Lawrence & Lorsch, 1978). Integration can be manifested as physical, cognitive, or emotional associations (connections) among the multiple elements that result in the reinforcement of the system's relationships (e.g., meanings).

Integration at the micro-individual level of the social system is achieved through cognitive and emotional development of the agent as they fulfill their biological and personality needs (Bandura, 1999; Cervone, Artistico, & Berry, 2006; Mischel & Shoda, 1995) such as reduction of equivocality (Weick, 1979). At the mesocollective level it is achieved through the establishment of social norms, culture, and structures to maintain positive goal attainment while reducing the negative aspects of human interaction (e.g., conflict).

Both of these levels of integration rely on the agent's structuring interactions as a bridge between them. Micro interactions influence the meso structure and actions, but in turn, those mesostructures influence future micro actions and interactions. Each interaction either reinforces or inhibits changes that influence future interactions. It is this ever-changing relational "dance" and coevolution of structure (McKelvey, 2002) that allows the organization to adapt as a system and survive in complex environments.

The actions and interactions of individuals, whether knowingly or not, jointly produce and reproduce the operating procedures, routines and norms for doing things both as individuals and as a collective. Structuring is present in all interactions and is manifested in acts of reflection, dialogue, inquiry, language, and sustaining of diversity as well as the traditional acts of direction and order. For example, by using language as action, social structuring can be accomplished by simply saying, "This is the way we do things here." These words (Habermas, 1987; Taylor & Van Every, 2000) influence the social structure of work routines, and influence future acts by the agent while reinforcing the collective's work procedures.

Individuals are free to make "informed choices" concerning their actions; however, they do it in situations that are heavily influenced by past and present social structuring that may encourage normative behaviors. This means that each actor is a potential player in the structuring process. Whether in a formal position or not, they have an opportunity to structure an equivocal environment in accordance with their values and sensemaking (Weick, 1995). Thus, the evolution of the individual constitutes a complex system with the potential to unpredictably change their personal values through learning, and to arrive at a different understanding at the micro level of the human system.

The collective's ability to systematically integrate and regenerate (Dooley & Van de Ven, 1999) its social patterns with environmental objects and its internal agents is highly dependent on its capacity to maintain structuring acts. Jantsch (1982) sees these structuring acts relating to dissolution and/or creation of related conditions and processes for the collective evolution. Dissolution is seen as being accomplished through actions that break the symmetry of current structures, thus increasing the degrees of freedom available to the system for restructuring. Creation is accomplished through actions of experimentation and alignment with deep collective social patterns that are irreversible. Actions of both dissolution and creation can be present simultaneously, thus resulting in paradoxical and complex social conditions.

The next two sections of this chapter explore the dynamics of the microindividual and mesocollective levels and the nature of social interaction as the structuring bridge. By incorporating an established social cognitive theory of personality development and a sociological theory of structuration, each section provides insights into the dynamic nature of their respective evolution.

MICROINDIVIDUAL STRUCTURING AS DEVELOPMENT AND UNDERSTANDING

This section focuses only on the coevolution of agents through personal development and understanding of self in the context of their dependence on human structuring interactions (Figure 5.2). McKelvey (2002) delineates the necessary and sufficient conditions for coevolution to occur; agents must be heterogeneous, have adaptive learning capability, be able to interact and mutually influence each other, be subject to higher level constraints that motivate adaptation processes, and must be open to initiating events. Using these conditions we find that the human agent does form a coevolutionary relationship with their structural context. Each action of an individual (heterogeneous personalities), whether it is an act of direction or an act of collaboration, with another individual, or objects (open to initiating events), results in a change to the their situation (either in conditions and/or means). When two individuals interact, they influence each other's lives as do predators and prey, and each normally becomes a major source of selection operating on the other; in such situations coevolution occurs (Ehrlich, 2000).

Each individual, as a complex adaptive system, requires interaction with their environment as a source of new information and feedback con-

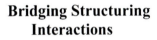

Figure 5.2.   Microindividual coevolving interactions.

cerning their actions (Bandura, 1982). The structuring interactions involve a series of double interlocking actions between and among the actors (Weick, 1979). All double interacts have social structuring potential, both intended and unintended, that contributes to the evolutionary process of the individual's development as a "person," and simultaneously to the coevolution of the structure of the collective. Because the individuals are changing their behaviors based on their individualized interpretations of the structuring actions (*Situation, Ends, and Norm/Values*), variation and selection (Axelrod & Cohen, 2000) make prediction very difficult.

The individual's personality and understanding of self coevolves as they interact with other individuals in the context of the collective's social structure. These interactions provide information and feedback for personal cognitive and emotional evolution. They are altered by their interactions, both through personal learning and growth of self-efficacy (personal orientation). This interaction contributes to the individual's personal capacities:

> People's ability to deliberate on the past and future, combined with the capacity to form a sense of self and social identity, enables them to select and shape the environments they encounter, develop skills to meet future challenges, pursue personal aims, and thereby function as causal agents. (Cervone et al., 2006, p. 170)

Bandura's (1977) social cognitive theory (social learning) provides a conceptual frame for understanding the agent's evolutionary dynamics. He explains psychosocial functioning in terms of triadic reciprocal causation (Wood & Bandura, 1989) among behavior (actions), personal factors (personality, cognition, emotions, self-efficacy), and the external environment (the collective). Social cognitive theory places an emphasis on the ability of the individual actors to drive and alter their behaviors (learn) based on environmental events, their personal knowledge structures (schemata), perceived self-efficacy, and mastery of the requisite competencies. Bandura sees "the feedback accompanying enactments as providing the information for detecting and correcting mismatches between conception and action. The behavior is thus modified, based on the comparative information to achieve a close match between conception and action" (1999, p. 26). A sense of mastery provides cognitive and emotional feedback concerning the order of one's environment (Ehrlich, 2000).

Of particular note is the relevance of this triadic interaction in decision making. The complexity of decision making is dependent on various dimensions such as number of relevant factors available for consideration, necessary tradeoffs, and the relative stability of different predictive factors in the probabilistic environment. Wood and Bandura's (1989) research has shown that the relationship of prior performance to subsequent performance is partly mediated by the actor's perceived self-efficacy, personal goals, and analytical strategies (schemata). Further these self-referent characteristics provide the cognitive regulators of moral conduct, altruism, and an appreciation for one's efforts for the collective beyond one's self interest (Mainemelis, 2001). However, "Self-regulatory mechanisms do not operate unless they are activated, and there are many processes by which moral self-sanctions can be disengaged from inhumane conduct" (Bandura, 1999, p. 33). Disengaging actions such as blaming the victim, minimizing injury, or justification through serving "worthy purposes" are seen as "dampening" the coevolution of moral behavior.

Individuals in organizations, even though subject to higher levels of constraint (norms and values), possess the cognitive capability to make choices (learn). These higher levels of constraints are also a product of the agent structuring interactions and represent emergent outcomes at the mesocollective level.

STRUCTURING INTERACTIONS AS MESOCOLLECTIVE STRUCTURE

This section examines the coevolving relationship between the structuring interactions of the agents, emerging collective structures, and the reciprocal effects of these structures on the structuring interactions. It provides a more detailed development of the mesocollective coevolution with the bridging interactions. Using established sociological concepts it

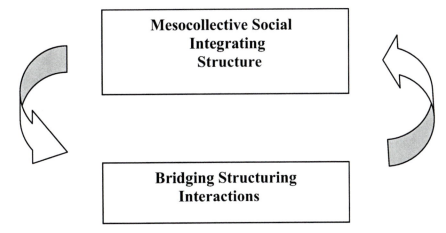

Figure 5.3.   Meso coevolving structures.

adds a "dynamic dimension" to the consideration of the collective as a complex adaptive system. Figure 5.3 illustrates this reciprocal-ongoing interaction between the mesocollective integrating structures and the bridging structuring interactions of the microindividuals.

As microindividual double interacts occur in a nonlinear fashion, collective structures emerge as outcomes in the form of norms, rules, structures, cultures and identities. These mesocollective structures emerge in response to the need for integration and reduction of equivocality, and influence the range and goals of future structuring actions of the agents. This reciprocal process is called "structuration" (Giddens, 1984) and represents the dual nature of social structuring. Microindividual interactions are simultaneously "structured by" and "are structuring" the mesocollective.

To add dynamic specificity to the coevolution of collective emergent structures and their reciprocal influence on the actor, Giddens functionally classifies emerging norms and rules as "modalities of structuration": signification, legitimation, and domination. The rules of *signification* enable and guide meaningful communication and sensemaking among the agents. It provides structure to clarify information and knowledge for the agents, in the context of the collective. Norms of *legitimation* provide the collective with the ability to morally sanction specific actions and reject others. They provide the rules of inclusion within the cultural boundaries of the collective. The modality of *domination* addresses the functions of command, power, and authority over people and resources. "The actors use appropriate 'rules and resources' (structures) to give 'form' to situations of action by interlacing ... meaning, normative elements and power" (Parker, 2000, p. 57). These modalities set limits on actions, provide focus for collective goals, and define the nature of interaction.

Participating in the collective necessitates the transfer of large portions of order over one's individual actions to the needs, norms and values of the collective. This is not a complete capitulation by the agent. They are simply attempting to gain personal utility by making the unilateral transfer to the will of the collective. Contrary to Giddens' premise of minimized free choice, actors do make informed choices concerning their commitment to the collective and its values; the choice may be to not act in accordance with the collective rules, thus preventing themselves from becoming mindless dupes of the culture (Coleman, 1990). This may begin a change in those collective norms. Herein lies the dynamics of the human interactions of structuring as the bridging mechanism for the coevolution of the microindividual level of the social system with its meso-collective level.

In many situations, the interactions of the agents, because of their self-serving orientation and therefore nonlinear nature, result in the possibility for adaptation to the currently accepted norms/values and collective structuring. For example, the lack of creativity and innovation in an organization may create a "situation" and "end" that forces the consideration of changes in norms that govern how structuring (leadership) interactions deal with information dissemination. Greater flexibility, rather than tight order, of information diffusion can lead to higher levels of knowledge creation (Schwandt & Marquardt, 2000). Thus, over time, new norms governing structuring of relationships within the collective may coevolve with the need for new knowledge and values concerning innovation.

The past two sections of this chapter have provided explanations for the dynamics of both the microindividual and mesocollective levels as they coevolve with each other. The next section analyzes these dynamics as complex adaptive systems.

COEVOLUTION OF COMPLEX ADAPTIVE SYSTEMS: STRUCTURING INTERACTIONS AS BRIDGING

The above delineation of the two complex adaptive systems and their human dynamics makes it clear that structuring interactions that bridge the micro and meso levels of the social system are necessary for the coevolution of the social system. It has explained the context surrounding the agent's actions, clarifying how the individual gains from structuring interactions and at the same time contributes to the formation of collective social structures. However, from a theoretical and research perspective, we must ask the question, "To what extent are the properties of complex adaptive systems invariant *across* the microindividual and mesocollective levels of the human system and are the functional outcomes of the structuring interactions isomorphic?"

Invariance of Complex Adaptive System's Properties

Previously the assertion was made that both the microindividual and mesocollective levels of the social system each constituted a complex adaptive system. This section establishes that assertion. Four properties of complex systems—emergence, schemata, non-linearity, and self organizing—provide the essences of the dynamic uniqueness of the human social system (Anderson, 1999; Cilliers, 1998; Holland, 1995; McKelvey, 2002). Emergence, or aggregation, is concerned with new phenomena emanating from interactions of less complex elements and refers to, "the patterns of elements and their relationships that reflect changing adaptations as time elapses and experience accumulates" (Holland, 1995, p. 23). The social system has the ability to manifest phenomena that are observable (or felt), but not clear as to the causal variables that contribute to the phenomena (Fararo, 2001). Although many authors include emergence (and coevolution) as a property of complexity, this chapter has incorporated it as part of its assumptions.

Related to emergence, three other properties reflect the complex nature of human interactions. Table 5.1 summarizes the comparison of these properties across both levels of analysis. To fully apply the concepts of complex adaptive systems and coevolution to human organizational systems, and move past using the concepts metaphorically, I will address the invariance of these properties across these levels of analysis (Klein et al., 1999).

Schemata. The dynamics of coevolution of structuring actions is influenced by sets of simple rules, at both micro and meso levels, that are fluid enough to be changed over time when subjected to repeated interactions of the agents. "Each agent's behavior (individual and/or collective) is dictated by a *schema*, a cognitive structure that determines what action the agent takes at time t, given its perception of the environment at $t - 1$" (Anderson, 1999, p. 219). Multiple schemas exist at both levels. Individual schemas lie within personal knowledge structures (values, meanings, relationships) and are manipulated through learning and personality development. Collective schemas, although also embedded in the knowledge structures of the individual, are contained within the routines, rules, norms and cultural values shared by the collective, "these patterns of ele-

Table 5.1.   Invariance of CAS Properties Across Coevolving Levels of Analysis

CAS Property	Individual—Micro	Collective—Meso
Influenced by schemata	Cognitive representations conveyed by modeling serve as guides for the production of skilled performances and as standards for making corrective adjustments in development of behavioral proficiency and self-understanding.	Routines, policy, and traditions guide collective interaction and provide the criteria for evaluating the achievement of collective goals.
Nonlinearity	Intuition and sensemaking are governed by nonadditive and non sequential brain functions as they relate to new information. In addition, individuals have the capacity to exercise forethought. This enables the agent to wield adaptive order anticipatorily rather than being simply reactive to the consequences of their actions. This human capacity results in double interacts that are also nonadditive.	The totality of the collective is greater than the sum of its elements. Symbiotic demands on the structuring interactions are not predictable, nonadditive, and are therefore open to mutation. Nonlinear interactions make the behavior of the collective more complicated than would be predicted by summing or averaging the individual behaviors. Progressive adaptations in the actions lead to the possibility for novel interactions.
Self-organizing	People create the nature of their situations to serve their purposes. To exercise self-influence, individuals have to monitor their actions, judge it in relation to personal standards of merit and react in a process of self-evaluation and learning. This leads to personal change and variations of personality contingent on situation.	Systems that consist of independent actors whose interactions are governed by a system of recursively applied rules generate stable structure. Variations in outcomes necessitates selection of new options (Axelrod & Cohen, 2000) When the interaction only involves positive feedback actors become locked into self-reinforcing behaviors. Negative feedback leads to adaptation of the actions.

ments and their relationships reflect changing adaptations as time elapses and experience accumulates" (Holland, 1995, p. 23). Thus, each system (micro and meso) has an inherent set of schemas that over time and repeated interactions can be altered to influence subsequent interactions and schema.

Nonlinearity. The property of nonlinearity assumes the nonadditive nature of the elements of the system and their relationships to each other. At the micro level, individuals are guided by their needs and goals. The existence of "choice" and the variation in human values assures interactions that are unpredictable.

At the meso level, the collective represents the essence of complexity in that elements of the system do not obey "single cause-effect" relationships. They are subject to "nonproportionality (small forces can result in large effects, etc.), and their behaviors cannot be aggregated through simple averaging of individual element values. The diversity of human nature, self-efficacy, and personality provide essentially new and unique context for each double interact. Although collective schemas may "guide" the interactions, the structuring that results may result in the potential for mutations in social patterns. Within the bridging interactions lies the potential for a small action, or double interacts, to influence (directly or indirectly) the path of evolution of the collective's structure and culture (Kaufman, 1985).

Self-Organizing. The inherent diversity and nonlinearity of both systems also contributes to their ability to self-generate and self-organize, thus creating new possibilities for further interactions. The triadic reciprocal relationship (Bandura, 1999) among agent actions, organizational environment, and personal cognitive, emotional, and efficacy factors regulate motivational, affective, and cognitive functioning of the actor, and over time and space simultaneously influence other actors and enable them to create beneficial organizational environments. Wallace (1961) refers to these interactions as "mutual equivalence structures" with minimal knowledge of other's motives. This allows for "mutual prediction" rather than just "mutual sharing." As the agent's values change based on their integration of environmental feedback with self-efficacy requirements, new perspectives, or different personality orientations occur. For the individual this process can be interpreted as learning and unlearning and may result in transformations or newly self-organized schemas.

New structuring interactions become opportunities for the critical examination of collective structures. "The self is socially constituted but, by exercising self-influence, human agency operates generatively and proactively on social systems, not just reactively" (Bandura, 1999, p. 24). These new interactions become the collective learning process (Schwandt & Marquardt, 2000) and may result in structural change (new routines or rules) or even cultural change (new values). The time needed for this self-organizing is dependent on the system's ability to change its values and norms that relate their goals to the situation. In most incidents, the change at the collective level is slower than at the individual level.

This analysis has demonstrated the complex adaptive nature of both the microindividual and the mesocollective systems. These properties describe two systems that are dependent on one another for their evolution. Although not predictable, the emergence of order at each level provides patterns of structuring functions that appear to be similar. However, within the context of the human social system, are these functions isomorphic across levels?

Isomorphic Nature of Cross Level Outcomes

In discussing the multilevel theoretical implications of the structuring actions of humans, one must be careful of committing fallacies of reification and personification (Morgeson & Hofmann, 1999, p. 249). Morgeson and Hofmann (1999) suggest that isomorphic constructs that span levels of analysis may have similar functions or causal outputs, but can differ in their nature of the variables that are involved in the functional processes. The processes we are interested in are those of structuring. The outcomes of social structuring, both for individuals and the collective, are the reduction of equivocality, the integration of interactions, and a framework for the assigning of meaning to the interactions. Although the outcomes (structuring) are isomorphic, the natures of the interactions differ. These structuring interactions account for the mutual coevolution of each system with the other and act as the "bridge" between the two. Three functional outcomes are supported at their respective levels with social theories that incorporate coevolution. Table 5.2 summarizes these outcomes; understanding meaning and sensemaking; understanding the role of culture and self-interest in maintaining integrity of the system; and the need for a sense of order. Each of these functional isomorphic relations is discussed below.

Individual-Micro Cognition and Collective-Meso Signification: Meaning. Structuring interactions contribute to the outcomes of cognition for the

Table 5.2.   Functional Outcomes of Coevolving Structuring Actions Across Levels of Analysis

Individual-Micro Structuring Outputs *(Bandura)*	*Collective-Meso Structuring Outputs* *(Giddens)*
Cognition—reasoning, comprehension, assignment of *meaning*, and understanding.	Signification—communications and ***meaning*** codes
Self-efficacy—sense of situational expectations, confidence, and motivation, and individual *integrity*.	Legitimation—sense of community expectations, morality, and collective ***integrity***.
Mastery—capability for action and self-determination, freedom, and *order* of ones self and environment.	Domination—conformity and power differentials contributing to ***order*** of the collective.

individual and signification for the collective. These functions are isomorphic in that they both result in the assignment of meaning and the reduction of equivocality. The individual actions, although stemming from cognitive/emotional sources that are emergent from biological brain functions of neurons and synapses (Milner, Squire, & Kandel, 1998) are dependent on "feedback accompanying enactment which provides the information for detecting and correcting mismatches between concepts and actions" (Bandura, 1999, p. 26). Individual meaning is based on extracted cues from their signified environment which triggers sensemaking (Weick, 1995). These cues, sometimes minor, have the power to launch new nonlinear cyclic actions that can change personal life courses, future interactions with other actors, and influence collective norms and values.

Although, in new situations, the actor's sensemaking is characterized more by plausibility than accuracy (Weick, 1995), individual actors maintain a course of action that is influenced not only by internal standards and sanctions, but also by collective signification in the form of external norms and organizational values. Social status, rules, cultural values, and physical structures guide the processes and frequencies of communication of the agents. These collective structures have emerged over time and influence the individual's selection of events and behaviors during interaction. "Cognitive factors partly determine the salience of environmental events, what meaning is conferred on them, whether they leave any lasting effects, what emotional impact and motivating power they have, and how the information they convey will be organized for future use" (Bandura, 1999, p. 27). These processes of integration and sense making are constituted through human actions, interactions, and communications (Habermas, 1987; Luhmann, 1995) that provide continuous "structuring and restructuring" of not only the social system, but also of the individual's personality by focusing their attention, increasing or decreasing human choice, and reducing equivocality. These meanings result in increased individual and collective knowledge (potentially good or bad) about the collective and self.

Individual Self-Efficacy and Collective Legitimation: Integrity. An individual's interactions are driven by his or her need for self-interest, gratification, and altruism in the context of collective structures. Individuals are expected to make judgments, matches, and selections as to the relationship between the "situation" and the "ends" using their values as influenced by the norms of the collective. Each action is associated with structuring of their environments in an attempt to add meaning, understanding, and sometimes order. This continuous process of differentiation and integration is accompanied by ever increasing elaborations that generate additional information and increased equivocality. The individual is always in the process, at some level, of self-exploration.

The evolution of the individual's development and understanding becomes part of their efforts to establish "wholeness" or the integrity of the self as a system. "Complex adaptive systems theories presume that the adaptation of a system to its environment emerges from the adaptive efforts of individual agents that attempt to improve their own payoffs" (Anderson, 1999, p. 223). This "payoff" or self-serving nature of individual actions within the context of the collective provides a potential motive (Cervone et al., 2006; Mischel & Shoda, 1995) for high or low amounts of participation in the collective actions. The motivation to participate in the double interact is initiated by the need to marshal the means to attain one's individual ends and self-efficacy. Collective action first converges around the "means" for action, not the "ends."

> Once the members converge on interlocked behaviors as the means to pursue diverse ends, there occurs a subtle shift away from diverse to common ends. The diverse ends remain, but they become subordinated to an emerging set of shared goals. (Weick, 1979, p. 92)

Diversity of personal goals and self-interest requires the collective to expend energy to maintain itself as a system. Smith (1986) describes this as dissipative self-organization that, "implies a system change that takes shape within turbulent conditions through the breakdown and rebuilding of structural arrangements" (p. 204). The dissipation of energy occurs as the collective legitimates itself through structuring its social interactions in support of internal equity, an exchange (market) and preservation of the individual's freedom to negotiate, and the need to coordinate and enhance mutual dependence (hierarchical) to alleviate the fear of failure to perform (Douglas, 1992).

Legitimation, or establishment of structures and norms, by the collective, assures itself of temporary continuity and integration. For the individual, structuring interactions provide continuing feedback for one's capacity as a developmental system. Thus, both self-efficacy and legitimation are the isomorphic outcomes of interactions in that they are directed at maintaining the system's integrity.

Individual-Micro Mastery and Collective-Meso Domination: A Sense of Order. Human conflict, both individual and collective, may arise from structuring interactions that have as outcomes meaning assignment and maintenance of system integrity. This conflict can be both constructive (e.g. disagreement around process or task) and and/or destructive (e.g. personal competition, or self interest over collective's goal) (Jehn, 1997). Therefore, the systems' structuring processes must self-generate the capacity for dampening (McKelvey, 2003; Weick, 1995) or controlling the tensions associated with destructive, or personal, conflict. Historically, conflict has been seen as an emerging dialectic, "dialectical theory begins with the Hegelian assumption that the organizational entity exists in a pluralistic world of colliding events, forces, or contradictory values that compete with each other for domination and order" (Van de Ven & Poole, 1995, p. 517). This emergence of order is manifested in collective cultural norms and in self-regulation of individual actions.

At the collective level we find the individual interacting in situations in which their personal values must conform, to a certain extent, with those collective norms and values that have emerged over time. For example, leadership, as structuring, is governed by a set norms accepted by the collective. If the norm is autocratic, then structuring for the collective may only occur when strong and frequent direction is verbalized and enacted by an individual. However, if the collective norm is open to multiple modes of structuring (e.g. distributed leadership), and can tolerate associated ambiguity, then multiple agents may be free to interact to provide the necessary collective structuring.

The actors' interactions are delimited by collective routines, yet they have the capacity to alter these routines, but at a potential cost, or possible sanctions. The probability of actors altering collective structuring interactions can be thought of as a function of the difference of individual's values ($V_{individual}$) from the collective's values ($V_{collective}$). That is;

Probability of altering structuring actions = $1 - (V_{collective} - V_{individual})/V_{collective}$

It is this inverse power relation and the recursive probabilistic nature of individual's values orientation that acts to dampen or order structuring interactions. It is also the source of cross level conflict during coevolution.

At the microindividual level, self-regulation of actions becomes a function of the agent's forethought, personal reward, self-gratification, and a need for self-efficacy. Situations and ends are moderated by the cognitive and emotional evaluation of the collective norms by the individual. "The belief system is the foundation of human agency. Unless people believe that they can produce desired effects by their actions they have little incentive to act or to persevere in the face of difficulties" (Bandura, 1999, p. 28). The potential for achievement of self-interests through structuring interactions creates order and a self-correcting system that is larger than any individual.

Interaction mastery at the individual level (e.g., developing self-efficacy as an outcome of structuring interactions in the social system context) involves having a sense of order over one's interactions with other agents. This order at the individual level (social interactions mastery) assures oneself of continuity and continuing ability to reduce equivocality and maintain integration through sensemaking. Domination at the collective is achieved through power distribution (rewards and sanctions), but still assures the collective the continuity of reduction in equivocality and integration. Both mastery and domination are isomorphic outcomes in that they contribute to the system's sense/or need for order.

In summary, this section has shown the invariance of the complex properties of schemas, non-linearity, and self-organizing for both the micro-individual and the meso-collective level of the human social system. The bridge between the two complex systems is comprised of structuring interactions that create isomorphic functions and outcomes that provide for the assignment of meaning, system's integrity, and a sense of order.

IMPLICATIONS FOR SYSTEMS LEADERSHIP/STRUCTURING

Complexity theory has implications for how we "think" about the leadership function in collectives and our need to control actions as the only answer to ambiguous environments (Marion, 1999; Thietart & Forgues, 1995; Von Krogh & Roos, 1994; Wheatley, 1992). Nonlinear explanations of the collective may still be in the metaphoric stage of theory building, however, it does provide interesting implications for understanding the unpredictability of the collective's actions, especially as they pertain to the debate concerning organizational order and individual development (Eden & Ackermann, 1998; Mintzberg, 1994; Pressman & Wildavsky, 1984; Schwandt, 1997).

The preceding discussions have laid out an argument for broadening our perspectives of leadership from a person/role-centered model to one that has a social interaction based framework. By focusing on the structuring that is inherent in human actions and treating these acts and interactions as comprising a complex adaptive system, we may not have to rely on, or default to, a person in position model of leadership. If we focus on structuring as an isomorphic function, then we find that many means for ordering emerge and are the responsibility of us all. This means that our interactions encompass many types of social structuring interactions such as critical inquiry, experimentation, dialog, knowledge sharing, and development of individual member's self-efficacy. It is not dependent on organizational position. This section examines three implications that emanate from the consideration of leadership as structuring actions; human meaning, integrity, and order.

Human Meaning

One of the major implications for systems leadership is the realization that sensemaking and judgment may be more dependent on the social aspects of the collective than on a universal management perspective (Johnson, Daniels, & Asch, 1998). The emergent structure of the collective and the personal needs of the individual are both necessary ingredients for establishing human meaning. This meaning is the critical component of the individual's value formation and the collective's basic cultural assumptions. However, it is temporal in nature and is an outcome of our interactions. If managers are to make sense of their environments, they must understand the complex dynamics of the collective as well as the individual as their social systems coevolve over time.

Understanding the relationship between social actions and knowledge creation is not only an implication for managers, but for all members of a collective. As participants in the collective, we all must search for new information, employ a social structure to reflect on that information, and, finally, make critical judgments concerning the plausibility of its value as it is applied to our situations. Because of the social nature of this process, it may threaten the collective's ability to create new knowledge and may lead to conflicting actions of the agents. Understanding the dynamics of systems leadership requires an analytic framework that takes into consideration structuration (Giddens, 1984), institutionalization (Archer, 1988; Douglas, 1981) and implications for interactions of actors (Bourdieu, 1977; Weick, 1995) in a highly complex environment.

System's Integrity

The emergence of coevolving system's integrity as an outcome of structuring interactions has two implications for systems leadership. First, it is necessary that individuals derive a sense of self and wholeness from their social interactions. We are just beginning to place emphasis on understanding "the cognitive antecedents of emotion and the cognitive consequences of affect for diverse processes such as memory, decision making, and language" (Davidson, Scherer, & Goldsmith, 2003, p. xv). This implication means that the collective system of structuring actions must constantly reflect a negotiated and dynamic emerging structure. It is the tension (McKelvey, 2002) between the individual and collective perspectives that is indicative of the non-linear nature of structuring.

Second, there should be no expectation that system's integrity equates with the ability to predict. Emergent structuring at both levels is not predictable based on a set of variables that can be observed. One could assume as equivocality increases, the structuring will also increase to maintain the integrity of self and/or the collective. However, "What transpires will be the unpredictable outcome of the mix of intended and unintended consequences of the strategic use of structures by agents" (Parker, 2000, p. 59). These implications challenge the "iron grip" of organizational behaviorist on describing the measurable functions of leadership in terms of role behaviors and attributes (Marion, 1999).

Sense of Order

Linking structure to agency, especially in the context of systems leadership (Hellgren & Lowstedt, 1998), has implications for how we view traditional constructs such as conflict and power—not in, and of themselves, but how they relate to patterns of collective actions and cognition. Systems leadership shifts structuring interactions from an expectation and valuing of order to one of enhancing flexibility. This entails a greater tolerance for novelty and exploration as opposed to exploitation (March, 1991). It has implications concerning the cultural values that must be maintained to take advantage of systems leadership. It means more trust than order, more tolerance of conflict, and less dependence on a false sense of security based on our ability to predict.

Of course, this argument for relaxing collective order must be tempered by the individual's self control based on their values concerning personal responsibility. If not, the "tragedy of the commons" could result from the distribution of structuring as opposed to concentration of leadership in a position. Tragedy stems from the concept that if structuring is not "owned" by each of the agents, even though it may raise conflict, it may not be owned by anyone. The result is possible disengagement and dropping-out that leads to decreases in coevolution. This may move the collective structure too far from equilibrium position and possible bifurcation, or increased entropy and eventual death of the system.

In this pursuit, we must remember that a better understanding of the micro-meso interactions and emergence of social phenomena such as systems leadership, may not necessarily lead to success of the firm, or even, more predictability. Our investigations may only provide insights to patterns of interactions and the probability of occurrences as opposed to measurable variables and direct cause-effect relationships. The future of the social system will remain quite unpredictable.

CONCLUSION

The fields of information technology and complexity are proceeding with vigor toward social systems as potential applications of their theories. The "knowledge management" and the "distributed intelligence" flags are providing the rally points for both complexity and information management theorists and practitioners. Advances in agent based models (Axelrod, 1997; Taylor & Greve, 2006) are enabling researchers to investigate issues of agent diversity, team performance, networks, and other micro-macro phenomena via computer simulations. Workshops such as those sponsored by the Santa Fe Institute are providing a medium for the discussion of collective cognition and theories of collectives that include understanding dialog and the role of inter-agent communications and interactions.

This chapter has scratched the surface of developing leadership as a broader system's function by delineating a model of social coevolution dependent on structuring interactions of its agents. By understanding the dynamic nature of human natures (both individual and collective) and their development in the context of the dynamics of complex adaptive systems, the dependence of social coevolution on structuring interactions becomes apparent. The purpose of these human interactions is two fold: the reduction in environmental equivocality and the enhancement of internal integration. If we don't balance our discussions of complexity with concerns for evolving human nature, then we may prove critics correct by treating individuals as, "mere automatons undergoing actions devoid of any conscious regulation, phenomenological life of personal identity" (Bandura, 1999, p. 22).

NOTES

1. This chapter uses interchangeably the terms "individual," "actor," and "agent" to represent the micro level of interaction and reserves the term "collective" to represent meso entities such as groups, teams, or organizations.

2. This chapter does not support Parsons' normative, stable systems, or equilibrium seeking, assumptions concerning social structure, however, his description of an action (situation, goal, value) provides a good starting point for the analysis of human interaction and emergence. This view is much more congruent with "early" Parsons than his later work (Buckley 1967).

3. Actions within the context of the collective do not stand in isolation of one another. They form patterns, or sets, of actions called "subsystems of actions," that fulfill prerequisite functions necessary for the survival of the

social system and are dependent on each other for their own coevolution. Thus, a dysfunction in one pattern of actions will jeopardize the effectiveness of the whole system because each subsystem requires inputs (or exchanges) from the other subsystems in order to perform their function for the social system (Blau, 2002; Parsons & Shils, 1952).

REFERENCES

Anderson, P. (1999). Complexity theory and organization science. *Organization Science, 10*(3), 216-232.

Archer, M. (1988). *Culture and agency: The place of culture in social theory.* New York: Cambridge University Press.

Axelrod, R. (1997). *The complexity of cooperation.* Princeton, NJ: Princeton University Press.

Axelrod, R., & Cohen, M. D. (2000). *Harnessing complexity: Organizational implications of a scientific frontier.* New York: Basic Books.

Bandura, A. (1977). *Social learning theory.* Englewood Cliffs, NJ: Prentice-Hall.

Bandura, A. (1982). Self-efficacy mechanism in human agency. *American Psychologist, 37*(2), 122-147.

Bandura, A. (1999). Social cognitive theory: An agentic perspective. *Asian Journal of Social Psychology, 2,* 21-41.

Blau, P. M. (2002). *Exchange and power in social life.* New Brunswick, NJ: Transaction.

Bourdieu, P. (1977). *Outline of a theory of practice* (R. Nice, Trans.). Cambridge, England: Cambridge Press.

Buckley, W. (1967). *Sociology and modern systems theory.* Englewood Cliffs, Prentice-Hall.

Cervone, D., Artistico, D., & Berry, J. M. (2006). Self-efficacy and adult development. In C. Hoare (Ed.), *Handbook of adult development and learning* (pp. 169-195). New York: Oxford University Press.

Cilliers, P. (Ed.). (1998). *Complexity and postmodernism: Understanding complex systems.* London: Routledge.

Coleman, J. S. (1990). *Foundations of social theory.* Cambridge, MA: The Belknap Press of Harvard University Press.

Davidson, R., Scherer, K. R., & Goldsmith, H. H. (Eds.). (2003). Introduction. In *Handbook of affective sciences* (pp. xiii-xvii). Cary, NC: Oxford University Press.

Davis, G. (2005). Mechanisms and the theory of organizations. *The Journal of Management Inquiry, 15*(2), 114-118.

Dooley, K. J., & Van de Ven, A. H. (1999). Explaining complex organizational dynamics. *Organization Science, 10*(3), 358-372.

Douglas, M. (1981). *How institutions think.* Syracuse, NY: Syracuse University Press.

Douglas, M. (Ed.). (1992). The normative debate and the origins of culture. In *Risk and blame: Essays in cultural theory* (pp. 125-148). London: Routledge.

Eden, C., & Ackermann, F. (1998). *Making strategy: The journey of strategic management.* London: Sage.

Ehrlich, P. R. (2000). *Human natures: Genes, cultures, and the human prospect.* New York: Penguin Books.

Fararo, T. J. (2001). *Social action systems: Foundation and synthesis in sociological theory.* Westport, CT: Praeger.

Giddens, A. (1984). *The constitution of society.* Los Angeles: University of California Press.

Graen, G. B., & Uhl-Bien, M. (1995). Relational-based approach to leadership: Development of the leader-member exchange (LMX) theory of leadership over 25 years. *Leadership Quarterly, 6,* 219-247.

Griffin, D. (2000). *The emergence of leadership.* London: Routledge.

Guastello, S. J. (1998). Self-organization in leadership emergence. *Nonlinear Dynamics, Psychology, and Life Sciences, 2*(4), 303-316.

Habermas, J. (1987). *Lifeworld and system: A critique of functionalist reason* (Vol. 2) (T. McCarthy, Trans.). Boston: Beacon Press.

Hedstrom, P., & Swedberg, R. (1998). *Social mechanisms: An analytical approach to social theory.* New York: Cambridge University Press.

Hellgren, B., & Lowstedt, J. (1998). Agency and organization: A social theory approach to cognition. In C. Eden & J. C. Spender (Eds.), *Managerial and organizational cognition* (pp. 40-57). London: Sage.

Holland, J. H. (1995). *Hidden order: How adaptation builds complexity.* Reading, MA: Helix Books, Addison-Wesley.

Jantsch, E. (1982). *The evolutionary vision.* Boulder, CO: Westview.

Jehn, K. (1997). A qualitative analysis of conflict types and dimensions in organizational groups. *Administrative Science Quarterly, 42,* 530-557.

Johnson, P., Daniels, K., & Asch, R. (1998). Mental models of competition. In C. Eden & J. C. Spender (Eds.), *Managerial and organizational cognition* (pp. 130-146). London: Sage.

Katz, D., & Kahn, R. L. (1978). Organizations and the system concept. In J. M. Shafritz & P. H. Whitbeck (Eds.), *Classics of organization theory* (pp. 161-173). Oak Park, IL: Moore.

Kaufman, H. (1985). *Time, chance, and organizations: Natural selection in a perilous environment.* Chatham, NJ: Chatham House.

Klein, K. J., Tosi, H., & Cannella, A. A. (1999). Multilevel theory building: Benefits, barriers, and new developments. *Academy of Management Review, 24*(2), 243-249.

Kuhn, T. S. (1970). *The structure of scientific revolutions* (2nd ed.). Chicago: University of Chicago Press.

Lawrence, P. R., & Lorsch, J. W. (1978). Organization environment interface. In J. M. Shafritz & P. H. Whitbeck (Eds.), *Classics of organization theory* (pp. 238-242). Oak Park, IL: Moore.

Lewin, A. Y., Long, C. P., & Carroll, T. N. (1999). The coevolution of new organizational forms. *Organizational Science, 10*(5), 535-550.

Luhmann, N. (1995). *Social systems* (J. J. Bednarz & D. Baecker, Trans.). Palo Alto, CA: Standford University Press.

Maguire, S., McKelvey, B., Mirabeau, L., & Oztas, N. (2006). Complexity science and organization studies. In S. R. Clegg, C. Hardy, T. Lawerence & W. Nord

(Eds.), *Sage handbook of organizational studies* (pp. 165-214). Thousand Oaks, CA: Sage.

Mainemelis, C. (2001). When the muse takes it all: A model for timelessness in organizations. *The Academy of Management Review, 26*(4), 548-566.

March, J. G. (1991). Exploration and exploitation in organizational learning. *Organization Science, 2*(1), 71-87.

Marion, R. (1999). *The edge of organization: Chaos and complexity theories of formal social systems.* Thousand Oaks, CA: Sage.

McKelvey, B. (2002). *Managing coevolutionary dynamics.* Paper presented at the 18th EGOS Conference, Barcelona, Spain.

McKelvey, B. (2003). Emergent order in firms: Complexity science vs. the entanglement trap. In E. Mitleton-Kelly (Ed.), *Complex systems and evolutionary perspectives on organisations: The application of complexity theory to organisations* (pp. 99-125). Amsterdam: Elsevier Science.

Milner, B., Squire, L. R., & Kandel, E. R. (1998). Cognitive neuroscience and the study of memory. *Neuron, 20*(3), 445-468.

Mintzberg, H. (1994). *The rise and fall of strategic planning.* New York: The Free Press.

Mischel, W., & Shoda, Y. (1995). A cognitive-affective theory of personality: Reconceptualizing situations, dispositions, dynamics, and invariance in personality structure. *Psychological Review, 102*(2), 246-268.

Morel, B., & Ramanujam, R. (1999). Through the looking glass of complexity: The dynaqmics of organizations as adaptive and evolving systems. *Organization Science, 10*(3), 278-294.

Morgeson, F. P., & Hofmann, D. A. (1999). The structure and function of collective constructs: Implications for multilevel research and theory development. *Academy of Management Review, 24*(2), 249-265.

Parker, J. (2000). *Structuration.* Philadelphia: Open University Press.

Parsons, T., & Shils, E. A. (1952). *Toward a general theory of action.* Cambridge, MA: Harvard University Press.

Pressman, J. L., & Wildavsky, A. (1984). *Implementation* (3rd ed.). Berkeley: University of California Press.

Rocher, G. (1975). *Talcott Parsons and American sociology.* New York: Barnes and Noble.

Schwandt, D. R. (1997). Integrating strategy and organizational learning: A theory of action perspective. In J. P. Walsh & A. S. Huff (Eds.), *Organizational learning and strategic management* (Vol. 14). Greenwich, CT: JAI Press.

Schwandt, D. R., & Marquardt, M. J. (2000). *Organizational learning: From world-class theories to global best practices.* New York: St. Lucie Press.

Smelser, N. J. (1995). *Problematics of sociology: The Georg Simmel lectures.* Berkeley: University of California Press.

Smith, C. (1986). Transformation and regeneration in social systems: A dissipative structure perspective. *Systems Research, 3*(4), 203-213.

Taylor, A., & Greve, H. R. (2006). Superman or the fantastic four? Knowledge combination and experience in innovative teams. *Academy of Management Journal, 49*(4): 723-740.

Taylor, J. R., & Van Every, E. J. (2000). *The emergent organization: Communication as its site and surface*. Mahwah, NJ: Erlbaum.

Thietart, R. A., & Forgues, B. (1995). Chaos theory and organization. *Organization Science, 6*(1), 19-31.

Uhl-Bien, M., Marion, R., & McKelvey, B. (2007). Complexity leadership theory: Shifting leadership from the industrial age to the knowledge age. *The Leadership Quarterly, 18*(4), 298-318.

Van de Ven, A. H., & Poole, M. S. (1995). Explaining development and change in organizations. *Academy of Management Review, 20*(3), 510-540.

Von Krogh, G., & Roos, J. G. (1994). An essay on corporate epistemology. *Strategic Management Journal, 15*, 53-71.

Wallace, A. F. C. (1961). *Culture and personality*. New York: Random House.

Weick, K. (1979). *The social psychology of organizing* (2nd ed.). New York: McGraw-Hill.

Weick, K. E. (1995). *Sensemaking in organizations*. Thousand Oaks, CA: Sage.

Wheatley, M. J. (1992). *Leadership and the new science*. San Francisco: Berrett-Koehler.

Wood, R., & Bandura, A. (1989). Social cognitive theory of organizational management. *Academy of Management Review, 14*(3), 361-384.

CHAPTER 6

DISPELLING THE MYTHS ABOUT LEADERSHIP

From Cybernetics to Emergence

Donde Ashmos Plowman and Dennis Duchon

ABSTRACT

Conventional views of leadership are based on the assumption that the world is knowable and that effective leaders can rely on planning and control mechanisms to bring about desired organizational futures. However, complexity science suggests that the world is not knowable, that systems are not predictable and that living systems cannot be forced to follow a linear path. We argue that conventional views of leadership have a *cybernetics* focus, that is, leaders are the regulators who control organizational behavior in order to achieve intended results. Based on the characteristics of complex adaptive systems we present an *emergent* view of leadership that dispels the following myths: leaders specify desired futures; leaders direct change; leaders eliminate disorder and the gap between intentions and reality; and leaders influence others to enact desired futures. The implications of emergent leadership for how organizational scientists consider the topics of conflict, information, teams, change, language, and relationships are discussed.

Complexity Leadership, Part I: Conceptual Foundations
pp. 129–153

"Doubt is not a pleasant condition, but certainty is absurd."

—Voltaire

Conventional notions of management and leadership are based on an assumption of certainty: the world is knowable, systems are predictable, and effective leaders can rely on formulaic approaches to planning, control, and organizational problems. But over the last decade ideas from complexity science have challenged the certainty approach by arguing that uncertainty is a better starting point. Ideas such as the inherent unpredictability of systems, the self-organizing nature of human systems, the nonlinearity of far-from-equilibrium states, the necessity of chaos for growth—are but a few observed in the physical sciences that Wheatley (1999), Stacey (1992), and other early adopters began to translate for managers and organization theorists. With a special issue of *Organization Science* in 1999, organizational scientists such as McKelvey, Anderson, Lewin, Boisot, Child, and others moved complexity science into traditional organizational literature. Subsequently, authors such as Marion (1999), Lichtenstein (2000), Chiles, Meyer, and Hench (2004), Meyer, Gaba, and Colwell (2005), and Marion and Uhl-Bien (2001) have conceptualized organizations as complex adaptive systems whose fundamental characteristics are in stark contrast to those on which most conventional leadership theories are based.

While the basic principles of complexity theory have not yet reached wide acceptance in organizational sciences, they have begun to appear in the theoretical frameworks of scholars not typically thought of as complexity theorists, such as Weick and Quinn's (1999) discussion of change, Nonaka's (1994) conception of knowledge creation, etc. However, we have yet to see a major reconceptualization of leadership based on the principles of complexity theory, although the need has been expressed by Marion and Uhl-Bien (2001), Wheatley (1999) and others.

A complexity view of organizations raises provocative questions about the conventional view of leadership where one person (leader) deliberately exerts influence over another (follower) in order to achieve an intended outcome (Yukl, 2006). For example, if organizations are inherently unpredictable due to factors beyond the control of the leader, then what do leaders, well-trained in the art of forecasting and strategic planning, do? If self-organization is an inherent characteristic of social systems, what role is there, if any, for formal leaders? If radical organizational change is often emergent rather than intended (Plowman, Baker, et al., 2007), what is the responsibility of leaders to bring about change? If behaviors *emerge*, including the behavior of leadership, then what does it mean to be the leader of an organization? These and other questions cast doubts about the traditional view of leaders as those formally responsible for creating order, for establishing organizational agendas, for influencing followers to achieve established goals and for directing them in how to do it (Marion & Uhl-Bien, 2001; Yukl, 2006).

In this paper we distinguish between traditional views of leadership—which we refer to as *cybernetic leadership*—and a complexity view of leadership—which we call *emergent leadership* and present some of the specific challenges to the study of leadership that a complexity view of organizations implies. We argue that traditional views of leadership focus on leadership as a *role* rather than as a *behavior*, and it is a role occupied by someone assigned to regulate the behaviors of others so that predictable outcomes can be achieved. We present the argument that leadership is a behavior that emerges in the context of ongoing interactions among individuals and groups in organizations. This emergent behavior is not limited to the formal leader but can manifest across different people depending on the nature of interactions. Max De Pree, former chief executive officer of Herman Miller, calls it "roving leadership" (De Pree, 1989), a behavior that results from self-organization and can vary from situation to situation. Leaders emerge, not from self-assertion, but because they make sense, given what a group or set of individuals need at the time in order to survive and grow (Wheatley, 1999). Thus, leadership emerges from self-organization and also encourages self-organization, which can lead to unknown but productive organizational futures. Based on an understanding of complexity theory as well as results from three empirical studies of leadership and change, we offer a view of *emergent leadership*, that dispels some of the myths about leadership and alters the way leaders and organization scientists conceptualize the following variables: conflict, information, teams, change, language and relationships. We begin with an overview of important principles of complexity theory that cast doubts on traditional views of leadership.

THEORETICAL BACKGROUND

Characteristics of Complex Adaptive Systems

Complex adaptive systems are made up of numerous interdependent agents, who, in parallel, purposely pursue individual plans based on local knowledge or rules and adapt to feedback about the behavior of others in the system (Chiles et al., 2004). In organizations, agents are autonomous individuals or groups that act simultaneously without explicit coordination or central communication (Anderson, 1999). A defining feature of a complex adaptive system is its ability to *learn* from the numerous interactions that are occurring and *adapt*. Four distinguishing characteristics of complex adaptive systems are important to consider and provide a conceptual framework for considering leadership in complex organizations: (1) sensitivity to initial conditions; (2) far-from-equilibrium state; (3) non-linear interactions; and (4) emergent self-organization.

Sensitivity to Initial Conditions

Small changes can produce disequilibrium. Lorenz' (1963) famous story of the flap of a butterfly's wings in one part of the world creating a storm somewhere else made popular the notion that small fluctuations in some variables can produce monumental and unpredictable consequences. Complexity scholars in the "hard sciences" remind us that because of the diversity and complexity of the universe it is impossible to predict the outcomes of most actions (Holland, 1995; Kauffman, 1993). Because complex systems are sensitive to initial conditions, a small fluctuation in one part of the system (an initial condition) can bring unexpected and consequential changes to other parts of the system. Because organizations are made up of individuals and groups who are connected to each other, small changes are likely to escalate when systems are under stress and the existing state of equilibrium is disrupted. When disruption occurs in organizations, people talk, controversy or interest mounts as connections among individuals and groups tighten. In the midst of disturbances these tightened connections make it easier for information or gossip or ideas (energy) to amplify and move through the system quickly.

Thus, for organizations uncertainty and unpredictability are not just functions of changing external conditions, but also come from inside organizations because of the ongoing uncontrollable interactions among a network of organizational members that produce unpredictable results. Each person in a network is a "node" and through talk and interaction "connections" among the nodes are formed. The addition of new nodes or changes in the nature of the connections between the nodes can lead to changes that have enormous consequences. Consultants working with Jack Welch describe how he instituted town hall meetings at GE so executives could listen to feedback from employees about the company's bureaucracy. Executives were then held responsible for removing the bureaucratic barriers identified by employees, and the organization increased the number of nodes (added employees) and altered the connections (fresh ideas). The changes that resulted from those town hall meetings redirected the company. (See interview with Richard Pascale in Pascale, Millemann, & Gioja, 2000.)

Far-From-Equilibrium State

Disequilibrium is not necessarily a bad thing. Prigogine and colleagues (Nicolis & Prigogine, 1989; Prigogine & Stengers, 1984) made famous the idea that chemical systems change only when they are pushed to a state far from equilibrium. When adaptive tensions increase and push a system towards disequilibrium, the system is injected with energy and information, and rather than dampening energy, it is dissipated through the system, breaking up existing patterns and creating disturbance. In the midst of this disorder, irregular and unpredictable patterns form, called dissipative structures, as the system shifts from an orderly phase to a disorderly one. When organizations move away from equilibrium toward instability, they display what some refer to as "highly complex behavior." That is, they are both orderly and disorderly at the same time (Kauffman, 1995), and these contradictory forces operate simultaneously, pulling the organization in different directions (Stacey, 1992).

When organizations move away from stability and toward disequilibrium into the "region of complexity" (Maguire & McKelvey, 1999), adaptive tensions enable opportunities for new order as a consequence of emergent self-organization. In fact, most argue that it is only as organizations move into disorderly states that emergent ideas about new adaptations are possible, and so give rise to innovation and creativity (Anderson, 1999; McKelvey, 1999). Innovations, for example, rarely arise from systems in equilibrium; that is, experiencing perfect order and balance. In business, Jack Welch has been described by consultants who work with him (Pascale et al., 2000) as someone who "fosters disequilibrium to evoke fresh ideas and innovative responses" (p. 28). Rather than seek stability he was instead something of an equilibrium buster.

Nonlinear Interactions

Complex systems are characterized as nonlinear because their components are constantly interacting with each other through a web of feedback loops (Stacey, 1995). There is no single pathway that all components share. Small changes to initial conditions create disorder that produces a series of locally coherent interactions. These interactions put new knowledge back into the system, thus creating a feedback loop that is unknown to but nonetheless influences the larger system. Moreover, these learning-adaptive cycles are essentially unpredictable. Thiétart and Forgues (1995, pp. 21-22) describe the nonlinear nature of interactions in organizations: "Multiple organizational actors, with diverse agenda, inside and outside the organization, try to coordinate their actions to exchange information and to interact in other ways and they do all this in a dynamic manner." In applying complexity theory to organizations, organizational scientists describe organizations as systems of nonlinear interactions where small changes can have large effects (Anderson, 1999). Lichtenstein (2000, p. 132), for example, states, "a single idea can provide the seed for self-organization—the beginnings of a new configuration" when a system moves beyond certain limits or certain thresholds of capacity.

As complex adaptive systems, the disequilibrium-learning-feedback cycle in organizations at the local level creates a kind of perpetual novelty. Sensitive to initial conditions, these nonlinear interactions can often occur far from an assumed stable pattern and surprise is likely. People and groups interact, exchange information, and take adaptive actions without the intervention of someone occupying the role of central controller. Each interaction, exchange, and adaptive reaction, changes the organization in unexpected ways, calling into question the purpose of leadership, as it is traditionally viewed.

Emergent Self-Organization

New forms will emerge. Chiles et al. (2004) describe the concept of emergent self-organization as complexity theory's "anchor point phenomenon." The ongoing interactions among entities at a lower level in the system can result in emergent order at a larger system level (Anderson, 1999). This is because systems are nested and in constant interplay (Ashmos & Huber, 1987). Agents at a lower level in the system exchange information, take actions, and continuously adapt to feedback about others' actions. The next larger part in the system reacts and so novel responses can bubble up and provide system level order without the imposition of an overall plan by a central authority (Chiles et al., 2004). *Self-organization* is the tendency of systems, especially in times of uncertainty or stress, to shift to a new state because the agents that make up the system interact, learn new things and modify their interconnections. A new order emerges locally from a previous one without constant direction from a higher level. This new order or condition is an *emergent* state.

Bees, ants, and termites are often cited as examples from nature of complex adaptive systems in which self-organization and emergence are central organizing principles. Each individual termite follows rather simple rules and yet what emerges from the collective efforts is an architecturally complex mound that is home to millions of termites. In business we see examples of companies that rely on self organization such as direct sales organizations like Tupperware, where each dealer is self-employed, and organizes sales parties independently, adapting to local circumstances as necessary to earn desired commissions. The complex networks of sales associates that emerge from each dealer's efforts are coherent and sufficiently adaptive that Tupperware has become the largest plastic supplier in the world.

Traditional Leadership—A Focus on Cybernetics

Organizational scientists have studied leadership for decades, and some have expressed disappointment that the proliferation of theories has occurred without an agreed-upon definition of leadership. However, (Yukl, 2006) points out that although definitions of leadership abound, there is general agreement that leadership involves the intentional influence by one person over others to direct them toward achievement of predetermined organizational goals. A quick review of some of the well-known definitions of leadership used by organizational scholars reveals the consistent emphasis on directing, controlling, and influencing the behavior of others in order to achieve a predetermined goal (see Table 6.1).

A dominant theme in each of the definitions in Table 6.1 is "influencing and controlling" the behavior of lower-level system members in order to move behavior toward system goals established to achieve predictable outcomes. Wheatley (1999) refers to this as the "Newtonion" organization in which reductionism, determinism, and control are central concepts and the leader's role is largely to "make sure that people know exactly what to do and when to do it" (1999, p. 131). There is little room in these conven-

Table 6.1.   Definitions of Leadership

Author	Definition
Hemphill and Coons (1957, p. 7)	The behavior of an individual ... *directing* the activities of a group toward a shared goal.
Katz and Kahn (1978, p. 528)	The *influential* increment over and above mechanical compliance with the routine directives of the organization.
Robbins (1997, p. 138)	The ability to *influence* a group toward the achievement of goals.
Rauch and Behling (1984, p. 46)	The process of *influencing* the activities of an organized group toward goal achievement.
Jacobs and Jaques (1990, p. 281)	The process of giving purpose (meaningful direction) to collective effort, and *causing willing effort to be expended* to achieve purpose.
House et al. (1999, p. 184)	The ability of an individual to *influence*, motivate and enable others to contribute toward the effectiveness and success of the organization.
Yukl (2006, p. 3).	Process whereby *intentional influence* is exerted by one person over other people to guide, structure and facilitate activities and relationships in a group or organization.

Source: Adapted from Yukl (2006, emphasis added).

tional notions of leadership to accommodate the concepts of emergence and self-organization. In fact, emergence and self-organizing behavior would likely be considered deviant and in need of correction. The leader's role would be to make the correction.

Although the open systems view of organizations has dominated the organizational literature for decades, traditional notions of leadership still place a heavy emphasis on regulating and controlling the system's behavior, reminiscent of Level 3 on Boulding's (1956) scale of system complexity—the cybernetic system (see Table 6.2).

Cybernetic systems are those dominated by control systems that contain a fixed point of reference and circular feedback loops. Cybernetic systems require negative feedback that indicates the presence and size of a gap between the system's goals (point of reference or point of equilibrium) and its current state. If a gap is seen to exist the system makes a choice among a limited number of acceptable, predetermined actions in order to bring the system back to the fixed point of equilibrium. Pondy and Mitroff (1979) criticized researchers for failing to consider the complexities of organizations. Complexity theorists mount the same criticism today, nearly 30 years later. The definitions of leadership presented in Table 6.1 reflect a lower order, mostly cybernetic view of leadership, that is, systems are controllable and the goals of the system (the leader's vision) become the reference points toward which leaders direct the behavior of followers.

Table 6.2.   Boulding's Scale of System Complexity

Level	System	Definition
9	Transcendental systems	Complex systems not yet imagined
8	Social organizations	Collections of individuals
7	Symbol processing systems	Systems of individuals acting in concert
6	Differentiated systems	Internal image systems with detailed awareness of the environment
5	Blueprinted growth systems	Systems with a division of labor among cells
4	Open systems	Self-maintaining structures in which life differentiates itself from nonlife
3	Control systems	Cybernetic systems which maintain any given equilibrium within limits
2	Clockworks	Simple dynamic systems with predetermined, necessary motions
1	Frameworks	Static structures

Source: Adapted from Boulding (1956), Pondy and Mitroff (1979), Ashmos and Huber (1987).

An exhaustive review of the leadership literature is beyond the scope of this paper (see Hunt, 1999), however, most management textbooks include a chapter on leadership which focuses around two debates: first, whether leadership is best viewed as traits vs. behaviors and second, what style of leadership is appropriate for particular situations or contingencies. Early studies of leadership focused on the desire to know which special traits were associated with leader effectiveness—such as physical, social and mental abilities (Steers, Porter, & Bigley, 1996). Producing little that could be established across organizations, these studies eventually gave way to studies of leader behaviors, with a focus on whether the leader's orientation toward task or toward people (Fleishman, 1962; Likert, 1961) resulted in better organizational outcomes. Later, contingency theories of leadership (e.g., Fiedler, 1967; Hersey & Blanchard, 1988; House, 1971) suggested that situations determine which combination of leadership traits, behavior, or style is most effective. Recent research on style side steps the "combination" approach and suggests a process approach. For example, the transformational leader process tries to influence followers to achieve goals by inspiring them to transcend their self-interest for the organization's sake (Bass, Aviolio, & Goodheim, 1987). The transactional process has leaders influence employees primarily by providing material rewards in return for their efforts (Bass, 1985).

All of the approaches to leadership briefly described above—the trait, behavioral, situational, contingency, and style models of leadership—derive from models that are deterministic, top-down and assume an equilibrium end state without the possibility for emergent self-organization. Each is based on the idea that effective leaders are largely in control of what happens in organizations and can direct people's behaviors towards some outcomes and away from others. Each of these models is based on assumptions that are incomplete for complex adaptive systems and altogether provide a set of nostrums we refer to as *myths of leadership*. We review each of these leadership myths below.

Myth 1: Leaders Specify Desired Futures

Conventional views of leadership are grounded in the notion that leaders are the visionaries in organizations; they alone are responsible for seeing the future of the organization and are responsible for charting the destination and guiding others towards that future. Kotter (1996), for example, claims that most change efforts fail due to leadership's failure to develop a vision, and he defines vision as "a picture of the future" (Kotter, 1996, p. 68), "an activity or organization as it will be in the future, often the distant future" (p. 71). Similarly, Nanus (1992), argues that leaders must develop a vision, and a vision is composed of "one part foresight, one part insight, plenty of imagination and judgment, and often, a healthy dose of chutzpah" (Nanus, 1992, p. 34). These quotes capture the prescriptions offered again and again for how to lead organizations: use personal insight and judgment to determine the organization's desired future, design actions needed to achieve that future, and remove any obstacles to claiming that future. Much of the emphasis in conventional views of leadership is on what the *individual* in the role of leader knows and thinks and does. From this perspective, the leader seems to have a view from outside the system and makes choices for it, planning actions for the organization according to predicted outcomes. It is as if the leader as an outsider *forms* the organization, directing and controlling the necessary actions required for achieving the organization's knowable future, but is not, in turn, *formed* by it (Stacey, 1992). In developing the organization's vision, leaders are advised to thoroughly scan the environment and anticipate changes, as if external factors are the primary source of unpredictability.

In contrast, complexity theory suggests that a major source of organizational unpredictability comes from inside the organization—from the ongoing interaction of individuals and groups within the organization whose actions, exchanges, interactions, and adaptations to each others' actions are not controlled (or even known) by organizational leaders. In complex adaptive systems, ideas that redirect the organization are likely to bubble up from below, without oversight by a central controller (Chiles et al., 2004). Leaders are not the sole "influencers" of organizations. Griffin (2002) and others, for example, argue that while an individual leader is autonomous, s/he is also an agent of the system who can be both outside and inside the system at the same time, attempting to form the system, yet at the same time being formed by it. Thus, organizations are capable of achieving productive futures because of ideas that grow out of the ongoing interactions of system members rather than from the vision of the leader at the top of the organization. Regine and Lewin (2000) capture this idea by describing leadership as "more like an improvisational dance with the system rather than a mechanistic imperative of doing things to the system, as if it were an object that could be fixed" (p. 17).

Marion and Uhl-Bien (2001) argue that "complex leaders" focus less on controlling futures and more on *enabling* productive futures. From interviews with executives of companies that follow complexity theory principles, Regine and Lewin (2000) report stories of leaders whose "power rested not so much in control but in their capacity to allow" (p. 19). Our own research provides preliminary empirical support of an alternative to leading by defining desired futures. Plowman, Baker, et al. (2007) observed the emergence of a radical new identity and transformation of an organization that resulted from the interactions of individuals low in the system, none of whom were formal leaders. An idea generated over dinner one evening among low level members in the organization—largely out of boredom—caught on and ultimately transformed an organization that had been dying. A careful analysis of the role of the formal leaders in the ultimate radical change revealed that while the leaders had been unsuccessful in the conventional approaches to change (i.e., create a sense of urgency, develop a vision, plan for its implementation, etc.), they had simultaneously spent much time fostering interactions and relationships among organizational members. Unintentionally, these rich connections among organizational members were a way of "fostering emergent, distributive intelligence" (Marion & Uhl-Bien, 2001, p. 391), and so a small idea grew, amplified, and ultimately transformed the organization. Thus, based on the principles of complexity theory and our own empirical findings we suggest replacing Myth # 1 with the following new reality:

New Reality #1: Leaders provide linkages to emergent structures by enhancing connections among organizational members.

Myth 2: Leaders Direct Change

Conventional views of leadership place a strong emphasis on the leader's role in directing and bringing about change. As Yukl (2006) points out, for many theorists leading change "is the essence of leadership and everything else is secondary" (p. 284). Almost immediately after Kotter published his article in *Harvard Business Review* (1995) titled "Leading Change: Why Transformation Efforts Fail," it became the top seller of reprints for the journal. Kotter speculated on the article's popularity a year later, and said "First managers read the list of mistakes organizations often make when trying to effect real change and said *Yes!* This is why we have achieved less than we had hoped" (Kotter, 1996, p. ix). We agree that managers are frustrated with efforts to lead change, but the "mistakes" may have something to do with the fact that in complex adaptive systems, managers falsely think they are in control and they alone can direct successful change. Thus, it is disappointing when the changes leaders want don't happen. But because of the inherent unpredictability of systems, neither better forecasting techniques nor improved lists of cybernetic-based "how to's" will improve leaders' ability to direct top-down change in organizations.

Studies of transformational leadership reflect the assumption that successful transformations occur when leaders clearly specify the future and the needed change. For example, typical items used by organizational scholars to measure transformational leadership (Podsakoff, Mackenzie, & Bommer, 1996; Podsakoff, MacKenzie, Moorman, & Fetter, 1990; Rubin, Munz, & Bommer, 2005) include the following: paints an interesting picture of the future for our group, has a clear understanding of where we are going, inspires other with his/her plans for the future, is able to get others committed to his/her dream of the future. The expectation of the leader is to know what the future should be, and what changes will take the organization to that desired place.

Complex adaptive systems are sensitive to small changes in initial conditions, meaning that because of the networked nature of the universe (and organizations) in which we live (Kauffman, 1995), a small change in one part of a system can have a rippling effect and lead to large unexpected outcomes for the system as a whole. In organizations, where individuals and groups are tightly connected, the experience of some stress or disorder produces small changes that can easily cascade and unleash an avalanche of change—none of which may be consistent with the change the leader wanted to direct. Kauffman (1995) offers the image of a sand pile on top of a table onto which sand is poured at a continuous slow rate as a way of conceptualizing small changes in initial conditions. Eventually the sand piles up and cascades begin, but it is impossible to know which cascade will lead to an eventual landslide. Poised between order and chaos, organizations and their leaders "cannot foretell the unfolding consequences of their actions" (Kauffman, 1995, p. 29).

In a study of leadership in emergent self-organization Plowman, Solansky, and colleagues (2007) examined what it is that leaders actually do in the midst of emergent change. In a case study of an organization that underwent unintended radical change they observed that rather than rely on vision statements and prescriptions for change, leaders successfully detected and labeled patterns in the small changes that emerged. For example, the organization studied was a church that accidentally happened on to what became the regenerating solution to its organizational decline. A handful of young people started a breakfast for homeless people on Sunday mornings. The Sunday morning breakfast quickly morphed into a full-scale ministry to the homeless with not only breakfasts, but medical clinics and a full range of social services. The Sunday morning program ultimately transformed the church into a thriving urban church with what the pastors started calling "ministry with the marginalized" and illuminating peoples' commonalities rather than differences. Their use of the label "marginalized" and development of a logo "Justice in Action" came from seeing a pattern in the changes and broadened the focus of the organization's efforts from homeless (narrow niche) to marginalized (includes anyone who has ever felt marginalized). The label gave meaning to the changes and helped capture people's attention, ultimately transforming the church's identity. Much as Weick and Quinn (1999) suggested, the leaders in Plowman, Solansky, et al.'s (2007b) study acted as sense-makers, using language and symbols to encourage coherence around and meaning to the emerging changes. This reinforces Pascale et al.'s (2000) notion that people find it easier to act their way into a new way of thinking than to think their way into a new way of acting. Much like the example Weick (1987) offers of the lost Hungarian soldiers finding their way out of the Alps with a map of the Pyrenees, the leaders in the Plowman et al. (2007b) study found their way out of decline by acting on an idea—feeding breakfast to the homeless—which then along with other ideas—providing medical care, providing weekday shelter—led to a new way of thinking about the organization's identity. Thus, based on complexity principles as well as some preliminary empirical evidence we suggest replacing Myth #2 with the following new reality:

New Reality #2: Leaders try to make sense of patterns in small changes.

Myth 3: Leaders Eliminate Disorder and the Gap Between Intentions and Reality

Traditional views of leadership focus on the leader's role in influencing others to accomplish tasks necessary for achieving goals. If the goal is to implement a major change, leaders are expected to recognize the forces for change, unfreeze the status quo, implement the change, and refreeze the new change so as to make it permanent (Lewin, 1952). And the expectation is that this will all be done in an orderly fashion—implementing "controlled change" (Mintzberg, 1973, p. 78). Effective leaders are often judged on the degree to which they are able to minimize conflict, and maintain order, or at least manage the impression that there is no conflict. Mintzberg's (1973) seminal work, *The Nature of Managerial Work*, still serves as a benchmark for describing what it is that managers actually do. In their role as "disturbance handlers" he (1973, p. 82) writes: "A disturbance occurs, a correction is necessary." Presiding over equilibrium, removing barriers of resistance to change, establishing order, and minimizing conflict are often seen as the hallmarks of effective leadership. Waldman, Ramirez, House, and Puranam (2001), for example, argue that leaders who "take action to correct mistakes and deviations from expectations should help to foster better organizational performance" (p. 135). All of these efforts rely on the application of negative feedback—feedback that reveals the gap between intentions and reality, and helps dampen deviations and move the system back to its starting point, away from disorder.

The emphasis on minimizing conflict appears in academic studies of leadership as well as in prescriptions to future leaders. For example, the leader-member-exchange (LMX) theory (Graen & Uhl-Bien, 1995) posits that high quality LMX relationships (relationships between leaders and followers) are characterized by mutual trust, respect, and obligation.

When these high quality relationships exist and exemplar performance contributions occur, not only is there no conflict, but followers receive special privileges. According to this theory high quality LMX, which gives importance to harmonious relationships, is the desirable state for leaders and followers to achieve.

Harmony and stability characterize equilibrium and in traditional models of organizations have been the desired state for any organization. Complexity theory argues that most organizations actually exist somewhere between instability and stability, and the dogged pursuit of stability, rather than being beneficial, is the sure way to organizational demise. When destabilizing forces move an organization toward greater instability (Prigogine & Stengers, 1984; Stacey, 1995) that organization enters the "region of complexity (Maguire & McKelvey, 1999) where new, emergent ideas about the system are created. Thus, leaders need not eliminate disorder and might even provide benefits by becoming a source of disorder. Stacey (1992) describes this area as bounded instability. It is an area that is not in equilibrium, but, driven by both negative and positive feedback, is both stable and unstable.

In Plowman, Solansky, et al.'s (2007) study of leadership in emergent self-organization they observed that leaders play a role in destabilizing a system by disrupting existing processes or patterns of behavior and pushing the system towards chaos (Regine & Lewin, 2000). From the moment the pastors were appointed to the dying church they began illuminating the church's dying status, forcing conversations about it, and the need for members to make changes. The pastors forced some changes, such as "we will welcome homosexuals to our church" and they longed for other changes that would start the turnaround. Rather than seize upon the solution for revitalization much of these early activities and conversations led to more conflict, as people who didn't want change left the church. The ultimate solution came not from the pastors but from an emergent idea from people (who might have been considered at the fringes of the organization because some were actual church members and others were nonmembers). In the study the formal leaders created and highlighted conflict, and openly embraced uncertainty. They functioned as "equilibrium busters" (Wheatley, 1999, p. 108) and grand disturbers of the system, which then made it easier for emergent ideas from the fringes of the organization to bubble forth and attract attention. Thus, based on complexity principles and our own empirical findings we suggest that Myth #3 be replaced with the following new reality:

New Reality #3: Leaders are destabilizers who encourage disequilibrium and disrupt existing patterns of behavior.

Myth 4: Leaders Influence Others to Enact Desired Futures

"Influence is the essence of leadership" writes Yukl (2006, p. 145) and he suggests that the way to evaluate an influence attempt is observe whether or not the immediate outcome is what the leader intended. A rather simple idea underlies this notion—leaders know what needs to be done (i.e., what action will bring about what outcome) and they use their power, personality, knowledge, authority, whatever they can call on, to influence others to bring about the desired future state. In conventional views of leadership leaders are expected to provide answers, to know cause-effect relationships, and to direct or "influence" others' behaviors based on such knowledge. Sage planning, detailed strategic plans, flawless execution of plans are the hallmarks of strategic leadership from a traditional perspective (Brown & Eisenhardt, 1998). All of these notions are steeped in the assumption of linearity: affecting or altering one variable will lead to anticipated changes in another variable. For example, studies such as Agle, Nagarajan, Sonnenfeld, and Srinivasan (2006) argue that under certain conditions the right amount of charismatic leadership produces positive firm performance.

Complexity science, on the other hand recognizes the ability of systems, nonlinear in nature, to learn. This means that people and groups in organizations are capable of learning from their experiences and from their interactions. As any classroom teacher knows learning often does not come from being told something by the teacher. Rather it comes from a combination of activities and experiences in which the learner is also shaping the experience. Similarly, in organizations leaders and others learn together. Most organizations are too complex and exist in too much uncertainty for the people at the top to know and prescribe to others what to do. Rather in complex adaptive systems, members help leaders find the way forward out of confusion and uncertainty. In a study of 32 organizations, (Solansky, Martinez, Duchon, & Plowman, 2006) observed that firm performance was better when leaders and members shared the same task mental model than when they did not. Specifically they observed that organizations in which members and leaders shared the same understanding of how decisions are made and how organizational processes unfold, performed better than organizations where leaders and followers were in less agreement about how things were done. This suggests that when leaders focus on clarifying processes rather than clarifying outcomes, organizations function better. Based on complexity principles and on our own empirical observations we suggest that Myth #4 be replaced with the following new reality:

New Reality #4: Leaders encourage processes that enable emergent order.

BEYOND THE MYTHS

In this chapter we have argued that conventional theories of leadership are based in control-oriented, cybernetic ideas that are inconsistent with the characteristics of living systems as described by complexity science. The myths of leadership presented here need to give way to new realities or frames of understanding based on the characteristics of living systems (see Table 6.3). The cybernetic model of leadership ignores the unpredictable nature of human beings who are not easily forced into machine-like functioning. In spite of cybernetic-based efforts and organizational policies, people do not stay in their functional silos or stick to their scripted job descriptions. They talk to each other, they develop relationships, they make observations and share information because social systems follow the principles of complex systems. They will self-organize;

Table 6.3.   Summary of Complexity Principles and Implications for Leadership

Complexity Theory Principal	Cybernetic Leadership— Role Functions (Myths)	Emergent Leadership— Enabling Behaviors (New Reality)
Emergent self-organization— system level order emerges as independent agents act, exchange information, and continuously adapt to feedback about others' actions.	Leaders specify desired futures.	Leaders provide linkages to emergent structures; enhance connections among organizational members (Plowman, Solansky, et al., 2007).
Sensitivity to initial conditions—Small fluctuations can have huge, unpredictable consequences.	Leaders direct change.	Leaders make sense of patterns in small changes (Plowman, Baker, et al., 2007).
Far-from-equilibrium is where change can occur; system imports energy and information which is dissipated through the system, creating disorder and ultimately leads to some new unpredictable order	Leaders eliminate disorder and gap between intentions and reality.	Leaders encourage disequilibrium; disrupt existing patterns of behavior (Plowman, Solansky, et al., 2006).
Nonlinear interactions in dynamic systems occur because multiple players with diverse agenda are interconnected and affect each others actions.	Leaders influence others to enact desired futures.	Leaders encourage processes that enable emergent order (Solansky et al., 2006).

Table 6.4. Reconceptualization of Organizational Variables

Organizational Variables	Cybernetics View	Emergent View
Conflict	Disruption is the result of flawed management or leadership mistakes.	Disruption is the result of self-organizing and can be the source of new order.
Information	Syntactic information, in which information is measured in bits, treated as a commodity.	Semantic information, in which emphasis is on what things mean.
Teams	Small task groups made up members with a shared purpose and interdependent roles.	Ensembles that often form independently due to interactions among autonomous agents in the system.
Change	Change occurs in distinct episodes as "planned replacements" intended to fix a problem, or achieve a goal.	Change occurs continuously, as minor adaptations, which can accumulate, amplify and become radical.
Language	Means of directing follower behavior.	Mechanism for giving meaning to emergent changes.
Relationships	Sources of power that leader can use to "get things done."	Key to mental models and team cognition that enables undirected actions by others.

small changes may cascade—sometimes to the benefit and sometimes to the harm of organizations. Rather than prescribe one more list of "how-to's" on leadership, it is time to reconceptualize it entirely. Complexity science offers important implications for leadership—we call it *emergent leadership*—and these implications alter how both leaders and leadership scholars alike consider other organizational variables. Table 6.4 summarizes how using an "emergence" frame changes our view of what leaders are and what they do.

First, complexity science challenges us to rethink the nature of *conflict*. The conventional cybernetics view of leadership suggests that conflict, that is disorder and disruptions, are the result of flawed leadership. Leaders are expected to eliminate or minimize disturbances and correct deviant behavior, bringing the system back in line with the established needs and goals. Emergent leadership, on the other hand, recognizes conflict and divergence as the first steps in a change process, and as the natural partner to self-organizing, can illuminate new order and revitalizing ideas. That is, the emergent leader needs to be alert not just to the source of the conflict, but also to the patterns it disrupts, and the new patterns that might be emerging. Emergent leadership might even create a disruption as a way of destabilizing the system and encouraging self-organization. A cybernetic leader would never purposely "cause problems."

The conventional (cybernetics) view of conflict, however, contains a built-in contradiction. While change can be welcomed as both healthy and necessary, conflict is not. Yet, conflict and change are the two sides of the same coin. A "change" is about disrupting a well-known pattern and replacing it with a different one. Change, by definition, requires conflict. Thus, conflict is not in itself a bad thing for the system. But both "big" clashes and "small" disruptions are "conflicts," and so a difference in scale needs to be noted. Cybernetic leaders are on the lookout for "big clashes" because in the cybernetic, linear view, big clashes cause big disruptions. In contrast, the emergent view understands that small disruptions can produce big changes, so the emergent leader is constantly monitoring the status of small disruptions. This does not mean that an emergent leader will ignore large events, but it does mean that a cybernetic leader pays less attention to small events. In the emergent view small events can matter. Of course, not all small disturbances will effect large changes: most will likely be absorbed by the system without much notice. But the important point is that the emergent leader will not only understand conflict differently from the conventional leader, but also will be alert to small scale patterns that might generate large changes.

Second, traditional views of organizations and their leaders treat *information* largely as "syntactic," in which information is measured in bits without regard to its meaning (Nonaka, 1994). Information theorists such as Shannon and Weaver (1949) focused on the form rather than the meaning of information and treated information as a "quantity, bits and bytes to be counted, transmitted, received and stored" (Wheatley, 1999, p. 94). Information is thus a commodity and the cybernetic leader determines the optimal placement and distribution of such information in the organization.

An emergent view of leadership changes the way we consider information and places higher value on the meaning of information. The "semantic" perspective of information (Nonaka, 1994) is critical for understanding knowledge creation and self-organization because it focuses not on what Wheatley (1999) refers to as the "thingness" of information but more on the character, content, and meaning of information. This is important because living networks pass on only information it determines is meaningful. Thus emergent leadership is about making sense of information and helping shape the meaning of unfolding events. Moreover, the emergent leader does not try to "control" information in the conventional sense. Rather, the emergent leader seeks to set free information to flow through the system. Self-organizing and emergence produce the most effective adaptations in information rich environments.

The leader cannot play the role of editor because if s/he does so the power of emergence is dampened.

Third, complexity science informs the way we consider *teams* in organizations. Teams are often defined as small task groups made up of members with a shared purpose and interdependent roles and who hold each other mutually accountable. From a cybernetics leadership perspective the expectation is that leaders determine team purposes and select members to the team who can best achieve the team's predetermined goals. See Katzenbach and Smith (1993) on how to build team performance. The first task for team leaders usually involves: "establish urgency, demanding performance standards and direction" (Katzenbach & Smith, 1993, p. 4). Additionally, managers are urged to create teams by carefully controlling membership, selecting those with the skills needed to complete team tasks, as envisioned by the manager. High performing teams have a clear goal, are task driven yet collaborative, have high standards of excellence, receive external support and have strong and principled leadership (Katzenbach & Smith, 1993). From a cybernetics perspective, there is a formula for effective teams and a major component of the formula is leadership that selects membership, establishes goals, and keeps team members on task.

In contrast a complexity perspective recognizes the fluidity of teams. In addition to the classical team that is formed and selected by the leader, the more important teams may be those "ensembles" (Marion & Uhl-Bien, 2001) that form independently due to interactions among autonomous agents in the system. Emergent leaders encourage *unplanned* interactions that can speed up the emergence of distributed intelligence throughout the organization. With the distribution of intelligence, through planned as well as unplanned interactions, through formal teams as well as ensembles, more novelty and innovation is possible. When information spreads throughout the organization and brings people together, novel ideas can bubble up from below in unexpected ways and help move the organization to a productive future. Teams are important, but their form and their makeup are often far beyond the control of the formal organizational leaders.

Fourth, complexity science dramatically alters the way we conceptualize *change*. From a traditional view of organizations transformational change occurs in distinct episodes where the leadership identifies a "planned replacement" (Weick & Quinn, 1999) that is, a new strategy, program, or structure intended to fix a problem or achieve a goal. The cybernetic leader's role is to determine the necessary replacements and monitor progress toward successful replacements. In this way, cybernetic leaders direct change. Complexity science, on the other hand, illuminates the continuous nature of change and because of sensitivity to initial conditions and amplifiers in the organization, small continuous changes can escalate and become radical over time. Plowman, Baker, et al. (2007) provide evidence of emergent, radical change that is continuous because of the ongoing interactions of contextual conditions and amplifying actions. What emergent leaders recognize is the importance of looking for patterns in small adaptations, labeling it and giving it meaning for others in the organization. They also encourage emergent change because it is often the source of innovation and organizational vitality.

Fifth, the way we consider *language* differs when we think of cybernetics versus emergent leadership. From a cybernetics leadership perspective language is a mechanism for control: alerting followers to responsibilities and directing their behavior. Cybernetic leaders use language to "tell and sell" their visions, which essentially means they are crafting language that will clearly communicate what they want and at the same time be motivating enough (or inoffensive enough) to achieve buy-in. The leader's assumption is: if I can be clear enough about what I want, and persuasive enough, people will do it. Thus, the leader focuses on clarity of message content (e.g., "I want you to do the following ..."). A leader's effectiveness as a communicator is measured by the extent to which people do what they are told. While such an approach may be "successful" in the short run, in that it ensures the control of the leader, it also ensures that the kind of creative and experimental ideas that characterize an emergent system will not be voiced.

In contrast, an emergent leader uses language not as a means of achieving control, but rather as a means for making sense, a means for discovering the emergent order. Clarity is important, but it is not the clarity of content that is important. Rather the emergent leader is trying to achieve clarity of meaning: what do our actions mean. Language is used not for compliance, but rather for understanding. Understanding is better achieved when many voices are heard, not just the voice of the leader, because many voices create a larger (more complex) conversation where different frames, different points of view can be considered. This does not suggest that all voices present useful ideas, but in the tradition of natural selection, the consideration of many different voices (frames) gives the system the best chance to identify a direction (an emergent order) that will be successfully adaptive. Thus, the emergent leader needs to be the enabler of many conversations because a broader and clearer understanding of "what we are" and "what we do" has a better chance of succeeding.

The emergent leader's success as a communicator will be measured not by compliance, but rather in the richness of the conversations, and success at "making meaning." Thus the leader does not have to control language or conversation. Instead, the leader should set free the conversation: make all information available, widely share interpretations of that information, and not be threatened or unnerved if things seem to become unruly. The desired result is making sense of the patterns of events and behaviors that might best achieve emergence to a new, more effective adaptation. The emergent leader does not control language or control people in the traditional sense. The emergent leader sets language free.

Finally, the way *relationships* are viewed differ sharply between the cybernetics and emergent views of leadership. From a cybernetics view, relationships are viewed as sources of power that the leader can use to get things done. From this perspective leaders rely on the power inherent in formal roles described by the hierarchy. But effective leaders go beyond the legitimate relationships described by the hierarchy and foster relationships in order to build power bases that will ensure domination. The leader's vision must be fulfilled, and s/he will try to use or manipulate relationships to achieve that end. Thus, the leader will rely on friendships, favors, or even calculated manipulation to achieve desired ends. While such a use of relationships is not necessarily counterproductive or unethical, it is limited because it is aimed at achieving the leader's singular view of what is desirable. Relationships are used to narrow the conversation, and, not coincidentally, maintain the status and power of the leader.

In contrast, an emergent leader uses relationships to expand the power of the entire system. Power in this sense is the power of capability, not the power of domination. Greater capability increases the chances for effective adaptation. Capability has the best opportunity to occur when information flows freely through the system while the system tries to make sense of it. This flow requires reliance on many processing nodes, each of which has its own interpretive capacity, its own inventive capacity, and its own knowledge base, and such a networked system is a contrast to the unitary leader-centered node found in cybernetic systems. Thus, the emergent leader fosters relationships not only to build more nodes, but also to help connect the nodes to each other. The system then has a richer, denser set of relationships, an expanded network of capability which is not leader-dependent.

CONCLUSION

Uncertainty, or doubt as Voltaire called it, may not be pleasant, but it is a better starting point for leaders than Certainty. Much of what the world expects successful leaders to do is grounded in assumptions of certainty, what we have termed a cybernetics view of leadership in which leaders are system regulators, determining the system's destination and then regulating behaviors that appear to take the system off-task. In his book, "Why Leaders Can't Lead," Bennis (1989, p. xii) argues that "within any organization, an entrenched bureaucracy with a commitment to the status quo undermines the unwary leader." We agree, but also suggest that leaders undermine themselves with a view of leadership, largely cybernetic, that is unrealistic. Leaders can't predict the future and take followers towards that future because the future is unpredictable. Leaders can't direct all the change, because they alone don't know what change is necessary. If leaders eliminate what surfaces as "conflict" or "disorder," they may eliminate the seed of an idea that can lead to a more productive future for the organization.

Cybernetic leadership is ultimately unfulfilling because it is not based on life-giving properties. Organizations are not that different from individuals, who when numb, do not experience pain (disorder or conflict) but they also do not experience pleasure (collective exhilaration from an idea that bubbled up). The continuous emphasis on control and regulation, on predictability and balance, drains energy from leaders and followers. Emergent leadership is energy—producing on the other hand, because it encourages the free flow of information and recognizes that organizational adversity cannot be avoided. Organizations will face challenges beyond the limits of what a handful of people at the top can understand. Organizations will experience the messiness of conflict, discomfort, and missteps. Emergent leadership recognizes that those can be opportunities for growth, for creativity and new ideas that can enable positive and exciting organizational futures. We couldn't agree more with Pascale et al. (2000, p. 286) who say "Keeping the life in a living system may be hard work, but it is exhilarating, rewarding, and *crucial*."

REFERENCES

Agle, B. R., Nagarajan, N. J., Sonnenfeld, J. A., & Srinivasan, D. (2006). Does CEO charisma matter? An empirical analysis of the relationships among organizational performance, environmental uncertainty, and top management team perceptions of CEO charisma. *Academy of Management Journal, 49*(1), 161-174.

Anderson, R. (1999). Complexity theory and organization science. *Organization Science, 10*, 216-232.

Ashmos, D. P., & Huber, G. (1987). The systems paradigm in organizational theory: Correcting the record and suggesting the future. *Academy of Management Review, 12*(4), 607-621.

Bass, B. M. (1985). *Leadership and performance beyond expectations*. New York: Free Press.

Bass, B. M., Aviolio, B. J., & Goodheim, L. (1987). Biology and the assessment of transformational leadership at the world-class level. *Journal of Management, 13*(1), 7-19.

Bennis, W. (1989). *Why leaders can't lead*. San Francisco: Jossey-Bass.

Boulding, K. E. (1956). General systems theory: The skeleton of a science. *Management Science, 2*, 197-207.

Brown, S. L., & Eisenhardt, K. M. (1998). *Competing on the edge*. Boston: Harvard Business School Press.

Chiles, T., Meyer, A., & Hench, T. (2004). Organizational emergence: The origin and transformation of Branson, Missouri's musical theaters. *Organization Science, 15*(5), 499-519.

De Pree, M. (1989). *Leadership is an art*. New York: Doubleday.

Fiedler, F. E. (1967). *A theory of effective leadership effectiveness*. New York: McGraw-Hill.

Fleishman, E. H. (1962). Patterns of leadership behavior related to employee grivances and turnover. *Personnel Psychology, 15*, 43-56.

Graen, G. B., & Uhl-Bien, M. (1995). Development of leader-member exchange (LMX) theory of leadership over 25 years: Applying a multi-domain perspective. *The Leadership Quarterly, 6*, 219-247.

Griffin, D. (2002). *The emergence of leadership*. London: Routledge.

Hemphill, J. K., & Coons, A. E. (1957). Development of the leader behavior description questionnaire. In R. M. Stogdill & A. E. Coons (Eds.), *Leader behavior: Its description and measurement* (pp. 6-38). Columbus: Bureau of Business Research, Ohio State University.

Hersey, P., & Blanchard, K. H. (1988). *Management and organizational behavior*. Englewood Cliffs, NJ: Prentice-Hall.

Holland, J. H. (1995). *Hidden order*. Reading, MA: Addison-Wesley.

House, R. J. (1971). A path goal theory of leader effectiveness. *Administrative Science Quarterly, 16*(3), 321-339.

House, R., Hanges, P. J., Ruiz-Quintanilla, S. A., Dorfman, P. W., Dickson, M. W., Jvidan, M., et al. (1999). Cultural influences on leadership and organizations: Project GLOBE. In W. H. Mobley, M. J. Gessner, & V. Arnold (Eds.), *Advances in global leadership* (pp. 171-233). Stamford, CT: JAI Press.

Hunt, J. G. (1999). Transformational/charismatic leadership's transformation of the field: An historical essay. *The Leadership Quarterly, 11*(4), 435-458.

Jacobs, T. O., & Jaques, E. (1990). Military executive leadership. In K. E. Clark & M. B. Clark (Eds.), *Measures of leadership* (pp. 281-295). West Orange, NJ: Leadership Library of America.

Katz, D., & Kahn, R. L. (1978). *The social psychology of organizations*. New York: John Wiley.

Katzenbach, J. R., & Smith, D. K. (1993). The discipline of teams. *Harvard Business Review, 83*(7/8), 1-9.

Kauffman, S. A. (1993). *The origins of order*. New York: Oxford University Press.

Kauffman, S. A. (1995). *At home in the universe: The search for the laws of self-organization and complexity*. New York: Oxford University Press.

Kotter, J. P. (1995). Leading change: Why transformation efforts fail. *Harvard Business Review*, 59-67.

Kotter, J. P. (1996). *Leading change*. Boston: Harvard Business School Press.

Lewin, K. (Ed.). (1952). *Group decision and social change*. New York: Holt, Rinehart.

Lichtenstein, B. B. (2000). Self-organized transitions: A pattern amid the chaos of transformative change. *Academy of Management Executive, 14*, 128-141.

Likert, R. (1961). *New patterns of management*. New York: McGraw-Hill.

Lorenz, E. N. (1963). The mechanics of vacillation. *Journal of the Atmospheric Sciences, 20*, 448-464.

Maguire, S., & McKelvey, B. (1999). Complexity and management: Moving from fad to firm foundations. *EMERGENCE, 1*(2), 19-61.

Marion, R. (1999). *The edge of organization*. Thousand Oaks, CA: SAGE.

Marion, R., & Uhl-Bien, M. (2001). Leadership in complex organizations. *The Leadership Quarterly, 12*, 389-418.

McKelvey, B. (1999). Avoiding complexity catastrophe in coevolutionary pockets: Strategies for rugged landscapes. *Organization Science, 10*, 294-324.

Meyer, A. B., Gaba, V., & Colwell, K. A. (2005). Organizing far from equilibrium: Nonlinear change in organizational fields. *Organization Science, 16*, 456-473.

Mintzberg, H. (1973). *The nature of managerial work*. New York: Harper & Row.

Nanus, B. (1992). *Visionary leadership*. San Francisco: Jossey Bass.

Nicolis, G., & Prigogine, I. (1989). *Exploring complexity: An introduction*. New York: W.H. Freeman.

Nonaka, I. (1994). A dynamic theory of organizational knowledge creation. *Organization Science, 5*, 14-37.

Pascale, R. T., Millemann, M., & Gioja, L. (2000). *Surfing the edge of chaos*. New York: New Rivers Press.

Plowman, D. A., Baker, L. T., Beck, T. E., Kulkarni, M., Solansky, S. T., & Travis, D. V. (2007). Radical change accidentally: The emergence and amplification of small change. *Academy of Management Journal, 50*(3), 515-543.

Plowman, D. A., Solansky, S., Beck, T., Baker, L., Kulkarni, M., & Travis, D. (2007). The role of leadership in emergent, self-organization. *The Leadership Quarterly, 18*(4), 341-356.

Podsakoff, P. M., Mackenzie, S. B., & Bommer, W. H. (1996). Transformational leader behaviors and substitutes for leadership as determinants of employee satisfaction, commitment, trust, and organizational citizenship behaviors. *Journal of Management, 22*, 259-298.

Podsakoff, P. M., MacKenzie, S. B., Moorman, R. H., & Fetter, R. (1990). Transformational leader behaviors and their effects on followers' trust in leader, satisfaction, and organizational citizenship behaviors. *Leadership Quarterly, 1*, 107-142.

Pondy, L. R., & Mitroff, I. I. (1979). Beyond open system models of organization. In B. M. Staw (Ed.), *Research in organizational behavior* (Vol. 1, pp. 3-39). Greenwich, CT: JAI Press.

Prigogine, I., & Stengers, I. (1984). *Order out of chaos: Man's new dialogue with nature*. Boulder, CO: New Science Library.

Rauch, C. F., & Behling, O. (1984). Functionalism: Basis for an alternative approach to the study of leadership. In J. G. Hunt, D. M. Hosking, C. A. Schriesheim, & R. Stewart (Eds.), *Leaders and managers: International perspec-*

tives on managerial behavior and leadership (pp. 45-62). Elmsford, NY: Pergamon Press.

Regine, B., & Lewin, R. (2000). Leading at the edge: How leaders influence complex systems. *EMERGENCE, 2*(2), 5-23.

Robbins, S. P. (1997). *Essentials of organizational behavior.* Upper Saddle River, NJ: Prentice Hall.

Rubin, R. S., Munz, D. C., & Bommer, W. H. (2005). Leading from within: The effects of emotion recognition and personality on transformational leadership behavior. *Academy of Management Journal, 48*(5), 845-858.

Solansky, S., Martinez, P., Duchon, D., & Plowman, D. A. (2006). *Team mental models across multiple levels of leadership: An empirical look at the impact on organizational performance.* Unpublished manuscript.

Shannon, C. E., & Weaver, W. (1949). *The mathematical theory of communication.* Urbana: University of Illinois Press.

Stacey, R. (1992). *Managing the unknowable.* San Francisco: Jossey-Bass.

Stacey, R. (1995). The science of complexity: An alternative perspective for strategic change processes. *Strategic Management Journal, 16*, 477-495.

Steers, R. M., Porter, L. W., & Bigley, G. A. (1996). *Motivation and leadership at work.* New York: McGraw-Hill.

Thietart, R. A., & Forgues, B. (1995). Chaos theory and organizations. *Organization Science, 6*, 19-31.

Waldman, D., Ramirez, G., House, R., & Puraham, P. (2001). Does leadership matter? CEO leadership attributes and poritability under conditions of perceived enviornmental uncertainty. *Academy of Management Journal, 44*(1), 134-143.

Weick, K., & Quinn, R. (1999). Organizational change and development. *American Review of Psychology, 50*, 361-386.

Weick, K. Q. R. (Ed.). (1987). *Substitutes for strategy.* Cambridge, MA: Ballinger.

Wheatley, M. (1999). *Leadership and the new science.* San Francisco: Berrett-Koehler.

Yukl, G. (2006). *Leadership in organizations.* Upper Saddle River, NJ: Pearson Prentice Hall.

CHAPTER 7

BEYOND TRANSACTIONAL AND TRANSFORMATIONAL LEADERSHIP

Can Leaders Still Lead When They Don't Know What to Do?

Robert G. Lord

ABSTRACT

This chapter develops a theory of leader influence on emergent structures in organizations. It proposes that structure emerges spontaneously from the interactions of units, and that this structure can be influenced by changes in thresholds or biases that make some patterns more likely to emerge than others. Leaders are conceptualized as influencing the structure emergence process through their effects on three types of biases, those associated with affect, goal orientations, and identities. The theory that is developed is applied on both an intra- and an interpersonal level to explain the emergence of structure. Consistent with an important aspect of complexity theory, effective leaders are seen as influencing the process by which structure

Complexity Leadership, Part I: Conceptual Foundations
pp. 155–184

emerges, but not necessarily directly controlling the specific outcome of the structure emergence process.

Leadership theory often contrasts two very different types of leadership. One approach to leadership emphasizes rule following, extrinsic incentives, close monitoring of outcomes, and rewarding subordinates for outcomes that are valued by the organization. On the opposite end of a continuum, visionary leaders can inspire followers so that they willingly contribute to an organization's goals and may even come to include their organizational identity as a central part of their self-concept. Tyler and Blader (2005) label these two contrasting approaches "command and control" versus the "self-regulatory" approach to leadership. An analogous distinction can be made between transactional and transformational leadership. Transactional leadership is oriented toward satisfying subordinate's self-interest through appropriate transactions with the work environment, and transformational leadership is grounded in higher moral values and ethics which can transform both organizations (Yukl, 2002) and the identities of followers (Lord, Brown, & Freiberg, 1999; Shamir, House & Arthur, 1993).

This chapter addresses a third, more general, aspect of leadership that is equally important. It may complement transformational and transactional leadership, amplifying their effects, or it may be effective in circumstances when neither transformational nor transactional leadership would work well. Specifically, in this chapter I propose that an important aspect of leadership that has not yet been systematically discussed in the leadership literature pertains to how leadership activities can shape the emergence of individual and interpersonal structures in organizations. It is argued that this form of leadership may be especially important in complex systems in which many structures and processes emerge spontaneously from the local interaction of individuals (or units).

LEADERSHIP AND EMERGENCE

Although transactional and transformational leadership differ in many fundamental ways, they are similar in that they both focus on the leader as initiating different forms of social organization, and they also emphasize the leader's vision or value system. Leaders are viewed as having a right to influence followers (Tyler, 1997; Tyler & Blader, 2005) and, even when followers are self-directed, they may identify with the leader's vision and values or with the organization symbolized by a leader. In other words, though very different, both transformational and transactional leadership still fit with top-down hierarchical structures in terms of how internal exchanges with employees are structured and in terms of how organizations achieve and maintain alignment with their external environment.

Complexity theory, however, suggests that many aspects of structure have an emergent, bottom-up quality (Holland, 1995; Marion, 1999; Marion & Uhl-Bien, 2001) and that no one fully understands or is able to fully predict the outcome of a specific action (Cilliers, 2001). Patterns emerge within individuals as they make sense of dynamic environments, and these internal patterns guide social interactions leading to the emergence of interpersonal structures that then foster the emergence of meta-structures and so on, until organizations, and even their environments, are fundamentally transformed (Cilliers, 1998; Hogue & Lord, 2007; Marion, 1999; Marion & Uhl-Bien, 2001). Such bottom-up processes may still exist within the top-down constraints coming from higher levels in organizations, yet complexity theory represents the role of leaders as being much more limited than is suggested by more traditional leadership theories: Leaders do not control emergent processes, although they may manage them to a certain extent (Marion & Uhl-Bien, 2001).

Viewing leaders as managers of complex processes may be appropriate in some situations, but in others it may imply too much knowledge and control from top-levels of organizations. Indeed, in many dynamic situations, top-level leaders are too isolated from critical environments (e.g., emerging markets, developing technologies, new knowledge, dynamic political processes, changing religious values, etc.) to be able to construct appropriate visions. As a consequence, the value of transformational leadership is limited. Similarly, in many situations leaders may not have the ability to monitor subordinates, or they may lack control over important rewards. These constraints may limit the appropriateness of transactional leadership. Other forms of leadership based on legitimate authority and the respect for rules and traditions that characterize bureaucratic organizations may also be inappropriate in complex and dynamic environments.

How can leaders be effective in such dynamic situations in terms of motivating and facilitating individual actions or in terms of encouraging effective organizational structures to emerge? The purpose of this chapter is to articulate ways that leaders can effectively influence emerging structures both within and among followers. These processes are especially important when leaders are themselves isolated from critical information on changing environments or when they lack the critical knowledge base that would allow them to appropriately interpret new information. The processes discussed are also important in other leadership situation where they can complement (or work against) more traditional, leader-focused activities.

Leadership, and its relation to emerging structures, is inherently a multilevel phenomenon (Kozlowski & Klein, 2001; Hogue & Lord, 2007). Leaders may influence emergent, individual-level cognitive, emotional, and motivation processes as well as the interpersonal structures that develop from individual level processes. I propose that it may be essential for leaders to *indirectly* facilitate and modulate the nature of these emergent processes. Further, I will suggest that leaders can be guided in doing this by an understanding of how complex systems operate and how complex systems can be influenced by leaders. The objective of this paper, then, is not to articulate an additional pattern of leadership behaviors, but rather to offer a more general perspective on leadership that can complement more traditional leader-focused approaches to managing organizations and also is appropriate when such leader-focused approaches would not work well. The concern is with how leaders can create a culture for understanding and adapting to complexity, or in other words, how they can help to develop organizations that can thrive in complex environments.

To address these issues, I first describe some of the properties of complex systems and explain why traditional transactional and transformational leadership behaviors may not be sufficient for leading complex organizations. Second, I identify the construct of emergent structures as a key point of leverage for leadership in complex systems, noting that structures can emerge both within an individual (e.g., goals are formed) and between individuals (e.g. communications networks develop). I also suggest in this section that emergence can be influenced by biasing factors. Third, I describe several types of "biasing factors" that can influence the way structures develop, and I suggest that influencing these biasing factors is a critical aspect of effective leadership in complex systems. Finally, I discuss the implications of this perspective for the traditional view that leadership roles should emphasize the knowledge, qualities, and values of specific leaders and contrast this view with a perspective that leadership itself can be an emergent, jointly constructed process.

LEADERSHIP THAT FACILITATES THE EMERGENCE OF ADAPTIVE STRUCTURES

Complex Systems and Challenges for Leadership

Marion and Uhl-Bien (2001) provide an excellent introduction to understanding leadership in complex systems. They stress that a critical feature of complex systems is that they are characterized by dynamic, nonlinear interactions among their constituent parts. This property has two important implications: causality is often uncertain and it is inappropriate to study the isolated parts of these holistic systems. These implications can be illustrated by recognizing that structures often develop spontaneously in complex systems through a cascading, bottom-up process in which the interactions of units (often called agents) creates emergent structures or aggregates, and these aggregates in turn create higher level meta-aggregates, which create still more aggregated meta-meta-aggregates. Further, at each new level, structures may be fundamentally transformed to reflect different qualities and processes than those which characterize their constituent parts. For example, affective and communication processes may create linkages among specific individuals, but over time such linkages spontaneously develop into networks involving many individuals, and those networks may then evolve to identify factions, groups, or collectives that interact on a still higher level. Thus, as Kozlowski and Klein (2001) stress, aggregation processes do not simply sum lower level processes, rather they often create a qualitatively different entity as aggregation occurs.

Because of the nonlinear, dynamic, and emergent quality of such systems, it is difficult to know in advance how they will develop or what types of structures should be encouraged by leaders (Marion, 1999). Further, because structures may emerge in a bottom-up manner, developing initially at lower levels in organizational hierarchies, top-level leaders may not have a sufficiently clear vision to transform the nature of organizational processes. Vision may also lag rather than lead organizational developments, and an outdated vision imposed from the top may prevent the emergence of more effective ways to adapt to environments. For example, the vision that automobiles should be powered by internal combustion engines rather than electric motors, which is shared by many influential government and industrial leaders, may hinder the emergence of more effective ways to reduce CO_2 emissions. Thus, while leaders can still ensure that some aspects of exchanges with organizations are perceived as being just, they may not be able to define, monitor, or reward effective behavior. Nor can they really create visions and goals that lead to effective outcomes. In other words, in some circumstances both transformational and transactional leadership activities may be ineffective and may not even be accepted by followers. Indeed, in some complex situations, the leader-follower role may even be reversed, with top-level leaders maintaining their power only by getting on board (albeit with reluctance and tardiness) the bandwagon that is created and propelled by follower knowledge, vision, or values.

Are such situations beyond effective leadership? Thinking from a complexity theory perspective helps us sort out the limits for leadership in evolving situations and what might be effective strategies for leaders to adopt. As Marion and Uhl-Bien (2001) stress, leaders cannot control the products of such emergent structures which often cannot be anticipated, but they can manage the process by which products emerge, enabling some types of outcomes and forestalling others. I propose that effective leaders should not attempt to micro-manage these processes, but instead may be more effective if they focus on what I call biasing factors, which constrain the manner in which emergence occurs. Others (Plowman, Solansky, Beck, Baker, Kulkarni, & Travis, 2007) make a similar point, proposing that leaders are more effective when they enable rather than attempt to control radical, emergent change. However, they still take a leader-centered approach that emphasizes the symbolic role of leaders as sensemakers and catalysts for change.

Biasing Factors and Emergence in Complex Systems

In this section I first explain what is meant by the emergence of structure, using goal emergence as an illustrative phenomenon. The relation of bias to structure emergence is then illustrated and bias is defined more formally. Following this, biases related to affect, goals, and self-identity are discussed, and research related to the mechanisms by which these processes can affect the emergence of structure is reviewed. Finally, the combined effects of these three types of biases are discussed.

Dynamics and the Emergence of Tractors

Structure emerges dynamically in complex systems through the cumulative effects of spontaneous, nonrandom interactions among constituent elements. As units interact over time, some linkages are strengthened and others are weakened, and through the local interaction of these units, more aggregate level structures can be created. These dynamic processes are often compared to movement about a phase space which tracks the output of a system over time. A *phase space* is a multidimensional surface that helps us visualize a system's behavioral trajectory over time. Trajectories on this surface often converge in areas called attractors, which are points of stability toward which related behaviors are drawn. Attractors also have basins, or regions of attraction. When a trajectory enters a basin it moves towards the attractor. Attractors often represent important mechanisms underlying the dynamics of a system, such as a particular state of organization among the local units that produce the more aggregate behavioral pattern.

An alternative, visual representation of attractors is shown in Figure 7.1. Here attractor basins are shown as wells or valleys in a surface, and regions of instability are shown as hills. In this representation, the behavior of the system at a particular moment is represented as a ball on the surface. As the ball rolls toward an attractor in a particular basin, it also moves toward a region of lower energy, and it takes additional energy to move the ball out of a basin in which it has become lodged. However, although such a landscape creates a useful analogy in terms of valleys being energy minima, it implies a degree of stability that is not characteristic of emergent dynamic systems. Because structure is created dynamically, it might be more appropriate to think of the emergence of structure as actually carving out the valleys as patterns of interaction are solidified (Eiser, 1994). However, it should also be recognized that emergent systems are continuously evolving, and past attractors could conceivably become new repellors (or vice versa) as the system evolves. For example, in the social dynamics of teenage dating, a girl's former boyfriend, who once functioned as an attractor for social behavior, may become a repellor after a breakup as social interactions with the former beau are avoided.

Goals spontaneously emerge through the interaction of individuals and environments (Carver & Scheier, 2002), and they can become points of stability that structure further interactions among individuals or guide the internal thought processes of an individual. Carver and Scheier explain that the notion of goals fits well with dynamic systems and phase spaces if goals are conceptualized as attractors. They note that people spend much time trying to keep behavior in accord with goals, just as dynamic systems spend much of their time near attractors. Consequently, Figure 7.1 portrays one's current goal as a global minimum, with a broad and deep basin. Because goals are systems that are continually emerging in a coherent manner, the representation shown in the top left portion of Figure 7.1 also shows a potential future goal as being a local minimum. For example, if one is about to go shopping, the future goal of driving to the store may have less capacity to guide one's attention and behavior at a particular moment than the current goal of finding one's car keys. When a goal such as finding one's keys is actively pursued, the pattern constituting the goal is actively maintained in working memory and goal-relevant information automatically becomes more accessible than it was before the goal was formulated. Consequently, this goal allows the production of relevant thoughts and search behaviors with minimal effort, which is consistent with the notion of valleys being an energy minima as well as being attractors. Yet, when completed, goals are actively suppressed as a means of clearing working memory and protecting it from interference, and the accessibility of the completed goal and related information drops below its baseline level (Johnson, Chang, & Lord, 2006). For example, after one's keys are found, alternative locations for keys are no longer easily accessible to conscious attention, and in fact, these alternative locations

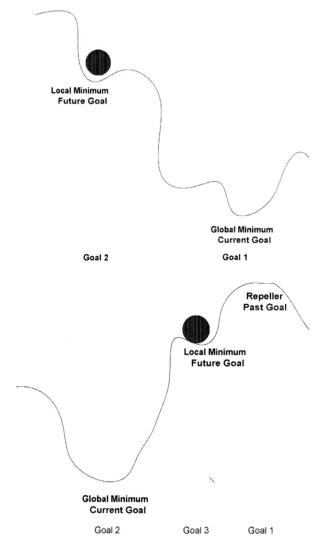

Local Minimum
Future Goal

Global Minimum
Current Goal

Goal 2   **Goal 1**

Repeller
Past Goal

Local Minimum
Future Goal

Global Minimum
Current Goal

Goal 2   Goal 3   Goal 1

Figure 7.1.   Changing structure of dynamic system as
goals emerge and are completed.

are even less accessible than they were before the goal of finding one's
keys was formulated. In short, as goals emerge, direct behavior, and are
attained, phase spaces are dynamically transformed.

The top and bottom panels of Figure 7.1 illustrate the dynamic
changes which occur as goals are formulated and accomplished over time.
The top portion of this figure depicts current goals (Goal 1) as a global

minimum or a strong attractor, whereas a related future goal (Goal 2) may only capture thought processes momentarily. However, when a goal is achieved (e.g., the keys are found), the stability accompanying a previously activated goal structure dissipates. In other words, the prior valley associated with a just completed goal (Goal 1), now becomes a hill or a point of instability as new thought patterns emerge and a new basis for social interaction takes hold. A person's thoughts or social processes may momentarily revisit a just-completed goal, but they are likely to quickly shift to more pressing current concerns. Such a change in structure is shown in the bottom panel of Figure 7.1. As a whole, these two panels represent the changes in the ability of goals to capture thoughts and direct actions, as one dynamically moves from pursuing one goal to completing it and developing a successive goal. In this example, mental effort associated with accessing goal-related information is analogous to the energy represented by the height of the behavioral surface.

To see how these same dynamics can be applied to a social as well as an individual cognitive process, consider the situation of a typical board meeting. As shown on the top of Figure 7.1, social interactions and individual thought processes tend to be focused on current agenda items (Goal 1), although thoughts and discussions may wander temporarily to future agenda issues (Goal 2). However, as shown in the bottom panel of Figure 7.1, once an agenda item is discussed and voted on, it becomes a past goal which no longer has the same capacity to focus individual thoughts or social processes. Instead, a new agenda item becomes an attractor that captures thoughts and social processes (Goal 2). Dynamically, goal completion can be thought of as a dramatic change in the phase space which simultaneously transforms a goal-related valley into a hill, and carves out another deep valley as new goals emerge and are directly pursued. As already noted, such changes can be seen by comparing the top and bottom panels in Figure 7.1. It is important to note that this change is different than a phase transition or a phase shift in which behavior shifts from one attractor basin to another, because when goals are completed they no longer serve as attractors.

Biasing factors are general properties of the context which influence the nature of the structures that emerge from the interaction of units. This idea is borrowed from the literature on neural networks (Churchland & Sejnowski, 1992; Hopfield, 1982). Biasing factors do not directly change outputs of systems, rather they change the functioning of the entire system by adding or subtracting a little to many interactions, and in the process biasing factors transform the higher level system that emerges. *Biases* can be thought of as changes in the thresholds for activating specific types of neurons when we are focusing on individual level cognitive processes (Churchland & Sejnowski, 1992), or they can be thought of as changes in

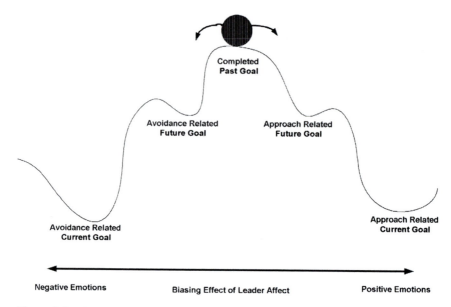

Figure 7.2.   Representation of two alternative affective biases of leaders and their potential effects on goal emergence.

the threshold for social behaviors when our concern is with the interaction of people. For example, when a new goal is emerging, positive affect can operate as a biasing factor which supports the emergence of an approach goal; whereas, negative affect may encourage the development of avoidance goals (Gray, 2001). In this way, affect can transform the nature of the developing phase space that describes the path of a dynamic system.

Figure 7.2 directly incorporates the effects of a leader's influence on biases. To return to our board meeting example, imagine that we are at a school board meeting and a chairperson turns the focus from the past goal of approving minutes of the prior meeting to the future goal of an upcoming school levy. If the leader expresses positive emotions and optimism, approach related goals pertaining to how to ensure passage of the levy are likely to spontaneously emerge. On the other hand, if the leader expresses negative emotions and pessimism, then a qualitatively different type of goal, one oriented towards figuring out how to cope with a future failure of the levy, is more likely to emerge. Thus, when the board members are at a point of instability associated with just completing a goal, biasing factors associated with a leader's expressed emotions can cause very different goal structures to emerge, which in graphic form is equivalent to the ball in Figure 7.2 rolling to the left or right. It is also important to recognize that the timing of emotional expression may be critical. Once the ball has moved in one direction or another and an approach or avoidance goal has emerged, it would be much more difficult to move social processes or individual cognition to the opposite goal type. It should be noted that Figure 7.2 is a bit misleading in that it shows both approach and avoidance goals as existing simultaneously, when in reality one or the other would be created by emergent processes.

There are two additional points related to this example which are worth emphasizing. One is that our board chairperson may not have the knowledge needed to directly formulate a vision regarding how the board should proceed. That information may exist at other levels of the organization—specific schools, individuals attuned to neighborhood opinions, etc. Consequently, attempting to directly control the strategy that emerges may not be very feasible. However, it may still be possible to guide the emergent processes in terms of approach or avoidance orientations. Second, I suggested that timing may be a critical issue in that biasing factors may have the greatest effect when systems are momentarily at points of instability. This would seem to imply that leaders need to be present at such points to exert their influence. Yet Dragoni's (2005) work suggests that this may not be the case. Specifically, she maintains that through repeated activities, leaders can create enduring goal orientations in followers, which may then operate as biasing factors in the leader's absence. In other words, through repeated interactions our school board chairperson might create and approach or avoidance climate, which would serve to influence the emergence of specific goal structures even when the leader was not physically present.

In the following section, I suggest that there are several types of biasing factors that can be influenced by leaders to guide the nature of emergent structures that spontaneously develop. Specifically, emotions, goal orientations, and identity levels are three important constructs that can be influence by leaders and which serve as biasing factors that can steer emergent structures in one direction or another. Further, I propose that these factors can operate both within an individual to create cognitive and emotional structures, and between individuals to create interpersonal structures. Each of these three types of biasing factors is discussed in turn. Finally, although these processes can be applied to a specific situation and may reflect the direct influence of a leader, I suggest that it is also common for leaders to have an indirect effect on biasing factors that is mediated by the enduring climates or individual level meta-structures they help create.

Three Types of Biasing Factors—
Emotions, Goal Orientations, and Identities

Emotions as a Biasing Factor

To more fully see how emotions can function as a biasing factor, it is useful to consider in more detail how scientists represent bias in emergent structures. Hopfield (1982), using an analogy to the physics of spin glass, showed how more aggregate structures can emerge through the local interaction of units. In essence, in spin glass the dynamic interaction among spinning molecules causes successive reorientation of specific molecules en route to creating an aggregate structure. Specifically, each spinning molecule flips in a physical sense so that there is aggregate consistency in whether the positively or negatively charged pole is up, creating an aggregate structure that is analogous to an external magnetic field. However, the orientation of molecules is dynamically created through local interactions rather than being externally directed. What essentially happens is that as molecules flip sequentially to a common orientation, the threshold of energy needed to cause each successive molecule to flip decreases, and the size of this decrease defines the *biasing function*.

Research shows that emotions can create similar biases that affect the way that networks of neurons function within an individual in constructing a more aggregate construct (e.g., an idea or a goal). To illustrate how this emotion-based biasing process works, consider the effects of dopamine, a neurotransmittor associated with positive affect. Dopamine has been shown to alter the activation function for sets of neurons, or in other words, its operates as a bias in Hopfield's (1982) terms. That is, as dopamine is released, some types of neurons can fire more easily, while other types of neurons are inhibited. This change associated with bias can also be thought of as a change in the threshold required for neurons to fire (Churchland & Sejnowski, 1992). Consequently, changes in dopamine levels can influence the emergence and maintenance of more aggregate neuronal structures (Ashby, Isen, & Turken, 1999), because patterns associated with facilitated neurons are more likely to occur, whereas those patterns created by the inhibited neurons are less likely to occur.

Dopaminergic pathways from midbrain structures associated with emotions branch out to many areas of the brain including the prefrontal cortex, allowing them to create diffuse but powerful organizing functions on many types of cognitions. Dopamanergic pathways have a critical role in modulating the emergence and maintenance of approach goals in the left prefrontal cortex (Rougier, Noelle, Braver, Cohen, & O'Reillly, 2005), and active goals in the prefrontal cortex, in turn, bias the access of consciousness to long-term memory structures (Johnson, Chang, et al., 2006;

O'Reilly, Braver, & Cohen, 1999). Thus, dopamine allows one to structure cognitions and actions in a purposeful manner. Dopamine also has more subtle effects, influencing creativity for example (Ashby et al., 1999). It is also important to recognize that these dynamic processes reflect a cascading emergence of structure from a dopaminergic system, to the prefrontal cortex (goal) system, to a memory system, and such multi-level structures are characteristic of complex systems.

Much of the research on affect and bias focuses on the prefrontal cortex because, as Arnsten and Robbins (2002) note, the prefrontal cortex (PFC), which is of critical importance for understanding learning or the regulation of behavior, is affected by a variety of neurotransmittors that are associated with emotions. The PFC functions include working memory, attentional focus, and planning for actions, functions which Arnsten and Robbins note are "the most fragile in our behavior repertoire" (p. 51) because they can be disrupted by neurochemical changes associated with fatigue, stress, or advancing age. This, of course, also means that the PFC is a highly dynamic system.

It also seems likely that the emotions communicated by leaders can affect PFC functioning, and thereby influence many cognitive and self-regulatory functions. Dragoni (2005) provides a thorough discussion of how leaders can influence the nature of goal emergence in followers, and De Shon and Gillespie (2005) develop an extensive theory of goal orientations as emergent structures. The critical point, though, is that positive emotion created by leaders can be a diffuse and often unrecognized factor that can facilitate the emergence of learning orientations and achievement goals. In other words, positive emotion operates as a biasing factor that affects intraindividual processes. Leaders can have such effects because emotions are themselves contagious, and positive affect expressed by leaders can "infect" followers with similar affect (Cherulnik, Donley, Wiewel, & Miller, 2001). Emotional contagion occurs through a two part process in which the facial expressions (e.g., smile) or body postures of leaders are automatically mimicked by followers, then these physical structures in followers feed back to affect followers' own emotions. Leaders can also affect the emotions of followers by using language that is high in concrete imagery rather than being highly abstract (Naidoo & Lord, in press).

There are also neurotransmittors such as serotonin and noradrenaline that trigger fear responses, and there are analogous pathways from the midbrain to the right prefrontal cortex for these neurotransmittors. Operating through these brain structures, expectations for negative outcomes can also structure cognitions, prompting immediate action and increased vigilance, while reducing flexibility and creativity (Bless, 2001). Leaders creating negative affect or the expectations for negative outcomes can trigger such avoidance processes, promoting the development of avoidance goals (Dragoni, 2005) and more careful processing of information. Because the left and right prefrontal cortex have mutual inhibitory connections (Tomarken & Keener, 1998), these biases toward the positive and negative emotions associated with rewards and punishments generally are not simultaneously active. Consequently, in most situations one type of emotion and associated motivation will predominate.

This reasoning implies that leaders may be most effective in specific contexts when they emphasize one orientation or the other rather than mixing positive and negative affect. That emotion, however, should be matched to the task at hand (Newcombe & Ashkanasy, 2002). For example, in managing learning, positive emotions may facilitate initial learning, whereas negative emotions may facilitate the vigilant application of prior knowledge. In short, by conveying or arousing appropriate affect, I propose that leaders can indirectly change how information is processed, the nature of goals that emerge, and the access of followers to information in their long-term memories. That is, leaders can bias the operation of many emergent cognitive processes, rather than directly trying to produce a specific type of output.

It should also be recognized that emotions can be used in conjunction with a leader's vision. Indeed, charismatic leaders may be particularly effective at using positive emotions to attract followers to their vision (Bono & Ilies, 2006; Naidoo & Lord, in press) or at using negative emotions to enhance vigilance in avoiding certain outcomes. For example, the Bush administration frequently uses the emotions associated with the threat of another terrorist attack as a means to promote the vigilant application of internal security measures, although President Bush also has changed his rhetoric in ways that emphasize optimism, collective orientations, and aggression (Bligh, Kohles, & Meindl, 2004). The coupling of vision with emotions may lead to particularly powerful charismatic leadership (Awamleh & Gardner, 1999), but the current concern is with the less focused, emergent effects of emotions. Such emergent processes are illustrated by the fact that the rhetoric used by the print media covering President Bush changed from pre to post 9/11 in ways that mimicked the president's own change, using more optimism, collectives, and aggressive language (Bligh et al., 2004).

It is important to recognize that aggregate affective structures also emerge among individuals who interact. George (2002) for example discusses affective regulation in groups and teams, noting that positive or negative climates develop in such units. Those climates, in turn, have effects on the nature of spontaneous behaviors that emerge, such that negative affect can inhibit prosocial behavior and positive affect can reduce absenteeism (George, 1990). In discussing the emergence of goal orientation, Dragoni (2005) also emphasizes that in addition to direct effects, leaders can have indirect effects that operate through the emergence of a common work group climate. Thus, a leader's affective orientation and expressed affect can influence the nature of emerging social structures as well as shape individual cognition and motivation. Through such biasing effects, leaders can have profound effects on followers even though they do not directly control particular outcomes. Leaders may benefit immensely from skill in understanding and using emotions, as research is beginning to show (Bono & Ilies, 2006; Kellett, Humphrey, & Sleeth, 2002; Pescosolido, 2002), and perceptions of leadership are intimately associated with the affect that perceivers experience (Brown & Keeping, 2005; Hall & Lord, 1995; Naidoo & Lord, in press). Part of the knowledge needed by leaders may pertain to how affect influences emergent structures.

By now the reader should recognize that I am describing a very different type of influence processes than the heroic, dramatic action often associated with leadership. Discussing the issue of whether this is a good or bad model for a leader to follow will be postponed until implications are addressed. The point that should be emphasized at this juncture is simply that leadership, which has a very small effect on the operation of many agents or units, may still have a very important net consequence in emerging systems, even though it is very difficult to directly associate these consequences with the leader.

Goals as Biasing Factors

Although we often view goals as being set by explicit, rational processes, recent research (Carver & Scheier, 2002; Chartrand & Bargh, 1996; Diefendorff & Lord, in press) indicates that goals often emerge spontaneously. Rather than being a random process, goals emerge in a manner that satisfies a number of active constraints from internal (emotions, values, personality) and external (tasks, social processes) sources (Thagard & Nerb, 2002). Biasing factors associated with leadership can be an important source of activation for many of these constraints, and thereby affect the goals that spontaneously emerge. Such leadership processes should not be confused with popular management by objectives techniques or with path goal theory (House & Mitchell, 1974), which attempt to directly influence the goals that are set rather than influencing the processes by which goals emerge.

The influence of constraints on goal emergent processes can most clearly be seen by considering two distinctions that underlie the nature of goals: promotion (approach) versus prevention (avoidance) regulatory focus (Higgins, 1997) and learning versus performance goal orientation (Dweck, 1986). Considering regulatory focus, it is important to note that the same goal content and performance level can be framed as either a promotion (try to attain a certain level of performance) or prevention (try not to fall below a certain level of performance) goal. I suggest that the spontaneous development of this regulatory framework reflects the combination of several components such as currently active emotions, social influence, and chronic individual differences. All of these factors can be influenced by leaders. Leaders can influence regulatory focus through framing situations in opportunity versus threat terms. Such framing effects have been discussed in the management literature (Dutton & Jackson, 1987). Leaders can also encourage a promotion focus through nurturing activities and a prevention focus through emphasizing security and avoiding loss.

Finally, just as there are chronic differences among individuals in the tendency to experience positive versus negative emotions, there are chronic regulatory focus differences among individuals. Individuals with a promotion focus seek to minimize differences between their ideal and actual selves, whereas individuals with a prevention focus seek to minimize differences between ought and actual selves. However, leaders can affect these enduring individual orientations through their cumulated effect on follower learning. For example, Ritter (2004) found that the chronic regulatory focus of leaders can affect followers through what has been labeled a transference processes, and Shah (2003a) has shown that representations of significant others can automatically affect the pursuit of ideal versus ought goals. Moreover, in an extensive series of five studies, Shah (2003b) showed that the effects of subliminally primed individuals extend to the activation and performance of a number of goals with which they were associated. He further identified goal accessibility as the mediating factor in these priming effects. Thus, one important enduring consequence of leadership may be on how a leader's subordinates represent task goals.

Turning to the dimension of goal orientation, Dweck (1986) proposed that individuals with a learning goal orientation seek to develop their knowledge, skills, and competencies through task achievements, and they believe that these qualities can be changed with practice. In contrast, individuals with a performance goal orientation seek to demonstrate competence in comparison to others, and that demonstration is particularly important because they believe that ability is fixed. De Shon and Gillespie (2005) developed a theoretical model for conceptualizing goal orientation as being an emergent quality derived from spreading activation among an individual's "massively interconnected" goal structures. Both momentary and chronic differences in goal orientation can reflect this emergent process. The important point for understanding leadership is that leaders can affect an individual's goal structures in a number of ways which operate directly on specific individuals or indirectly through team or work group climate (Dragoni, 2005). Thus, without directly controlling the products of goal setting processes, leaders can have profound and enduring effects on motivation by biasing the processes that affect goal emergence in terms of learning versus performance goal orientations.

In short, the underlying dimensions of goal orientation and regulatory focus can exert powerful constraints on the nature of emerging goals. I propose that leaders can influence self-regulatory processes by influencing these dimensions. Because goals focus attention and influence the information that can be easily accessed from long-term memory (Johnson, Chang, et al., 2006) or maintained in working memory (O'Reilly et al., 1999), leaders can profoundly affect cognitive as well as motivational processes through activities that bias the emergence of one form of goal versus another.

I have focused extensively on internal, cognitive processes, but complexity theory maintains that emerging internal processes can, over time, affect the nature of the interpersonal social structures that develop. Although it is easy to imagine how goals can emerge through internal processes, it is less obvious how they can operate through social interactions. In discussing emotions, I referred to an emotional contagion process through which one person infects others with their emotions. Do goals have a similar capacity to infect observers? Recent neurological research suggests that they might because humans (and primates) have specific neural structures that mirror the goal structures of others. Rizzolatti, Fogassi and Gellese (2006) describe the operation of mirror neurons, which seem to fulfill this role.

Mirror neurons fire when someone performs a simple goal-directed action, helping an individual to understand the meaning of his or her action. Surprisingly, neurological evidence indicates that these neurons also fire when we observe others performing goal-directed actions. Thus, comprehension of the other person's actions occurs in part by activating the same meaning system used in understanding our own actions These sets of neurons are also sensitive to the intent and outcomes of actions, as well as specific contexts. Rizzolatti et al. (2006) note that different sets of neurons fire when actions imply different intentions and when contexts differ. Further, knowledge of outcomes feeds back to activate the actions that are likely to produce these outcomes.[1]

The critical aspects of mirror neurons for understanding goal contagion is that they provide a mechanism by which one person can develop a sophisticated understanding of other peoples' actions by tapping into the same mechanisms by which one's own actions are understood. In this manner, individuals who interact frequently may develop a common structure for generating and understanding action, and this understanding may then serve as a basis for developing more elaborate interpersonal structures. In other words, internal motivational structures can become the sources of interpersonal motivational structures. Shah (2003a) provides evidence supporting this logic by showing that priming a significant other (one's father), affects the extent to which one's own regulatory focus matches that of one's father. Following Dragoni (2005), I suggest that leaders can play a key role in this process, in that subordinates are likely to mirror the regulatory focus that is frequently exhibited by their leaders. Aggregation processes may then build on such dyadic processes to create similar group or organizational level structures. Although one needs to be cautious in suggesting that aggregation preserves qualities such as regulatory focus or goal orientation (Kozlowski & Klein, 2001), the fact that mirror neurons operate in nonhuman species (e.g., macaque monkeys) in a manner quite similar to humans, suggests that they may create powerful and general organizing structures.

Identity as a Biasing Factor

An individual's self-identity is a rich collection of more specific cognitive schema, which can help to guide both intra- and interindividual processes (Markus & Wurf, 1987). Importantly, different self-identities can be active at different times depending on context, and Markus and Wurf have labeled the currently active identity the *working self-concept*. The working self-concept, in turn, can be a powerful constraint on cognitions, emotions, behavior, and goal structures. Thus, it can influence the emergence of cognitive and motivational structures through multiple routes. Leaders, particularly transformational leaders, are theorized to affect subordinate behavior in part through the activation of different working self-concepts (Lord & Brown, 2004; Lord et al., 1999; Shamir et al, 1993). One's working self-concept, in turn, then constrains the nature of goals that emerge.

It is helpful to distinguish among three different levels of identity to understand how this process works. When *individual level identities* are active, self views emphasize attributes that are personally important and which differentiate the self from others. Further, a sense of self-worth stems from favorable comparisons with others (Brewer & Gardner, 1996). When *relational level identities* are active, self views often reflect feedback from significant others and significant others are often included in one's self view (Aron & McGlaughlin-Volpe, 2001). A sense of self-worth depends on fulfilling the role relationships with one's dyadic partner and creating favorable outcomes for them. Self-worth also depends on reflected appraisals communicated by significant others. When *collective level identities* are active, self-views are defined in terms of group or collective prototypes, and a sense of worth depends on matching behavior and characteristics to this prototype as well as on creating favorable group outcomes.

Importantly, these different identity levels tend to foster different goals and motivations. For example, De Cremer (2002) has shown that when individual identities are active, proself motives tend to predominate and competitive behavior emerges; whereas, when collective identities are active, prosocial motives predominate and cooperative behavior is more likely. Johnson, Selenta and Lord (2006) also illustrated the importance of relational identities, showing that individuals who were higher on relational identities were more likely to report engaging in organizational citizenship behaviors at work, and they were more likely to base satisfaction on interpersonal justice.

Recent experimental research shows that leaders can influence the emergence of identities through a variety of priming activities. Chang and Hall (2006) found that leaders can activate collective follower identities by stressing shared values and cooperation, and this in turn, increases motivation for group tasks and enhances the perceived utility of group feedback. In contrast, when leaders emphasized individual level values, motivation for individual tasks was enhanced and participants preferred individual level feedback. Similarly, Paul, Costley, Howell, Dorfman, and Trafimow (2001) showed that reading about leaders could affect identity level. They had subjects read written vignettes describing a charismatic leader, an individually considerate leader, or a combination of both of these styles. They found that compared to the individual consideration condition, subjects who read about a charismatic leader had a more active collective identity. Other cross-sectional research in organizations shows that charismatic leadership tends to be associated with greater identification with one's organization and a greater willingness to contribute to group goals (Shamir, Zakay, Breinin, & Popper, 2000), but identification also has been shown to have different effects on follower self-esteem when it involved the development of personal compared to social identities (Kark, Shamir, & Chen, 2003). Identity levels have also been shown to influence the source of intentions, with individual attitudes predicting intentions when individual identities have been primed and group norms influencing intentions when collective identities have been primed (Ybarra & Trafimow, 1998).

In short, when different identities are active, people base their behavior and intentions on different mental constructs, they interpret social justice differently, and they shift social motives and behavior to be competitive or cooperative. Moreover, research shows that leaders can prime different identities through their use of language or their interaction with subordinates. Although this work has mainly been done with individual level subjects, research by Ritter (2004) also shows that effects associated with one leader can transfer to similar leaders, evoking self-with- leader schema that affected regulatory focus, goal levels, and task behavior. This suggests that individual level schema can structure new social interactions. Work by social identity theorists also shows that leaders can affect group identities and ensuing work behavior (van Knippenberg, van Knippenberg, De Cremer, & Hogg, 2004). For example, De Cremer and van Knippenberg (2004) have also shown that leader self-sacrificing compared to self-benefiting behavior can foster different identity levels which, in turn, produces competitive compared to cooperating behavior. Thus, there is empirical literature which shows that identities cued by leaders can cause different work and social structures to emerge.

Combined Effects of Biases

I have suggested that leaders can change the nature of emergent individual and social structures by actions that elicit different emotions, different types of goal structures, or different identities in others. Literature demonstrating each of these processes has developed in isolation, but in reality, to be effective leaders may need to combine these potential biases. A few studies support this argument. For example, Gray (2001) shows that positive or negative emotions support different types of memory structures (verbal versus spatial, respectively), and that these structures, in turn, allow the maintenance of information related to approach or avoidance goals. Similarly, because identities affect the types of behaviors that are desirable to individuals, and anticipated reward allows the maintenance of patterns in the prefrontal cortex (O'Reilly et al., 1999), different identity levels may also influence the nature of information that is easily maintained in memory.

Although suggestive, we certainly need more information concerning the potential interaction of biases in influencing emerging structures both within and between individuals. One intriguing possibility suggested by research on mirror neurons (Rizzolatti et al., 2006) is that emotions can also *directly* elicit mirror responses in observers. This being the case, combining emotions with actions may convey a more refined understanding of another's actions or goals because observers partially experience the actions, goals, and emotions of the person being observed. Indeed, individuals who are deficient in terms of mirror neuron activity in the inferior frontal gyrus are less empathetic and also less able to assess the intentions of others (Ramachandran & Oberman, 2006).

One might immediately think of the articulation of a leader's vision as an area for examining the combination of such biases, particularly since charismatic leaders create positive affect when communicating their vision (Bono & Ilies, 2006; Naidoo & Lord, in press), visions often specify the nature of desired goals, and they also create more collective identities

(De Cremer & van Knippenberg, 2004; Paul et al., 2001; Shamir et al., 2000). However, the communication of a vision is an example of a leader's top-down influence. The effects of leaders operating through organizational climates may be more consistent with the orientation of this chapter because leaders may help create a particular type of climate, e.g., one emphasizing learning versus performance goals, without specifying the specific goal that is desired. With respect to climate, we would expect affect, goal orientation, and identity level to interact in biasing the emergence of a variety of individual and collective structures.

IMPLICATIONS

Thinking of leadership as involving the creation of biases that can shape the emergence of emotions, goals, and identities raises a number of theoretical and practical implications, some of which concern the dynamics of individual level processes and some of which involve more interpersonal structures. There are also potential inconsistencies between short- and long-run consequences that may be practically important.

Individual Level Implications

One obvious implication of the perspective developed in this chapter is that leadership can occur through diffuse processes that are very different from the typical actions associated with leaders. To observers and potential leaders, changing biasing factors associated with emotions, goals, or identities may not seem like leadership at all. It may create effects that are far removed from the leader in terms of time, structures, and outcomes. When this occurs, observers may substitute romantic ideas regarding leadership for a precise understanding of leadership processes (Lord & Maher, 1991; Meindl, 1995), and romantic ideas that are common in Western society suggest that leaders are active, dynamic individuals that directly change followers and are the source of organizational institutions (Marion, 1999). Thus, for both leaders who believe dramatic actions are needed, and for observers whose perceptual structures are geared to salient actions, managing biases in others would not seem like effective leadership. Consequently, it may be hard to convince potential leaders that knowing how to manage biases in emergent process is an important leadership skill, and it may be difficult for observers to notice this skill in leaders (although they may respond automatically to it). In addition, teaching this type of leadership skill would also seem to present a substantial challenge. However, this perspective on leadership is consistent with an understanding of complexity theory and the emergence of structure within complex systems. My premise is simply that this aspect of leadership deserves more attention than it has been given. It may require an approach to leadership that is less leader-centered and views leaders as merely participants, albeit important ones, who along with followers jointly construct many crucial organizational systems and processes. As stressed in the following section on aggregate structures, such constructions play out over time and involve many interacting components of organizations.

The evidence reviewed suggests that affect and identities influence the nature of goals that emerge, and goals in turn affect many other cognitive and emotional processes. Further, many traditional concerns with leadership seem to influence these factors, although the focus of such theories is more on leader-centered actions. I began with the proposition that leadership that influences emergent structures may be appropriate in dynamic situations where individuals in lower levels of organizations had a better idea of the type of changes needed than did higher level leaders. However, we can now raise the question of whether explicit direction from leaders or indirect leadership effects that operate through emergent processes have greater importance.

Certainly, direct actions by leaders can have dramatic short-run outcomes; however, the long-run effects associated with how leaders influence biases may be more important because they can change the structures that emerge spontaneously. Consider the effects of a leader who bluntly and insensitively demands a particular action from subordinates. The action may be performed by subordinates, but the lack of interpersonal justice may elicit hostility, negative affect, avoidance goals, and an individual instead of a collective identity. The long-run effects of these latter changes may far outweigh the value of the action that was demanded. This is particularly likely if, as complexity theory suggests, individual level structures develop into more aggregate interpersonal level structures, such as, coworkers tell each other what a lousy boss they have and destructive work group climates develop. Similar arguments can be developed in the political domain. For example, pragmatic political decisions may have short-run benefits, and yet at the same time, they may elicit processes that cumulate to yield negative long-term consequences. Political cover-ups are one famous illustration. Business practices based on questionable ethics provide another. Although as these examples illustrate, the short- and long-run consequences of a leader's actions may be antagonistic, ideally they serve to complement rather than conflict with each other. Effective leaders are likely to manage emergent processes in ways that support their direct actions.

If there is merit in the perspective on leadership developed in this chapter, an obvious questions need to be addressed. Why hasn't understanding the effects of such biases been a central aspect of leadership theory? Part of the answer is that learning about the effects of biasing factors is very difficult for leaders who are immersed in managing short-run problems or for researchers who observe such behaviors. Leaders may develop an implicit understanding of such processes with years of experience and the development of leadership expertise (Lord & Hall, 2005). However, the importance of such actions can't really be fully appreciated without the emphasis on emergent processes that is provided by complexity theory, and the integration of leadership and complexity theory has only recently been a topic of interest to leadership theorists.

Interpersonal and Aggregate Implications

Emergent Aggregate Structures and the Analogy to Neural Networks

Although we have rich psychological theory that suggests how leaders can prime individual affect, goals, and identities, there is much less literature on how emerging higher level structures are affected by such processes. This is in part because the effects of primes on individual processes occur quite quickly, but the effects of similar primes on the development of interpersonal structures involve much slower processes. Also, rather than laboratory research, such research depends on detailed observations of actual work organizations. Nevertheless, research does demonstrate that collective group structures (Weick & Roberts, 1993) and collective group moods (Barsade, 2002; Bartel & Saavedra, 2000) emerge from interaction patterns among work group members. Further, Hutchins (1991, 1996) has carefully developed the argument that interpersonal work systems can be viewed as parallel information processing systems with many similarities to neural network models. He maintains that work teams can be viewed as constraint satisfaction networks in which the global systems that are needed for task performance emerge from the local interactions of team members. In such systems, structure emerges from connections among individuals in terms of interrelated task activities (Weick & Roberts, 1993), emotions (Barsade, 2002) and cognitions (Porac, Thomas, and Baden-Fuller, 1989). In the terminology we have developed, systems function as dynamic, adaptive structures in which the needed solutions for task activities emerge through collective actions which create and discard attractors as context continually changes.

It is critical to recognize that in many systems although there is formal authority, no specific individual has sufficient knowledge to coordinate actions. As Weick and Roberts (1993) note in describing the collective mind in work organizations, "Portions of the envisaged system are known to all, but all of it is known to none" (p. 365). Further, Hutchins (1996, chapter 8) provides a detailed analysis of organizational learning, explaining that it occurs at the subsystem level as the representations that guide the actions of one unit adapt in response to the actions of other units, which in turn, are guided by their representations. Thus, learning inside a system is guided by the context created by the other systems with which it interacts. In complexity theory terms, this seems to aptly describe the process by which structures emerge through dynamic interaction among units. The principal point made in this chapter is that leaders can bias the dynamic processes that create, and recreate structures, affecting first the representation that develop within units, and then the adaptations that occur within related units. This form of influence, though diffuse, may have a profound impact on the structures that continually emerge. Such effects of leaders can be described in terms of organizational climates or the nature of emerging group identities. However, both of these constructs imply a degree of stability that is somewhat inconsistent with the recognition from complexity theory that structures are continually adapting. Thinking of leaders as biasing the continual adaptation of processes in organizations avoids this limitation.

This perspective developed in this chapter, however, also implies that leaders can have enduring effects because they influence emergent structures in others. I have reviewed evidence showing that leaders can have lasting effects on subordinate's regulatory focus (Ritter, 2004; Shah, 2003a, 2003b) and goal orientation (Dragoni, 2005). Further, research shows that leaders can be critical links in organizational networks (Bono & Anderson, 2005; Sparrowe & Liden, 2005). The nature of such linkages may depend in turn on the quality of affective relations that develop between leaders and followers (Liden, Wayne, & Stillwell, 1993). Such network effects may be particularly important in modern organizations because as organizations become flatter, formal structures are less able to handle administrative demands, and organizations tend to become increasingly reliant on the informal structures that emerge (Sparrowe & Liden, 2005).

Network theory has tended to focus on the various types of positions leaders hold in networks such as their degree of centrality or their ability to link disparate clusters in organizations. However, this is still a leader-centered approach to understanding influence and communication. The extension of the perspective I have developed here would be to suggest that leaders can foster climates that support the emergence of different types of networks. For example, whether linkages tend to form between groups or within groups may be affected by identity level, regulatory focus, and affective orientations of leaders. Collective orientations may be particularly helpful in developing networks in which ideas flow freely among various organizational units. Leadership researchers are just beginning to understand the importance of relational quality and LMX in influence and trust networks, and certainly more research is needed to understand how leaders can affect the nature of developing networks or other aggregate organizational structures. My argument is that they can do this in part by biasing the nature of emergent processes.

Emergence and Organizational Performance

At the outset of this chapter, it was suggested that managing various biases might be one way that leaders could promote a particular type of emergent organization when they lacked insight into specific actions or structures that are needed for organizational success. However, as structures emerge and form higher level aggregates, their consequences tend to be less and less understandable to individuals. Further, many times structures emerge spontaneously without external direction. Yet complexity theory sees leaders as catalysts for change, and describes the effects of leaders on emerging networks in terms of "tags" (Holland, 1995; Marion & Uhl-Bien, 2001). An obvious question is whether this type of leadership is likely to be effective in promoting adaptive organizational structures. One danger is that leaders will respond in terms of their own preferences for particular types of structures, rather than from an understanding of the demands of a particular situation. Thus, leaders may perpetuate a particular type of culture, rather than facilitate needed adaptations (see Porac et al., (1989) for an illustration of such processes). Further, many organizations may have subcomponents that demand different types of structures—research and development may benefit from a very different type of structure than is required by production departments. For this reason the biases that facilitate the emergence of effective structures in one area may be counterproductive in another.

These possibilities imply that there are important limitations in the effect that leaders can, or should, have on emergent structures. Adaptive processes may sometimes be more effective than leadership in designing informal systems (Marion, 1999); yet it also seems likely that there are many instances where leaders could appropriately influence the emergence of effective organizational structures. To do so, we need a better understanding of how biases activated by leaders can guide emergent structures. Complexity theory prompts us to pay attention to such processes, and in this chapter I have suggested several means that leaders can use to influence emergent structures that are derived from an understanding of intra-individual processes. Yet, further research is needed to more fully articulate the emergent interpersonal consequences of leader influence that operates through affective, goal-relevant, or identity-based biases.

NOTE

1. This process may explain a well-known research result in the leadership literature which has been labeled the Performance Cue Effect (Lord, 1985). Extensive research shows that knowledge of outcomes typically associated with leadership actions affects observer descriptions of behaviors that they have seen, with good performance leading to descriptions of behavior that are more prototypical of leaders in general. Presumably, if there are mirror neurons used to understand the goal related behaviors of leaders, then outcome knowledge could activate these comprehension systems, leading to the inference that certain types of behaviors actually occurred.

REFERENCES

Awamleh, R., & Gardner, W. L. (1999). Perceptions of leaders charisma and effectiveness: The effects of vision content, delivery, and organizational performance. *The Leadership Quarterly, 10*, 345-373.

Aron, A., & McLaughlin-Volpe, T. (2001). Including others in the self: Extensions to own and partner's group membership. In C. Sedikides & M. B. Brewer (Eds.) *Individual self, relational self, collective self* (pp. 89-108). Philadelphia: Psychology Press.

Arnsten, A. F. T., & Robbins, T. W. (2002). Neurochemical modulation of prefrontal cortical function in humans and animals. In D. T. Studd & R. T. Knight (Eds). *Principles of frontal lobe function* (pp. 51-84). New York: Oxford University Press.

Ashby, F. G., Isen, A. M., & Turken, A. U. (1999). A neuropsychological theory of positive affect and its influence on cognition. *Psychological Review, 106*, 529-550.

Barsade, S. G. (2002). The ripple effect: Emotional contagion and its influence on group behavior. *Administrative Science Quarterly, 47*, 644-675.

Bartel, C. A., & Saavedra, R. (2000). The collective construction of work group moods. *Administration Science Quarterly, 45*, 197-231.

Bless, H. (2001). The consequences of mood on the processing of social information. In A. Tesser & N. Schwarz (Eds.), *Blackwell handbook of social psychology: Intraindividual processes* (pp. 391-412). Malden, MA: Blackwell.

Bligh, M. C., Kohles, J. C., & Meindl, J. R. (2004). Charting the language of leadership: A methodological investigation of President Bush and the crisis of 9/11. *Journal of Applied Psychology, 89*, 562-574.

Bono, J. E., & Anderson, M. H. (2005). The advice and influence networks of transformational leaders. *Journal of Applied Psychology, 90*, 1306-1314.

Bono, J. E., & Ilies, R. (2006). Charisma, positive emotions and mood contagion. *The Leadership Quarterly, 17*, 317-334.

Brewer, M. B., & Gardner, W. (1996). Who is this "we"? Levels of collective identity and self representations. *Journal of Personality and Social Psychology, 71*, 83-93.

Brown, D. J., & Keeping, L. M. (2005). Elaborating the construct of transformational leadership: The role of affect. *The Leadership Quarterly, 16*, 245-272.

Carver, C. S., & Scheier, M. E. (2002). Control processes and self-organization as complementary principles underlying behavior. *Personality and Social Psychology Review, 6*, 304-315.

Chang, C. -H., & Hall, R. J. (2006). *Follower self-identity activation as the processes underlying leadership effects.* Manuscript submitted for publication.

Chartrand, T. A., & Bargh, J. A. (1996). Automatic activation of impression formation and memorization goals: Nonconscious goal priming reproduces the effects of explicit task instructions. *Journal of Personality and Social Psychology, 71*, 464-478.

Cherulnik, P. D., Donley, K. A., Wiewel, T. S. R., & Miller, S. R. (2001). Charisma is contagious: The effects of leader's charisma on observers' affect. *Journal of Applied Social Psychology, 31*, 2149-2159.

Churchland, P. S., & Sejnowski, T. J. (1992). *The computational brain.* Cambridge, MA: The MIT Press.

Cilliers, P. (1998). *Complexity and postmodernism: Understanding complex systems.* New York, Routledge.

Cilliers, P. (2001). Boundaries, hierarchies, and networks in complex systems. *International Journal of Innovation Management, 5*, 135-147.

De Cremer, D. (2002). Charismatic leadership and cooperation in social dilemmas: A matter of transforming motives. *Journal of Applied Social Psychology, 32*, 997-1016.

De Cremer, D. & van Knippenberg, D. (2004). Leader self-sacrifice and leadership effectiveness: The moderating role of leader self-confidence. *Organizational Behavior and Human Decision Processes, 95, 140-155.*

De Shon, R. P., & Gillespie, J. Z. (2005). A motivated action theory account of goal orientation. *Journal of Applied Psychology, 90*, 1096-1127.

Diefendorff, J. M., & Lord, R. G. (in press). Goal striving and self-regulation processes. In R. Kanfer & G. Chen, (Eds). *Work motivation: Past, present, and future.* San Francisco: Jossey-Bass.

Dragoni, L. (2005). Understanding the emergence of state goal orientation in organizational work groups: The Role of leadership and multilevel climate perceptions. *Journal of Applied Psychology, 90*, 1084-1095.

Dutton, J. E., & Jackson, S. E. (1987). Categorizing strategic issues: Links to organizational action. *Academy of Management Review, 12*, 76-90.

Dweck, C. S. (1986). Motivational processes affecting learning. *American Psychologist, 41*, 1040-1048.

Eiser, J. R. (1994). *Attitudes, chaos and the connectionist mind.* Oxford, United Kingdom: Blackwell.

Gray, J. R. (2001). Emotional modulation of cognitive control: Approach-withdrawal states double-dissociate spatial from verbal two-back task performance. *Journal of Experimental Psychology: General, 130*, 436-452.

George, J. M. (1990). Personality, affect, and behavior in groups. *Journal of Applied Psychology, 75,* 107-116.

George, J. M. (2002). Affect regulation in groups and teams. In R. G. Lord, R. J. Klimoski, & R. Kanfer (Eds.), *Emotions in the workplace: Understanding the structure and role of emotions in organizational behavior* (pp. 183-217). San Francisco: Jossey-Bass.

Hall, R. J., & Lord, R. G. (1995). Multi-level information—processing explanations of followers' leadership perception. *The Leadership Quarterly, 6,* 265-287.

Higgins, E. T. (1997). Beyond pleasure and pain. *American Psychologist, 52,* 1280-1300.

Hogue, M., & Lord, R. (2007). A complex explanation gender bias in leadership emergence. *The Leadership Quarterly, 18*(4), 370-390.

Holland, J. H. (1995). *Hidden order.* New York: Helix Books.

Hopfield, J. (1982). Neural networks as physical systems with emergent collective computational abilities. *Proceedings of the National Academy of Science USA, 79,* 2254 - 2258.

House, R. J., & Mitchell, T. R. (1974). Path-goal theory of leadership. *Contemporary Business, 3,* 81-98.

Hutchins, E. (1991). The social organization of distributed cognition. In L. B. Resnick, J. M. Levine, & S. D. Teasley (Eds.), *Perspectives on socially shared cognitions* (pp. 283- 307). Washington, DC: American Psychological Association.

Hutchins, E. (1996). *Cognition in the wild.* Cambridge, MA: MIT Press.

Johnson, R. E., Chang, C. -H. D., & Lord, R. G. (2006). Moving from cognition to behavior: What the research says. *Psychological Bulletin, 132,* 381-415.

Johnson, R. E., Selenta, C., & Lord, R. G. (2006). When organizational justice and the self- concept meet. *Organizational Behavior and Human Decision Processes, 99,* 175-201.

Kark, R., Shamir, B., & Chen, G. (2003). The two faces of transformational leadership: Empowerment and dependency. *Journal of Applied Psychology, 88,* 246-255.

Kellett, J. B., Humphrey, R. H., & Sleeth, R. G. (2002). Empathy and complex task performance: Two routes to leadership. *The Leadership Quarterly, 13,* 523-544.

Kozlowski, S. W. J., & Klein, K. J. (2001). A multilevel approach to theory and research in organizations: Contextual, temporal, and emergent processes. In S. W. J. Kozlowski & K. J. Klein (Eds.), *Multilevel theory, research and methods in organizations: Foundations, extensions, and new directions* (pp. 3-90). San Francisco: Jossey-Bass.

Liden, R. C., Wayne, S. J., & Stilwell, D. (1993). A longitudinal study on the early development of leader-member exchanges. *Journal of Applied Psychology, 78,* 662-674.

Lord, R. G. (1985). An information processing approach to social perceptions, leadership perceptions and behavioral measurement on organizational settings. In B. M. Staw & L. Cummings (Eds.), *Research in organizational behavior* (pp. 87-128). Greenwich, CT: JAI Press.

Lord, R. G., & Brown, D. J. (2004) *Leadership processes and follower self-identity.* Mahwah, NJ: Erlbaum.

Lord, R. G., Brown, D. J., & Freiberg, S. J. (1999). Understanding the dynamics of leadership: The role of follower self-concepts in the leader/follower relationship. *Organizational Behavior and Human Decision Processes, 78,* 167-203.

Lord, R. G., & Hall, R. J. (2005). Identity, deep structure and the development of leadership skills. *The Leadership Quarterly, 16,* 591-615.

Lord, R. G., & Maher, K. J. (1991/93) *Leadership and information processing.* Cambridge, MA: Unwin Hyman.

Marion, R. (1999). *The edge of organization: Chaos and complexity theories of formal social systems.* Thousand Oaks, CA: Sage.

Marion, R., & Uhl-Bien, M. (2001). Leadership in complex organizations. *The Leadership Quarterly, 12,* 389-419.

Markus, H., & Wurf, E. (1987). The dynamic self-concept: A social psychological perspective. *Annual Review of Psychology, 38,* 299-337.

Meindl, J. R. (1995). The romance of leadership as a follower-centric theory: A social constructionist approach. *The Leadership Quarterly, 6,* 329-341.

Naidoo, L. J., & Lord, R. G. (in press). Speech imagery and perceptions of charisma: The mediating role of positive affect. *The Leadership Quarterly.*

Newcombe, M. J., & Ashkanasy, N. M. (2002). The role of affect and affective congruence in the perception of leaders: An experimental study. *The Leadership Quarterly, 13,* 601-614.

O'Reilly, R. C., Braver, T. S., & Cohen, J. D. (1999). A biologically based computational model of working memory. In A. Miyake & P. Shah (Eds.), *Models of working memory: Mechanisms of active maintenance and executive control* (pp. 375-411). Cambridge, United Kingdom: Cambridge University Press.

Paul, J., Costley, D. L., Howell, J. P., Dorfman, P. W., & Trafimow, D. (2001). The effects of charismatic leadership on followers' self-concept accessibility. *Journal of Applied Social Psychology, 31,* 1821-1844.

Pescosolido, A. (2002). Emergent leaders as managers of group emotion. *The Leadership Quarterly, 13,* 583-599.

Plowman, D. A., Solansky, S., Beck, T., Baker, L., Kulkarni, M., & Travis, D. (2007). The role of leadership in emergent, self-organization. *The Leadership Quarterly, 18*(4), 341-356.

Porac, J., Thomas, H., & Baden-Fuller, C. (1989). Competitive groups as cognitive communities: The case of Scottish knitwear manufacturers. *Journal of Management Studies, 26,* 397-416.

Ramachandran, V. S., & Oberman, L. M. (2006). Broken mirrors: A theory of autism. *Scientific American, 295*(5), 63-69.

Rizzolatti, G., Fogassi, L., & Gallese, V. (2006). Mirrors in the mind. *Scientific American, 295*(5), 54-61.

Ritter, B. A. (2004). *Leadership transference: The generalization of affective and motivational processes.* Unpublished doctoral dissertation, The University of Akron.

Rougier, N. P., Noelle, D. C., Braver, T. S., Cohen, J. D., & O'Reilly, R. C. (2005). Prefrontal cortex and flexible cognitive control: Rules without symbols. *Proceedings of the National Academy of Sciences of the United States of America, 102*(20), 7338-7343.

Shah, J. (2003a). The motivational looking glass: How significant others implicitly affect goal appraisal. *Journal of Personality and Social Psychology, 85,* 424-439.

Shah, J. (2003b). Automatic for the people: How representations of significant others implicitly affect goal pursuit. *Journal of Personality and Social Psychology, 84*, 661-681.

Shamir, B., House, R. J., & Arthur, M. B. (1993). The motivational effects of charismatic leadership: A self-concept based theory. *Organizational Science, 4*, 577-594.

Shamir, B., Zakay, E., Breinin, E., & Popper, M. (2000). Leadership and social identification in military units. *Journal of Applied Social Psychology, 30*, 612-640.

Sparrowe, R. T., & Liden, R. C. (2005). Two routes to influence: Integrating leader-member exchange and social network perspectives. *Administrative Science Quarterly, 50*, 505- 535.

Thagard, P., & Nerb, J. (2002). Emotional gestalts: Appraisal, change, and the dynamics of affect. *Personality and Social Psychology Review, 6*, 274-282.

Tomarken, A. J., & Keener, A. D. (1998). Frontal brain asymmetry and depression: A self- regulatory perspective. *Cognition and Emotion, 12*, 387-420.

Tyler, T. R. (1997). The psychology of legitimacy: A relational perspective on voluntary deference to authorities. *Personality and Social Psychology Review, 4*, 323-345.

Tyler, T. R., & Blader, S. L. (2005). Can businesses effectively regulate employee conduct? The antecedents of rule following in work settings. *Academy of Management Review, 48*, 1143-1158.

van Knippenberg, D., van Knippenberg, B., De Cremer, D., & Hogg, M. A. (2004). Leadership, self, and identity: A review and research agenda. *The Leadership Quarterly, 15*, 825-856.

Weick, K. E., & Roberts, K. H. (1993). Collective mind in organizations: Heedful interrelating on flight decks. *Administrative Science Quarterly, 38*, 357-381.

Ybarra, O., & Trafimow, D. (1998). How priming the private self or collective self affects the relative weights of attitudes and subjective norms. *Personality and Social Psychology Bulletin, 24*, 362-370.

Yukl, G. (2002). *Leadership in organizations* (5th ed.). Upper Saddle River, NJ: Prentice Hall.

CHAPTER 8

COMPLEXITY LEADERSHIP THEORY

Shifting Leadership From the Industrial Age to the Knowledge Era

Mary Uhl-Bien, Russ Marion, and Bill McKelvey

ABSTRACT

Leadership models of the last century have been products of top-down, bureaucratic paradigms. These models are eminently effective for an economy premised on physical production but are not well-suited for a more knowledge-oriented economy. Complexity science suggests a different paradigm for leadership—one that frames leadership as a complex interactive dynamic from which adaptive outcomes (e.g., learning, innovation, and adaptability) emerge. This chapter draws from complexity science to develop an overarching framework for the study of complexity leadership theory, a leadership paradigm that focuses on enabling the learning, cre-

Editor's Note: This chapter is reprinted with permission from Elsevier. It was originally published in Vol. 18, No. 4, of *The Leadership Quarterly.* Copyright Elsevier, 2007.

Complexity Leadership, Part I: Conceptual Foundations
pp. 185–224

ative, and adaptive capacity of complex adaptive systems (CAS) within a context of knowledge producing organizations. This conceptual framework includes three entangled leadership roles (i.e., adaptive leadership, administrative leadership, and enabling leadership) that reflect a dynamic relationship between the bureaucratic, administrative functions of the organization and the emergent, informal dynamics of complex adaptive systems (CAS).

As we advance deeper in the knowledge economy, the basic assumptions underlining much of what is taught and practiced in the name of management are hopelessly out of date.... Most of our assumptions about business, technology and organization are at least 50 years old. They have outlived their time. (Drucker, 1998, p. 162)

We're in a knowledge economy, but our managerial and governance systems are stuck in the Industrial Era. It's time for a whole new model. (Manville & Ober, 2003, p. 48)

According to Hitt (1998), "we are on the precipice of an epoch," in the midst of a new economic age, in which twenty-first century organizations are facing a complex competitive landscape driven largely by globalization and the technological revolution. This new age is about an economy where knowledge is a core commodity and the rapid production of knowledge and innovation is critical to organizational survival (Bettis & Hitt, 1995; Boisot, 1998). Consistent with these changes, much discussion is taking place in the management literature regarding challenges facing organizations in a transitioning world (Barkema, Baum, & Mannix, 2002; Bettis & Hitt, 1995; Child & McGrath, 2001).

Yet, despite the fact that leadership is a core factor in whether organizations meet these challenges, we find little explicit discussion of leadership models for the Knowledge Era. As noted by Davenport (2001), while it has become clear that the old model of leadership was formed to deal with a very different set of circumstances and is therefore of questionable relevance to the contemporary work environment, no clear alternative has come along to take its place. Osborn, Hunt, and Jauch (2002) argue that "a radical change in perspective" about leadership is necessary to go beyond traditionally accepted views, because "the context in which leaders operate is both radically different and diverse. The world of traditional bureaucracy exists but it is only one of many contexts" (p. 798).

We begin to address this shortcoming by developing a framework for leadership in the fast-paced, volatile context of the Knowledge Era (Marion & Uhl-Bien, 2001; Schneider & Somers, 2006). Our model extends beyond bureaucracy premises by drawing from complexity science, the "study of the behaviour of large collections of ... simple, interacting units, endowed with the potential to evolve with time" (Coveney, 2003, p. 1058). Using the concept of complex adaptive systems (CAS), we propose that leadership should be seen not only as position and authority but also as an *emergent, interactive dynamic*—a complex interplay from which a collective impetus for action and change emerges when heterogeneous agents interact in networks in ways that produce new patterns of behavior or new modes of operating (cf. Heifetz, 1994; Plowman & Duchon, in press; Plowman, Solansky, et al., 2007).

Complex adaptive systems (CAS) are a basic unit of analysis in complexity science. CAS are neural-like networks of interacting, interdependent agents who are bonded in a cooperative dynamic by common goal, outlook, need, and so on. They are changeable structures with multiple, overlapping hierarchies, and like the individuals that comprise them, CAS are linked with one another in a dynamic, interactive network. Hedlund (1994) describes a generally similar structure relative to managing knowledge flows in organizations that he called "*temporary constellations* of people and units" (p. 82). CAS emerge naturally in social systems (cf. Homans, 1950; Roy, 1954). They are capable of solving problems creatively and are able to learn and adapt quickly (Carley & Hill, 2001; Carley & Lee, 1998; Goodwin, 1994; Levy, 1992).

The leadership framework we propose, which we call complexity leadership theory, seeks to take advantage of the dynamic capabilities of CAS. Complexity leadership theory (CLT) focuses on identifying and exploring the strategies and behaviors that foster organizational and subunit creativity, learning, and adaptability when appropriate CAS dynamics are enabled within contexts of hierarchical coordination (i.e., bureaucracy). In CLT, we recognize three broad types of leadership: (1) leadership grounded in traditional, bureaucratic notions of hierarchy, alignment and control (i.e., administrative leadership), (2) leadership that *structures* and *enables* conditions such that CAS are able to optimally address creative problem solving, adaptability, and learning (referring to what we will call, enabling leadership); and (2) leadership as a *generative dynamic* that underlies emergent change activities (what we will call, adaptive leadership).

The complexity leadership perspective is premised on several critical notions. First, the informal dynamic we describe is embedded in context (Hunt, 1999; Osborn et al., 2002). Context in complex adaptive systems is not an antecedent, mediator, or moderator variable; rather, it is the ambiance that spawns a given system's dynamic persona—in the case of complex system personae, it refers to the nature of interactions and interdependencies among agents (people, ideas, etc.), hierarchical divisions, organizations, and environments. CAS and leadership are socially constructed in and from this context—a context in which patterns over time must be considered and where history matters (Cilliers, 1998; Dooley, 1996; Hosking, 1988; Osborn et al., 2002).

Second, a complexity leadership perspective requires that we distinguish between *leadership* and *leaders*. Complexity leadership theory will add a view of *leadership* as an emergent, interactive dynamic that is productive of adaptive outcomes (which we call adaptive leadership, cf. Heifetz, 1994). It will consider *leaders* as individuals who act in ways that influence this dynamic and the outcomes. Leadership theory has largely focused on *leaders*—the actions of individuals. It has not examined the dynamic, complex systems and processes that comprise *leadership*. Because of this, earlier models have been criticized for being incomplete and impractical (Gronn, 1999; Osborn et al., 2002; see also Hunt, 1999). Rost (1991) refers to this as the problem of focusing on the "periphery" and "content" of leadership with disregard for the essential nature of what leadership is—a *process* (cf. Hunt, 1999; Mackenzie, 2006).

Third, complexity leadership perspectives help us to distinguish leadership from managerial positions or "offices" (a bureaucratic notion, see Heckscher, 1994). The vast majority of leadership research has studied leadership in formal, most often managerial, roles (Bedeian & Hunt, 2006; Rost, 1991) and has not adequately addressed leadership that occurs throughout the organization (Schneider, 2002). To address this, we will use the term *administrative leadership* to refer to formal acts that serve to coordinate and structure organizational activities (i.e., the bureaucratic function), and introduce the concept of *adaptive leadership* to refer to the leadership that occurs in emergent, informal adaptive dynamics throughout the organization (cf. Heifetz, 1994; Heifetz & Linsky, 2002).

Finally, complexity leadership occurs in the face of adaptive challenges (typical of the Knowledge Era) rather than technical problems (more characteristic of the Industrial Age). As defined by Heifetz (1994; Heifetz & Laurie, 2001), adaptive challenges are problems that require new learning, innovation, and new patterns of behavior. They are different from technical problems, which can be solved with knowledge and procedures already in hand (Parks, 2005). Adaptive challenges are not amenable to authoritative fiat or standard operating procedures, but rather require exploration, new discoveries, and adjustments. Day (2000) refers to this as the difference between management and leadership development. Management development involves the application of proven solutions to known problems, whereas leadership development refers to situations in which groups need to learn their way out of problems that could not have been predicted (e.g., disintegration of traditional organizational structures).

In the sections below we lay out the framework and dynamics we call complexity leadership theory. This framework describes how to enable the learning, creative, and adaptive capacity of complex adaptive systems

(CAS) within a context of knowledge producing organizations. Complexity leadership theory seeks to foster CAS dynamics while at the same time enabling control structures for coordinating formal organizations and producing outcomes appropriate to the vision and mission of the organization. We begin by describing the leadership requirements of the Knowledge Era and the limitations of current leadership theory for meeting these requirements. We then describe why CAS dynamics are well suited for the needs of the Knowledge Era, and how leadership can work to enable these dynamics. We conclude with a presentation of the complexity leadership theory framework and a description of the three key leadership functions and roles that comprise this framework: adaptive leadership, enabling leadership, and administrative leadership.

LEADERSHIP IN THE KNOWLEDGE ERA

The Knowledge Era is characterized by a new competitive landscape driven by globalization, technology, deregulation, and democratization (Halal & Taylor, 1999). Many firms deal with this new landscape by allying horizontally and vertically in "constellations" (Bamford, Gomes-Casseres, & Robinson, 2002). In the process, they actively interconnect the world, creating what some have called a *"connectionist era"* (Halal, 1998; Miles, 1998; see Hogue & Lord, 2007, for an extensive discussion). Through multinational alliances, firms in developing countries now find themselves engaging increasingly in manufacturing activities as producers or subcontractors, while firms in developed economies focus more on information and services (Drucker, 1999). The latter face the need to exhibit speed, flexibility, and adaptability, with the organization's absolute rate of learning and innovation and the pace of its development becoming critical to competitive advantage (Eisenhardt, 1989; Jennings & Haughton, 2000; Prusak, 1996). In other words, firms in developed economies sustain superior performance in the Knowledge Era by promoting faster learning (Child & McGrath, 2001).

This new age creates new kinds of challenges for organizations and their leaders (Barkema et al., 2002; Schneider, 2002). In this postindustrial era, the success of a corporation lies more in its social assets—its corporate IQ and learning capacity—than in its physical assets (McKelvey, 2001; Quinn, Anderson, & Finkelstein, 2002; Zohar, 1997). In the industrial economy, the challenge inside the firm was to coordinate the physical assets produced by employees. This was mainly a problem of optimizing the production and physical flow of products (Boisot, 1998; Schneider, 2002). In the new economy, the challenge is to create an environment in which knowledge accumulates and is shared at a low cost. The goal is to cultivate, protect, and use difficult to imitate knowledge assets as com-pared to pure commodity-instigated production (Nonaka & Nishiguchi, 2001). It is a problem of enabling intellectual assets through distributed intelligence and cellular networks (Miles, Snow, Matthews, & Miles, 1999) rather than relying on the limited intelligence of a few brains at the top (Heckscher, 1994; McKelvey, in press). Moreover, the focus is on speed and adaptability (Schilling & Steensma, 2001). Rather than leading for efficiency and control, appropriate to manufacturing (Jones, 2000), orga-nizations find themselves leading for adaptability, knowledge and learn-ing (Achtenhagen, Melin, Mullern, & Ericson, 2003; Volberda, 1996).

To achieve fitness in such a context, complexity science suggests that organizations must increase their complexity to the level of the environ-ment rather than trying to simplify and rationalize their structures. Ashby (1960) refers to this as the law of requisite variety; McKelvey and Boisot (2003) customized this law for complexity theory and call it the law of req-uisite complexity. This law states simply that it takes complexity to defeat complexity—a system must possess complexity equal to that of its envi-ronment in order to function effectively. Requisite complexity enhances a system's capacity to search for solutions to challenges and to innovate because it releases the capacity of a neural network of agents in pursuit of such optimization. That is, it optimizes a system's capacity for learning, creativity, and adaptability.

As Cilliers (2001) observed, traditional approaches to organization have done the opposite: they have sought to simplify or to rationalize the pursuit of adaptation. He argues that simplifying and rationalizing strate-gies lead to structures that define fixed boundaries, compartmentalized organizational responses, and simplified coordination and communica-tion (e.g., Simon, 1962). However, such approaches are limited because they do not represent reality—boundaries are not fixed perimeters, but rather, are sets of functions that dynamically interpenetrate one another (Cilliers, 2001). To meet the needs of requisite complexity, Knowledge Era leadership requires a change in thinking away from individual, con-trolling views, and toward views of organizations as complex adaptive sys-tems that enable continuous creation and capture of knowledge. In short, knowledge development, adaptability, and innovation are optimally enabled by organizations that are complexly adaptive (possessing requi-site complexity).

Limitations of Current Leadership Theory

Despite the needs of the Knowledge Era, much of leadership theory remains largely grounded in a bureaucratic framework more appropriate for the Industrial Age (Gronn, 1999). One such element of the bureaucratic concept is the traditional assumption that control must be rationalized. Much of leadership theory is developed around the idea that goals are rationally conceived and that managerial practices should be structured to achieve those goals. As Chester Barnard (1938) framed it, the role of leadership is to align individual preferences with rational organizational goals. Philip Selznick (1948) observed that irrational social forces tend to subvert the formal goals of an institution.

Consistent with this, the dominant paradigm in leadership theory focuses on how leaders can influence others toward desired objectives within frameworks of formal hierarchical organizational structures (Zaccaro & Klimoski, 2001). This paradigmatic model centers on issues such as motivating workers toward task objectives (House & Mitchell, 1974), leading them to produce efficiently and effectively (Zaccaro & Klimoski, 2001) and inspiring them to align with and commit to organizational goals (Bass, 1985). Macrolevel theories, such as those that address "upper-echelon leadership," are further premised in bureaucratic notions (Heckscher, 1994) that likewise mute uncontrolled behaviors; other models advocate a charismatic, visionary approach that is said to cascade down from the CEO to lower levels (Conger, 1999; Yukl, 2005). Leadership research has explored the implementation of these top-down organizational forms by drilling deeper and deeper into human relations models (aimed at alignment and control; Gronn, 1999; Huxham & Vangen, 2000).

Without realizing it, the inability to move beyond formal leaders and control inherent in traditional bureaucratic mindsets (Heckscher, 1994) limits the applicability of mainstream leadership theories for the Knowledge Era (Stacey, Griffin, & Shaw, 2000; Streatfield, 2001). There seems to be a contradiction between the needs of the Knowledge Era and the reality of centralized power (Child & McGrath, 2001) that leadership theory has not yet addressed. "The dominant paradigms in organizational theory are based on stability seeking and uncertainty avoidance through organizational structure and processes.... We believe that those paradigms are inadequate for global, hyper-competitive environments, although their replacements are not clear yet" (Ilinitch, D'Aveni, & Lewin, 1996, p. 217). As noted by Child and McGrath (2001), "Scholars, managers, and others face a widespread challenge to bureaucracy's central benefit, namely, its utility as a vehicle for strong economic performance in the new era" (p. 1136). Leadership scholars face the same challenge:

The ... challenge is to identify alternatives [to bureaucracy] and develop theories that account for them. It is not trivial. How can we improve upon, even replace, such a painstakingly well-developed concept of how human beings collectively best accomplish their objectives? (Child & McGrath, 2001, p. 1136)

We address this challenge by developing a model of leadership grounded not in bureaucracy, but in complexity. This model focuses on leadership in contexts of dynamically changing networks of informally interacting agents. As will be elaborated below, the premise of complexity leadership is simple: Under conditions of knowledge production, managers should *enable*, rather than suppress or align, informal network dynamics. Early researchers, such as K. Lewin (1952) and Homans (1950), glimpsed the potential of such informal dynamics (however vaguely, by complexity theory standards); but the thrust of many follow-up studies of their findings assumed that such informal dynamics were problematic for achieving organizational goals (Roy, 1954; Selznick, 1957). Several recent initiatives have explored the potential of decentralized authority or leadership, including Pearce and Conger's work with shared leadership (Pearce & Conger, 2003), Gronn's work on distributed leadership (Gronn, 2002), and Fletcher (2004) and Volberda (1996) on flexible forms. None, however, have developed a model that addresses the nature of leadership for enabling network dynamics, one whose epistemology is consistent with *connective*, *distributed*, *dynamic*, and *contextual* views of leadership.

We propose such a model in this article, one that we call, complexity leadership theory. This new perspective is grounded in a core proposition: *Much of leadership thinking has failed to recognize that leadership is not merely the influential act of an individual or individuals but rather is embedded in a complex interplay of numerous interacting forces.*

There are several orienting assumptions that underlie the complexity leadership model; these assumptions will be developed further in this chapter:

- Complexity leadership theory (CLT) is necessarily enmeshed within a bureaucratic superstructure of planning, organizing, and missions. CLT seeks to understand how enabling leaders can interact with the administrative superstructure to both coordinate complex dynamics (i.e., adaptive leadership) and enhance the overall flexibility of the organization (Marion & Uhl-Bien, 2007).
- Complexity leadership theory presumes hierarchical structuring and differing enabling and adaptive functions across levels of the hierarchy.
- The unit of analysis for complexity leadership theory is the CAS. The boundaries of CAS are variously defined depending on the intent of the researcher, but however identified, they are, without exception, open systems.

- Leadership, however it is defined, only exists in, and is a function of, interaction.

Before we elaborate these ideas in our framework below, however, we first must understand why complex adaptive systems are well suited for the Knowledge Era and the dynamics that drive these systems. Therefore, we turn next to an overview of CAS dynamics that will serve as a basis for discussion in subsequent sections.

The Argument for Complexity Leadership Theory: CAS Dynamics

Earlier we defined complex adaptive systems (or CAS) as open, evolutionary aggregates whose components (or *agents*) are dynamically interrelated and who are cooperatively bonded by common purpose or outlook. We also introduced complexity leadership theory as a model for leadership in and of complex adaptive systems (CAS) in knowledge-producing organizations. We now ask, "What is so unique about complex adaptive systems theory that it fosters a fresh look at leadership?" and "Why would we want to enable CAS dynamics anyway?"

To answer these questions we need to better understand the structure of CAS and how they are different from systems perspectives offered previously in the organizational literature. As described by Cilliers (1998), complex adaptive systems are different from systems that are merely complicated. If a system can be described in terms of its individual constituents (even if there are a huge number of constituents), it is merely *complicated*; if the interactions among the constituents of the system, and the interaction between the system and its environment, are of such a nature that the system as a whole cannot be fully understood simply by analyzing its components, it is *complex* (for example, a jumbo jet is *complicated*, but mayonnaise is *complex*, Cilliers, 1998).

Dooley (1996) describes a CAS as an aggregate of interacting agents that "behaves/evolves according to three key principles: order is emergent as opposed to predetermined, the system's history is irreversible, and the system's future is often unpredictable." In CAS, agents, events, and ideas bump into each other in somewhat unpredictable fashion, and change emerges from this dynamic interactive process. Because of this randomness, and the fact that complex dynamics can exhibit sensitivity to small perturbations (Lorenz, 1993), CAS are rather organic and unpredictable (Marion & Uhl-Bien, 2001). Change in complex adaptive systems occur nonlinearly and in unexpected places, and, as Dooley (1996) observed, their history cannot be revisited (one cannot return a system to a previous state and rerun its trajectory).

Complexity science has identified a number of dynamics that characterize the formation and behaviors of CAS. For example, complexity science has found that interactive, adaptive agents tend to bond in that they adapt to one another's preferences and worldviews (Marion & Uhl-Bien, 2001). From this, they form aggregates (i.e., clusters of interacting agents engaged in some measure of cooperative behavior). Mature social systems are comprised of a complex of hierarchically embedded, overlapping and interdependent aggregates, or CAS (Kauffman, 1993).

Complexity science has also found that the behaviors of interactive, interdependent agents and CAS are productive of *emergent creativity and learning*. Emergence refers to a nonlinear suddenness that characterizes change in complex systems (Marion, 1999; see also Plowman, Solansky, et al., 2007a). It derives from the collapse (or, more technically, dissipation) of built up tensions (Prigogine, 1997), sudden mergers (or divergences) of formerly separate CAS (Kauffman, 1993), or a cascade of changes through network connections (Bak, 1996). Creativity and learning occur when emergence forms a previously unknown solution to a problem or creates a new, unanticipated outcome (i.e., adaptive change).

CAS are unique and desirable in their ability to *adapt* rapidly and creatively to environmental changes. Complex systems enhance their capacity for adaptive response to environmental problems or internal demand by diversifying their behaviors or strategies (Holland, 1995; McKelvey, in press). Diversification, from the perspective of complexity science, is defined as increasing internal complexity (number and level of interdependent relationships, heterogeneity of skills and outlooks within CAS, number of CAS, and tension) to the point of, or exceeding, that of competitors or the environment (i.e., "requisite variety," Ashby, 1960 or "requisite complexity," McKelvey & Boisot, 2003). Adaptive responses to environmental problems include counter-moves, altered or new strategies, learning and new knowledge, work-around changes, new allies, and new technologies. By increasing their complexity, CAS enhance their ability to process data (R. Lewin, 1992), solve problems (Levy, 1992), learn (Carley & Hill, 2001; Levy, 1992), and change creatively (Marion, 1999).

Certain conditions will affect the capacity of CAS to emerge and function effectively in social systems. Agents must, for example, be capable of interacting with each other and with the environment. Agents must be interdependently related, meaning that the productive well being of one agent or aggregate is dependent on the productive well being of others. Moreover, they must experience tension to elaborate.

This capacity to rapidly explore solutions can be illustrated with a problem solving scenario called annealing, which is found in the evolution and simulation complexity literature (Carley, 1997; Carley & Lee, 1998; Kauffman, 1993; Levy, 1992; A. Lewin, 1999). In this scenario, multiple agents struggle with localized effects created by a given environmental perturbations (or tension; this is called localized because an agent cannot usually perceive a problem as a whole nor do they typically have the capacity to deal with an environmental problem in its entirety). As these agents develop localized solutions, work-arounds, or related responses, they affect the behaviors of other interdependently related agents, who subsequently build on the original response to create higher-order responses. This process extends to broader network levels, to the fabric of interdependent agents, and to the CAS that define the system or subsystem. In this process interdependent agents and CAS experiment, change, combine strategies, and find loopholes in other strategies—and, occasionally, unexpected solutions emerge that address the problem at some level.

Information flows in the annealing process are not necessarily efficient and agents are not necessarily good information processors. Nor does annealing imply that structural adaptations are embraced as official strategy by upper echelon administrators or that the process finds perfect solutions. The annealing process is imperfect and somewhat messy—as Carley (1997) puts it, "it may not be possible for organizations of complex adaptive agents to locate the optimal form, [but] they can improve their performance by altering their structure" (p. 25). The annealing process (and other processes described in the complexity literature; e.g., McKelvey, in press; Prigogine, 1997)[1] does, however, find solutions that individuals, regardless of their authority or expertise, could not find alone. Levy (1992), for example, describes bottom-up simulations that out-performed humans at finding solutions to mazes. Marion (1999) argued that technological and scientific advances inevitably emerge from a movement involving numerous individuals rather than from the isolated minds of individuals.

In sum, complexity describes the interdependent interactions of agents within CAS, agents with CAS, and CAS with CAS. The primary unit of analysis in these interactive dynamics is, however, the CAS itself, and the behaviors of agents are always understood within the context of CAS. CAS are unique and desirable in that their heterogeneous, interactive, and interdependent structures allow them to quickly explore and consolidate solutions to environmental pressures. They require new models of leadership because problem solving is performed by *appropriately structured social networks* rather than by groups coordinated by centralized authorities. As Mumford and Licuanan (2004) put it, effective leadership influence in conditions requiring creativity occurs through *indirect mechanisms* and through *interaction*.

Complexity is a science of mechanisms and interaction and is embedded in context. *Mechanisms* can be described as the dynamic behaviors that occur within a system such as a complex adaptive system. As defined by Hernes (1998), mechanisms are "a set of interacting parts—an assembly of elements producing an effect not inherent in any of them" (p. 74). They are "not so much about 'nuts and bolts' as about 'cogs and wheels' ... —the "wheelwork" or agency by which an effect is produced" (Hernes, 1998, p. 74). *Contexts* are structural, organizational, ideational, and behavioral features—the ambiance of interactions among agents (people, ideas, etc.), hierarchical divisions, organizations, and environments—that influence the nature of mechanism dynamics. Examination of mechanisms and contexts will pry back the cover on leadership, so to speak, and help us to understand *how* and *under what conditions* certain outcomes occur.

To further explain this, we turn next to presentation of our framework for complexity leadership theory. Complexity leadership theory is about setting up organizations to enable adaptive responses to challenges through network-based problem solving. It offers tools for knowledge producing organizations and subsystems dealing with rapidly changing, complex problems. It also is useful for systems dealing with less complex problems but for whom creativity is desired.

COMPLEXITY LEADERSHIP THEORY

Complexity leadership theory is a framework for leadership that enables the learning, creative, and adaptive capacity of complex adaptive systems (CAS) in knowledge producing organizations or organizational units. This framework seeks to foster CAS dynamics while at the same time enabling control structures appropriate for coordinating formal organizations and producing outcomes appropriate to the vision and mission of the system. It seeks to integrate complexity dynamics and bureaucracy, enabling and coordinating, exploration and exploitation, CAS and hierarchy, and informal emergence and top-down control.

Accomplishing this balance poses unique challenges for leadership, however: *How can organizations enable and coordinate CAS dynamics and informal emergence (where appropriate), without suppressing their adaptive and creative capacity?*

As described above, complex adaptive systems are intensely adaptive and innovative (Cilliers, 1998; Marion, 1999). CAS obtain the flexibility to adapt that has been attributed to loose coupling (Weick, 1976) and the capacity to coordinate from a more interdependent structure that is best described as moderately coupled (Kauffman, 1993; Marion, 1999). Moderately coupled interdependency (the actions of one agent are dependent on or limited by those of another) imposes restrictions on behavior. Thus flexibility and what might be called, autocoordination, derives from informal but interdependent structures and activities (autocoordination emerges from the nature of system dynamics and is not imposed by authorities). Complexity theorists refer to such informal interactive interdependency as bottom-up behavior, defined as behaviors and changes that emerge spontaneously from the dynamics of neurallike networks. However, the term bottom-up evokes images of hierarchy in organizational studies, so we will substitute the term *informal emergence* to describe these CAS dynamics in social systems (Lichtenstein et al., 2006; Plowman, Baker, et al., 2007; Plowman & Duchon, in press; Plowman, Solansky, et al., 2007).

Informal emergence and autocoordination are seemingly incompatible with administrative coordination, but in reality it depends on the nature of the coordination. In complex adaptive systems, coordination comes from two sources: from informal emergent constraints imposed by interdependent relationships themselves (auto-coordination) and from constraints imposed by actions *external* to the informal dynamic, including environmental restrictions (Kauffman, 1993; Marion, 1999) and administrative controls (McKelvey, Marion, & Uhl-Bien, 2003). *Internal* controls are imposed by a sense of common purpose that defines complex adaptive systems and from an interagent accountability that is inherent in interdependent systems (Marion & Uhl-Bien, 2001; Marion & Uhl-Bien, 2003; Schneider & Somers, 2006). Osborn and Hunt (2007) evocatively describe internal coordination in their discussion of the Highlander tribes of New Zealand. *External* constraints and demands are imposed by environmental exigencies and relationships; indeed the core of Stuart Kauffman's (1993) influential descriptions of complex activities in biological evolution involves the interinfluence of multiple interacting species.

In organizational systems, administrators in formal positions of authority likewise influence complex adaptive systems by imposing external coordinating constraints and demands. Such constraints are valuable for (among other things) controlling costs, focusing efforts, allocating resources, and planning. However, authority imposed (top-down) coordination is not necessarily responsive to the potent dynamics of interdependent learning, creativity, and adaptability inherent in complex adaptive systems, and it tends to impose the understanding of a few on the "wisdom" of a neural network (Heckscher, 1994; McKelvey, in press). That is, top-down control (i.e., administrative leadership) can hamper the effective functioning of complex adaptive systems. This is particularly evident in systems with only top-down, hierarchical chains of authority, in systems with closely monitored, centralized goals, or in systems whose dominant ideology is authoritarian.

How, then, can organizations capitalize on the benefits of administrative coordination *and* of complex adaptive dynamics? Complexity leadership theory suggests that the role of managers should not be limited to aligning worker preferences with centralized organizational goals. Rather, managers, particularly under conditions of knowledge production, should act to *enable* informal emergence and to coordinate the contexts within which it occurs.

A FRAMEWORK FOR COMPLEXITY LEADERSHIP THEORY

This leads us to our overarching framework for complexity leadership theory. This framework envisions three leadership functions that we will refer to as adaptive, administrative, and enabling. *Adaptive leadership* refers to adaptive, creative, and learning actions that emerge from the interactions of CAS as they strive to adjust to tension (e.g., constraints or perturbations). Adaptive activity can occur in a boardroom or in workgroups of line workers; adaptive leadership is an informal emergence dynamic that occurs among interactive agents (CAS) and is not an act of authority. *Administrative leadership* refers to the actions of individuals and groups in formal managerial roles who plan and coordinate activities to accomplish organizationally prescribed outcomes in an efficient and effective manner. Administrative leadership (among other things) structures tasks, engages in planning, builds vision, allocates resources to achieve goals, manages crises (Mumford, Bedell-Avers, & Hunter, in press) and conflicts, and manages organizational strategy (see Yukl, 2005). Administrative leadership focuses on alignment and control and is represented by the hierarchical and bureaucratic functions of the organization. *Enabling leadership* works to catalyze the conditions in which adaptive leadership can thrive and to manage the *entanglement* (described below) between the bureaucratic (administrative leadership) and emergent (adaptive leadership) functions of the organization. Managing entanglement involves two roles: (1) creating appropriate organizational conditions (or *enabling conditions*) to foster effective adaptive leadership in places where innovation and adaptability are needed, and (2) facilitating the flow of knowledge and creativity from adaptive structures into administrative structures. Enabling leadership occurs at all levels of the organization (as well as within the adaptive dynamic), but the nature of this role will vary by hierarchical level and position.

In complexity leadership theory, these three leadership functions are intertwined in a manner that we refer to as *entanglement* (Kontopoulos, 1993). Entanglement describes a dynamic relationship between the formal *top-down, administrative forces* (i.e., bureaucracy) and the informal, *com-*

plexly adaptive emergent forces (i.e., CAS) of social systems. In organizations, administrative and adaptive leadership interact and may help or oppose one another. Administrative leadership can function in conjunction with adaptive leadership or can thwart it with overly authoritarian or bureaucratic control structures. Adaptive leadership can work to augment the strategic needs of administrative leadership, it can rebel against it, or it can act independently of administrative leadership. The enabling leadership function helps to ameliorate these problems; it serves primarily to enable effective adaptive leadership, but to accomplish this it must tailor the behaviors of administrative and adaptive leadership so that they function in tandem with one another.

In formal organizations, one cannot disentangle bureaucracy from CAS. Earlier we stated that CAS are the basic unit of analysis in a complex system. However, as all organizations are bureaucracies (there are no such things as "postbureaucratic" organizations, see Hales, 2002), CAS necessarily interact with formal bureaucratic structures in organizations. Moreover, there are times and conditions in which rationalized structure and coordination (e.g., hierarchical authority) need to be emphasized in sub-units (e.g., when the environment is stable and the system seeks to enhance profits). At other times or conditions, firm may prefer to emphasize complexity and CAS (e.g., when environments are volatile or the competition's flexibility is threatening).

A role of enabling leadership at the strategic level (Jaques, 1989), then, is to manage the coordination rhythms, or oscillations, between relative importance of top-down, hierarchical dynamics and emergent complex adaptive systems (Thomas, Kaminska-Labbé, & McKelvey, 2005). Ultimately, neither can be separated from the other in knowledge producing organizations, for such firms must nurture both creativity and exploitation to be fit.

Based on this, we can summarize the main points we have developed thus far as follows:

- Complexity leadership theory provides an overarching framework that describes administrative leadership, adaptive leadership and enabling leadership; it provides for entanglement among the three leadership roles and, in particular, between CAS and bureaucracy.
- *Adaptive leadership* is an emergent, interactive dynamic that is the primary source by which adaptive outcomes are produced in a firm. *Administrative leadership* is the actions of individuals and groups in formal managerial roles who plan and coordinate organizational activities (the bureaucratic function). *Enabling leadership* serves to enable (catalyze) adaptive dynamics and help manage the entanglement between administrative and adaptive leadership (by fostering

enabling conditions and managing the innovation-to-organization interface). These roles are *entangled* within and across people and actions.

We now expand the elements introduced by complexity leadership theory, beginning with administrative leadership and then moving into the adaptive and enabling roles.

Administrative Leadership

Administrative leadership refers to the actions of individuals in formal managerial roles who plan and coordinate organizational activities (e.g., the bureaucratic function). Administrative leaders (among other things) structure tasks, engage in planning, build vision, acquire resources to achieve goals (Dougherty & Hardy, 1996; Shalley & Gilson, 2004), manage crises (Mumford & Licuanan, 2004) and personal conflicts (Jehn, 1997), and manage organizational strategy. The nature of this administrative leadership varies within the hierarchical level of the system. Administrators at Jaques' (1989) strategic level engage in planning, coordination, resource acquisition (Osborn & Hunt, 2006), and structuring conditions related to strategy (Marion & Uhl-Bien, 2007). At Jaques' organizational level, administrators implement more focused planning and coordination of creative operations, manage resource allocation, and structure conditions within which adaptive leadership occurs.

Administrative leadership is a top-down function based on authority and position, thus it possess the power to make decisions for the organization. However, within the structure described by complexity leadership theory, administrative leadership is advised to exercise its authority with consideration of the firm's need for creativity, learning, and adaptability (i.e., adaptive leadership), for its actions can have significant impact on these dynamics. A decision, for example, to exercise profitable efficiency in a volatile environment could deprive a firm of much needed adaptive capacity.

Adaptive Leadership

Adaptive leadership is an emergent, interactive dynamic that produces adaptive outcomes in a social system. It is a collaborative change movement that emerges nonlinearly from interactive exchanges, or, more specifically, from the "spaces between" agents (cf. Bradbury & Lichtenstein, 2000; Drath, 2001; Lichtenstein et al., 2006). That is, it originates in struggles among agents and groups over conflicting needs, ideas, or preferences; it results in movements, alliances of people, ideas, or technologies, and cooperative efforts. Adaptive leadership is a complex dynamic rather than a person (although people are, importantly, involved); we label it leadership because it is *a*, and, arguably, *the*, proximal source of change in an organization.

Adaptive leadership emerges from asymmetrical interaction (the notion of complexity and asymmetry is developed by Cilliers, 1998). We propose two types of asymmetry: that related to *authority* and that related to *preferences* (which include differences in knowledge, skills, beliefs, etc.). If an interaction is largely one sided and authority based, then the leadership event can be labeled as top-down. If authority asymmetry is less one-sided and more preference oriented, then the leadership event is more likely based on interactive dynamics driven by differences in preferences.

Struggles over asymmetrical preference differences foster adaptive change outcomes (thus the earlier statement that change emerges from the spaces between agents). Adaptive change is produced by the clash of existing but (seemingly) incompatible ideas, knowledge, and technologies; it takes the form of new knowledge and creative ideas, learning, or adaptation. A familiar form of this change occurs when two interdependent individuals who are debating conflicting perceptions of a given issue suddenly, and perhaps simultaneously, generate a new understanding of that issue—this can be considered an "aha" moment. The "aha" is a nonlinear product of a combination of the original perceptions, of the discarding of untenable arguments and the fusion of what is tenable, or perhaps of the rejection of original ideas as untenable and the creation of a totally new idea. It represents a process of seeing beyond original assumptions to something not bounded by those assumptions. Moreover, it cannot be claimed by any one individual, but rather is a product of the interactions among individuals (i.e., it is produced in the "spaces between"; Bradbury & Lichtenstein, 2000).

Adaptive leadership is recognized as such when it has significance and impact— significance is the potential usefulness of new, creative knowledge or adaptive ideas and impact refers to the degree to which other agents external to the generative set embrace and use the new knowledge or idea. The significance of an adaptive moment is related to the expertise of the agents who generate that moment (Mumford, Scott, Gaddis, & Strange, 2002; Weisberg, 1999) and to their capacity for creative thinking (Mumford, Connelly, & Gaddis, 2003). Expertise and creativity are not necessarily co-resident in an adaptive event, of course. Quite obviously, creative individuals without training in physics are not going to advance that field, but neither are, one might argue, two physicists who are unable or unwilling to break out of their paradigmatic assumptions. Complex systems depend on the former (expertise) and stimulate the latter (creativity).

Moreover, impact can be independent of significance because impact is influenced by (among other things) the authority and reputation of the agents who generated the idea, the degree to which an idea captures the imagination or to which its implications are understood, or whether the idea can generate enough support to exert an impact (see Arthur, 1989, for discussion). Thus an insignificant idea can have considerable circulation.

Complexity leadership theory describes dynamics in which adaptive dynamics emerge and generate creative and adaptive, knowledge that exhibits sufficient significance and impact to create change. Adaptive leadership is not an act of an individual, but rather a dynamic of interdependent agents (i.e., CAS). To exhibit significance and impact, adaptive leadership must be embedded in an appropriately structured, neural-like network of CAS and agents (within the context of CAS; i.e., network dynamics) and exhibit significance and impact that generate change in the social system.

Network Dynamics

Network dynamics refer to the contexts and mechanisms that enable adaptive leadership. As defined above, *context* is the interactive ambiance within which complex dynamics occur, and *mechanisms* are the dynamic patterns of behavior that produce complex outcomes. In interactive and interdependent networks, adaptive ideas, whether small or large, emerge and interact in much the same way that pairs or groups of agents interact. The contexts that shape those ideas include networks of interaction, complex patterns of conflicting constraints, patterns of tension, interdependent relationships, rules of action, direct and indirect feedback loops, and rapidly changing environmental demands. The mechanisms that emerge include resonance (i.e., correlated action; see below) and aggregation of ideas, catalytic behaviors (behaviors that speed or enable certain activities; Kauffman, 1993), generation of both dynamically stable and unstable behaviors, dissipation of built up tension as phase transitions (Prigogine, 1997), nonlinear change, information flow and pattern formation, and accreting nodes[2] (ideas that rapidly expand in importance and which accrete related ideas) (see Figure 8.1). In complex networks, ideas emerge, combine, diverge, become extinct, conflict with one another, adapt and change, and increase in complexity. The primary outputs of this complex dynamic are adaptability, creativity, and learning.

Adaptive leadership emerges within this complex milieu of contexts and mechanisms—it exists in complex network contexts and produces (and is produced by) complex mechanisms. There are two interactive and

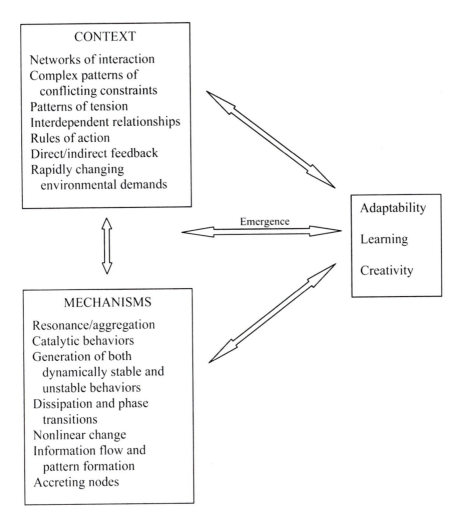

Figure 8.1.   The emergence dynamic.

interdependent levels of pertinent activity: (1) the interaction of agents and CAS that produce ideas and knowledge, and (2) the interaction of the ideas and knowledge to produce even more complex ideas and knowledge. Loosely adapting Cohen, March, and Olsen's (1972) garbage can metaphor, we can envision this as a complex garbage can in which agents and CAS and contexts and mechanisms and ideas and knowledge swirl. The end result is emergent creativity, learning, and adaptability at all levels of the system and at multiple scales of importance.

Emergence

Earlier we defined the complex change process in terms of "spaces between" and struggles over diverse ideas. We now define it more precisely in terms of emergence. Emergence involves two, interdependent mechanisms: (1) the reformulation of existing elements to produce outcomes that are qualitatively different from the original elements; and (2) self-organization. Reformulation competes with theories of natural selection or human intelligence as a source of unique change (but, importantly, it does not preempt the involvement of other such dynamics; see Kauffman, 1993, for example). Reformulation is defined as the expansion, parsing, amplification, transformation, and combination of multiple interacting, often conflicting, elements under conditions of tension and asymmetrical information. It is produced by complex (as opposed to complicated) interactive mechanisms within appropriately structured contexts; thus reformulation is intimately linked to the random nature of interaction in complex networks and outcomes can be unpredictable and nonlinear. The essence of the original elements is transformed in a manner that gives new meaning or interpretation to the resulting outcome. That is, the system changes in a fundamental way.

Wikipedia defines self-organization as a process in which the "internal organization of a system, normally an open system, increases in complexity without being guided or managed by an outside source" (Wikipedia, n.d.) This phenomenon is well documented in physics, biology, and the social sciences (see the above Wikipedia entry on self-organization for examples). We modify this definition for leadership studies, defining it in terms of resonating reformulation events (Marion & Uhl-Bien, 2001). Resonance is defined as acting in concert; it refers more specifically to situations in which the behaviors of two or more agents are interdependent. Thus clusters of cars speeding down a highway are resonating together. Self-organization, then, is a movement in which different reformulation activities find common cause. The modern terrorist movement, for example, is a self-organized event (Marion & Uhl-Bien, 2003). Importantly, human volition (e.g., managerial coordination) can play important roles in our definition of self-organization; however, volition is not necessarily determinative of self-organizing behaviors but is rather an actor in this dynamic.

We now formally define adaptive leadership:

Definition: Adaptive leadership is defined as emergent change behaviors under conditions of interaction, interdependence, asymmetrical information, complex network dynamics, and tension. Adaptive leadership manifests in CAS and interactions among agents rather than in individuals, and is recognizable when it has significance and impact.

Multilevel Adaptive Leadership

CAS, occur in all hierarchical levels of an organization. The emergent outcomes and the significance and impact of adaptive behaviors differ across hierarchical levels of course (Boal, Whitehead, Phillips, & Hunt, 1992; Hunt & Ropo, 1995; Phillips & Hunt, 1992). Broadly addressed, the adaptive outputs for the upper level of a hierarchy (what Jaques, 1989, called the strategic level) relates largely to emergent planning, resource acquisition, and strategic relationships with the environment (for discussion, see Marion & Uhl-Bien, 2007; see also Child & McGrath, 2001, for a useful discussion of interdependency among organizations). Adaptive outputs for the middle hierarchical levels (middle management, or what Jaques, 1989, called the organizational level) relates to emergence of focused planning, resource allocation, etc. That for the lower levels (Jaques' production level) relates to development of the core products of the organization; for knowledge producing organizations, this includes knowledge development, innovation, and adaptation (Osborn & Hunt, 2007, provide an extensive discussion of complexity and the levels perspective).

Enabling Leadership

The role of enabling leadership in the CLT framework is to directly foster and maneuver the conditions (e.g., context) that *catalyze* adaptive leadership and allow for emergence. Middle managers (Jaques, 1989) are often in a position to engage in enabling behaviors because of their access to resources and their direct involvement in the boundary conditions for the system's production level (see Osborn & Hunt, 2007). However, enabling leadership can be found anywhere. Its role seemingly overlaps, at times, that of administrative leadership in that it may be performed by agents acting in more managerial capacities. Moreover, a single agent or aggregate can perform either adaptive or enabling roles by merely changing hats as needed.

The roles of enabling leadership can be summarized as follows:

- Enabling leadership enables effective CAS dynamics by fostering *enabling conditions* that catalyze adaptive leadership and allow for emergence.
- Enabling leadership manages the entanglement between administrative and adaptive leadership; this includes (1) managing the organizational conditions in which adaptive leadership exists, and (2) helping disseminate innovative products of adaptive leadership

upward and through the formal managerial system (i.e., the innovation-to-organization interface, Dougherty & Hardy, 1996).

Enable Conditions That Catalyze Adaptive Leadership

One function of enabling leadership is to catalyze CAS dynamics that promote adaptive leadership. Catalyzing refers to activities that bring together the *enabling conditions (mechanisms and contexts)* necessary for adaptive leadership to emerge. As described earlier, complex networks conducive to adaptive leadership are (among other things) interactive, moderately interdependent, and infused with tension. Enabling leadership, then, fosters complex networks by (1) fostering interaction, (2) fostering interdependency, and (3) injecting adaptive tension to help motivate and coordinate the interactive dynamic.

Interaction.   Effective network conditions are catalyzed first by **interaction**. Interaction produces the network of linkages across which information flows and connects. Enabling leaders cannot create the sophisticated dynamic linkages that characterize complex networks, nor can they accurately precalculate what constitutes the right amount of coupling. Rather, such networks are self-organizing. They can, however, create the general structure of complex networks and the conditions in which sophisticated networks can evolve. For example, from an organizational level (Jacques, 1989), enabling leadership can foster interaction through such strategies as open architecture work places, self-selected work groups, electronic work groups (email, etc.), and by management-induced scheduling or rules structuring.

Moreover, the interactive imperative is not bounded to the immediate work group, but extends to interactions with other groups (CAS) and with the environment. Interaction with other CAS fosters cross-group initiatives, possible aggregation of different ideas into larger ideas, a degree of coordination across efforts, and the importation of information that may inform the target work group.

Further, at Jaques (1989) strategic level, enabling leadership helps foster interactions of organizational CAS with environmental dynamics. This serves at least two purposes: it enables importation of fresh information into the creative dynamic (Boisot, 1998), and it broadens the organization's capacity to adapt to environmental changes and conditions beyond the adaptive capacity of strategic leadership acting alone. Marion and Uhl-Bien (2007) propose that organizational adaptability should even be a significant element of strategic planning because of its capability to adapt quickly and competently to environmental changes; a particularly potent example is evident in the adaptive strategies of terrorist networks (see Marion & Uhl-Bien, 2003). For a more extensive discussion of complexity and strategic leadership, see Boal and Schultz (2007).

Individual agents in adaptive networks can act in an enabling role by adopting behaviors that enhance their interactive contributions. For example, they can enlarge their personal networks to increase the amount of access and network resources they can bring to the table. Moreover, they can contribute to the flow of information across CAS by keeping themselves informed and knowledgeable on issues important to the firm and their field and by framing issues appropriate to the perspectives of the others with whom they are interacting. They can also monitor the environment (e.g., political, economic, social, national, international, technological) to understand the nature of the forces that are influencing the adaptive dynamic.

Interdependency.   Interaction alone is insufficient for complex functioning; the agents in a system must also be **interdependent**. While interaction permits the movement and dynamic interplay of information, interdependency creates pressure to act on information. Interdependency's potency derives from naturally occurring (emergent) networks of conflicting constraints. Conflicting constraints manifest when the well-being of one agent is inversely dependent on the well-being of another, or when the information broadcasted by one agent is incompatible with that broadcasted by another agent. Such constraints pressure agents to adjust their actions and to elaborate their information.

At the organizational level (Jacques, 1989) there are a number of ways to manage conditions that catalyze interdependency mechanisms. One useful tool for promoting interdependency is to allow measured autonomy for informal behavior (see also Shalley & Gilson, 2004). Autonomy permits conflicting constraints to emerge and enables agents to work through those constraints without interference from formal authorities. Nordstrom illustrates this approach in a statement in their employee handbook:

> We also encourage you to present your own ideas. Your buyers have a great deal of autonomy, and are encouraged to seek out and promote new fashion directions at all times ... and we encourage you to share your concerns, suggestions and ideas. (Pfeffer, 2005, p. 99)

A major function of leaders has historically been to solve problems, to intervene when dilemmas arise or when individuals differ on task-related activities. Such action, however, can stifle interdependency and limit adaptive mechanisms. Complexity leadership theory proposes circumspection by administrative leaders in such matters, to resist the temptation to create an atmosphere in which workers bring their work problems to management (see Alvesson & Sveningsson, 2003). Enabling leaders fosters such circumspection by mediating this issue with administrative leaders who are overly involved, by stifling one's own desire in administrative roles to act in this way, or even by implementing policy regarding the resolution of problems and task conflicts (see, for example, Snyder's, 1988, description of such implementation).

At the strategic level enabling leaders can foster interdependency with rules—not limiting bureaucratic rules but rules or conditions that apply pressure to coordinate (Eisenhardt, 1989; McKelvey et al., 2003). Microsoft's strategy for developing software, for example, is built on interactive work groups and rule-enabled interdependencies (Cusumano, 2001). Programmers operate independently and in small groups, but are periodically required to run their code against the code of other programmers. If there are problems, the team must repair the incompatibility before moving on. Microsoft calls this "sync and stabilize." The process imposes interdependency that can create cascading changes and elaboration in Microsoft's software. Microsoft gains the benefit of flexibility, adaptability, speed, and innovation while maintaining coordinated action.

At the individual level, agents engaging in enabling leadership recognize the importance of interdependency and they can function to foster coordinated efforts. Enabling agents refine or realign their information relative to the information of the other agents (Kauffman, 1993; Marion & Uhl-Bien, 2001) in ways that contribute to coevolution or coelaborating of ideas and information such that new, sometimes surprising information can emerge (Kauffman, 1993).

Tension.   Finally, since tension creates an imperative to act and to elaborate strategy, information, and adaptability, enabling leadership also works to foster **tension**. *Internal* tension can be enhanced by heterogeneity, a stimulus of interdependency and conflicting constraints. Heterogeneity refers to differences among agents in such things as skills, preferences, and outlooks (McKelvey, in press; Schilling & Steensma, 2001). When couched within a context of interdependency, heterogeneity pressures agents to adapt to their differences. At the upper echelon and organizational levels, enabling leadership promotes heterogeneity by (among other things) building an atmosphere in which such diversity is respected, with considered hiring practices, and by structuring work groups to enable interaction of diverse ideas. Enabling leadership also fosters internal tension by enabling an atmosphere that tolerates dissent and divergent perspectives on problems, one in which personnel are charged with resolving their differences and finding solutions to their problems (cf. Heifetz & Laurie, 2001).

Enabling leadership not only fosters internal tension, it judiciously injects tension as well—tension that derives *externally* in that it is not a natural function of informal dynamics. Upper- and midlevel enabling leaders inject tension with managerial pressures or challenges, by distributing resources in a manner that supports creative movements, and by creating demands for results. Enabling leaders can impose tension by dropping "seeds of emergence" (Marion & Uhl-Bien, 2001; McKelvey et al., 1999), or perturbations that have the potential of fostering learning and creativity. Such "seeds" include ideas, information, judiciously placed resources, new people, and the capacity to access unspecified resources (i.e., gateways that permit exploration; access to the Internet is an obvious example). Seeds are intended to stimulate the networked system, and their impact may be unpredictable.

At the individual level, agents can engage in enabling leadership by recognizing the creative value of tension and using it to foster productive discussions and interaction. They would not look to authority for answers, but rather commit to engaging in the process of adaptive problem solving. Enabling agents recognize the difference between task (or ideational) conflict (which can produce creative outcomes; Jehn, 1997), and interpersonal conflict (which is disruptive to social dynamics) and work to promote productive, task conflicts (Heifetz, 1994; Jehn, 1997; Lencioni, 2002). They contribute ideas and opinions, they play devil's advocate, and they address the "elephants on the table" that others try to ignore (Parks, 2005). They also recognize when a group is bogged down by consensus (Lencioni, 2002) that comes from lack of diversity, and expose the group to heterogeneous perspectives, bringing other people and ideas into the dynamic as necessary.

Enabling leadership can also emerge from within the adaptive function. Schreiber (2006), in a study of complexity leadership and risk factors, identified several interesting enabling dynamics in work groups (measurements from these observations were used in a follow-up multi-agent based simulation). Certain agents emerged, for example, who tended to induce interactions and establish interdependencies. Others were boundary spanners, or "agent[s] who most likely connect … to otherwise disjoint groups" (p. 136). Some agents emerged who were "likely to have the most interactions and to learn more knowledge" (p. 136). There were also agents "who can most quickly communicate to the organization at large" (p. 136). Lastly, some agents were "most likely to communicate new knowledge" (p. 136). Such agent-roles represent nodes in a neural network of agents (see, for example, Carley & Ren, 2001) and serve to enable (and operationalize) interaction, interdependency, and learning within CAS.

Managing the Entanglement Between Adaptive and Administrative Structures

A second function of the enabling leadership role is to manage the entanglement between CAS dynamics and formal administrative systems and structures. This involves using authority (where applicable), access to resources, and influence to keep the formal and informal organizational systems working in tandem rather than counter to one another (Dougherty, 1996). In this function, enabling leaders:

1. work to prevent administrative leaders from stifling or suppressing beneficial interactive dynamics and foster adaptive dynamics that are consistent with the strategy and mission of the organization (the administrative-adaptive interface); and
2. facilitate the integration of creative outcomes into the formal system (i.e., the innovation-to-organization interface; Dougherty & Hardy, 1996).

Managing the Administrative-Adaptive Interface. Regarding the first of these roles, enabling leaders help protect the CAS from external politics and top-down preferences. They serve to influence the policies and decisions of administrative leadership, including planning and resource allocation, to accommodate the needs of adaptive structures (Dougherty & Hardy, 1996). They also help align organizational strategy to the needs of CAS dynamics and convince administrative leadership when CAS dynamics are important for organizational strategy (Marion & Uhl-Bien, 2007).

Managing the conditions for adaptive leadership requires a different focus on planning and resource allocation. With regard to **planning,** Mumford et al. (in press) note a lack of consensus in the leadership literature about whether creativity is enabled or hampered by administrative planning (Bluedorn, Johnson, Cartwright, & Barringer, 1994; Finkelstein & Hambrick, 1996). Some scholars argue that planning provides the resources and structure that creative initiatives require while others argue that administrators cannot anticipate and plan the directions in which creative dynamics will flow (Mumford et al., in press). Complexity leadership theory (CLT) has similar concerns about planning. On the one hand, emergence is the product of informal adaptive behavior that would be hampered by top-down restrictions (Krause, 2004). On the other hand, the need to focus creative behaviors is legitimate; indeed unrestrained adaptive behavior would be expensive to support and could compromise rather that enhance the organization's strategic mission.

Framing the question for complexity leadership theory, we ask: Does planning enable or inhibit nonlinear emergence? Our short answer is: It depends on the nature of the plan. Planning for creativity must deal with significant uncertainties, including the fact that creativity by definition involves development of ideas that are currently unknowable (Popper, 1986), changing future environmental uncertainties, and uncertainty about whether creative ideas will become viable market solutions. Mumford and colleagues (Mumford et al., in press; Mumford, Schultz, & Osborn, 2002) propose evolving and flexible plans to deal with such uncertainties. They divide their planning model into five stages: (1) scanning, (2) template planning, (3) plan development, (4) forecasting, and (5) plan execution. These stages can be summarized as idea identification (scanning and template planning), plan development (including forecasting), and plan execution. Mumford et al. (2002) argue that plans should be adapted to the needs of each stage and that planning within these stages should be a continuous process in order to adjust for changes and unknowns that are certain to arise. Mumford et al. (in press) further argue that R&D programs must be understood in the long term and that leaders of R&D are managers of systemic dynamics rather than of day-to-day details.

Mumford et al. (in press) propose that organizational plans should impose limits that assure creative emergence is consistent with the core competencies (or theme) of the system. This focuses creativity around practical constraints without unduly dampening the creative spirit. We further propose that planners separate the creative process from the structure in which it occurs: The creative process itself (e.g., adaptive behaviors) should not be unduly managed or constrained by administrative planning and coordination; however that process should be couched within a larger planning structure similar to that proposed (above) by Mumford and his colleagues.

Therefore, our framework proposes that enabling leadership, in general, assumes a systemic relationship with complex dynamics, one in which the responsibility is to provide the framework and conditions within which enabling and adaptive leadership function. At Jaques' (1989) strategic level enabling leaders plan a trajectory for the adaptive process and have a long-term outlook (Marion & Uhl-Bien, 2007). Enabling leaders at Jaques' (1989) organizational level, in contrast, plan the context surrounding work; their function is more short-term than that of strategic leaders and is focused on the given stage of a plan at any given time.

With regard to **resources,** the literature on creativity has noted the importance of increasing the availability of information resources (Reiter-Palmon & Illies, 2004). Similarly, complex adaptive systems depend on flows of information resources, and when such flows are hindered, they do not operate effectively. Therefore, enabling leaders provide resources that enhance access to information (e.g., access to electronic databases). They coordinate acquisition and allocation of resources (money, supplies, information, personnel, etc.) that support creative, learning, and adaptive behaviors of CAS. Bonabeau and Meyer (2001) add that leaders can enhance the adaptive process by allowing physical resources (e.g., money, supplies, etc.) to follow emergent ideas (see also Dougherty & Hardy, 1996). This fosters motivation and creates tension related to scarce resources. Since personnel are resources, and diversity of personnel skills and preferences are important to the creative and adaptive functions of CAS, enabling leaders also promote diversity in hiring practices and policy actions.

Enabling leadership manages conditions consistent with the **strategy and mission** of the organization by articulating the mission of a project (e.g., Kennedy's mission to put Americans on the moon by 1970; see, for example, Jaussi & Dionne, 2003). Complexity leadership theory adds (as does Mumford et al., in press), however, that such missions should not be so specific that they restrict the creative process. They should be sufficiently flexible to change with changing conditions.

Strategy and mission consistency is fostered by discouraging non-useful adaptations. Adaptive leadership is, by design, unpredictable, and its emergent activities can evolve in directions that are contrary to the strategic mission of the organization. Enabling leaders help realignment of nonuseful adaptations by (for example) periodically evaluating adaptive outputs for a given stage of development relative to organizational mission-themes (see Mumford et al., in press), by clearly articulating the mission (described above), or by offering technical support that is consistent with organizational themes.

Enabling leaders promote behavior that advances strategic goals by dealing with crises that threaten to derail adaptive functions (Mumford et al., in press); by protecting the creative process from forces (e.g., boards or directors, other administrators, environmental pressures) that would limit the capacity of the organization or its subsystems to engage in creativity, learning, and adaptation; and by structuring conditions such as missions, physical conditions, crises, personal conflicts, and external threats in ways that support creative adaptive behaviors.

Managing the Innovation-to-Organization Interface.   In the second role identified above, enabling leaders help in the innovation-to-organization interface. Howell and Boies (2004) refer to this as championing. They argue, describing creative ideas, that:

> To overcome the social and political pressures imposed by an organization and convert them to its advantage, champions demonstrate personal com-

mitment to the idea, promote the idea ... through informal networks, and willingly risk their position and reputation to ensure its success.... [They] establish ... and maintain ... contact with top management, to keep them informed and enthusiastic about the project.... [A] new venture idea require[s] a champion to exert social and political effort to galvanize support for the concept. (p. 124)

As noted by Dougherty and Hardy (1996), formal organizational systems are often not structured to foster internal dissemination of innovation—rather, they tend to inhibit it. Because formal structures present obstacles for innovation-to-organization transference, power is needed to facilitate, orchestrate, and share innovative ideas and outcomes throughout the organization. "Unless product innovation has an explicit, organization-wide power basis, there is no generative force, no energy, for developing new products continuously and weaving them into ongoing functioning" (Dougherty & Hardy, 1996, p. 1146). They suggest that organizations adopt a "proinnovation" approach by moving beyond reliance on networks of personal power (a focus on individuals) and toward an organization-system base of power. Such a system would foster processes that "link the right people" and "emphasize the right criteria," as well as "allow resources to begin to flow to the right places" (Dougherty & Hardy, 1996, p. 1149). Enabling leaders can play an integral role in helping design and protect such a "pro-innovation" organizational system.

Enabling leadership also works with adaptive and administrative leadership to decide which creative outputs of the adaptive subsystem are the most appropriate to move forward into the broader bureaucratic structure. In conducting this function, Mumford et al. (in press) caution administrators to avoid assessing the creative output itself and to instead focus on assessing the degree to which activities are accomplishing the functions of the given stage of development. "Evaluation," they argue, "should be viewed as a developmental exercise with multiple cycles of evaluation and revision occurring in any stage before planning progresses to the next stage" (in press). Therefore, enabling leadership helps coordinate the interface between adaptive and administrative leadership by working for policies and strategies that enable complex dynamics and by adopting a "pro-innovation" environment that facilitates innovation-to-organization transference.

Summary
Complexity leadership theory, then, is a framework for studying emergent leadership dynamics in relationship to bureaucratic superstructures. CLT identifies three types of leadership, adaptive, enabling, and administrative, and proposes that they differ according to where they occur in the larger organizational hierarchy. A basic unit of analysis of CLT is complex

adaptive systems, which exist throughout the organization and are entangled with the bureaucratic functions such that they cannot be separated. CLT proposes that CAS, when functioning appropriately, provide an adaptive capability for the organization, and that bureaucracy provides an orienting and coordinating structure. A key role of enabling leadership is to effectively manage the entanglement between administrative and adaptive structures and behaviors in a manner that enhances the overall flexibility and effectiveness of the organization (Marion & Uhl-Bien, 2007). By focusing on emergent leadership dynamics, CLT implies that *leadership* only exists in, and is a function of, interaction; despite this, there are roles for individual *leaders* in interacting with (i.e., *enabling*) this dynamic.

CONCLUSION

As described by Rost (1991), leadership study has been bogged down in the periphery and content of leadership, and what is needed is "a new understanding of what leadership is, in a postindustrial school of leadership" (Rost, 1991, p. 181). In the present article we attempt to move toward such an understanding by developing a model of leadership based in complexity science. Complexity science is a modern "normal" science, the assumptions of which fit the dynamics of social, managerial, and organizational behavior in high velocity, knowledge-type environments (Henrickson & McKelvey, 2002). Complexity science allows us to develop leadership perspectives that extend beyond bureaucratic assumptions to add a view of leadership as *a complex interactive dynamic through which adaptive outcomes emerge*. This new perspective, which we label complexity leadership theory, recognizes that leadership is too complex to be described as only the act of an individual or individuals; rather, it is a complex interplay of many interacting forces.

Complexity leadership theory focuses primarily on the complex interactive dynamics of CAS and addresses how individuals interact with this dynamic to enable adaptive outcomes. CAS are the basic unit of analysis in complexity leadership theory. CAS are comprised of agents, however, and their roles in the CAS dynamic is important. Further, individuals (particularly those in positions of authority) can influence the CAS function and are likewise of interest in complexity leadership theory.

Research on CAS in complexity leadership theory should examine the dynamic (i.e., changing, interactive, temporal), informal interactive patterns that exist in and among organizational systems. This generates interesting questions for leadership research. For example, what patterns of behavior (what Allen, 2001, calls, structural attractors) do organizational CAS gravitate to and are there "patterns to those patterns" across systems? What is the specific generative nature of asymmetry and how does it function within a network dynamic? What enabling functions emerge from a complex network dynamic (such as those found by Schreiber, 2006)? What psychosocial dynamic occurs in the "spaces between agents" emergent dynamic? What are the mechanisms by which a social system moves from one stable pattern to another? What contexts are conducive to given patterns of interaction and how do enabling and administrative leaders help foster or stifle those contexts?

A complexity leadership approach adds to leadership research a consideration of the *mechanisms* and *contexts* by which change occurs and systems elaborate rather than a predominant focus on *variables*. To understand mechanisms requires methodology that is capable of analyzing the interactions of multiple agents over a period of time (see Hazy, 2007). Developing an understanding of the mechanisms that underlie complexity leadership theory and the conditions in which such mechanisms will emerge is critical as we move our theorizing forward into embedded context approaches in leadership (Osborn et al., 2002). There can be any number of mechanisms underlying the complexity leadership theory function. In this article we focus on such mechanisms as interaction among heterogeneous agents, annealing, requisite variety, information flows, catalyzing activities, and nonlinear emergence.

Research regarding complexity dynamics needs to capture the nature of mechanisms, which are nonlinearly changeable, unpredictable in the long term (and sometimes in the short-term), temporally based, and interactively and causally complex. We suggest two methodological strategies for doing this. First, qualitative procedures allow temporal evaluations and have been used in complexity studies (Bradbury & Lichtenstein, 2000). Second, various computer modeling procedures have been utilized for complexity research (see Hazy, 2007), the most common being agent based modeling (Carley & Svoboda, 1996) and system dynamic modeling (Sterman, 1994).

In agent based modeling, individual, computerized agents are programmed to interact according to certain defined rules of sociological and organizational engagement (Carley & Svoboda, 1996). Systems dynamics model the interaction of more global variables and dynamics with equations that define their relationships. In either case, a common approach is to measure certain characteristics of a social group (e.g., organizational work groups) and to use that data as initial conditions in a simulation. This obviates the need to make detailed, onsite observations across time and permits the researcher to experiment with "what-if" scenarios (e.g., what if hierarchical centralization is increased). Jim Hazy has provided an excellent review of simulation procedures elsewhere in this edition; see also Guastello's article in this edition for a statistics-based, research strategy, and Plowman, Baker, et al. (2007) and Plowman, Solansky, et al. (2007) for a qualitative methodology.

In sum, in this chapter we develop and outline key elements of complexity leadership theory. We argue that while the knowledge era calls for a new leadership paradigm, much of leadership theory still promotes an approach aimed at incentivizing workers to follow vision-led, top-down control by chief executive officers (Bennis, 1999; Zaccaro & Klimoski, 2001). Though this approach fits recent trends toward performance management and accountability, it can stifle a firm's innovation and fitness (Marion & Uhl-Bien, 2001; Schneider & Somers, 2006). We propose that complexity leadership theory offers a new way of perceiving leadership—a theoretical framework for approaching the study of leadership that moves beyond the managerial logics of the Industrial Age to meet the new leadership requirements of the Knowledge Era.

ACKNOWLEDGMENT

We wish to express deep appreciation to Richard Osborn at Wayne State University, who served as editor for this paper. His insight and attention to detail was of tremendous help in developing the argument for complexity leadership theory.

NOTES

1. There are other problem-solving approaches in the literature. Complex systems can, for example, respond to the accumulation of tension with phase transitions to new states (McKelvey, 2006; Prigogine, 1997). All problem-solving strategies, however, are, in some fashion, driven by tension.
2. The notion of accreting nodes is derived from related work in fractal geometry; see, for example Mandelbrot (1983).

REFERENCES

Achtenhagen, L., Melin, L., Mullern, T., & Ericson, T. (2003). Leadership: The role of interactive strategizing. In A. Pettigrew, R. Whittington, L. Melin, C. Sanchez-Runde, F. A. J. Van Den Bosch, W. Ruigrok & T. Numagami (Eds.), *Innovative forms of organizing: International perspectives* (pp. 49-71). London: Sage.

Allen, P. (2001). A complex systems approach to learning in adaptive networks. *International Journal of Innovation Management, 5,* 149-180.

Alvesson, M., & Sveningsson, S. (2003). The great disappearing act: Difficulties in doing "leadership." *The Leadership Quarterly, 14,* 359-381.

Arthur, W. B. (1989). The economy and complexity. In D. L. Stein (Ed.), *Lectures in the sciences of complexity* (Vol. 1, pp. 713-740). Redwood City, CA: Addison-Wesley.

Ashby, W. R. (1960). *Design for a brain* (2nd ed.). New York: Wiley.

Bak, P. (1996). *How nature works.* New York: Copernicus.

Bamford, J. D., Gomes-Casseres, B., & Robinson, M. S. (2002). *Mastering alliance strategy.* San Francisco: Jossey-Bass.

Barkema, H. G., Baum, J. A. C., & Mannix, E. A. (2002). Management challenges in a new time. *Academy of Management Journal, 45*(5), 916-930.

Barnard, C. I. (1938). *The functions of the executive.* Cambridge, MA: Harvard University Press.

Bass, B. M. (1985). *Leadership and performance beyond expectations.* New York: Free Press.

Bedeian, A. G., & Hunt, J. G. (2006). Academic amnesia and vestigial assumptions of our forefathers. *The Leadership Quarterly, 17*(2), 190-205.

Bennis, W. G. (1999). Becoming a leader of leaders. In R. Gibson (Ed.), *Rethinking the future* (pp. 148-163). London: Brealey.

Bettis, R. A., & Hitt, M. A. (1995). The new competitive landscape. *Strategic Management Journal, 7*(13), 7-19.

Bluedorn, A. C., Johnson, R. A., Cartwright, D. K., & Barringer, B. R. (1994). The interface and convergence of the strategic management and organizational environment domains *Journal of Management, 20*(2), 201-262.

Boal, K., & Schlultz, P. (2007). Storytelling, time, and evolution: The role of strategic leadership in complex adaptive systems. *The Leadership Quarterly, 18*(4), 411-428.

Boal, K., Whitehead, C. J., Phillips, R., & Hunt, J. (1992). *Strategic leadership: A multiorganizational-level perspective.* Westport, CT: Quorum.

Boisot, M. H. (1998). *Knowledge assets: Securing competitive advantage in the information economy.* Oxford, England: Oxford University Press.

Bonabeau, E., & Meyer, C. (2001). Swarm intelligence: A whole new way to think about business. *Harvard Business Review, 79*(5), 107-114.

Bradbury, H., & Lichtenstein, B. (2000). Relationality in organizational research: Exploring *the space between. Organization Science, 11,* 551-564.

Carley, K. (1997). Organizational adaptation. *Annals of Operations Research, 75,* 25-47.

Carley, K., & Hill, V. (2001). Structural change and learning within organizations. In A. Lomi & E. R. Larsen (Eds.), *Dynamics of organizational societies* (pp. 63-92). Cambridge, MA: AAAI/MIT Press.

Carley, K., & Lee, J. S. (1998). Dynamic organizations: Organizational adaptation in a changing environment. *Advances in Strategic Management: A Research Annual, 15,* 269-297.

Carley, K., & Ren, Y. (2001). *Tradeoffs between performance and adaptability for c^3i architectures* (part of the A2C2 project supported in part by the Office of Naval Research). Pittsburg, PA: Carnegie Mellon University.

Carley, K., & Svoboda, D. M. (1996). Modeling organizational adaptation as a simulated annealing process. *Sociological Methods and Research, 25*(1), 138-168.

Child, J., & McGrath, R. G. (2001). Organizations unfettered: Organizational form in an information-intensive economy. *The Academy of Management Journal, 44*(6), 1135-1149.

Cilliers, P. (1998). *Complexity and postmodernism: Understanding complex systems.* London: Routledge.

Cilliers, P. (2001). Boundaries, hierarchies and networks in complex systems. *International Journal of Innovation Management, 5*, 135-147.

Cohen, M. D., March, J. G., & Olsen, J. P. (1972). A garbage can model of organizational choice. *Administrative Science Quarterly, 17*, 1-25.

Conger, J. A. (1999). Charismatic and transformational leadership in organizations: An insider's perspective on these developing streams of research. *The Leadership Quarterly, 10*(2), 145-179.

Coveney, P. (2003). *Self-organization and complexity: A new age for theory, computation and experiment.* Paper presented at the Nobel symposium on self-organization, Karolinska Institutet, Stockholm.

Cusumano, M. (2001). Focusing creativity: Microsoft's "synch and stabilize" approach to software product development. In I. Nonaka & T. Nishiguchi (Eds.), *Knowledge emergence: Social, technical, and evolutionary dimensions of knowledge creation* (pp. 111-123). Oxford, England: Oxford University Press.

Davenport, T. H. (2001). Knowledge work and the future of management. In W. G. Bennis, G. M. Spreitzer & T. G. Cummings (Eds.), *The future of leadership: Today's top leadership thinkers speak to tomorrow's leaders* (pp. 41-58). San Francisco: Jossey-Bass.

Day, D. V. (2000). Leadership development: A review in context. *The Leadership Quarterly, 11*(4), 581-613.

Dooley, K. J. (1996, 10.26.96). *Complex adaptive systems: A nominal definition.* Retrieved September, 2006, from http://www.eas.asu.edu/~kdooley/casopdef.html

Dougherty, D. (1996). Organizing for innovation. In S. R. Clegg, C. Hardy, & W. Nord (Eds.), *Handbook of organization studies* (pp. 424-439). London: Sage.

Dougherty, D., & Hardy, C. (1996). Sustained product innovation in large, mature organizations: Overcoming innovation-to-organization problems. *Academy of Management Journal, 39*, 1120-1153.

Drath, W. (2001). *The deep blue sea: Rethinking the source of leadership.* San Francisco: Jossey-Bass & Center for Creative Leadership.

Drucker, P. F. (1998). Management's new paradigms. *Forbes, 162*(7), 152-170.

Drucker, P. F. (1999). *Management challenges for the 21st century.* New York: HarperCollins.

Eisenhardt, K. (1989). Making fast strategic decisions in high-velocity environments. *Academy of Management Journal, 32*, 543-576.

Finkelstein, S., & Hambrick, D. C. (1996). *Strategic leadership: Top executives and their effects on organizations.* St. Paul, MN: West.

Fletcher, J. K. (2004). The paradox of postheroic leadership: An essay on gender, power, and transformational change. *Leadership Quarterly, 15,* 647-661.

Goodwin, B. (1994). *How the leopard changed its spots: The evolution of complexity.* New York: Charles Scribner's Sons.

Gronn, P. (1999). *A realist view of leadership.* Paper presented at the educational leaders for the new millennium—Leaders with soul. ELO-AusAsia On-line Conference.

Gronn, P. (2002). Distributed leadership as a unit of analysis. *The Leadership Quarterly, 13,* 423-451.

Guastello, S. (in press). Nonlinear dynamics and leadership emergence. *The Leadership Quarterly.*

Halal, W. E. (Ed.). (1998). *The infinite resource: Mastering the boundless power of knowledge.* New York: Jossey-Bass.

Halal, W. E., & Taylor, K. B. (Eds.). (1999). *Twenty-first century economics: Perspectives of socioeconomics for a changing world.* New York: Macmillan.

Hales, C. (2002). "Bureaucracy-lite" and continuities in managerial work. *British Journal of Management, 13,* 51.

Hazy, J. (2007). Computer models of leadership: Foundations for a new discipline or meaningless diversion? *The Leadership Quarterly, 18*(4), 391-410.

Heckscher, C. (1994). Defining the post-bureaucratic type. In C. Heckscher & A. Donnellon (Eds.), *The post-bureaucratic organization: New perspectives on organizational change* (pp. 14-62). Thousand Oaks, CA: Sage.

Hedlund, G. (1994). A model of knowledge management and the N-form corporation. *Strategic Management Journal, 15,* 73-90.

Heifetz, R. A. (1994). *Leadership without easy answers.* Cambridge, MA: Harvard University Press.

Heifetz, R. A., & Laurie, D. L. (2001). The work of leadership. *Harvard Business Review, 79*(11), 131-141.

Heifetz, R. A., & Linsky, M. (2002). *Leadership on the line: Staying alive through the dangers of leading.* Boston: Harvard University Press.

Henrickson, L., & McKelvey, B. (2002). Foundations of new social science: Institutional legitimacy from philosophy, complexity science, postmodernism, and agent-based modeling. *Proceedings of the National Academy of Sciences, 99*(Supp. 3), 7288-7297.

Hernes, G. (1998). Real virtuality. In P. Hedström & R. Swedberg (Eds.), *Social mechanisms: An analytical approach to social theory* (pp. 74-101). Cambridge, England: Cambridge University Press.

Hitt, M. A. (1998). Presidential address: Twenty-first century organizations: Business firms, business schools, and the academy. *The Academy of Management Review, 23,* 218-224.

Hogue, M., & Lord, R. G. (2007). A multilevel, complexity theory approach to understanding gender bias in leadership. *The Leadership Quarterly, 18*(4), 370-390.

Holland, J. H. (1995). *Hidden order.* Reading, MA: Addison-Wesley.

Homans, G. C. (1950). *The human group.* New York: Harcourt, Brace & World.

Hosking, D. M. (1988). Organizing, leadership and skilful process. *Journal of Management Studies, 25,* 147-166.

House, R. J., & Mitchell, T. (1974). A path-goal theory of leader effectiveness. *Journal of Contemporary Business*, 81-97.

Howell, J. M., & Boies, K. (2004). Champions of technological innovation: The influence of contextual knowledge, role orientation, idea generation, and idea promotion on champion emergence. *The Leadership Quarterly*, *15*(1), 123-143.

Hunt, J. (1999). Transformational/charismatic leadership's transformation of the field: An historical essay. *The Leadership Quarterly*, *10*(2), 129-144.

Hunt, J., & Ropo, A. (1995). Multi-level leadership—grounded theory and mainstream theory applied to the case of general motors. *The Leadership Quarterly*, *6*(3), 379-412.

Huxham, C., & Vangen, S. (2000). Leadership in the shaping and implementation of collaboration agendas: How things happen in a (not quite) joined-up world. *Academy of Management Journal*, *43*(6), 1159-1175.

Ilinitch, A. Y., D'Aveni, R. A., & Lewin, A. (1996). New organizational forms and strategies for managing in hypercompetitive environments. *Organization Science*, *7*, 211-220.

Jaques, E. (1989). *Requisite organization*. Arlington, VA: Cason Hall.

Jaussi, K. S., & Dionne, S. D. (2003). Leading for creativity: The role of unconventional leadership behavior. *The Leadership Quarterly*, *14*, 475-498.

Jehn, K. A. (1997). A qualitative analysis of conflict types and dimensions in organizational groups. *Administrative Science Quarterly*, *42*, 530-557.

Jennings, J., & Haughton, L. (2000). *It's not the big that eat the small … it's the fast that eat the slow*. New York: HarperBusiness.

Jones, G. R. (2000). *Organizational theory* (3rd ed.). Reading, MA: Addison-Wesley.

Kauffman, S. A. (1993). *The origins of order*. New York: Oxford University Press.

Kontopoulos, K. M. (1993). *The logics of social structure*. Cambridge, England: Cambridge University Press.

Krause, D. E. (2004). Influence-based leadership as a determinant of the inclination to innovate and of innovation-related behaviors: An empirical investigation. *The Leadership Quarterly*, *15*(1), 79-102.

Lencioni, P. (2002). *The five dysfunctions of a team: A leadership fable*. San Francisco: Jossey-Bass.

Levy, S. (1992). *Artificial life: The quest for new creation*. New York: Random House.

Lewin, A. (1999). *Complexity: Life at the edge of chaos* (2nd ed.). Chicago: University of Chicago Press.

Lewin, K. (1952). Group decision and social change. In G. E. Swanson, T. M. Newcomb & E. L. Hartley (Eds.), *Readings in social psychology* (Rev. ed., pp. 459-473). New York: Holt.

Lewin, R. (1992). *Complexity: Life at the edge of chaos*. New York: Macmillan.

Lichtenstein, B., Uhl-Bien, M., Marion, R., Seers, A., Orton, D., & Schreiber, C. (2006). Complexity leadership theory: An interactive perspective on leading in complex adaptive systems. *Emergence: Complexity and Organization*, *8*(4), 2-12.

Lorenz, E. (1993). *The essence of chaos*. Seattle: University of Washington Press.

Mackenzie, K. (2006). The LAMPE theory of organizational leadership. In F. Yammarino & F. Dansereau (Eds.), *Research in multi-level issues* (Vol. 5, pp. 345-428). Oxford, England: Elsevier Science.

Mandelbrot, B. B. (1983). *The fractal geometry of nature.* New York: W.H. Freeman.

Manville, B., & Ober, J. (2003, January). Beyond empowerment: Building a company of citizens. *Harvard Business Review,* 48-53.

Marion, R. (1999). *The edge of organization: Chaos and complexity theories of formal social organizations.* Newbury Park, CA: Sage.

Marion, R., & Uhl-Bien, M. (2001). Leadership in complex organizations. *The Leadership Quarterly, 12,* 389-418.

Marion, R., & Uhl-Bien, M. (2003). Complexity theory and al-Qaeda: Examining complex leadership. *Emergence: A Journal of Complexity Issues in Organizations and Management, 5,* 56-78.

Marion, R., & Uhl-Bien, M. (2007). Complexity and strategic leadership. In R. Hooijberg, J. Hunt, J. Antonakis, K. Boal, & N. Lane (Eds.), *Being there even when you are not: Leading through structures, systems, and processes* (pp. 273-287). Amsterdam: Elsevier.

McKelvey, B. (2001). Energizing order-creating networks of distributed intelligence. *International Journal of Innovation Management, 5,* 181-212.

McKelvey, B. (in press). Emergent strategy via Complexity Leadership: Using complexity science and adaptive tension to build distributed intelligence. In M. Uhl-Bien & R. Marion (Eds.), *Complexity and leadership, Part I. Conceptual foundations.* Charlotte, NC: Information Age.

McKelvey, B., & Boisot, M. H. (2003). *Transcendental organizational foresight in non-linear contexts.* Paper presented at the INSEAD Conference on Expanding Perspectives on Strategy Processes, Fontainebleau, France.

McKelvey, B., Marion, R., & Uhl-Bien, M. (2003). *A simple-rule approach to CEO leadership in the 21st century.* Paper presented at the University of Lecce Conference on New Approaches to Strategic Management, Ostuni, Italy.

McKelvey, B., Mintzberg, H., Petzinger, T., Prusak, L., Senge, P., & Shultz, R. (1999). The gurus speak: Complexity and organizations. *Emergence: A journal of complexity issues in organizations and management, 1*(1), 73-91.

Miles, R. E. (1998). The spherical network organization. In W. E. Halal (Ed.), *The infinite resource: Creating and leading the knowledge enterprise* (pp. 111-121). San Francisco: Jossey-Bass.

Miles, R. E., Snow, C. C., Matthews, J. A., & Miles, G. (1999). Cellular-network organizations. In W. E. Halal & K. B. Taylor (Eds.), *Twenty-first century economics* (pp. 155-173). New York: Macmillan.

Mumford, M., Bedell-Avers, K. E., & Hunter, S. T. (in press). Planning for innovation: A multi-level perspective. In M. D. Mumford, S. T. Hunter & K. E. Bedell (Eds.), *Research in multi-level issues.* Oxford, England: Elsevier.

Mumford, M., Connelly, S., & Gaddis, B. (2003). How creative leaders think: Experimental findings and cases. *The Leadership Quarterly, 14*(4/5, Pt. 1), 411-432.

Mumford, M. D., & Licuanan, B. (2004). Leading for innovation: Conclusions, issues, and directions. *The Leadership Quarterly, 15*(1), 163-171.

Mumford, M. D., Schultz, R. A., & Osborn, H. K. (2002). Planning in organizations: Performance as a multi-level phenomenon. In F. J. Yammarino & F. Dansereau (Eds.), *Research in multi-level issues: The many faces of multi-level issues* (pp. 3-35). Oxford, England: Elsevier.

Mumford, M. D., Scott, G. M., Gaddis, B., & Strange, J. M. (2002). Leading creative people: Orchestrating expertise and relationships. *The Leadership Quarterly, 13*(6), 705-750.

Nonaka, I., & Nishiguchi, T. (2001). Introduction: Knowledge emergence. In I. Nonaka & T. Nishiguchi (Eds.), *Knowledge emergence: Social, technical, and evolutionary dimensions of knowledge creation* (pp. 3-9). Oxford, England: Oxford University Press.

Osborn, R., & Hunt, J. (2007). Leadership and the choice of order: Complexity and hierarchical perspectives near the edge of chaos. *The Leadership Quarterly, 18*(4), 319-340.

Osborn, R., Hunt, J. G., & Jauch, L. R. (2002). Toward a contextual theory of leadership. *The Leadership Quarterly, 13*, 797-837.

Parks, S. D. (2005). *Leadership can be taught: A bold approach for a complex world.* Boston: Harvard Business School Press.

Pearce, C. L., & Conger, J. A. (2003). *Shared leadership: Reframing the hows and whys of leadership.* Thousand Oaks, CA: Sage.

Pfeffer, J. (2005). Producing sustainable competitive advantage through the effective management of people. *The Academy of Management Executive, 19*(4), 95-108.

Phillips, R., & Hunt, J. (Eds.). (1992). *Strategic leadership: A multiorganizational-level perspective* Westport, CT: Quorum Books.

Plowman, D., Baker, L. T., Beck, T., Kulkarni, M., Solansky, S., & Travis, D. (2007). Radical change accidentally: The emergence and amplification of small change. *Academy of Management Journal, 50*(3), 515-543.

Plowman, D., & Duchon, D. (in press). Dispelling the myths about leadership: From cybernetics to emergence. In M. Uhl-Bien & R. Marion (Eds.), *Complexity and leadership volume I: Conceptual foundations.* Charlotte, NC: Information Age Publishing.

Plowman, D., Solansky, S., Beck, T., Baker, L. T., Kulkarni, M., & Travis, D. (2007). The role of leadership in emergent, self-organization. *The Leadership Quarterly, 18*(4), 341-356.

Popper, K. R. (1986). *The poverty of historicism.* London: Routledge.

Prigogine, I. (1997). *The end of certainty.* New York: The Free Press.

Prusak, L. (1996). The knowledge advantage. *Strategy & Leadership, 24*, 6-8.

Quinn, J. B., Anderson, P., & Finkelstein, S. (2002). Managing professional intellect: Making the most of the best. In S. Little, P. Quintas & T. Ray (Eds.), *Managing knowledge: An essential reader* (pp. 335-348). London: Sage.

Reiter-Palmon, R., & Illies, J. J. (2004). Leadership and creativity: Understanding leadership from the creative problem-solving perspective. *The Leadership Quarterly, 15*, 55-77.

Rost, J. C. (1991). *Leadership for the twenty-first century.* London: Praeger.

Roy, D. (1954). Efficiency and "the fix": Informal intergroup relations in a piecework machine shop. *American Journal of Sociology, 60*, 255-266.

Schilling, M. A., & Steensma, H. K. (2001). The use of modular organizational forms: An industry-level analysis. *Academy of Management Journal, 44*(6), 1149-1168.

Schneider, M. (2002). A stakeholder model of organizational leadership. *Organization Science, 13*(2), 209-220.

Schneider, M., & Somers, M. (2006). Organizations as complex adaptive systems: Implications of complexity theory for leadership research. *The Leadership Quarterly, 17*(4), 351-365.

Schreiber, C. (2006). *Human and organizational risk modeling: Critical personnel and leadership in network organizations.* Unpublished doctoral dissertation, Carnegie Mellon, Pittsburgh, PA.

Selznick, P. (1948). Foundations of the theory of organizations. *American Sociological Review, 13*, 25-35.

Selznick, P. (1957). *Leadership in administration.* New York: Harper and Row.

Shalley, C. E., & Gilson, L. L. (2004). What leaders need to know: A review of social and contextual factors that can foster or hinder creativity. *The Leadership Quarterly, 15*(1), 33-53.

Simon, H. A. (1962). The architecture of complexity. *Proceedings of the American Philosophical Society, 106*, 467-482.

Snyder, R. C. (1988). New frames for old: Changing the managerial culture of an aircraft factory. In M. O. Jones, M. D. Moore & R. C. Snyder (Eds.), *Inside organizations: Understanding the human dimension* (pp. 191-208). Newbury Park, CA: Sage.

Stacey, R. D., Griffin, D., & Shaw, P. (2000). *Complexity and management: Fad or radical challenge to systems thinking.* London and New York: Routledge.

Sterman, J. D. (1994). Learning in and about complex systems. *System Dynamics Review, 10*, 291-330.

Streatfield, P. J. (2001). *The paradox of control in organizations.* London: Routledge.

Thomas, C., Kaminska-Labbé, R., & McKelvey, B. (2005). Managing the MNC and exploitation/exploration dilemma: From static balance to dynamic oscillation. In G. Szulanski, Y. Doz, & J. Porac (Eds.), *Advances in strategic management: Expanding perspectives on the strategy process* (Vol. 22, pp. 213-250). Amsterdam: Elsevier.

Volberda, H. W. (1996). Toward the flexible form: How to remain vital in hypercompetitive environments. *Organization Science, 7*(4), 359.

Weick, K. E. (1976). Educational organizations as loosely coupled systems. *Administrative Science Quarterly, 21*, 1-19.

Weisburg, R. (1999). Creativity and knowledge: A challenge to theories. In R. J. Sternberg (Ed.), *Handbook of creativity* (pp. 226–259). Cambridge, England: Cambridge University Press.

Wikipedia. (n.d.). *Self-organization* [Electronic Version]. Retrieved September 15, 2006, from http://en.wikipedia.org/wiki/Self-organization.

Yukl, G. (2005). *Leadership in organizations* (6th ed.). Englewood Cliffs, NJ: Prentice-Hall.

Zaccaro, S. J., & Klimoski, R. J. (Eds.). (2001). The nature of organizational leadership: An introduction. In *The nature of organizational leadership* (pp. 3-41). San Francisco: Jossey-Bass.

Zohar, D. (1997). *Rewiring the corporate brain*. San Francisco: Berrett-Koehler.

CHAPTER 9

EMERGENT STRATEGY VIA COMPLEXITY LEADERSHIP

Using Complexity Science and Adaptive Tension to Build Distributed Intelligence

Bill McKelvey

ABSTRACT

Generation of economic rents requires stimulating coevolution and distributed intelligence within firms. The question becomes, How to improve the corporate brain's IQ? Intelligence *is the network* among neurons, thereby setting up social capital appreciation in firms as the means of improving corporate IQ. Heroic visionary leadership theory is dysfunctional because of the problem of "leading down" through several intervening levels—it destroys networking thereby diminishing corporate IQ—cascading charisma does not work; it creates instead a vision-led command-and-control hierarchy. Complexity theory offers a more dynamical means of explaining social phenomena and explicit methods by which CEOs may improve corporate IQ. Complexity leadership improves corporate IQ without emergent authoritarian command-and-control structures; it does so by speeding up intrafirm coevolving network dynamics rather than focusing on leader

Complexity Leadership, Part I: Conceptual Foundations
pp. 225–268

attributes. Complexity leadership theory moves macro-level economic, ecological, and evolutionary theories about organizational function and process into the "microrealm" heretofore left in the hands of psychologists. Effective CEO-level complexity leadership, thus, rests on a joint micro/macro theoretical footing. Various methods by which chief executive officers (CEOs) can improve corporate IQ are presented.

When share prices fall, CEOs often lose their jobs. The best way to keep share prices high is to produce economic *rents*—defined as profits above the industry average (Besanko, Dranove, & Shanley, 1996). Traditionally corporate strategy theorists advised CEOs in terms of economists' theory of the firm—CEOs invest capital and then order labor, as muscle, to carry out those tasks that cannot be turned over to machines—and aimed firms at the low cost or high differentiation ends of the efficiency curve (Porter, 1985). Now, hitting the efficiency curve is not seen as a guarantee of sustained rents; these come from staying ahead of the curve (Hamel & Prahalad, 1994; Porter, 1996). To accomplish this, CEOs are advised to add *human capital* (Becker, 1975) and *social capital* (Burt, 1992) to the production function.

But how should CEOs lead firms toward speedier human and social capital appreciation? Jack Welch (1991) realized that aggressive command-and-control leaders do not work well in the modern world because their top-down management style shuts down the emergent intelligence and social networking of their employees. Current leadership theory (Daft & Lengel, 1998; Ulrich, Zenger, & Smallwood, 1999) does not respond to this problem. Bennis (1996) and other leadership theorists focus on the "heroic visionary leader" atop a firm's command-and-control structure (Waldman & Yammarino, 1999). Not only does this approach put all of the rent-seeking "eggs" in one visionary basket, the charisma of the heroic visionary leader may bring human and social capital appreciation among lower-level participants to a standstill, as Welch recognizes, and opposite what modern strategic thinking calls for. Most leadership theorists focus on lower-level group or dyadic relations (Dansereau & Yammarino, 1998a, 1998b) and hence are irrelevant to firm-wide CEO leadership.

New Science leadership theory proposes an alternative (Wheatley, 1992), "New Science" being a popularized application of chaos/complexity theory to management (Maguire & McKelvey, 1999; Maguire, McKelvey, Miribreau, & Oztas, 2006). New Science authors typically couple the emergent structure aspect of complexity theory (Nicolis & Prigogine, 1989) with leadership theories aimed at enhancing motivation via employee empowerment (Galbraith, Lawler, & Associates, 1993). In contrast to empowering managerially defined groups or teams by giving them increased responsibility or self-leadership (Markham & Markham,

1998), my focus is on how to foster and speed up the emergence of *distributed intelligence* (DI) in firms. DI is a function of strategically relevant human and social capital assets—the networked intellectual capabilities of human agents (Argote, 1999; Ferber, 1999; Masuch & Warglien, 1992). The question is: *What should CEOs do to foster emergent DI in their firms, speed up its appreciation rate, and steer it in strategically important directions, all the while negating emergent bureaucracy?* Hereinafter, I refer to this as "complexity leadership" (see Uhl-Bien, Marion, & McKelvey, 2007). I build from Prigogine's (Nicolis & Prigogine, 1989) concept of "dissipative structures" and Kauffman's (1993) "spontaneous order-creation" theory.

This chapter is organized as follows. I first argue that rent generation stems mostly from speeding up rates of intrafirm change. Then I propose the emergence of optimal levels of DI as a New Science-based CEO objective. Existing leadership theories are found inadequate. Next I introduce basic elements of complexity science, focusing on *adaptive tension* and the *critical values* in firms that serve to create the emergent phenomena studied by complexity science. This identifies a number of managerial activities CEOs can use to produce and steer emergent rent-generating dynamics in their firms.

COEVOLUTIONARY DYNAMICS

> The true and stunning success of biology reflects the fact that organisms do not merely evolve, they *coevolve* both with other organisms and with a changing abiotic environment. (Kauffman, 1993, p. 237, italics in original)

The term, coevolve, originates in an article by Ehrlich and Raven (1964), in which they focus on "the joint evolution of two (or more) taxa that have close ecological relationships but do not exchange genes and in which *reciprocal selective pressures* operate to make the evolution of either taxon partially dependent on the evolution of the other" (quoted in Pianka, 1994, p. 329, emphasis added). Futuyma (1979) emphasizes the *evolution of interactions* and *reciprocal evolution*. Of late it has come to be even more broadly applied, as Kauffman indicates, to a variety of *intra*- as well as interpopulation and organism-abiotic environment interactions. Coevolution has now become an umbrella term "for a variety of processes and outcomes of reciprocal evolutionary change" (Thompson, 1994, p. viii).[1]

Biological coevolutionary analysis has become a study of *adaptive agents* at various levels of analysis (Slatkin, 1983). "Agents" may be nucleotides, acids, genes/proteins, chromosomes, molecules, organelles, cells, organs, organisms, and species. At the human level of analysis, "agents" may be people, cognitive elements, groups, firms, societies, and so on. Coevolution typically exists at multiple levels within an organism, with "micro" coevolution applying to microagents, that is, agents at the lowest levels representing the behaviors of the most fundamental components. Biologists analyze the coevolutionary relations of agents and their networks from the most micro levels to macro levels, often using the same models. For example, Kauffman (1993) applies his *NK* model at gene, chromosome, cell, and species levels. Maynard Smith and Szathmáry (1995, p. 7) observe that the same agent-based model may be used for both micro- and macrolevels. This point sets up the realization that interagent networks and their relative rates of coevolutionary change apply at all levels of analysis in biology.

Higher rates of reproduction and mutation cause faster coevolution between bacteria and mites than between koala bears and eucalyptus trees (Futuyma, 1979). Since the 1930s, biologists have debated the principle causes of selection, whether individual, species, population, or geographical. Fisher's (1930) fundamental theorem of natural selection holds that *"the rate of evolution of a character at any time is proportional to its additive genetic variance"* (Slatkin, 1983, p. 15, emphasis added). Density- and frequency-dependent effects, that is, population-level effects, moderate this theorem, however. This focuses our attention on the relative rates of *intra*individual variation versus population/ecological/geographic variation (Slatkin, 1983).

Microcoevolution is defined as coevolution of biomolecules or other components (agents) at various levels *within* organisms or populations. *Rapid microcoevolution among microagents within* two ecologically similar populations increases the probability that the inferior population (in the current niche) will survive by evolving toward a different population/niche configuration and stop competing directly against the stronger population. The populations avoid the Red Queen Paradox (Van Valen, 1992) since, instead of running faster and faster in place, one moves into a new niche. Again, we see the effects of the differing rates of *micro*coevolution based individual selection versus population, ecological, or geographical *macro*coevolution. Slow microcoevolution means either that population regulation effects will balance the size of the populations or that the inferior one will suffer competitive exclusion. Needless to say, the "inertia argument" on which population ecology depends (Levins, 1968) is the opposite of rapid microcoevolutionary capability.

Forgotten, however, is Levins' observation that the mutation rates driving microcoevolution are higher in changing environments (1968, p. 97). Genes are the "memory of a population;" it follows, that old unchanging genetic memories are not favored in changing environments. But, even where populations are in more stable situations and competing head-to-head over a fixed resource, it follows that the population with the higher mutation rate has the potential to more quickly drift into a separate niche rather than continue head-to-head competition.

Premise[2] 1a: *As the microcoevolution of agents speeds up, localized niche separation effects predominate over broader environmental context or population-level selection effects.*

Premise 1b: *As the microcoevolution of agents speeds up, adaptive changes within a population (and within its members) negate the death and replacement of populations due to broader environmental changes.*

Micro and macro selection appear in organization science (Aldrich, 1979, 1999; McKelvey, 1982, Nelson & Winter, 1982). Population ecologists (Baum, 1996; Baum & Shiplilov, 2006; Hannan & Freeman, 1977) and institutional theorists (Scott, 1995) claim that population designs are the result of downward selection pressure—competitive ecological contexts and institutional structures determine firms' fates. This is the invisible hand. Visible hand proponents (Chandler, 1977; Child, 1972) claim the opposite—that individuals (mostly managers and visionary leaders) create internal causal pressures leading to the survival of their firm.

But the invisible hand works among agents inside firms as well (Burgelman & Mittman, 1994; McKelvey, 1997; Miller, 1999; Miner, 1994). Microcoevolutionary perspectives also appear in organization science (Baum & McKelvey, 1999; Koza & Lewin, 1998; March, 1991; McKelvey, 1997). Microcoevolutionary agents could be: discourse or process elements; and people, units, departments, or divisions—all within firms. Two points relate to strategy.

Premise 2a: *The rate at which agent fitness and connections coevolve at any given level determines the relative importance of lower versus higher levels of analysis.*

Premise 2b: *Rent generation at a given level is always a function of the rate of coevolution within and between lower levels within it.*

As in biology, the relative importance of intrafirm versus interfirm selection depends on the rate of microcoevolution. March (1991) focuses on different learning rates of employee/agents within simulated firms. Rosenkopf and Nerkar (1999) illustrate the general point that the rate of coevolution at one level affects the rate of coevolution at other levels. Ingram and Roberts (1999) theorize that the rate at which firms introduce new products depends on intrafirm dynamics—specifically the rate at which internal selection takes place. Madsen, Mosakowski, and Zaheer (1999) link internal rate of variation with firm performance. Lomi and Larson (1999) and McKelvey (1999a, 1999b) both use computational agent-based models to explore the relation between rates of microcoevolution and firm-level outcomes. Firms also avoid the Red Queen Paradox (Barnett & Hansen, 1996) by moving into new product/niche configurations.

Premise 3:   *As the rate of microagent coevolution increases, at some point microcoevolution dominates macrocoevolution for increasing the likelihood of rent generation.*

Biologists can study microcoevolution where time is measured in weeks (Futuyma, 1979, p. 461). But, in the coevolution of laptop computer manufacturers—a rapidly changing population of firms—weeks may be too short a time span. There is enough evidence of structural inertia (Hannan & Freeman, 1989; Meyer & Zucker, 1989) and resistance to change (Kotter, 1996) in firms to suggest that the speed of microcoevolution in most firms may be attenuated, though Baum (1996) finds limits to the inertia claim as well. Individual resistance to change, strong culture rigidities, personal chemistry effects, boundary rigidities, "not invented here" attitudes, limited absorptive capacity, and so forth, all serve to inhibit learning, knowledge accumulation, and network development. How fast is fast when it comes to microcoevolutionary effects on firm-level adaptation? At a minimum, it is a function of the rate of technological, market, and institutional changes and the rate at which competitors make their moves. To have an effect, microcoevolution in PC firms must be grossly faster than in violin makers, for example.

Can microcoevolution rates be increased? Jack Welch, GE's CEO, has "created more shareholder wealth than any other CEO in history." How? (1) "It is the story of how GE leverages its intellectual capital" and (2) "There is nothing so special about these changes except the speed with which GE does them" (Stewart, 1999, pp. 124, 127). The cover story of *The Economist* ("The revolutionary," 1999) spotlights "speed and adaptability" (p. 17). Speed is also critical at Hewlett-Packard: "We've got to beat the Japanese through speed of development" (Schoonhoven & Jelinek, 1990, p. 106). While stories in *Fortune* and *The Economist* good science do not make, nevertheless, no one is saying these things about GM, which has gone in the opposite direction in wealth creation during the time that Welch has run GE.[3] More generally, *How should CEOs accelerate microcoevolution?*

Premise 4:   *To be effective in increasing the probability of creating rent-generating initiatives, microcoevolution rates must exceed technology, mar-*

ket, and institutional change rates as well as the microcoevolutionary rates of a firm's niche competitors.

Strategy as a Microcoevolutionary Problem

The only thing that gives an organization a competitive edge—the only thing that is sustainable—is what it knows, how it uses what it knows, and how fast it can know something new! (Prusak, 1996, p. 6)

Good strategy is no longer just picking the right industry; it is being at the right place in the industry—at the cutting edge of industry evolution—new technology, new markets, new moves by competitors. For firms in high-velocity environments this shifts competitive dynamics from industry selection and interfirm competition to intrafirm rates of change.

Recent writing about competitive strategy and sustained rent generation parallels Prusak's emphasis on how fast a firm can develop new knowledge. Rents are seen to stem from seeing industry trends (Hamel & Prahalad, 1994), staying ahead of the efficiency curve (Porter, 1996), winning in hypercompetitive environments (D'Aveni, 1994), and keeping pace with high-velocity environments (Eisenhardt, 1989) and value migration (Slywotzky, 1996). Further, advocates of the resource- and competence-based view emphasize unique resources, distinctive/dominant/core competencies, dynamic capabilities, learning, and knowledge creation (Barney, 1991; Heene & Sanchez, 1997; Prahalad & Hamel, 1990; Rumelt, 1987; Teece, Pisano & Shuen, 1994; Wernerfelt, 1984). It advocates moving firms toward more sophisticated skills and technologies. As a result, the increased level of causal ambiguity (Mosakowski, 1997), and complexity (ogilvie, 1998), learning and innovation are not only more essential (Ambrose, 1995), but also more difficult (Auerswald, Kauffman, Lobe, & Shell, 1996). Dynamic ill-structured environments and learning opportunities become the basis of competitive advantage if firms can be *early* in their industry to unravel the evolving conditions (Stacey, 1995). Drawing on Weick (1985), ogilvie (1998, p. 12) argues that strategic advantage lies in developing new useful knowledge from the continuous stream of "unstructured, diverse, random, and contradictory data" swirling around firms. Becker (1975) defines knowledge/skills held by employees and their intellectual capabilities as *human capital* (*H*), and having given knowledge and capability economic value, adds it to the production function.

Human capital is a property of individual employees. Taken to the extreme, even geniuses offer a firm only minimal adaptive capability if they are isolated from everyone else. A firm's knowledge requisite for competitive advantage increasingly appears as *networks* of human capital holders. These knowledge networks also increasingly appear throughout firms rather than being narrowly confined to upper management. Employees have become responsible for adaptive capability rather than just being bodies to carry out orders. Here is where networks become critical. Especially in the last two decades, much of the effectiveness and economic value of human capital held by individuals has been shown to be subject to the nature of the social networks in which the human agents are embedded (Granovetter, 1985, 1992; Burt, 1997), as a reading of the various chapters in Nohria and Eccles (1992) also suggests. Burt (1992) goes so far as to move networks into the realm of economic value by terming them *social capital* (S), saying that competitive advantage is a function of network relations, not individual knowledge attributes. Combining the need for both H and S, the Cobb Douglas production function, thus, becomes $Y = f(K, L, H, S)$, where K = capital; L = labor; Y = income. But, since Porter (1996) now argues that the K and L portions of the equation no longer guarantee sustainable rents, this leaves the emphasis on H and S.

Premise 5:   *Human and social capital appreciation (relevant to a competitive context) is a necessary, though not sufficient, condition for sustained rent generation.*

As high-velocity product life-cycles (Eisenhardt, 1989) and hypercompetition (D'Aveni, 1994) have increased in recent decades, speed of knowledge appreciation has become a central attribute of competitive advantage (Leonard-Barton, 1995; Prusak, 1996) with learning fundamental to change in knowledge (Argote, 1999). Learning is seen as a key element of core competence (Barney, 1991). Much of the concern about human capital appreciation bears on high-technology based industries (Leonard-Barton, 1995; Boisot, 1998). Eisenhardt and colleagues have focused on "high-velocity" high-tech firms for some time (Eisenhardt & Tabrizi, 1995). In these firms the classic "organic" organizing style is just too slow to keep pace with changes in high-velocity firms, as Eisenhardt (1989) and Brown and Eisenhardt (1997) observe.

Premise 6: *In high-velocity firms, rent generation rests primarily on speeding up the development of H and S.*

Distributed Intelligence Versus Leadership Theory

"Why is it that whenever I ask for a pair of hands, a brain comes attached?" (Henry Ford) [4]

Enhancing rent generation by improving H (human capital) and S (social capital) is alien not only to strategy science but also to organization science and leadership theory as well. True, speeding up the knowledge, skills, or intellectual capabilities of employees and improving interpersonal communications and networking in groups are old ideas, dating back at least to the use of individual and group incentives in autonomous workgroups (Herbst, 1970; Trist & Bamforth, 1951). But the emphasis in those days was on productivity. Micro OB added social influence, interpersonal and group dynamics, satisfaction, and felt-worth to theories about motivating employees (Katz, Kahn & Adams, 1980). Now there is self-, charismatic, visionary, and transformational leadership (Dansereau & Yammarino, 1998a, 1998b). In all of this, strategic corporate intelligence—and ideas for rent generation—remains in the brain of the heroic visionary CEO (Bennis, 1996; Bennis & Nanus, 1985). For neoclassical economists as well, a firm's strategic intelligence is in the head of the owner, with capital and labor's muscle employed to bring it to life, hence: $Y = f(K, L)$. But at GE they say it is more than just Jack. They say it's the *collective brainpower* of people throughout the firm (Slater, 2001, pp. 112-113). If so, then, *What is organizational intelligence?* and *How to improve the corporate brain?*

Distributed Intelligence

My work is in a building that houses three thousand people who are essentially the individual "particles" of the "brain" of an organization that consists of sixty thousand people worldwide. (Andrew Stone)

Zohar (1997, p. xv) starts her book by quoting Andrew Stone, the director of the retailing giant, Marks & Spencer: Each particle has some intellectual capability—Becker's H. And some of them talk to each other—Burt's S. Together, H and S comprise *distributed intelligence*. I draw on both brain and distributed computer systems research to demonstrate that Becker and Burt each are half right. They naïvely could be interpreted to imply that "isolated geniuses" or "networked idiots" can generate rents. Surely they would agree that H and S are *both* important. If so, the theory of the firm most relevant to rent generation appears as: $Y = f(K, L, D)$, where D stands for the configuration of H and S likely to produce optimal DI for a particular firm. DI—in brains and in parallel processing computer systems—is a function of both knowledge in the nodes (minimal in brains) and emergent connections among nodes (primitive in computer systems).

Intelligence in brains rests entirely on the production of emergent networks among neurons—intelligence "*is* the network" (Fuster, 1995, p. 11).

Neurons behave as simple "threshold gates" that have one behavioral option—fire or not fire (p. 29). As intelligence increases, it is represented in the brain as *emergent* connections (synaptic links) among neurons. Human intelligence is "distributed" across really dumb agents!

Premise 7:   *DI in a brain is entirely a function of its capability for producing emergent networks among neurons.*

In computer DI systems, computers play the role of neurons. They are more "node-based" than "network-based." Artificial intelligence resides in the *intelligence capability* of the computers as agents, with emergent network-based intelligence rather primitive (Garzon, 1995). Garzon's analysis notwithstanding, the distributed computer literature shows only marginal progress toward computer-embedded *emergent* DI, whether in agents *or* networks.

Artificial intelligence (AI) computational models increasingly are used to simulate learning processes in firms, though their intelligence capability is not fully connectionist and the intelligence of their agents is minimal—far below that, even, of PCs (Carley & Prietula, 1994; Ferber, 1999; Masuch & Warglien, 1992). My focus on DI as emergent order places most of the emphasis on the emergence of constructive networks. Of course, firms that have constructive networks among geniuses usually will fare better than those having great networks among idiots.

Premise 8: *DI in parallel processing computer systems is mostly a function of the built-in intelligence capability of computers-as-agents, with minimal DI improvement stemming from emergent networks among the computer/ agents.*

The lesson from brains and computers is that organizational intelligence is best seen as "distributed" and that increasing it depends on fostering network development along with increasing agents' human capital. Is there an actual optimal mix of H and S in D? In general? In a specific firm? Optimality could result from independent linear increases in H and S to the point where DI is maximized, but there is no reason to believe that, like "area," optimality always results from equal amounts of the two dimensions. Optimality seems more likely the nonlinear result of mutually causal emergence depending on specific agents and firm contexts. Zucker and Darby (1996; Darby, Liu, & Zucker, 1999) find that one genius appropriately networked is superior to larger networks comprised of less talented agents. Oppositely, knowledge transfers via networks among workers from "lesser schools or the armed forces" "lie at the heart of GE's success" according to *The Economist* ("General Electric," 1999, p. 24). *D* operates as a nonlinear mutual causal function of H and S with optimality the "multifinal" outcome, to use an old systems term (Buckley, 1967).

There are also thresholds and redundancy effects. Genius may not automatically lead to denser networks—though this could be implicit in the Zucker/Darby findings and could be concluded from the Liebeskind, Oliver, Zucker, and Brewer (1996) study. Nor do "social" agents automatically become smarter. A firm starting with the extremes of "isolated geniuses" or "networked idiots" cannot assume that the missing dimension will willy-nilly appear. At GE, for example, H and S are embedded within an hospitable organizational culture. Redundancy is a critical element in DI, both in brains and in parallel processing computers. Holographic[5] H formations can withstand some agent losses without performance deterioration, meaning that not all holders of H need to be in the network all the time. And structurally equivalent network formation (Lorrain & White 1971) means that some network links can fail without performance deterioration. Once achieved, optimality often may be quite robust against agent and network deterioration. But, given some highly capable holders of H, the intelligence of an entire firm likely correlates quite well with the density of their connections to other less endowed agents.

Premise 9: *Above threshold levels of H and S yet to be identified, the optimum amounts, and ratio, of H to S, that is, D, for rent generation is equifinal, nonlinearly mutual causal, and subject to local firm idiosyncrasies.*

Emergent DI Versus Visionary Charismatic Leadership

Is it true, as I claim in the Introduction, that leadership theory is irrelevant to rent seeking CEOs trying to create DI and increase its appreciation rate? Leadership theory is old—Merrill (1960) cites Jethro in *Exodus* on delegation. It has a vast empirical base (Bass, 1981) and continues richly diverse in its theories (Dansereau & Yammarino, 1998a, 1998b) (DY). Surely every nuance of leadership has been studied. How could leadership aimed at improving DI be overlooked?

Dansereau and Yammarino's summary table (1998a, p. xxxix) shows leadership theory to be focused on attributes of leaders and their effects on groups of followers and on individual followers in dyads—corroborated by Klein and House (1998, p. 9). To use Dubin's (1979) phrases, this is mostly "leadership in organizations" rather than "leadership of organizations." In the Dansereau/Yammarino (DY) books, only Hunt and Ropo (1998) concentrate on leadership *of* organizations via their case analysis of Roger Smith's years as CEO of General Motors. The Klein and House (1998) chapter on charismatic leadership focuses on leadership of subordinates at different levels *in* firms—leader-subordinate dyads at different levels—rather than leadership *down through* a firm's several levels.

From Fayol (1916), who defined leadership as "command," to most of the 34 "complexity-theory-applied-to-management" books reviewed in the *Emergence* special issue (Maguire & McKelvey, 1999), "leadership" has routinely appeared in the context of "command-and-control" structures. Every single chapter in the DY books focuses on how leaders influence followers within the frame of an existing command-and-control structure. Markham and Markham's (1998) chapter on self-leadership assumes a stable formal structure with followers taking responsibility for self-admin-istering rewards as a means of cutting out first-line supervisors. Their chapter builds mainly on the earlier work of Manz and colleagues who define self-leadership in terms of self-reinforcement, self-observation/ evaluation, self-expectation—all within an unchanging formal structure (Manz & Sims, 1987, p. 120). Avolio and Bass (1998, p. 58) note that transactional leadership works within existing rules and then, drawing on Bass (1985), they define transformational leadership as redefining the rules to *better connect the leader's vision to follower needs.* "Rules" for them are in organizational culture. Left intact are the rules of the formal structure of command and control. They invoke the notion of "cascading" (Bass, Waldman, Avolio, & Bebb, 1987; Yammarino, 1994) in explaining that transformation moves down the hierarchy one level at a time.

One ray of hope in the DY books is Day (1998, p. 195), who translates Hall and Lord's (1998) view of multi-level information processing into *dis-tributed sensemaking*, building on Weick (1993, 1995). Troubling, however, is his quote of Weick (1993, p. 643): "When formal structure collapses, there is no leader, no roles, no sense." Day broadens this to say "no struc-ture therefore no distributed sensemaking." Presuming that the latter applies to firms puts it in direct conflict with the complexity-applied-to-management books, which say, "command-and-control kills emergence." Consequently, traditional leadership theory faces a dilemma: It says lead-ers need to create structure to foster distributed sensemaking, but it also says that if they create structure they suppress distributed sensemaking.

Leadership in the DY books, is multilevel, yes, but always cascading down across only one level at a time. Weick's quote comes from his study of the Mann Gulch disaster, a one-level group situation. Waldman and Yammarino (1999) get closer to strategic upper echelon leadership in considering leadership across several levels, where followers are not direct-reports—followers are separated from the CEO by levels of inter-vening managers. Bennis and colleagues (Bennis & Nanus, 1985; Bennis & Biederman, 1996) zero in on leaders who successfully reorient multi-level sets of followers in organizations. They abandon trait and situational/contingency theories for a skill-based theory built around leaders who are able to get subordinates to follow their vision.

Presaging my concern about how CEOs can increase DI, Bennis (1996, p. 149) says:

> The problem facing almost all leaders in the future will be how to develop their organization's social architecture so that it actually generates intellectual capital."

He calls for "organized anarchy" saying leadership is like *"herding cats."* True, he begins by zeroing in on how CEOs might foster DI. Consider the following quotes (1996, pp. 149-151):

> Human resources people will have to … develop ways of trying to generate intellectual capital.

> Major challenge for leaders … how to release the brainpower of their organizations.

> Leaders … have to make sure that they are constantly reinventing the organization.

> How do you deploy your workforce so that it … can start reinventing [the firm] and creating new ideas?

So far he is with me. But, when he gets to defining leader attributes, trouble begins:

> Leaders need to have a strongly defined sense of purpose. A sense of vision.

> Leading means doing the right things … creating a compelling, overarching vision."

> The capacity clearly to articulate a vision.

> It's about *living* the vision, day in day out—embodying it—and empowering every other person … to implement and execute that vision." (emphasis in original)

> The vision has to be shared. And the only way that it can be shared is for it to have meaning for the people who are involved in it. Leaders have to specify the steps that behaviorally fit into that vision, and then reward people for following those steps."

Bennis follows the charismatic leadership theory of House (1977) and Nanus (1992). Klein and House (1998, p. 3) say "charisma is a fire that ignites followers' energy, commitment, and performance." In dwelling primarily on the "mythic," "heroic," "visionary," upper echelon leaders, such as Jack Welch, Bennis works at cross purposes with distributed sensemaking and speeding up the rate of DI formation. In the last quote above it is the brain of the leader that creates the vision and followers are rewarded (in the context of command-and-control structure) for carrying it out. And yet, as Bennis himself says, "people at the periphery of organizations are usually the most creative and often the least consulted" (1996, p. 152). Bennis does not answer the question: *How to lead the corporate brain without shutting it down?*

How does the visionary CEO suppress emergent DI? First, heroic visionary leaders tend to create "strong cultures" (Peters & Waterman, 1982; Schein, 1990). The role of entrepreneurs as visionary creators of organizational culture has been noted (Siehl, 1985). Kotter and Heskett (1992) observe that organizational performance is connected to adaptive cultures and that leaders play a key role in culture change. Sorensen (2002) shows that strong cultures are assets in stable environments but liabilities in changing times. Leaders are seen as molding employees' views about a firm and defining their roles within it (Bryman, 1996). Willmott (1993) claims that culture management is simply a new form of managerial control. Bryman (1996, p. 285) notes that Martin's (1992) "integration perspective" points to leaders who go about "creating, maintaining or changing cultures" in the normative manner outlined by the foregoing authors.

Some leaders have visions that are always correct, innovative, and up-to-date in high velocity environments. But what if the heroic leader's brain is not up to the job? Upper echelon visionary charismatic leadership produces cohesion and leader defined "groupthink" (Janis, 1972) across intervening levels, where one would instead want to see emergent novelty and new product-market combinations. Charismatic leadership, thus, produces a corporate brain mirroring the CEO's.

A possible alternative to the heroic visionary CEO appears as "*dispersed leadership*" (Bryman, 1996). Hosking (1988) emphasizes the network building functions of effective leadership and the cultivation of social influence. Katzenbach and Smith (1993) focus on a kind of leader who fosters the emergence of small teams in which members have common purpose and performance goals. These leaders help the teams build commitment, create opportunities, remove obstacles, and facilitate team solidarity. Kouzes and Posner (1993, p. 156) move even closer to a DI perspective when they say that good leaders "turn their constituents into leaders" and liberate employees "so that they can use their abilities to lead themselves and others" (Bryman, 1996, p. 283). Bryman also connects Martin's (1992) "fragmentation perspective" with a de-centering of leadership and the "imaginative consumption of culture" idea suggested by Linstead and Grafton-Small (1992). They view culture formation as "dispersed" rather than flowing monolithically from the vision of a heroic leader. Thus, depending on conditions—largely unspecified and unresearched—organizational cultures may comprise: (1) a homogeneous solidarity group flowing from a leader's vision; (2) a group fairly uniformly resisting the leader's normative efforts; (3) a group fragmented in many directions; or (4) in the same power-equalized manner of fragmented cultures, a group may respond to environmentally imposed problems as a result of the dispersed efforts of its members in a process outlined by Schein (1985). At this reading, I do not see that dispersed leadership theory provides a focused offset to the suppressive effects of aggressive top-down visionary leadership. For a corroborating analysis, see Marion and Uhl-Bien (2001). One recent study supporting my position is by Brown and Gioia (2002) who, agreeing with Avolio, Kahai, and Dodge (2001), say that "...leadership is not solely a set of characteristics possessed by an individual, but an emergent property of a social system, in which 'leaders' and 'followers' share in the process of enacting leadership" (quote taken from Parry & Bryman, 2006, p. 455). But the prevailing view is summarized as follows:

Premise 10: *The visionary, charismatic CEO strategist, given the condition of intervening levels, creates a climate within the firm of intra- and intergroup homogeneity that inhibits (1) diversity in H appreciation; by (2) inhibiting emergence of S connecting employees holding the diverse human capital; that in turn (3) inhibits the creation of the kinds of new product/ niche strategies most likely to lead to sustainable rent generation.*

SOME NEW SCIENCE 'COMPLEXITY LEADERSHIP' ACTIVITIES

Complexity Theory

How should CEOs accelerate the rate of DI increase? Most New Science authors say "Take away the command-and-control-structure." They equate the *emergence process* in complexity theory with the *empowerment process* that has existed for years in the Organization Development (OD) literature—hardly a new idea. This is like picking a mattress up off the grass—the grass, having gone flat, straightens back up again. But suppose a CEO needs more growth than what lifting the command-and-control "mattress" leads to? *What is the "fertilizer" that speeds up DI growth?*

Complexity science studies how and under what conditions networks such as DI come about. These are termed *"complex adaptive systems"* (Cowan, Pines, & Meltzer, 1994). Gell-Mann (2002, p. 17) says they "seem to have some connection with life." They consist of *heterogeneous agents* having some propensity to connect. Surowiecki (2004) and Page (2007) both present evidence substantiating the superiority of collectivities of heterogeneous agents over appointed experts. More specifically, how do heterogeneous agents (whether biomolecules, genes, neurons, organisms, people, firms, societies, etc.), self-organize into emergent aggregate structure? Cowan (1994) observes:

> Complexity ... refers to systems with many different parts which, by a rather mysterious process of self-organization, become more ordered and more informed than systems which operate in approximate thermodynamic equilibrium with their surroundings. (p. 1)

> Complex systems contain many relatively independent parts which are highly interconnected and interactive and that a large number of such parts are required to reproduce the functions of truly complex, self-organizing, replicating, learning, and adaptive systems. (p. 2)

I focus on *agents* and what creates the region of emergent complexity "*at the edge of chaos.*" For a review of relevant theories on the "0th law"—the order-creation law, see McKelvey (2004a).

Arthur, Durlauf, and Lane (1997, pp. 3-4; adapted from Holland, 1988, p. 118) set out the basic elements of complex adaptive systems at the edge of chaos, as follows:

1. *"Dispersed Interaction"*—dispersed, possibly heterogeneous, agents active in parallel;

2. *"No Global Controller or Cause"*—coevolution of agent interactions;

3. *"Many Levels of Organization"*—agents at lower levels create contexts at higher levels;

4. *"Continual Adaptation"*—agents revise their adaptive behavior continually;

5. *"Perpetual Novelty"*—by changing in ways that allow them to depend on new resources, agents coevolve with resource changes to occupy new habitats; and

6. *"Out-of-Equilibrium Dynamics"*—economies operate "far from equilibrium," meaning that economies are induced by the pressure of trade imbalances, individual to individual, firm to firm, country to country, and so forth.

Kauffman (1993) holds that all that is needed for "*spontaneous*" order creation is some set of heterogeneous agents, motive to connect (such as improved fitness, performance, learning, etc.) and some number of connections with other agents—collectively, all three are necessary and sufficient for order creation. Take any one of these three away and new order does not appear. Below, I add reducing adaptive tension as one of the motives to connect.

Cramer (1993) identifies three levels of complexity—defined in Table 9.1—depending on how much information is necessary to explain the complexity: *Newtonian complexity, emergent complexity,* and *stochastic complexity*. Complexity science (Nicolis & Prigogine, 1989) shows that the separation of the region of emergent complexity from the other kinds is a function of the exogenous energy impinging on a system of agents. Emergent structures are created and maintained by negentropy[6] and eroded by entropy. Negentropic effects create or maintain order in the face of entropic energy/order destroying effects within any system.

Complexity theorists define systems in the emergent complexity category as being in a state "*far from equilibrium*" (Prigogine & Stengers, 1984) and "*at the edge of chaos*" (Lewin, 1992/1999). Prigogine and colleagues observe that energy importing, self-organizing, open systems create structures that in the first instance increase negentropy, but nevertheless ever

Table 9.1. Definitions of Kinds of Complexity by Cramer (1993)*

"**Newtonian complexity**" exists when the amount of information necessary to describe the system is less complex than the system itself. Thus a rule, such as $F = ma = md^2s/dt^2$ is much simpler in information terms than trying to describe the myriad states, velocities, and acceleration rates pursuant to understanding the force of a falling object. "Systems exhibiting subcritical [Newtonian] complexity are strictly deterministic and allow for exact prediction" (1993, p. 213). They are also "reversible" (allowing retrodiction as well as prediction thus making the "arrow of time" irrelevant (Eddington, 1930; Prigogine & Stengers, 1984).

At the opposite extreme is "**stochastic complexity**" where the description of a system is as complex as the system itself—the minimum number of information bits necessary to describe the states is equal to the complexity of the system. Cramer lumps chaotic and stochastic systems into this category, although deterministic chaos is recognized as fundamentally different from stochastic complexity (Morrison, 1991), since the former is 'simple rule' driven, and stochastic systems are random, though varying in their stochasticity. Thus, three kinds of stochastic complexity are recognized: **purely random, probabilistic**, and **deterministic chaos**. For this essay I narrow stochastic complexity to deterministic chaos, at the risk of oversimplification.

In between Cramer puts "**emergent complexity**." The defining aspect of this category is the possibility of emergent simple deterministic structures fitting Newtonian complexity criteria, even though the underlying phenomena remain in the stochastically complex category. It is here that natural forces ease the investigator's problem by offering intervening objects as 'simplicity targets' the behavior of which lends itself to simple rule explanation. Cramer (1993, pp. 215-217) has a long table categorizing all kinds of phenomena according to his scheme.

*For mnemonic purposes I use "Newtonian" instead of Cramer's "subcritical," "stochastic" instead of "fundamental," and "emergent" instead of "critical" complexity.

after become sites of energy or order dissipation. Consequently they are labeled *"dissipative structures."* Self-organized—and self-contained[7]—dissipative structures may exhibit persistence and nonlinearity. Complexity caused self-organizing structures are now seen as a ubiquitous natural phenomenon (Mainzer, 1994/2004) and presumed broadly applicable to firms (Anderson, 1999; Goldstein, 1994; Levy, 1994; McKelvey, 1998, 1999a, 2004b; Stacey, 1995; Thiétart & Forgues, 1995; Zimmerman & Hurst, 1993). Maguire, McKelvey, Mirabeau, and Oztas (2006) offer a comprehensive review of complexity theory applied to organizations.

> **Premise 11:** *A system of agents subject to the tension, T, of an energy differential[8] will form emergent structures showing different kinds of complexity that (1) form as a result of importing energy into themselves; and (2) dissipate this energy (and eventually themselves) as they act to reduce the impinging adaptive tension.*

The boundaries of emergent complexity in Premise 12 are defined by *"critical values"* (Mainzer, 1994/2004). Nicolis & Prigogine (1989, ch. 1) describe the function of critical values in natural science. Nothing is so basic to their definition of complexity science as the Bénard (1901) cell—two plates with fluid in between. An exogenous *energy* (heat) *differential* between the plates—defined here as **adaptive tension**, *T*—creates a circular molecular motion as hotter molecules move toward the colder plate when the energy level rises above the 1st critical value. The energy differential in the Bénard cell parallels that between (1) a teapot: when the heat under the pot reaches the 1st critical value we get what cooks call a rolling boil—the water molecules change their rules *from* vibrating in place at a higher rate as the heat increases, *to* circulating from the hot to the cool part of the pot so as to dissipate the heat even faster; and (2) the hot surface of the earth and cold upper atmosphere: hotter air molecules move upward and if they move fast enough, create storm cells. If *T* increases beyond the 2nd critical value, the agent system jumps into the region of chaotic complexity. Complexity science cannot be understood without appreciating the role that *T* plays in defining the *region* of complexity between the 1st and 2nd critical values. Here the system is likely to oscillate between different states—centered around different *basins of attraction*—thereby creating chaotic behavior. Definitions of *attractors* are given in Table 9.2. Thus, for molecular agents:

- **Below the 1st critical value** of *T*—the *edge of order*, agents show minimal response in reducing *T*—molecules vibrate in place but "conduct" energy by colliding with each other.

- **Above the 1st critical value** of T—the *edge of order*, agents show collective action toward reducing T. Gas molecules start bulk currents of "convection" movement, as the molecules actually circle around from hot to cold and back to hotter plate, or generate strong bulk currents of air flowing up and down from earth's surface to upper atmosphere—the air turbulence and storm cells that create rough airplane rides.

- **Above the 2nd critical value** of T—the *edge of chaos*, the molecular movement becomes chaotic. For example, if T between hot lower air and cold upper air increases further, perhaps by the conflation of warm moist air from the south and cold air from the north, say over Kansas, the *2nd critical value* may be exceeded; the storm cell may then oscillate between two basins of attraction, tornado-producing and non-tornado-producing behavior.

Table 9.2.   Definitions of Attractors by Gleick (1987)

"**Point attractors**" act as equilibrium points. A system, even though oscillating or perturbed, eventually returns to repetitive behavior centered around the point attractor—traditional control style management decision structures may act in this manner (appearing as Newtonian complexity);

"**Periodic attractors**" or "limit cycles" (pendulum behavior) foster oscillation predictably from one extreme to another—recurrent shifts in the centralization and decentralization of decision making, or functional specialization vs. cross-functional integration fit here (also appearing as Newtonian complexity);

If adaptive tension is raised beyond some critical value, systems may be subject to "**strange attractors**" in that, if plotted, they show never intersecting, stable, low-dimensional, non-periodic spirals and loops, that are not attracted by some central equilibrium point, but nevertheless appear constrained not to breach the confines of what might appear as an imaginary bottle. If they intersected, the system would be in equilibrium (Gleick, 1987, p. 140) following a point attractor. The attractor is "strange" because it "looks" like the system is oscillating around a central equilibrium point, but isn't. Instead, as an energy importing and dissipating structure, it is responding with unpredictable self-organized structure to tensions created by imposed external conditions, such as tension between different heat gradients in the atmosphere caught between a hot surface of the earth and a cold upper atmosphere, or constraints in a fluid flow at the junction of two pipes, or tension created by newly created dissipative structures, such as eddies in a turbulent fluid flow in a canyon below a waterfall, or "MBA terrorist" structural changes imposed in an attempt to turnaround an acquired firm.

As a metaphor, think of a point attractor as a rabbit on an elastic tether—the rabbit moves in all directions but as it tires it is drawn toward the middle where it lies down to rest. Think of a strange attractor as a rabbit in a pen with a fox on the outside—the rabbit keeps running to the side of the pen opposite from the fox but as it tires it comes to rest in the middle of the pen. The rabbit ends up in the "middle" in either case. With the tether the cause is the pull of the elastic. In the pen the cause is repulsion from the fox unsystematically attacking from all sides.

Translating to firms, suppose a large firm acquires another firm need-ing a turnaround. Suppose T stays below the 1st critical value, in which existing management stays in place and the acquiring firm imposes little change. There is little reason for people in the acquired firm to create new structures. Instead, there might be only "conduction" type changes in the sense that new turnaround ideas percolate slowly from one person to another person adjacent in a network.

If T goes above the 2nd critical value, complexity theory predicts chaos. Suppose the acquiring firm changes several of the acquired firm's top managers and sends in "MBA terrorists" to change the management systems "over-night"—new budgeting and information systems; new chain of command, new personnel procedures, promotion approaches, and benefits packages; new production and marketing systems. And sup-pose the acquired firm's day-to-day interaction patterns are changed as well. In this circumstance, two basins of attraction could emerge: one basin defined around demands of the MBA terrorists and the other cen-tered around the comfortable preacquisition ways of doing business and resistance to change. The activities of the system could oscillate between these two basins, seemingly exhibiting the characteristics of a strange attractor.

Premise 12: *The region of emergent complexity exists when T stays between the 1st and 2nd critical values, with the 1st value defining the "edge of order" and the 2nd value defining the "edge of chaos."*

Between the 1st and 2nd critical values lies the organizational equiva-lent of Cramer's emergent complexity—the region of complexity at the edge of chaos that Brown and Eisenhardt (1998) aim at. Here, network structures emerge to solve T problems. Using the storm cell metaphor, in this region the "heat conduction" of interpersonal dynamics between spo-radically communicating individuals is insufficient to reduce the observed T. To pick up the adaptive pace, the equivalent of organizational storm cells consisting of "bulk" adaptive work-flows starts. Formal or informal structures emerge, such as new network formations, informal or formal group activities, departments, entrepreneurial ventures, and so on.

Though the Ts in organization science are unlikely to have the precise values they appear to have in some natural sciences (Johnson & Burton, 1994) it seems likely that a probability distribution of such values will exist for individual firms and each of their subunits. Though precise values of T for firms do not exist, we do know about symptoms indicating whether a firm is below the 1st, in between, or above the 2nd critical value (Brown & Eisenhardt, 1998).

Proposition 1: *Emergent social capital dissipative structures in firms form in a region of complexity bounded by the 1ˢᵗ and 2ⁿᵈ critical values of T (T being probabilistically defined).*

CEO Activities

My analysis takes strategy out of the hands of economists and population ecologists and turns it into a ***complexity leadership challenge***—rents are more apt to come from speeding up microcoevolution within firms—that is, speeding up the DI appreciation rate and boosting the corporate brain's IQ. In addition, the typical heroic visionary CEO at the top of a large hierarchical firm could easily be out of touch with changing technology, markets, and competitor moves, and even worse, could inadvertently create command-and-control conditions inhibiting emergent DI. Complexity theory emphasizes the role of the critical values in defining and enlarging the region of emergent social capital structures. I identify T, the adaptive tension energy gradient, as the factor controlling whether a firm's DI system is within the region of emergent complexity or not. Now the question is, *How can CEOs use adaptive tension and other related activities to speed up the DI appreciation rate and steer it away from the least promising directions without inadvertently creating the negative effects of an emergent command-and-control structure?*

The activities I emphasize are (1) adaptive tension and critical values, which produce emergent DI, and (2) attractors and the agency problem, which pertain to "steering" the emergence. I ignore four relevant issues due to space limitations, recognizing that there could be others as well:

- Modular design—discussed by Sanchez (1995) and Schilling (2000);
- The (auto)catalytic process—discussed as the "coaching" process in the OD literature for decades and is covered very well in the New Science context in books by Goldstein (1994) and Kelly and Allison (1998);
- Dysfunctional anxiety—discussed in depth in Stacey's (1996) book;
- Kauffman's (1993) complexity catastrophe—discussed by Levinthal (1997), McKelvey (1999a, 1999b), and Rivkin (2000, 2001), among many others (see Maguire et al., 2006).

Defining and Managing Adaptive Tension

A CEO's first task in mobilizing the corporate brain is to make sure it is exposed to the full range of "Ts" "out there"—that surround the agents—

that might energize emergence. But a T that is "out there" but ignored by agents has no impact on agents' behavior. In natural systems, so far as we know, agents—particles, molecules, cells—do not ignore Ts impinging on them. Agents in firms can. Welch uses "Be #1 or 2 in your industry," with a very clear motivational **activator**—respond to the T "or your division will be sold!"[9] Thus, Ts need to have an intrinsic or extrinsic motivational activator attached before they can be felt as tension by agents. Ts are the root motivation causing agents to import negentropy—from whatever source available—that is, the cause of emergent networks aimed at dissipating them.

Definition 1:   *T is the product of (1) the difference between a firm's or agent's current state and a different, more desirable state relevant to the firm or agent; times (2) the intrinsic or extrinsic motivation of an agent to respond.*

While agents in a Bénard cell face just one T, the adaptive tension confronting the many agents within a firm—as receivers—may appear as countless Ts. In addition, there are many Ts reflecting forces and constraints in the environment, not to mention Ts created by numerous agents within firms—from the CEO down to the people in engineering, production, marketing, sales, and so on. An agent network could emerge virtually anywhere in a firm around an initiative to produce a better part, product, marketing approach, new strategy, and so forth. Consequently, there is danger in a priori trying to focus certain kinds of Ts toward specific kinds of agents. This might preclude the emergence of the most effective new networks. But there is an equal danger in trying to flood every agent with every kind of T. It is also clear that "selecting" the nature of the incoming Ts based on preconceived CEO-level notions, as Roger Smith did at GM for a decade (Hunt & Ropo, 1998) puts blinders on the corporate brain. Toyota is well known for its system of increasing the awareness of workers about how well their designs and products compete against the competition—a small set of narrowly defined Ts. Welch accomplishes the same objective by defining Ts very broadly as, "Be #1 or 2 in your industry!" This is a perfect example of using a simple piece of information to focus attention on a particular aspect of the competitive environment—everything is boiled down to one T that *drives* the lower level systems without the command-and-control structure *defining* them. Strong corporate leadership is shown without setting up a suppressive command-and-control-structure or otherwise inhibiting emergent DI.

Definition 2:   *Adaptive tension is defined by "an effective sampling" of Ts that agents at various levels within the firm can use to define their adaptive state relative to that of competing agents/firms.*

Definition 3:   *"An effective sampling" is defined as ranging "adroitly" between (1) a set of Ts (a) not delimited by the CEO's or others' visions; (b) not narrowly defined by the specific responsibilities of a specific agent; and (c) not mindlessly flooding all agents indiscriminately with all kinds of information, on the one hand, and (2) T prioritizations based on (a) indications of value migration and industry, technological, and market trends; (b) the firm's path dependencies, idiosyncratic resources and competencies, and (c) larger groupings of agents (the sampling of Ts relevant to agents in one division may be reasonably different from Ts relevant to another).*

Definition 4:   *"Adroitly" is defined as that **portfolio** of Ts getting the corporate brain to produce emergent initiatives showing the highest probability of rent generation over time.*

Another aspect of tension is the felt sense of urgency, defined as the rate at which adaptive events take place—a firm's metabolic (energy conversion) *rate* (McKelvey, 1997). This is the rate at which the DI system seeks to reduce the *T*s. A cursory review of the OD literature (see French, Bell, & Zawacki, 1994) suggests that little attention is paid to *rates* at which organizational events happen. An exception is an article by Beatty and Ulrich (1991) in which they talk about "re-energizing" mature firms. They mention in passing Welch's interest in "speed" of event flows at GE, a point noted again by Stewart (1999). Schoonhoven and Jelinek (1990) bear witness to the concern over speed at Hewlett-Packard. Eisenhardt and colleagues (Brown & Eisenhardt, 1998; Eisenhardt & Tabrizi, 1995) zero in on the use of "time pacing" strategies for cranking up the metabolic rates of firms.

Definition 5:   *Ts may also be defined as rates of: product introductions, positive and negative bottom-up leadership events, process improvement events, network transaction events, novelty occurrences; rates at which dysfunctional events are reduced; rates of effective coordination events; information flow rates, etc.*

If a firm is construed as a place where events take place that improve fitness, then, how often do these take place—process improvement events in general, bottom-up leadership events, network transaction events, novelty occurrence rates, dysfunctional-event reduction rates, and so forth? CEOs have used "management by walking around" to raise metabolic levels while staying outside the bureaucratic command-and-control structure. Rates at which DI systems check in with top leaders are important and may be speeded up as appropriate. Ashkenas, Ulrich, Jick, and Kerr (1995) identify four critical elements that serve to raise or lower metabolic flow rates in the DI system: information, competence, authority, and incentives—they call them leverage points. Information flow rates may be managed, as can rates at which learning, knowledge accumulation, and as a result, competence, improve. The relative mix of point attractors and strange attractors used also may be managed (more on this in Section 2.2.3). And surely incentives have a tremendous effect on the rate at which events take place in organizations. In the secondary value chain, differentials in rates of new product research and products brought to market, human and social capital accumulation, requisite variety development, and so forth, are important.

> **Proposition 2:** *Tension management that is "adroit" in confronting agents with appropriate sets of adaptive tension Ts (each of which includes an appropriate intrinsic or extrinsic motivational activator) will show the highest probability of rent generation.*

Managing Around the Critical Values

Assuming agents are confronted by an adroitly defined portfolio of *T*s, managing the critical values aspect of adaptive tension requires three basic activities: (1) checking whether the behavioral symptoms (see next paragraph) of *T*s impinging on one or more agents are below, between, or above the critical values; (2) altering motivational activators to move the *T* levels into the region between the 1st and 2nd critical values; and (3) widening the distance between the critical values.[10] For now I assume *T*s impinging on an agent are averaged, though in real life some *T*s have far more adaptive significance than others and agents may respond to some more than others with heightened intrinsic motivation.[11]

Critical values are not precisely determined in firms—as they are in natural science. Nor does research indicate what levels of *T*s are below, between, or above the critical values. For now we have to rely on behavioral *"symptoms"* for evidence about *T* effects. Brown and Eisenhardt (1998) (BE)[12] identify some symptoms. As indications that *T* is *below the 1st critical value*, BE point to:

- *High bureaucratic level*: all rules followed, overbearing structure, strictly channeled communication (p. 30);
- *Too low alliance coadaptation*: fiefdoms, overlapping effort, little coordination or learning, uncoupled strategies (p. 60);

- *Too low a regeneration level*: no modular structures, little novelty, too much path dependency, too many rules (p. 94);
- *Kind of experimentation*: little agent vision, reactive, focused on present competition (p. 130).

For evidence that T is *above the 2nd critical value* BE point to

- *Minimal bureaucracy*: rule breaking, loose structure, random communication (p. 30);
- *Too high alliance coadaptation*: over coordination, politics, poorly adapted products (p. 60);
- *Too high a regeneration level*: too much novelty, no building on the past, modular structures disconnected (p. 94);
- *Kind of experimentation*: intense experimentation but too narrowly focused, sporadic (p. 130).

The BE symptoms do not identify the full range of Ts I define earlier, but they make a good start and point the way toward a broader set of symptoms. Some other indications of the system tipping over into the chaotic region could be: emergent groups that subsequently inhibit intergroup networks—the groups become isolates themselves; emergent structure gone wild; the breaking down of structures—such that individual agents tend toward more isolation; oscillation between individual or network domination; and unstable emergent groups.

BE focus on symptoms showing when a system is *outside* the region of emergence. There are also direct symptoms *of* emergence. In general T between the critical values produces emergent dissipative structures, which then start reducing T, at which point they dissipate. Examples are:

- Emergent social networks such as dyadic or triadic communication channels, informal or formal teams, groups, or other network configurations;
- More effective networks within or across groups, more structural equivalence, better proportions of strong and weak ties, more networks emerging between hostile groups—marketing with engineering, or with production, with suppliers, with customers, etc.;
- Emergent networks of any kind, networks that produce novel outcomes, new strategies, new product ideas, new directions of knowledge accumulation; and
- Networks that speed up metabolic (energy or adaptive tension conversion) rates of event occurrence.

Proposition 3: *Tension management that is "adroit" moves the firm into the emergent complexity region by altering the portfolio of Ts impinging on the relevant agent(s) (and attached motivational activators) as evidenced by observable behaviors between the 1st and 2nd critical values.*

Not only does the level of an imposed *T* fall below, between, or above the critical values, the *felt adaptive tension* and the consequent behavioral symptoms could be a function of the number and nature of *T*s hitting any given agent. One *T* per agent, even though significant may not get the agent's behavior above the 1st critical value and too many may shoot it over the 2nd value. This augments the definition of "adroitly" mentioned in Definition 4.

Proposition 4: *Tension management that is "adroit" includes managing the portfolio of Ts impinging on one or more agents so that the total effect of the several Ts produces observable behavioral symptoms landing between the critical values.*

In addition to the BE material, symptoms showing the agent system oscillating from below the 1st to above the 2nd critical value, and vice versa—thereby missing the region of emergence—are worth noting. Oscillation could be a sign that either:

1. An agent system is above the 2nd value and subject to a strange attractor in which the two basins of attraction are agent oscillations in (a) response to the more extreme values of the impinging *T*s; or (b) moves back and forth across the 1st and 2nd critical values;
2. The region between the two values is so narrow that the only response possible is cycling between order and chaos; and
3. The *T*s themselves are fluctuating to the point where the agent system does not stay in the emergence region long enough for emergent structure to form coherently or with stability—that is, the environment is chaotic (Ashby, 1962).

Leaders can deal with (1) above simply by reducing *T* to the point where it falls below the 2nd value. A better strategy is to widen the region of emergent structures as much as possible—the larger the region of emergence the easier it is for the system to avoid oscillating or bifurcating.

Widening the region of emergence requires operating on the location of the critical values themselves—lowering the 1st, raising the 2nd—rather than only trying to adjust the *T*s to fall in between. Much of OD is aimed at getting employees to communicate more—"Increased interaction and communication ... underlies almost all OD interventions. The rule of thumb is: Get people talking and interacting in new, constructive ways and good things will result" (French & Bell, 1995, p. 161). Anything that gets networks to form more easily is essentially lowering the 1st critical value. Raising the 2nd critical value requires training agents to develop (1) more effective emergent structures—so tension stops rising and starts dissipating; and (2) higher tension tolerance to handle higher tension levels before "going chaotic." For example, employees in high-velocity firms in Silicon Valley work routinely in an atmosphere of adaptive tension far higher than might ever appear in large dinosauric firms or government agencies. What seems above the 2nd value in Detroit or Washington may be below the 1st value in Silicon Valley. What seems chaotic to agents with little experience at managing adaptation and forming new networks may seem well below the 2nd critical value to agents experienced in adapting to high-velocity environments. Many OD methods also respond to this issue as well. In fact, most of the 34 "complexity-theory-applied-to-management" books reviewed in Maguire and McKelvey (1999) apply elements of OD to these issues.

Proposition 5: *Lower the 1st critical value by using various OD methods, for example, to increase the ease and pace at which agents form new networks.*

Proposition 6: *Raise the 2nd critical value by (1) increasing: requisite variety (Ashby, 1956) and strength of human capital, experience in adaptation and change, networking capability, tolerance for ambiguity; and (2) using related OD methods aimed at raising the adaptive skills of agents.*

Managing the Attractors

Speeding up the corporate brain's search for new initiatives, could easily lead to lots of newly empowered agents running around out of control wasting funds on silly projects. The previous two sections work on the "fostering-and-speeding-up-emergence" part. Now I turn to the problem of "steering" without inadvertently fostering the emergence of a suppressive command-and-control-bureaucracy. Recall the definitions of *point* and *strange attractors* in Table 9.2.

Bureaucratic negative feedback systems center on point attractors. A visionary leader operates as one—the vision is the goal, which becomes the equilibrium point toward which managerial negative feedback and control processes define the system. Since firms do need strong leaders, and since some people like being strong leaders and behave like strong leaders, it is pointless to think of avoiding point attractors. The trick is to aim these "strong leader types" toward using point attractors that "*drive*" the system toward reducing the *T*s but do not "*define*" the system in the command-and-control ways that inhibit emergence—as I have already noted that Jack Welch did. *T*s *are* point attractors; activities that serve to reduce *T*s, thus, are point attractors. The *portfolio* of *T*s should become the focus of strong leaders' attentions. In managing DI it is essential to have point attractors limited to the *T* symptoms relevant to agents in the DI system. Any other use of point attractors by strong charismatic leaders seems most likely to start defining lower level behaviors, thus working against constructive emergence.

Proposition 7:   *Leader activities are best limited to managing the *T*s, which includes portfolio design and motivational activators.*

Strong leader activities are best redefined to be strange attractors. This is probably the best way in which to view Bennis's "herding cats" meta-phor—the "cage" effect of the rabbit and fox metaphor in Table 2. We may use what Morgan (1996, p. 98) refers to as *"cybernetic reference points"* and *"avoidance of noxiants"* to define the reflective cage of a strange attractor without defining goals that act as point attractors. Strange attractor "definitions of the cage" must be created without determining specific or repeating paths—characteristics of point attractors and opposite the defi-nition of novelty. Core values, core ideologies (Collins & Porras, 1994), and Hewlett-Packard style strong cultures (Schoonhoven & Jelinek, 1990), that keep agent systems from falling off the track of seeking emergent networks and novel approaches to rent generation, can be particularly effective in defining limits without setting up point attractors.

Proposition 8:   *To Improve DI, leader behaviors are best limited to man-aging strange attractors.*

Proposition 9:   *Reference points and noxiants used to define strange attractor cages are best defined so as to avoid moves (1) away from building on existing core competencies and idiosyncratic resources; and (2) away from the more easily discerned "dry wells," and activities apt to endanger the firm.*

Incentives should encourage the proper delineation, separation, and development of point and strange attractors. It is easy to define point attractor incentives—"Here is the goal and I will pay more if you achieve it." Saying "No" is all too easy in firms and seldom needs to be encour-aged. Setting up "inexpensive experiment" strange attractor systems seems more risky and learning when to say "No" to continuing an experi-mental product development activity is problematic (Royer, 2003). Strange attractors also need to be made attractive for agents "inside the cage." Entrepreneurial incentive systems and strange attractor champions seem relevant, following the new product champion idea (Clark & Wheelwright, 1993). Selection processes seem relevant since goal-setting theory (Locke & Latham, 1990) indicates that some people thrive better in basins created by point attractors than by strange attractors. As Stacey (1996) discusses at great length, operating in a strange attractor organization could raise anxiety to dysfunctional levels and, thus, needs to be managed carefully. For a general review of managing incentives and innovation, see Tushman and Anderson (1997).

Proposition 10:   *Incentive systems for strange attractor management are necessarily of the long term variety, encouraging "No's" only to emergent network initiatives likely to endanger the firm, while avoiding easy "No's" that would shut down emergent networks and inexpensive experiments.*

Managing the Agency Problem

Visionary leadership theorists could say that a strong vision at the top (with stock options) is the best defense against the agency problem. Absent this, the DI system will tend to seek the missions of its own agents rather than shareholder wealth. Economists agree, putting their faith in the owner/operator who presumably has the vision (Jensen & Meckling, 1976; Besanko, Dranove, & Shanley, 1996). However, if sustainable competitive advantage and rent generation lies within the DI system, adhering to strong visions held by leaders at the top surely works against shareholder interests—witness Smith's decade of isolated vision at GM (Hunt & Ropo, 1998). Strong visions that create conditions of emergent DI can work for shareholders—as in the shareholder wealth resulting from Welch's approach toward "workouts,"—the empowerment of lower participants (Tichy & Sherman, 1993), and the Hewlett-Packard vision. Even so, if responsibility for strategy lies within the DI system, then the agency problem is relevant. Human and social capital holders could choose to put their own interests ahead of shareholder interests.

If slack resources (March & Simon, 1958) are made available for DI development, then there is the possibility that the slack could be used against shareholder interests. Agency theorists define slack as resources used for non-owner purposes. But slack may be seen constructively as resources available for importation into an emergent system as negentropy, thereby putting dissipative structures in motion. So viewed, slack is another means, in addition to managing the Ts, to tune agents' behaviors and their symptoms toward the emergent complexity region. High Ts that would produce symptoms above the 2nd value without slack—because developing emergent structures without negentropy is more difficult—could produce symptoms between the values if more slack was available.

Slack targeted for DI development should be managed by strange attractors rather than allocated to point attractors. Slack imported into basic research parks is adaptive, but the tension is low as the agents are disconnected from market defined Ts. Connecting slack with specific Ts, but still steering the DI system by strange rather than point attractors seems optimal. The more that market-connected Ts are used to create the conditions leading to emergence, the more likely networks will emerge in response to market-related adaptive problems rather than in response to the interests of individual agents. In most organizations, lack of effective strange attractors (leader activities that define the "cage" without creating an emergent command-and-control bureaucracy), coupled with strong bureaucratically driven point attractors, are the forces giving rise to the classic anti-management informal groups and pursuit of aberrant individual interests. Random agent interests—lacking a unity of response toward Ts—are not likely to give rise to emergent networks absent oppressive command-and-control point attractors uniformly seen as undesirable by the agents. In short, Ts serving to heighten and steer the adaptive tension felt by agents, if designed properly—meaning an adroit mix of point and strange attractors—also serve to mitigate the agency problem.

In light of our goal of finding ways that leaders can produce sustainable rents, leader activities that inhibit DI appreciation actually contribute to the agency problem. DI appreciation depends on staying in the region between the critical values, which in turn depends on "pointing" agents' attention toward the Ts (defined to include incentives). Failure to do this leaves more leeway for agents to pursue their own interests. Furthermore, energetic agent campaigns of experimentation, novelty generation, and new product initiations are less likely to deviate from shareholder interests if they are "caged" within a strange attractor framework.

Proposition 11: *Connecting slack resources to the Ts—as point attractors (that have incentives attached)—aids the reduction of adaptive tension while at the same time mitigating the agency problem—by focusing agent interests toward activities aimed at increasing shareholder wealth.*

Proposition 12: *The mechanics of stimulating the corporate brain toward speedier DI appreciation rates foster more effective adaptation and rent generation while at the same time reducing the agency problem.*

CONCLUSION

Narrowly, I suggest that CEOs wishing to generate sustainable rents in a changing world would be more successful if they used a "microevolutionary theory of the firm" focused on human and social capital appreciation rates, distributed intelligence, complexity theory, and "complexity leadership" activities. More broadly, I show how the relevance of several disciplines bearing on organization science reduces to dependence on dynamics, thereby producing a single overarching framework. The several literatures, dynamically integrated, boil down to the following lessons:

1. Economic rents and competitive advantage depend on human and social capital microstrategy.

2. Rapid microcoevolution of distributed intelligence (DI)—a function of optimal levels of human capital and emergent social networks—forms the basis of novelty, and offsets competitor effects.

3. High-velocity and hypercompetitive contexts require rapid microcoevolution of human and social capital.

4. Current leadership theories, if followed, are more likely to suppress than enhance DI.

5. In firms, the "critical values" of adaptive tension—most likely identified by behavioral symptoms—define the complexity region that stimulates the emergent social capital networks necessary for improving DI.

6. Complexity leadership activities are identified for CEOs to use in speeding up DI appreciation rates for the purpose of producing rents and shareholder wealth.

While New Science advocates still see leadership as crucially important in a rapidly changing nonlinear world, many writers also see a disconnect between a vision-led command-and-control hierarchy and the kind of emergent distributed intelligence giving rise to sustainable economic rents. I use complexity theory's adaptive tension to show how CEOs can speed up the rate of DI appreciation while at the same time suppressing the emergence of bureaucracy. Complexity science recognizes that kinds of complexity are not immutable; they are the result of adaptive tension. Knowing this, if leaders alter the adaptive tension imposed on a system, its kind of complexity changes. Specifically, tuning adaptive tension to between the 1st and 2nd critical values produces emergent network structures. Complexity science, thus, not only offers a more comprehensive means of explaining social phenomena but also offers explicit methods by which CEOs may create fundamental changes in the intrafirm systems for which they are responsible.

I argue that heroic visionary leadership is dysfunctional because of the problem of "leading down" through several intervening levels—it is more apt to suppress the corporate brain than increase its IQ. In contrast, *com-*

plexity leadership produces emergent DI without emergent command-and-control structures. Complexity leadership theory (Uhl-Bien et al., 2007) is not just another multi-level approach to leadership, many of which appear in Dansereau and Yammarino (1998a, b). It builds on the distributed leadership notions discussed by Bryman (1996) and upper echelon leadership ideas by Waldman and Yammarino (1999). It identifies activities for CEOs to use who have to lead entire firms, that is, "lead down" through several intervening levels of organization. It avoids the cascading leader-follower, incremental, one-level-at-a-time approaches of existing leadership writers (see chapters in Dansereau & Yammarino, 1998a, b).

Though my use of microcoevolution, DI, and complexity theory to identify strategic complexity leadership activities is novel, the activities themselves reflect the OD literature. Given this, my essay places CEO-level leadership theory on a joint micro/macro theoretical footing and connects it to rent generation as a common objective for both CEOs and researchers. While not rejecting the psychological and social psychological bases of extant leadership theory and OD, nevertheless, I present a complexity leadership theory that moves macrolevel economic, ecological, and evolutionary theories about organizational function and process into the "microrealm" heretofore left in the hands of psychologists—a new definition of micro OB!

Complexity leadership theory offers promise because it better connects to social system dynamics, specifically, microcoevolution, DI, and complexity theory—rather than just to followers' emotions. It steers leadership theory toward speeding up dynamics rather than focusing on leader attributes. In modern science, agent-based modeling approaches (Carley & Prietula, 1994; Ferber, 1999; North & Macal, 2007) are increasingly pervasive and nowhere is this more true than in studies of coevolution, intelligence, and complexity. These disciplines suggest that effective leaders must focus on how to accelerate their firms' DI appreciation rates—especially in the modern world and especially for the United States, as it grows increasingly dependent on knowledge intensive industries. Leadership theory needs to get on board with the "dynamic" approach.

Theories of bureaucracy and organization (Scott, 1998) put intelligence *in the positions* and in the people holding them, and emphasize human capital appreciation as the basis of competitive advantage. Parallel-processing distributed computer systems put intelligence mostly in the agents with primitive emergent connectionism possible. In contrast, theories of the brain and human intelligence say intelligence *is the network*, a view taken up by Burt (1992) in his emphasis of social capital appreciation as the basis of competitive advantage. None of these views is correct by itself. Combined brain and computer-based distributed systems place intelligence *both* in the agents and in the network. My view of DI in firms builds on both brain and computer analogies.

Given rapidly changing technologies and markets, the use of knowledge in rapidly changing competitive contexts depends on high levels of corporate DI at organizational levels below the CEO. I argue that human and social capital in firms are the basic building blocks of corporate DI. Given this, social networks are critical. Using a Prigogine-based interpretation of complexity theory, I outline some basic activities that CEOs can set in motion to improve stimulate the emergence of social networks, that is, emergent order. Specifically: (1) They allow CEOs to stimulate the emergent order/intelligence process without introducing the kind of strong command-and-control structure that tends to shut down emergent networks and the creation of new ideas; (2) CEO tendencies to set up point attractors are limited to identifying adaptive tensions and the strange attractor notion is used to prevent emergent DI networks from going too far afield; (3) Attention is paid to enlarging the region of emergent complexity; and (4) CEO focus on adaptive tension reduces the agency problem.

AUTHOR NOTE

This chapter has circulated for several years and been cited in other papers under the title of "MicroStrategy from MacroLeadership: Distributed Intelligence from New Science."

ACKNOWLEDGMENTS

I wish to thank Paul Adler, Joel Baum, Chris Earley, Jina Kang, Konstantina Kiousis, Arie Lewin, Mike Lissack, Elaine Mosakowski, and Olav Sorenson for reading the paper and offering many helpful comments. I have also benefited from exchanges at various conferences and workshops where I presented portions of this material: the *New England Complex Systems Institute Conferences*—Nashua, NH, October 1998, Boston, March 1999; the *Organization Science Winter Conference*, Keystone, CO, January 1999; the *MESO Conference*, Duke University, April/May, 1999; the *EIASM Workshop on Complexity and Organization*, Brussels, June 1999; the *MOBS Conference*, Northwestern University, October 1999, the *Knowledge Dynamics Workshop*, Anderson School at UCLA, November 1999; the *Complexity Workshop, Centre for Complexity and Organization*, London School of Economics, March 2000; *Center for the Study of Evolution and the Origin of Life*, UCLA, February 2000; workshops at Cranfield, UK, HEC-Paris, University of Paris-Dauphine, INSEAD, and IMD, March 2000; the *3rd Intangibles Conference on Knowledge*, NYU, May 2000; and the workshop on *Organizational Networks as Distributed Systems of Knowledge*, Otranto, Italy, July 2000; the *Complexity and Complex Systems in Industry Conference*, Warwick University, Coventry, UK. All errors remaining are my responsibility.

NOTES

1. A more detailed definition of coevolution appears in Futuyma and Slatkin (1983). Of particular importance is their attention to the rates at which organisms coevolve and when "coevolution" stops being coevolution and turns into mimicry, evolution, or preadaptive development of traits found, later, to have selective advantage.
2. I follow each argument with a *premise*. Following evolutionary epistemology (Azevedo, 1997; McKelvey, 1999c), a *premise* stands as the *best current collective belief* in the pertinent literature. My premises summarize elements of the more solidly researched literature. Starting in the second section, I state the summaries as *propositions*—seen as one step before refutable hypotheses—which call for research corroboration.
3. For more detail about how Welch unknowingly uses complexity theory to run GE see Mackey, McKelvey, & Kiousis (2006).
4. Quoted in Hamel (2000, p. 102).
5. Meaning that the ability to recreate the whole is carried in redundant parts. For example, the human genome resides in every cell and when appropriately activated can create any aspect of the whole.
6. Schrödinger (1944) coined negentropy to refer to energy importation into an open system.
7. According to a recent conversation between Mike Lissack and Ilya Prigogine, the latter has long regretted not having originally included "self-contained" along with "self-organized" when defining dissipative structures (personal communication from Mike Lissack, Brussels, June 26, 1999).
8. The force leading to a phase transition may be measured as T, the energy (temperature) imposing on, say, a teapot or the earth's atmosphere, or as R, the Reynolds number (the measure of the rate of fluid flow). In latter case it is a direct function of the energy, T, causing the flow. In fluid dynamics, given a T-level causing an increased rate of R, fluid flow becomes turbulent—the phase transition. This "critical value" of R is termed the Rayleigh number, R_c (Lagerstrom, 1996). Hereinafter, I will simply use T in referring to an imposing force or tension to which a system responds, which I will call *adaptive tension*.
9. Actually, "we would fix, sell, or close" (Tichy & Sherman, 1994, p. 108).
10. How wide should the region of emergence be? If a firm spends all of its time above the *edge of order* it could spend all of its energy on self-organization [March's (1991) exploration] and not on being efficient and making profits (March's exploitation). Thomas, Kaminska-Labbé, and McKelvey

(2005) call for oscillation above and below the edge of order. It doesn't seem that there is a limit to raising the 2nd critical value so as to avoid crossing the *edge of chaos*.

11. More likely, *T*s are Pareto-distributed—meaning that most *T*s are small (almost everyday) tensions, but infrequently there is an extreme *T* in the form of avoiding bankruptcy (Ford Motor Co.), or fighting off or making an acquisition, or taking advantage of a new technology (Intel, Google). See Andriani and McKelvey (in press) for a discussion of Gaussian averages versus Pareto distributions.

12. Though the BE book offers useful advice to practicing managers the impression they give of complexity theory could be misleading to naïve readers. They argue that managers should balance their firms between too much rigid bureaucratic structure and chaos—as if these are God-given and etched in stone. Instead, complexity science shows that a complex adaptive system is caused to exist below, between, or above the 1st and 2nd critical values by an adaptive tension (energy differential) acting on the system as an exogenous variable, that naturally (as in the weather) or artificially (as with a Bénard cell) is subject to change and/or manipulation. Put simply, CEOs don't respond to complex adaptive systems as fixed entities—they can inadvertently or purposefully create all three kinds of them!

REFERENCES

Aldrich, H. (1979). *Organizations and environments*. Englewood Cliffs, NJ: Prentice Hall.

Aldrich, H. (1999). *Organizations evolving*. Thousand Oaks, CA: Sage.

Ambrose, D. (1995). Creatively intelligent post-industrial organizations and intellectually impaired bureaucracies. *Journal of Creative Behavior, 29*, 1-15.

Anderson, P. (1999). Complexity theory and organization science. *Organization Science, 10*, 216-232.

Andriani, P., & McKelvey, B. (in press). Beyond Gaussian averages: Extending organization science to extreme events and power laws. *Journal of International Business Studies, 38*(November-December).

Argote, L. (1999). *Organizational learning: Creating, retaining and transferring knowledge*. Norwell, MA: Kluwer.

Arthur, W. B., Durlauf, S. N., & Lane, D. (Eds.) (1997). Introduction. In *The economy as an evolving complex system II* (pp. 1-13). Proceedings of the Santa Fe Institute, Vol. XXVII. Reading, MA: Addison-Wesley.

Ashby, W. R. (1956). *An introduction to cybernetics*. London: Chapman & Hall.

Ashby, W. R. (1962). Principles of the self-organizing system. In H. von Foerster & G. W. Zopf (Eds.), *Principles of self-organization* (pp. 255-278). New York: Pergamon.

Ashkenas, R., Ulrich, D., Jick, T., & Kerr, S. (1995). *The boundaryless organization*. San Francisco: Jossey-Bass.

Auerswald, P., Kauffman, S., Lobo, J., & Shell, K. (2000). A production recipe approach to modeling technological innovation: An application to learning by doing. *Journal of Economic Dynamics and Control, 24*, 389-450.

Avolio, B. J., & Bass, B. M. (1998). Individual consideration viewed at multiple levels of analysis: A multi-level framework for examining the diffusion of transformational leadership. In F. Dansereau & F. J. Yammarino (Eds.), *Leadership: Multiple-level approaches: Contemporary and alternative* (pp. 53-74). Stamford, CT: JAI Press.

Avolio, B. J., Kahai, S., & Dodge, G. E. (2001). E-leadership: Implications for theory, research, and practice. *The Leadership Quarterly, 11*, 615-618.

Azevedo, J. (1997). Mapping reality: An evolutionary realist methodology for the natural and social sciences. Albany: State University of New York Press.

Barnett, W. P., & Hansen, M. T. (1996). The Red Queen in organizational evolution. *Strategic Management Journal, 17*, 139-157.

Barney, J. B. (1991). Firm resources and sustained competitive advantage. *Journal of Management, 17*, 99-120.

Bass, B. M. (1981). *Stogdill's handbook of leadership: A survey of theory and research* (rev. ed.). New York: Free Press/Macmillan.

Bass, B. M. (1985). *Leadership and performance beyond expectations.* New York: Free Press.

Bass, B. M., Waldman, D. A., Avolio, B. J., & Bebb, M. (1987). Transformational leadership and the falling dominoes effect. *Group and Organization Studies, 12*, 73-87.

Baum, J. A. C. (1996). Organizational ecology. In S. R. Clegg, C. Hardy & W. R. Nord (Eds.), *Handbook of organization studies* (pp. 77-114). Thousand Oaks, CA: Sage.

Baum, J. A. C., & Shipilov, A. V. (2006). Ecological approaches to organizations. In S. Clegg, C. Hardy, T. Lawrence & W. Nord (Eds.), *Handbook of organization studies* (2nd ed., pp. 55-110). Thousand Oaks, CA: Sage.

Baum, J. A. C., & McKelvey, B. (Eds.). (1999). *Variations in organization science: In honor of Donald T. Campbell.* Thousand Oaks, CA: Sage.

Beatty, R. W., & Ulrich, D. (1991). Re-energizing the mature organization. *Organizational Dynamics, 20*, 16-30.

Becker, G. S. (1975). *Human capital* (2nd ed.). Chicago: University of Chicago Press.

Bennis, W. G. (1996). Becoming a leader of leaders. In R. Gibson (Ed.), *Rethinking the future* (pp. 148-163). London: Brealey.

Bennis, W. G., & Nanus, B. (1985). *Leaders: Strategies for taking charge.* New York: Harper & Row.

Bennis, W. G., & Biederman, P. W. (1996). *Organizing genius: The secrets of creative collaboration.* Reading, MA: Addison-Wesley.

Bénard, H. (1901). Les tourbillons cellulaires dans une nappe liquide transportant de la chaleur par convection en régime permanent [Turbulent cells in a liquid phase subjected to a convection heat transmission under an established regime]. *Annales de Chimie et de Physique, 23*, 62-144.

Besanko, D., Dranove, D., & Shanley, M. (1996). *The economics of strategy.* New York: Wiley.

Boisot, M. (1998). *Knowledge assets.* New York: Oxford University Press.

Brown, M. E., & Gioia, D. A. (2002). Making things click: Distributive leadership in an online division of an offline organization. *The Leadership Quarterly, 13,* 297-419.

Brown, S. L., & Eisenhardt, K. M. (1997). The art of continuous change: Linking complexity theory and time-paced evolution in relentlessly shifting organizations. *Administrative Science Quarterly, 42,* 1-34.

Brown, S. L., & Eisenhardt, K. M. (1998). *Competing on the edge: Strategy as structured chaos.* Boston: Harvard Business School Press.

Bryman, A. (1996). Leadership in organizations. In S. R. Clegg, C. Hardy & W. R. Nord (Eds.), *Handbook of organization studies* (pp. 276-292). Thousand Oaks, CA: Sage.

Buckley, W. (1967). *Sociology and modern systems theory.* Englewood Cliffs, NJ: Prentice-Hall.

Burgelman, R. A., & Mittman, B. S. (1994). An intraorganizational ecological perspective on managerial risk behavior, performance, and survival: Individual, organizational and environmental effects. In J. A. C. Baum & J. V. Singh (Eds.), *Evolutionary dynamics of organizations* (pp. 53-75). New York: Oxford University Press.

Burt, R. S. (1992). *Structural holes: The social structure of competition.* Cambridge, MA: Harvard University Press.

Burt, R. S. (1997). The contingent value of social capital. *Administrative Science Quarterly, 42,* 339-365.

Carley, K. M., & Prietula, M. J. (Eds.). (1994). *Computational organization theory.* Hillsdale, NJ: Erlbaum.

Chandler, A. D., Jr. (1977). *The visible hand: The managerial revolution in American business.* Cambridge, MA: Belknap/Harvard University Press.

Child, J. (1972). Organizational structure, environment and performance: The role of strategic choice. *Sociology, 6,* 2-22.

Clark, K. B., & Wheelwright, S. C. (1993). *Managing new product and process development.* New York: Free Press.

Collins, J. G., & Porras, J. I. (1994). *Built to last.* New York: HarperCollins.

Cowan, G. A. (1994). Conference opening remarks. In G. A. Cowan, D. Pines & D. Meltzer (Eds.), *Complexity: Metaphors, models, and reality* (pp. 1-9). Proceedings of the Santa Fe Institute, Vol. XIX. Reading, MA: Addison-Wesley.

Cowan, G. A., Pines, D., & Meltzer, D. (Eds.). (1994). *Complexity: Metaphors, models, and reality.* Proceedings of the Santa Fe Institute, Vol. XIX. Reading, MA: Addison-Wesley.

Cramer, F. (1993). *Chaos and order: The complex structure of living things* (D. L. Loewus, Trans.). New York: VCH.

D'Aveni, R. A. (1994). *Hypercompetition: Managing the dynamics of strategic maneuvering.* New York: Free Press.

Daft, R. L., & Lengel, R. H. (1998). *Fusion leadership.* San Francisco: Berrett-Koehler.

Dansereau, F., & Yammarino, F. J. (Eds.). (1998a). *Leadership: Multiple-level approaches: Classical and new wave.* Stamford, CT: JAI Press.

Dansereau, F., & Yammarino, F. J. (Eds.). (1998b). *Leadership: Multiple-level approaches: Contemporary and alternative.* Stamford, CT: JAI Press.

Darby, M. R., Liu, Q., & Zucker, L. G. (1999). *Stakes and stars: The effect of intellectual human capital on the level and variability of high-tech firms' market values.* Working paper # 7201, Cambridge, MA: National Bureau of Economic Research.

Day, D. V. (1998). Leadership sensemaking—Parts, wholes, and beyond. In F. Dansereau & F. J. Yammarino (Eds.), *Leadership: Multiple-level approaches: Contemporary and alternative* (pp. 191-198). Stamford, CT: JAI Press.

Dubin, R. (1979). Metaphors of leadership: An overview. In J. G. Hunt & L. L. Larson (Eds.), *Cross-currents in leadership* (pp. 225-238). Carbondale: Southern Illinois University Press.

Eddington, A. (1930). *The nature of the physical world.* London: Macmillan.

Ehrlich, P. R., & Raven, P. H. (1964). Butterflies and plants: A study in coevolution. *Evolution, 18,* 586-608.

Eisenhardt, K. M. (1989). Making fast strategic decisions in high-velocity environments. *Academy of Management Journal, 32,* 543-576.

Eisenhardt, K. M., & Tabrizi, B. N. (1995). Accelerating adaptive processes: Product innovation in the global computer industry. *Administrative Science Quarterly, 40,* 84-110.

Fayol, H. (1916). *Administration industrielle et générale.* [Reprinted as *General and industrial management* (C. Storrs, Trans.). London: Pitman.]

Ferber, J. (1999). *Multi-agent systems: An introduction to distributed artificial intelligence.* London: Addison-Wesley.

Fisher, R. A. (1930). *The genetical theory of natural selection.* Oxford, England: Clarendon.

French, W. L., & Bell, C. H., Jr. (1995). *Organization development* (5th ed.). Englewood Cliffs, NJ: Prentice-Hall.

French, W. L., Bell, C. H., Jr., & Zawacki, R. A. (Eds.). (1994). *Organization development and transformation.* Burr Ridge, IL: Irwin.

Fuster, J. M. (1995). *Memory in the cerebral cortex: An empirical approach to neural networks in the human and nonhuman primate.* Boston: MIT Press.

Futuyma, D. J. (1979). *Evolutionary biology.* Sunderland, MA: Sinauer Associates.

Futuyma, D. J., & Slatkin, M. (1983). Introduction. In D. J. Futuyma & M. Slatkin (Eds.), *Coevolution* (pp. 1-13). Sunderland, MA: Sinauer.

Galbraith, J. R., & Lawler, E. E., III, & Associates. (1993). *Organizing for the future: The new logic for managing complex organizations.* San Francisco: Jossey-Bass.

Garzon, M. (1995). *Models of massive parallelism.* Berlin: Springer-Verlag.

Gell-Mann, M. (2002). What is complexity? In A. Q. Curzio & M. Fortis (Eds.), *Complexity and industrial clusters: Dynamics and models in theory and practice* (pp. 13-24). Heidelberg, Germany: Physica-Verlag.

General Electric: The house that Jack built. (1999a, September 18-24). *The Economist, 352,* 23-26.

Gleick, J. (1987). *Chaos: Making a new science.* New York: Penguin.

Goldstein, J. (1994). *The unshackled organization.* Portland, OR: Productivity Press.

Granovetter, M. (1985). Economic action and social structure: A theory of embeddedness. *American Journal of Sociology, 82,* 929-964.

Granovetter, M. (1992). Problems of explanation in economic sociology. In N. Nohria & R. G. Eccles (Eds.), *Networks and organizations: Structure, form, and action* (pp. 25-56). Boston: Harvard Business School Press.

Hall, R. J., & Lord, R. G. (1998). Multi-level information-processing explanations of followers' leadership perceptions. In F. Dansereau & F. J. Yammarino (Eds.), *Leadership: Multiple-level approaches: Contemporary and alternative* (pp. 159-183). Stamford, CT: JAI Press.

Hamel, G. (2000, June). Reinvent your company. *Fortune*, 99-118.

Hamel, G., & Prahalad, C. K. (1994). *Competing for the future*. Boston: Harvard Business School Press.

Hannan, M. T., & Freeman, J. (1977). The population ecology of organizations. *American Journal of Sociology, 83*, 929-984.

Hannan, M. T., & Freeman, J. (1989). *Organizational ecology*. Cambridge, MA: Harvard University Press.

Heene, A., & Sanchez, R. (Eds.). (1997). *Competence-based strategic management*. Chichester, England: Wiley.

Herbst, P. G. (1970). *Behavioural worlds: The study of two cases*. London: Tavistock.

Holland, J. H. (1988). The global economy as an adaptive system. In P. W. Anderson, K. J. Arrow, & D. Pines (Eds.), *The economy as an evolving complex system* (pp. 117-124). Proceedings of the Santa Fe Institute, Vol. V. Reading, MA: Addison-Wesley.

Hosking, D. M. (1988). Organizing, leadership and skilful process. *Journal of Management Studies, 25*, 147-166.

House, R. J. (1977). A 1976 theory of charismatic leadership. In J. G. Hunt & L. L. Larson (Eds.), *Leadership: The cutting edge* (pp. 189-207). Carbondale: Southern Illinois University Press.

Hunt, J. G., & Ropo, A. (1998). Multi-level leadership: Grounded theory and mainstream theory applied to the case of General Motors. In F. Dansereau & F. J. Yammarino (Eds.), *Leadership: Multiple-level approaches: Classical and new wave* (pp. 289-327). Stamford, CT: JAI Press.

Ingram, P., & Roberts, P. W. (1999). Suborganizational evolution in the U. S. pharmaceutical industry. In J. A. C. Baum & B. McKelvey (Eds.), *Variations in organization science: In honor of Donald T. Campbell* (pp. 155-168). Thousand Oaks, CA: Sage.

Janis, I. L. (1972). *Victims of groupthink*. Boston: Houghton Mifflin.

Jensen, M. C., & Meckling, W. H. (1976). Theory of the firm: Managerial behavior, agency costs, and ownership structure. *Journal of Financial Economics, 3*, 305-360.

Johnson, J. L., & Burton, B. K. (1994). Chaos and complexity theory for management. *Journal of Management Inquiry, 3*, 320-328.

Katz, D., Kahn, R. L., & Adams, J. S. (Eds.). (1980). *The study of organizations*. San Francisco: Jossey-Bass.

Katzenbach, J. R., & Smith, D. K. (1993). *The wisdom of teams: Creating the high-performance organization*. Boston: Harvard Business School Press.

Kauffman, S. A. (1993). *The origins of order: Self-organization and selection in evolution*. New York: Oxford University Press.

Kelly, S., & Allison, M. A. (1999). *The complexity advantage*. New York: McGraw-Hill.

Klein, K. J., & House, R. J. (1998). On fire: Charismatic leadership and levels of analysis. In F. Dansereau & F. J. Yammarino (Eds.), *Leadership: Multiple-level approaches: Contemporary and alternative* (pp. 3-21). Stamford, CT: JAI Press.

Kotter, J. P. (1996). *Leading change.* Boston: Harvard Business School Press.

Kotter, J. P., & Heskett, J. L. (1992). *Corporate culture and performance.* New York: Free Press.

Kouzes, J. M., & Posner, B. Z. (1993). *Credibility: How leaders gain and lose it, why people demand it.* San Francisco: Jossey-Bass.

Koza, M. P., & Lewin, A. Y. (1998). The co-evolution of strategic alliances. *Organization Science, 9,* 255-264.

Lagerstrom, P. A. (1996). *Laminar flow theory.* Princeton, NJ: Princeton University Press.

Leonard-Barton, D. (1995). *Wellsprings of knowledge.* Boston: Harvard Business School Press.

Levins, R. (1968). *Evolution in changing environments.* Princeton, NJ: Princeton University Press.

Levinthal, D. A. (1997). Adaptation on rugged landscapes. *Management Science, 43,* 934-950.

Levy, D. (1994). Chaos theory and strategy: Theory, application and managerial implications. *Strategic Management Journal, 15,* 167-178.

Lewin, R. (1999). *Complexity: Life at the edge of chaos.* Chicago: University of Chicago Press. (Original work published 1992)

Liebeskind, J. P., Oliver, A. L., Zucker, L., & Brewer, M. (1996). Social networks, learning, and flexibility: Sourcing scientific knowledge in new biotechnology firms. *Organization Science, 7,* 428-443.

Linstead, S., & Grafton-Small, R. (1992). On reading organizational culture. *Organization Studies, 13,* 331-355.

Locke, E. A., & Latham, G. P. (1990). *Goal setting: A motivational technique that works.* Englewood Cliffs, NJ: Prentice-Hall.

Lomi, A., & Larsen, E. R. (1999). Evolutionary models of local interaction: A computational perspective. In J. A. C. Baum & B. McKelvey (Eds.), *Variations in organization science: In honor of Donald T. Campbell* (pp. 255-278). Thousand Oaks, CA: Sage.

Lorrain, F., & White, H. C. (1971). Structural equivalence of individuals in social networks. *Journal of Mathematical Sociology, 1,* 49-80.

Mackey, A., McKelvey, B., & Kiousis, P. K. (2006, August). Can the CEO churning problem be fixed? Lessons from complexity science, Jack Welch & AIDS. Presented at the Academy of Management Meeting, Atlanta, GA.

Madsen, T. L., Mosakowski, E., & Zaheer, S. (1999). Static & dynamic variation and firm outcomes. In J. A. C. Baum & B. McKelvey (Eds.), *Variations in organization science: In honor of Donald T. Campbell* (pp. 213-236). Thousand Oaks, CA: Sage.

Maguire, S., & McKelvey, B. (1999). Complexity and management: Moving from fad to firm foundations. *Emergence, 1*(2) 19-61.

Maguire, S., McKelvey, B., Mirabeau, L., & Oztas, N. (2006). Complexity science and organization studies. In S. Clegg, C. Hardy, T. Lawrence & W. Nord

(Eds.), *Handbook of organization studies* (2nd ed., pp. 165-214). Thousand Oaks, CA: Sage.

Mainzer, K. (2004 1994). *Thinking in complexity: The complex dynamics of matter, mind, and mankind* (4th ed.). New York: Springer-Verlag. (Original work published 1994)

Manz, C. C., & Sims, H. P. (1987). Leading workers to lead themselves: The external leadership of self-managing work teams. *Administrative Science Quarterly, 32,* 106-129.

March, J. G. (1991). Exploration and exploitation in organization learning. *Organization Science, 2,* 71-87.

March, J. G., & Simon, H. A. (1958). *Organizations.* New York: Wiley.

Marion, R., & Uhl-Bien, M. (2001). Leadership in complex organizations. *The Leadership Quarterly, 12,* 389-418.

Markham, S. E., & Markham, I. S. (1998). Self-management and self-leadership reexamined: A levels-of-analysis perspective. In F. Dansereau & F. J. Yammarino (Eds.), *Leadership: Multiple-level approaches: Classical and new wave* (pp. 193-210). Stamford, CT: JAI Press.

Martin, J. (1992). *Cultures in organizations: Three perspectives.* New York: Oxford University Press.

Masuch, M., & Warglien, M. (1992). *Artificial intelligence in organization and management theory.* Elsevier Science, Amsterdam, The Netherlands.

Maynard Smith, J., & Szathmáry, E. (1995). *The major transitions in evolution.* Oxford, England: Freeman and Spektrum.

McKelvey, B. (1982). *Organizational systematics: Taxonomy, evolution, classification.* Berkeley, CA: University of California Press.

McKelvey, B. (1997). Quasi-natural organization science. *Organization Science, 8,* 351-380.

McKelvey, B. (1998). Complexity vs. selection among coevolutionary firms. *Comportamento Organizacionale Gestão, 4,* 17-59.

McKelvey, B. (1999a). Avoiding complexity catastrophe in coevolutionary pockets: Strategies for rugged landscapes. *Organization Science, 10,* 294-321.

McKelvey, B. (1999b). Self-organization, complexity catastrophe, and microstate models at the edge of chaos. In J. A. C. Baum & B. McKelvey (Eds.), *Variations in organization science: In honor of Donald T. Campbell* (pp. 279-307). Thousand Oaks, CA: Sage.

McKelvey, B. (1999c). Toward a Campbellian realist organization science. In J. A. C. Baum & B. McKelvey (Eds.), *Variations in organization science: In honor of Donald T. Campbell* (pp. 383-411). Thousand Oaks, CA: Sage.

McKelvey, B. (2004a). Toward a 0th law of thermodynamics: Order creation complexity dynamics from physics & biology to bioeconomics. *Journal of Bioeconomics, 6,* 65-96.

McKelvey, B. (2004b). Toward a complexity science of entrepreneurship. *Journal of Business Venturing, 19,* 313-341.

Meyer, M. W., & Zucker, L. G. (1989). *Permanently failing organizations.* Newbury Park, CA: Sage.

Merrill, H. F. (1960). *Classics in management.* New York: American Management Association.

Miller, D. (1999). Selection processes inside organizations: The self-reinforcing consequences of success. In J. A. C. Baum & B. McKelvey (Eds.), *Variations in organization science: In honor of Donald T. Campbell* (pp. 93-109). Thousand Oaks, CA: Sage.

Miner, A. S. (1994). Seeking adaptive advantage: Evolutionary theory and managerial action. In J. A. C. Baum & J. V. Singh (Eds.), *Evolutionary dynamics of organizations* (pp. 76-89). New York: Oxford University Press.

Morgan, G. (1996). *Images of organization* (2nd ed.). Thousand Oaks, CA: Sage.

Morrison, F. (1991). *The art of modeling dynamic systems.* New York: Wiley Interscience.

Mosakowski, E. (1997). Strategy making under causal ambiguity: Conceptual issues and empirical evidence. *Organization Science, 8,* 414-442.

Nanus, B. (1992). *Visionary leadership.* San Francisco, CA: Jossey-Bass.

Nelson, R. R., & Winter, S. (1982). *An evolutionary theory of economic change.* Cambridge, MA: Belknap.

Nicolis, G., & Prigogine, I. (1989). *Exploring complexity: An introduction.* New York: Cambridge, MA: Freeman.

Nohria, N., & Eccles, R. G. (Eds.). (1992). *Networks and organizations: Structure, form, and action.* Boston: Harvard Business School Press.

ogilvie, d. (1998). *Creativity and strategy from a complexity theory perspective.* Presented at the 10th International Conference on Socio-Economics, Vienna, Austria.

Page, S. E. (2007). *The difference: How the power of diversity creates better groups, firms, schools, and societies.* Princeton, NJ: Princeton University Press.

Parry, K. W., & Bryman, A. (2006). Leadership in organizations. In S. R. Clegg, C. Hardy, T. B. Lawrence & W. R. Nord (Eds.), *Handbook of organization studies* (2nd ed.), pp. 447-468. London: Sage.

Peters, T. J., & Waterman, R. H. (1982). *In search of excellence: Lessons from America's best-run companies.* New York: Harper & Row.

Pianka, E. R. (1994). *Evolutionary ecology* (5th ed.). New York: HarperCollins.

Porter, M. E. (1985). *Competitive advantage.* New York: Free Press.

Porter, M. E. (1996). What is strategy? *Harvard Business Review, 74,* 61-78.

Prahalad, C. K., & Hamel, G. (1990). The core competence of the corporation. *Harvard Business Review, 68,* 78-91.

Prigogine, I., & Stengers, I. (1984). *Order out of chaos: Man's new dialogue with nature.* New York: Bantam.

Prusak, L. (1996). The knowledge advantage. *Strategy & Leadership, 24,* 6-8.

The revolutionary spirit. (1999b, September 18-24). *The Economist, 352,* 17-18.

Rivkin, J. W. (2000). Imitation of complex strategies. *Management Science, 46,* 824-844.

Rivkin, J. W. (2001). Reproducing knowledge: Replication without imitation at moderate complexity. *Organization Science, 12,* 274-293.

Rosenkopf, L., & Nerkar, A. (1999). On the complexity of technological evolution: Exploring coevolution within and across hierarchical levels in optical disc technology. In J. A. C. Baum & B. McKelvey (Eds.), *Variations in organization science: In honor of Donald T. Campbell* (pp. 169-183). Thousand Oaks, CA: Sage.

Royer, I. (2003). Why are bad projects so hard to kill? *Harvard Business Review*, *81*(2) 48-56.

Rumelt, R. P. (1987). Theory, strategy, and entrepreneurship. In D. J. Teece (Ed.), *The competitive challenge* (pp. 137-158). Cambridge, MA: Ballinger.

Sanchez, R. (1995). Strategic flexibility in product competition. *Strategic Management Journal, 16*, 135-159.

Schein, E. H. (1985). *Organizational culture and leadership*. San Francisco: Jossey-Bass.

Schein, E. H. (1990). Organizational culture. *American Psychologist, 45*, 109-119.

Schilling, M. (2000). Toward a general modular systems theory and its application to interfirm product modularity. *Academy of Management Review, 25*, 312-334.

Schoonhoven, C. B., & Jelinek, M. (1990). Dynamic tension in innovative, high technology firms: Managing rapid technological change through organizational structure. In M. A. Von Glinow & S. A. Mohrman (Eds.), *Managing complexity in high technology organizations* (pp. 90-118). New York: Oxford University Press.

Schrödinger, E. (1944). *What is life? The physical aspect of the living cell*. Cambridge, England: Cambridge University Press.

Scott, W. R. (1995). *Institutions and organizations*. Thousand Oaks, CA: Sage.

Scott, W. R. (1998). *Organizations: Rational, natural, and open systems* (4th ed.). Upper Saddle River, NJ: Prentice-Hall.

Siehl, C. (1985). After the founder: An opportunity to manage culture. In P. F. Frost, L. F. Moore, M. R. Louis, C. C. Lundberg & J. Martin (Eds.), *Organizational culture* (pp. 125-140). Newbury Park, CA: Sage.

Slater, R. (2001). *Get better or get beaten: 29 leadership secrets from GE's Jack Welch*. New York: McGraw-Hill.

Slatkin, M. (1983). Genetic background. In D. J. Futuyma & M. Slatkin (Eds.), *Coevolution* (pp. 14-32). Sunderland, MA: Sinauer.

Slywotzky, A. (1996). *Value migration*. Boston: Harvard Business School Press.

Sorensen, J. B. (2002). The strength of corporate culture and the reliability of firm performance. *Administrative Science Quarterly, 47*, 70-91,

Stacey, R. D. (1995). The science of complexity: An alternative perspective for strategic change processes. *Strategic Management Journal, 16*, 477-495.

Stacey, R. D. (1996). *Complexity and creativity in organizations*. London: Berrett-Koehler.

Stewart, T. A. (1999, September 27). See Jack. See Jack run Europe. *Fortune, 140*, 124-136.

Surowiecki, J. (2004). *The wisdom of crowds: Why the many are smarter than the few and how collective wisdom shapes business, economies, societies and nations*. New York: Doubleday.

Teece, D. J., Pisano, G., & Shuen, A. (1994). Dynamic capabilities and strategic management. *Strategic Management Journal, 18*, 509-533.

Thiétart, R. A., & Forgues, B. (1995). Chaos theory and organization. *Organization Science, 6*, 19-31.

Thomas, C., Kaminska-Labbé, R., & McKelvey, B. (2005). Managing the MNC and exploitation/exploration dilemma: From static balance to irregular oscillation. In G. Szulanski, Y. Doz & J. Porac (Eds.), *Advances in strategic management* (Vol. 22, pp. 213-247). Oxford, England: Elsevier.

Thompson, J. N. (1994). *The coevolutionary process.* Chicago: University of Chicago Press.

Tichy, N. M., & Sherman, S. (1994). *Control your destiny or someone else will.* New York: HarperCollins.

Trist, E. L., & Bamforth, K. W. (1951). Social and psychological consequences of the longwall method of coal-getting. *Human Relations, 4*, 3-28.

Tushman, M. L., & Anderson, P. (1997). *Managing strategic innovation and change: A collection of readings.* New York: Oxford University Press.

Uhl-Bien, M., Marion, R., & McKelvey, B. (2007). Complexity leadership: Shifting leadership from the industrial age to the knowledge era. *The Leadership Quarterly, 18*(4), 298-318.

Ulrich, D., Zenger, J., & Smallwood, N. (1999). *Results-based leadership.* Boston: Harvard Business School Press.

Van Valen, L. (1992). Ecological species, multispecies, and oaks. In M. Ereshefsky (Ed.), *The units of evolution: Essays on the nature of species* (pp. 69-77). Cambridge, MA: MIT Press.

Waldman D. A., & Yammarino, F. J. (1999). CEO charismatic leadership: Levels-of-management and levels-of-analysis effects. *Academy of Management Review, 24*, 266-285.

Weick, K. E. (1985). Systematic observational methods. In G. Lindzey & E. Aronson (Eds.), *The handbook of social psychology* (3rd ed., Vol. 1, pp. 567-634). New York: Random House.

Weick, K. E. (1993). The collapse of sensemaking in organizations: The Mann Gulch disaster. *Administrative Science Quarterly, 38*, 628-652.

Weick, K. E. (1995). *Sensemaking in organizations.* Thousand Oaks, CA: Sage.

Welch, J. (1991). *Annual report.* General Electric Corporation.

Wernerfelt, B. (1984). A resource-based view of the firm. *Strategic Management Journal, 5*, 171-180.

Wheatley, M. J. (1992). *Leadership and the new science: Learning about organization from an orderly universe.* San Francisco: Berrett-Koehler.

Willmott, H. (1993). Strength is ignorance: Slavery is freedom: Managing culture in modern organizations. *Journal of Management Studies, 30*, 515-552.

Yammarino, F. J. (1994). Indirect leadership: Transformational leadership at a distance. In B. M. Bass & B. J. Avolio (Eds.), *Improving organizational effectiveness through transformational leadership* (pp. 26-47). Thousand Oaks, CA: Sage.

Zimmerman, B. J., & Hurst, D. K. (1993). Breaking the boundaries: The fractal organization. *Journal of Management Inquiry, 2*, 334-355.

Zucker, L. G., & Darby, M. R. (1996). Star scientists and institutional transformation: Patterns of invention and innovation in the formation of the biotechnology industry. *Proceedings of the National Academy of Sciences, 93*, 12,709-12,716.

Zohar, D. (1997). *Rewiring the corporate brain.* San Francisco: Berrett-Koehler.

CHAPTER 10

RESEARCH METHODS FOR STUDYING THE COMPLEXITY DYNAMICS OF LEADERSHIP

Kevin J. Dooley and Benyamin Lichtenstein

ABSTRACT

Significantly, novel leadership theory can be developed by examining the dynamics of leadership processes. Leadership dynamics are temporal patterns of leadership action and interaction which may impact group performance positively or negatively. Leadership dynamics can exist in multiple time scales—from minutes to hours to days to months. This chapter presents an integrated research methodology for studying leadership dynamics at 3 time scales: real-time observation for microscale dynamics, social network analysis for mesoscale dynamics, and event history analysis for macroscale dynamics. Examples are presented from a case study, the ASU Software Factory, where the methodology was employed.

INTRODUCTION

In the new view of complexity leadership, leading is a process that occurs in the interactions between any two individuals (Lichtenstein, Uhl-Bien, et al., 2006; Uhl-Bien, 2006). In contrast to the old view of a single leader

Complexity Leadership, Part I: Conceptual Foundations
pp. 269–290
Copyright © 2008 by Information Age Publishing
All rights of reproduction in any form reserved.

who takes independent actions aimed at changing individual and organizational behavior, complexity leadership focuses on the dynamics of leadership as it emerges over time in all arenas of an organizational system. Each interchange and every connection provide opportunities for leading, as peers individually and collectively learn, grow and engage in the continuous process of organizing (Weick, Sutcliffe, & Obstfeld, 2005; Uhl-Bien, 2006).

Seeing leadership as a relational phenomenon that is distributed across individuals goes beyond current conceptions of shared leadership (Pearce & Conger, 2003), collective leadership (Weick & Roberts, 1993), distributed leadership (Gronn, 2002), or relational leadership (Drath, 2001; Uhl-Bien, 2006). The new complexity view recognizes the dynamic interplay of leading in organizations, attending to the way leadership emerges across multiple levels and multiple time scales (Lichtenstein, Uhl-Bien, et al., 2006). Complexity leadership focuses on these processes of change in individuals, groups, ventures, organizations and institutions occurring in daily interactions, interventions that occur in weekly or monthly time scales, and macrosocial events that accrue over months and years. Two good examples of emergent leadership at multiple levels are Chiles, Meyer and Hench's (2004) analysis of how entrepreneurial and institutional interactions led to the emergence and transformation of Branson, MO; and Plowman and colleagues' (Plowman, Baker, et al., 2007; Plowman, Solansky, et al., 2007) exploration of multiple levels of activity that led to the continuous-radical transformation at "Mission Church."

Given the importance of understanding how leadership emerges through specific interchanges—differently in every interaction—we need to develop methodologies for identifying and measuring these complex and temporally-based leadership dynamics. A variety of methods have been offered that might accomplish this task, but until now these approaches have not be categorized or brought together. For example, Dooley, Daneke, and Pathak (2005) have tracked the daily media interactions of Motorola's Iridium venture, showing how its failure was related to certain errors of leadership timing during start-up. Alternatively, social networks have been used to explore the interactions leading to long-term changes within a leadership context (e.g. Carley, Lee, & Krackhardt, 2001; Schreiber, Singh, & Carley, 2004). Additionally, an event history analysis approach was used by Lichtenstein, Dooley, and Lumpkin (2006) to explore the leadership activities of one entrepreneur who was trying to start-up a new business venture. The objective of chapter is to present an integrated research methodology which studies the dynamics of leadership interactions over time.

Leadership Dynamics as a Fractal Time Ecology

According to the recent research in complexity leadership, the essence of leading occurs in the interactions between individuals, interactions that by their nature are dynamic, that is, they occur *in* time and *across* time(s). Time and temporal dynamics have been shown to have a critical effect in explaining emergence (Lichtenstein, Carter, Dooley & Gartner, in press) and the leadership of emergence (Plowman, Baker, et al., 2007; Plowman, Solansky, et al., 2007). What we present is a broader framework that recognizes three differing scales of time—micro, meso, and macro—and how these interact to create what Koehler (2001) has termed a "fractal time ecology."

Leadership can occur in minute-by-minute interactions—the microlevel conversations and interactions of individuals working together in a focused way. Methodologically, such microlevel interactions can be shown to have a dynamical signature (Dooley & Van de Ven, 1999), representing an underlying pattern of order. This pattern can inform us of the underlying drivers of the process, which is a crucial component of what we are seeking in a complexity theory of leadership.

Leadership also occurs in interactions and outcomes at a mesolevel, that is, through daily and weekly small-scale changes in relationships and processes within an organization. Similarly, leadership can occur in macrolevel time—over weeks and even months through significant events and emergent sensemaking that can guide the cognitive and behavioral routines of individuals and whole organizations. Like interactions at a microlevel, an analysis of mesolevel and macrolevel interactions and their outcomes may reveal patterns which help explain exactly how leadership emerged in those interactions, as well as other causal dynamics in the system.

In a fractal time ecology (Koehler, 2001) the assumption is that dynamical patterns at one level of interaction are linked to emergent patterns at other levels. For example, dynamical patterns at a microlevel time horizon may be linked to emergent patterns in meso- and macrolevel time horizons. In the context of a group, we suggest that patterns of leadership interaction enacted minute-by-minute may be connected to the patterns observed over days, weeks, months, and years. In this way, the patterns are "fractal," since the same patterns may be repeated at multiple scales. For the same reasons, macropatterns may constrain meso- and micropatterns. These links between levels reflect an ecology of interactions, which is at the heart of a complexity model of leadership.

In this chapter we discuss specific research methods for studying leadership interaction at these three different time scales:

- Microscale interactions can be studied with real-time observation techniques (Dooley, Corman, McPhee, & Kuhn, 2003);
- Mesoscale interactions across days and weeks can be studied using social network analysis (Wasserman & Faust, 1994), and
- Macroscale interactions across weeks, months and even longer can be studied using event history analysis (Poole, Van de Ven, Dooley, & Holmes, 2000).

Our goal is to provide examples of how these methods can be used to study leadership dynamics, and discuss practical implementation issues. (However, the chapter is not meant to be a methods tutorial, nor do we attempt to develop specific theory from our analyses.)

Studying leadership processes at multiple time-scales provides several benefits. First, comparison across time-scales allows us to study processes of emergence and structuration, which offer a much more in-depth view of the dynamics of leadership in interactions. Second, most existing leadership theories were developed outside of time, based on a cross-sectional view of leadership being directed from one person. A view of leadership that emerges in interactions requires a highly dynamic methodology which can capture the nuanced and multiplex nature of those interactions and their results. These approaches, combining temporality and multiple levels, are likely to generate novel insights into leadership and its emergence throughout organizations.

Research Context: The Software Factory at ASU

As we explain each of the three methods, we will draw examples from a single context: the Arizona State University "Software Factory" (Dooley & Corman, 2002). The ASU Software Factory (SF) provided software development services to the research scientists within Arizona State University (ASU). The development group was managed by a single professional manager, who oversaw 6 to 18 employees (student programmers) at a time, organized into project teams of one to six people. Typical work projects involved reengineering existing software code to extend functionality or translate to a new technology platform, and development of new software, primarily involving complex computation or equipment control.

The SF used "agile development methods" (Boehm & Turner, 2004) that included pair programming and frequent customer interaction. These methods reflect certain qualities that we see in complexity leadership, especially the phenomenon of leadership emergence (Guastello, 1995; Guastello, Hyde, & Odak, 1998). Specifically, aside from the single professional manager, there were no other defined roles, so any leadership network that emerged was due to the dynamic interaction of personalities and tasks. As the research methodology proposed in this paper was employed within the SF, we can speak directly to implementation issues. To our knowledge, the ASU SF represents the first setting in which all three of these time-scales were observed over years. Given this fact, and the qualities of leadership emergence within the SF, it is a useful and interesting context for us to draw on for this chapter.

STUDYING LEADERSHIP MICRODYNAMICS WITH REAL-TIME OBSERVATION

Many researchers believe that the best way to understand a human system is to directly observe it (Denzin & Lincoln, 2000). Real-time observation of human systems can occur in many ways, including through ethnography, field studies, conversation analysis, interaction analysis, discourse analysis, direct observation, high resolution broadband discourse analysis, etc. (Dooley et al., 2003). The common thread across these different approaches is that communication and interaction amongst the agents in the system is observed in the smallest time-scale possible. Using real-time observation (RTO) a researcher can begin to understand the microlevel thoughts and actions of organizational actors, and thus microlevel leadership interaction (Marion & Uhl-Bien, 2001). RTO enables cause and effect to be inferred between microlevel work patterns (e.g., patterns of communication during problem solving) and organizational performance (Senge, 1990). Within a leadership context, RTO can provide insight into how the group gains situational awareness, how it negotiates and coordinates action, and how social bonds that enhance trust and understanding are created or destroyed.

There are two challenges to RTO. First, collecting RTO data can be very time-consuming and expensive. If one wishes to capture all of the communication and interaction occurring within an organization, then one must have the means to "see" and "hear" everything that is going on. Traditionally, researchers have seen and heard via human observers. A "field researcher" attempts to observe and make sense of group behavior in real-time through note-taking, synthesis, and reflection. Aside from issues of bias and incompleteness, depending solely on human observers creates research logistics challenges; in order to capture microlevel behavior in a reliable way, one may need as many observers as there are participants, at which point we cannot assume the observation process itself is not impacting behavior. Human observers can be supplemented or even supplanted by technology (although humans still need to be involved in data interpretation). Due to advances in audio and video technology, researchers can capture a real-time record of group behavior and analyze it "off-line."

Even though technology can create efficiencies in observation of real-time behavior, the second challenge is that the volume of data generated is so large that it creates challenges in conversion (e.g., creating transcripts from audio tapes, or creating activity histories from video tapes), storage and retrieval, and analysis. Corman, Kuhn, McPhee, and Dooley (2002) estimated that approximately twenty thousand pages of transcripts are created from the conversations within a fifty person organization over one week of time. *Until significant, additional breakthroughs occur in speech and video recognition, RTO will continue to be resource-intensive.*

Within the ASU SF, three RTO methods were used. First, researchers did field observations within the facility. Because the facility was a single room, all workers could be seen from a single locale. Also, because conversation was not constant, it was possible to hear and take notes on what was being said between individuals. As much as possible, observers worked in pairs in order to increase reliability and interpretive capability. Second, a camera captured a picture of the facility every five minutes, and these pictures could be examined to see how people were configuring themselves in the facility, and how "socially active" the organization was at a given time.

Third—and most importantly for RTO—each participant wore a microphone for the entire period they were at work in the SF. When a worker came into the facility, they "checked in" at a PC which had software that (a) logged their name and time, and (b) created an identification stamp and a time stamp on their digital audio recorder, so exact (correct) times could be associated with the communication data on the recorder. At the end of the day, the worker would "check out" by hooking up the recorder to the PC, which in turn would download all of the audio data to disk. Once a week a researcher then grabbed all of the audio files and uploaded them to a database which could be searched according to participant and day.

Logistics and Methods for Real Time Observation

Practically, we did not note any work-related problems with RTO of participants. All participants could request that certain taped data be erased (per human subjects agreement), but no requests were ever made. Participants were asked several times over the 3 years whether the recording equipment caused them to change their behavior, and the answer was always no; and field researchers never saw any evidence that RTO was generating a "Hawthorne" effect. Practically though, sustaining RTO was challenging. First, as time went on compliance by workers dropped off when the SF went from salaried to hourly employees. Second, there are many ways in which recorders can not do what they are supposed to—batteries can be dead, an off button can be pushed accidentally, microphones can break or not be plugged in. We found that a regular maintenance program, including reliability tests, was necessary to ensure good data. Third, while we captured almost all conversational data that occurred in the organization over a 3-year period, we did not realize ahead of time that much of the conversational data would be in Mandarin or Hindi rather than English. This in turn caused significant challenges with transcription.

We shall demonstrate the use of RTO with an example from part of a study examining pair programming (Boehm & Turner, 2004). Pair programming is a software engineering practice in which pairs program rather than individuals. The "driver" commands the keyboard and writes the software code while an "observer" watches for mistakes and generally helps out. Pair programming has been shown to have a positive, significant impact on software code quality and programmer job satisfaction (Nosek, 1998). From a leadership perspective, we might be interested in how the pair manages its own work activities, and how it coordinates with other pairs.

In this example we used actual conversational data to understand the leadership dynamics within a project team. The team had been given a task which had two parallel subtasks, and the conversational data highlights how the group tackled those two tasks, and who was leading the coordination efforts. The conversational data was collected via microphones, as described above. Signal processing methods similar to those described by Choudhury (2004) were used on the raw audio streams in order to identify discrete conversational bits, and within each bit, who was talking to whom; the same data could have been generated by direct observation. Note that since there is no formal leader on the project, this methodological approach can provide unique insights into how leadership was enacted within and across each interaction of the pair.

RTO Data, Results and Analysis

Table 10.1 shows a portion of the data—the "bits" of conversations between the two pairs of programmers on this particular project. Each "bit" is indicated by a start time, a duration (in milliseconds), a speaker (S), and listener(s) (L). The two pairs were (M2 and M2) and (M3 and M4). Because concurrent conversations were captured, any conversation bit may have two, three, or four members.

Table 10.2 aggregates the data in Table 10.1 over two 5-minute time segments. For example, the table indicates that between 13:20 and 13:25, M1 initiated interactions with M2 (their pair member) five times; however during this time period M2 is relatively silent, only listening to M1 (receiving). M1 also actively initiated interactions with the other pair members as well: M1 → M3 four times, and M1 → M4 three times. Again during this same 5-minute segment M3 and M4 primarily talk to themselves, they also—to a much lower degree—initiated with M1, who initiates and receives interactions with both of them significantly. Note that M2 initiates only two of the 35 initiations across the members (i.e., less than 6% of the total).

In the second 5-minute time segment these patterns change in an intriguing way. On the surface it is clear that M2 becomes more involved in the interactions, tripling his level of initiated interactions from two to six. In addition, every member initiates at least one interaction with every other member, in contrast to the previous time segment in which 3 of the 12 possible initiations were unexpressed. At the same time, the total number of initiated interactions is virtually the same in both time periods: 37 in T1 versus 38 in T2, indicating a similar lever of overall interaction. Moreover, the average number of initiated and received interactions is similar in both time periods—8.8 in T1 versus 9.5 in T2, indicating that the average level of interactions between members was not largely changed.

However, a deeper analysis suggests a significantly greater coherence of interaction across the group during the second time segment. Specifically, we compare the initiated interactions in T1 with the initiated interactions in T2, and similarly the received interactions in T1 with those in T2. In both cases the variance and the standard deviation of those interaction levels across the four members *drops* precipitously between T1 and T2. Specifically, the standard deviation of initiated interactions drops by 44% from T1 to T2, and the standard deviation of receptions drops by 56%. In other words, the second time period shows a much greater balance of interactions across all members, suggesting that they were working much more as a 4-person team than as two 2-person teams.

From a leadership standpoint, this difference at a microlevel may be the result of an aggregated shift in the leadership happening within each interaction (Lichtenstein, Uhl-Bien, et al., 2006). At a mesolevel the shift may be a response to some environmental influence such as a jolt, a punctuation, or an oscillation (Meyer, Gaba, & Colwell, 2005). By studying these patterns over multiple work sessions, we can begin to understand whether these leadership patterns are persistent or contextual. It is worthwhile to note that we can make these inferences without direct examination of the content of their interactions; while coreferencing content

Table 10.1.   Raw Data Showing Conversation Bites

Start Time	Duration	1111	2222	3333	4444
13:15:34	8112	S		L	
13:16:18	4500	S		L	L
13:16:26	6330	L		L	S
13:16:31	6797			L	S
13:16:37	5979	L		S	L
13:16:42	5760			S	L
13:16:54	11539	S			L
13:16:57	11206			S	L
13:17:02	11139	S	L		
13:17:07	9975	S	L		
13:17:17	11606	S	L	L	L
13:17:22	5996			S	L
13:17:29	10180		S		L
13:17:29	5905	S	L		
13:17:43	5699			L	S
13:17:50	9879	L	S		
13:17:55	5651			L	S
13:18:00	8966	S		L	
13:18:07	6743	L		S	
13:18:13	5905			S	L
13:18:18	6271	S		L	

S = Speaker; L = Listener

would no doubt help validate or disconfirm these inferences, they emanate from a description of the dynamics only.

In summary, microlevel dynamics infer the action and communication patterns that characterize numerous behavioral constructs such as problem solving, decision making, creativity, conflict, cooperation, and coordination. Techniques and methods associated with real-time observation provide a more process-oriented view of leadership than the more traditional view of leadership as personality or power. Instead, these models characterize leadership as a process of interaction.

STUDYING LEADERSHIP MESODYNAMICS
WITH SOCIAL NETWORK ANALYSIS

Whereas real-time observation emphasizes observing reality, mesolevel analysis emphasizes metric and perceptual data. In order to study dynamics at a mesolevel (e.g., daily, weekly), a researcher can collect project, pro-

Table 10.2.   Analysis of Interaction Bits

T1: 13:20 to 13:25

To →	M1	M2	M3	M4	Initiated
M1		5	4	3	12
M2	1		0	1	2
M3	3	0		9	12
M4	2	0	7		9
Received	6	5	11	13	

T2: 13:25 to 13:30

To →	M1	M2	M3	M4	Initiated
M1		3	4	5	12
M2	3		2	1	6
M3	2	1		6	9
M4	5	3	3		11
Received	10	7	10	11	

	M1	M2	M3	M4	Average	Variance	SD
Initiated T1	12	2	12	9	8.8	22.3	4.7
Initiated T2	12	6	9	11	9.5	7.0	2.6
Received T1	6	5	11	13	8.8	14.9	3.9
Received T2	10	7	10	11	9.5	3.0	1.7
Combined T1	18	7	23	23	17.8	56.9	7.5
Combined T2	22	13	19	22	19.0	18.0	4.2

cess, and performance data aggregated to whatever time frame is most useful for the context. In the SF we collected data such as hours worked per day, software changes made per week, customer contacts per week, etc. A researcher can also collect perceptual data from the participants through daily or weekly surveys or interviews. One particularly useful type of model for examining mesolevel patterns of leadership is social network analysis (Wasserman & Faust, 1994). Social network analysis (SNA) conceptualizes a social system as a set of nodes (agents) and connections between nodes. The structure of the social network, and the position of any particular agent's node, can be used to infer relational roles (Freeman, 1979). Most often, social networks are constructed based on individuals' perceptions of interaction, communication, or influencing. While SNA is well-established in social science, the study of dynamic networks is still developing (Monge & Contractor, 2003; Snijders, 2001).

From a leadership standpoint, SNA provides a relational model of leadership. Individuals with many connections, or connections that create boundary spanning, can be important in terms of enhancing social cohesion, facilitating information flow, and establishing cultural norms. Several leadership-related studies have SNA. For example, Balkundi and Kilduff (2006) explore how the network cognitions of leaders affect the pattern of interactions between themselves and other leaders in their networks. The social networks of group leaders have been shown to positively affect the group's performance and the leader's reputation (Mehra, Dixon, Brass, & Robertson, 2006), as well as the perceived effectiveness of transformational leaders (Bono & Anderson, 2005).

Social Network Data and Analysis

Within the ASU SF, social network data was collected via a weekly survey which asked how often the respondent had communicated with all other employees and researchers. To smooth out the noise caused by missing data, we assumed that if one survey indicated communication with any person during the week, then the communication was bidirectional. From a practical standpoint, the only problem with collecting social network data was non-compliance with responding to the survey. This improved when we standardized the process of sending out the surveys and survey reminders. When confronted with missing data, we conferred with the official SF roster at that moment in time and if the person whose survey was missing was employed and not on leave, then the connections from the previous week's network were carried forward.

In this example, we are using SNA to examine how the SF's social network changed from week to week. By determining where change is greatest and relating that to known events, one can infer what type of events are likely to lead to change in social structure, and thus leadership patterns (Burkhart & Brass, 1990). A total of 62 weeks of social networks was captured and analyzed. In order to look for changes in communication and thus social structure, we calculated the correlation between each network using the QAP procedure (Wasserman & Faust, 1994). A graph of the correlation between 2 weeks' networks is shown in Figure 10.1. Low values of correlation (less than 0.30) correspond to significant changes in the social network structure, and thus the potential onset of (new) emergent leadership. In order to determine the reasons behind changes, we

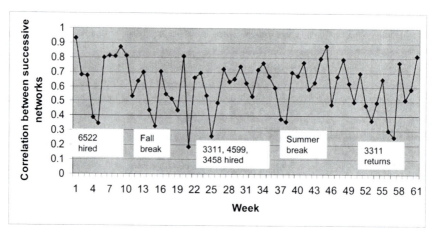

Figure 10.1.   Correlation between successive social networks.

examined a timeline of SF-related events and were able to find tentative explanations for these changes.

We see that changes in social structure occur when significant personnel changes occur. Participant 6522 has an important influence when they join the organization in week 5; likewise, a number of new employees are hired around week 15, corresponding to the beginning of the fall semester, and this leads to changes in structure. Participants 3311, 4599, and 3458 have an impact when they join and leave for the summer, and return after the summer (3311). It is important to note that over thirty individuals joined and left the organization during this time frame, so only a small fraction of participants had a significant impact on the social structure. By exploring more deeply we could identify to what degree this impact was due to that individual's leadership in interactions, which has been shown to increase the quality of their social network (Balkundi & Kilduff, 2006).

For example, examination of the individual networks indicates that 6522 was at the center of the SF's first clique, while 3311, 4599, and 3458 were important in creating social coherence and a sense of pride (and competition) amongst employees. These three were relatively extroverted compared to the rest of the employees, and had a greater desire for the quality of their work to be known and appreciated by others. Our argument is supported by the fact that two of these three received a coveted acknowledgement of their performance: They were the only SF employees that year to obtain a summer internship from Microsoft.

In summary, mesolevel dynamics infer organizational routines, networks of communication and influence, leadership emergence among sets (or cliques) of individuals, and the influence of macrolevel (institutional) dynamics such as planning or hiring cycles. Social network analysis creates a model of leadership that is relational and relative; an arrival or departure of a single individual can cause ripples in how leading is distributed within the group, and create opportunities for new leadership emergence. Here again we demonstrate a method based on process, without the usual focus on content. Certainly more in-depth explanations could be developed for these network changes; our goal here is simply to show how temporally based methods, even without much content, provide a unique view into the dynamics of leadership at ASU's Software Factory.

STUDYING LEADERSHIP MACRODYNAMICS WITH EVENT HISTORY ANALYSIS

When leadership interactions occur across multiple constituencies over time, focusing on each individual interaction or on specific interactions across network ties can lead to an overload of data without any basis for generating insight at a larger time-scale. Thus, a third approach to exploring the dynamics of leadership interactions uses the "event" as a unit of analysis (Abbott, 1992). More commonly called "event history analysis" (EHA), this method is designed to capture the aggregated leadership actions across multiple individuals, the emergence of which signals some substantive change in the nature of the system as a whole (Poole et al., 2000). That is, by defining an "event" as a macrolevel emergent phenomenon which creates some long-term change in the system, a dynamic structure is created that integrates a vast amount of data over long periods of time (Van de Ven & Engleman, 2004). Further, by identifying key events over time, the evolution of leadership in the system can be readily explored (Chiles et al., 2004; Lichtenstein, Dooley, et al., 2006).

EHA involves three steps: collection of event data, coding of event data, and analysis of event codes. EHA facilitates study of the leadership process to the extent that events are coded with respect to a construct or set of constructs that relates to a leadership theory-frame. Defining these constructs—agreeing on what "counts" as a significant leadership event—would be a critical aspect of this overall process. Several previous leadership studies have used EHA, including Chiles et al. (2004).

Event History Data and Analysis

Within the SF, events were noted by the SF research and administration teams, who had constant oversight into SF operations. Events were defined and coded for four types of leadership: influential, transactional,

Table 10.3.   Event Codes for Event History Analysis (Portion)

Event Date	Influential	Transactional	Strategic	Participatory
8/23/2002		X		
8/26/2002				X
8/27/2002		X		
9/4/2002		X		
9/5/2002			X	X
9/9/2002				X
9/10/2002	X			
9/11/2002		X		
9/12/2002		X		
9/16/2002			X	
9/16/2002		X		
9/18/2002		X		
9/18/2002		X		
9/20/2002		X		X
9/23/2002			X	
9/26/2002		X		
9/27/2002		X		X
9/30/2002				X
9/30/2002	X			
9/30/2002				X
9/30/2002	X			
9/30/2002		X		

strategic, or participatory leadership. Events were entered into a database, and at a later time several coding schemes were developed to examine different research questions. Table 10.3 shows a list of events as they occur on a day-to-day basis; here an X indicates that *at least* one event occurred in that time period. Table 10.4 shows the aggregated event counts per week.

EHA suggests different dynamics for different types of leadership amongst participants. Influence leadership in this case was aimed at developing strategic relationships with key internal research laboratories. Most of this was concentrated in the first month of operations; since the hiring cycle primarily operates on a semester-to-semester basis, we would expect this pattern to repeat in subsequent semesters. We also see that transactional leadership events occur more frequently in the beginning of the semester, indicative of the need to implement new processes and systems within the SF as a new semester commences. Strategic leadership events are spread uniformly throughout the time frame, indicating that

Table 10.4. Week-by-Week Event Counts for Event History Analysis

	Influence	Transactional	Strategic	Participatory	Total
8/26/02	0	2	0	1	3
9/2/02	0	2	1	1	4
9/9/02	1	1	0	1	3
9/16/02	0	4	1	1	6
9/23/02	0	1	1	1	3
9/30/02	3	5	1	2	11
10/7/02	0	0	1	0	1
10/14/02	0	1	0	0	1
10/21/02	0	1	2	0	3
10/28/02	0	0	0	0	0
11/4/02	0	2	1	1	4
11/11/02	0	0	1	0	1
11/19/02	0	1	0	0	1
11/25/02	0	0	1	0	1
12/2/02	0	1	0	0	1
12/9/02	1	1	0	1	3
12/16/02	0	1	2	1	4
12/23/02	0	1	0	0	1
Total	5	24	12	10	

strategic-level issues were considered as part of normal administrative overview. Participatory leadership also peaked in the first months; as work continued, less attention was paid to improving the social structure until end of semester events were planned. Overall the results show that while strategic leadership was constant over the period, other forms of leadership diminished as work loads increased.

However, a deeper analysis again shows an intriguing macropattern—a change point within this semester-long period of data. We assume as before that leadership emerges through interactions, and we suggest that the four types of leadership we have coded here do represent a kind of leadership interaction. By adding all leadership events each week and presenting these in a graph, a very distinct pattern of leadership emerges (see Figure 10.2). Essentially the number of leadership events rises dramatically in the first 6 weeks of the semester, from 3 per week to 11 in week 6; then they drop precipitously for the rest of the semester, to an average of 1.75 per week from the previous 6-week average of 5 per week.

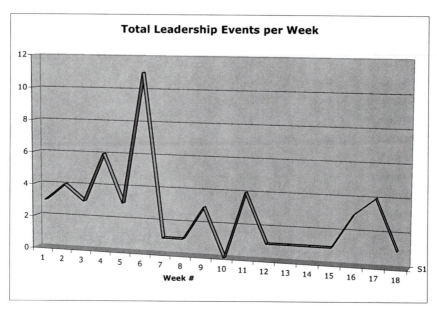

Figure 10.2.   Changes in leadership events during an 18-week period.

The size of this drop, coupled with the very distinct qualities before the change point and afterwards, suggests that a very different type of leadership is being enacted in these two phases of activity. In the first phase the sheer volume of leadership suggests that the system is out of balance, and requires a significant amount of internal leadership to bring it back into coherence. This process work appears to reach a critical threshold in week 6, after which the system appears to shift into a much more stable period, perhaps reflecting a sense of balance which allows the employees to focus much more on task behaviors rather than on group-maintenance behaviors.

Previous work using EHA has shown similar results (e.g., Lichtenstein, Dooley, et al., 2006), suggesting that the nature and quality of leadership in interactions may shift over time. These shifts may indicate macrolevel punctuated changes in the direction or orientation of the project, or they may reflect internal oscillations that are directed from the environment— in this case, the pattern of the semester. Either way, by comparing the events semester by semester, some intriguing insights may be gained in terms of how leadership is affected by these macrolevel changes, and how it may be a cause of the macrolevel patterns.

In summary, macrolevel dynamics infer the roles that individuals play within the larger system, how the organization as a whole strategically adapts to changes in the environment, the impact of institutional events such as planning and hiring cycles, and how micro- and mesolevel patterns (such as emergent leadership) impacts longer time-scale dynamics. EHA facilitates multiple theoretical perspectives to help explain macrolevel data, as each event can be coded in numerous ways, depending on the constructs being used relative to the research question(s) at hand. EHA characterizes leadership as a path dependent sequence of events, and by examining how event tallies change over time, we can observe different types of macrolevel patterns.

GOING THE NEXT STEP: INTERACTIONS BETWEEN TIME SCALES

As we have seen, studying leadership dynamics at different time scales will yield different insights. While each level can be examined independently, researchers should develop research plans which allow one to examine the co-occurring dynamics at all three levels. Only by understanding linkages across time scales can we paint a complete picture of how leadership emerges and evolves in a complex system.

In our case, and even with a minimal amount of analysis, a faint pattern may be discernable across the three time scales. At the microlevel there was a clear distinction between the first and the second time segments. In the first segment, the interaction patterns showed a separation between the two teams, where M1 mostly initiated conversation with M2 (although M2 did not much respond), whereas M3 and M4 had the majority of their interactions between themselves. In contrast the second time segment showed far more balance in the interchanges between all four members; this concordance across interactions was reflected in the significantly decreased standard deviations of both initiations and receptions amongst all four participants.

Second, at the mesolevel we saw a pattern of significant shifts in the network's structure over time. These shifts reflected in part the large influence of a small number of key individuals who brought a great deal of coherence to the networks; this coherence was disrupted when they left (e.g., for the summer) and it returned on their reentry. Third, at the macrolevel we again see a pattern of increased turbulence at the beginning, followed by a distinct change point that ushers in a period of relative coherence.

A deeper analysis would explore this pattern more carefully at all three levels. On the surface it appears to be fractal, that is, the dynamics at the microlevel seem to be repeating themselves at the mesolevel, and again at the macrolevel. If so, we have evidence of a fractal time ecology, which helps us understand and support interactive leadership in a much more subtle and potentially effective way.

In general, two mechanisms explain potential linkages between micro-, meso-, and macrotime scales. First, stable patterns of microactivity may emerge due to endogenous and exogenous effects which *entrain* these patterns across time-scales. That is, human agents choose archetypal patterns of interaction and then enact these patterns at different time-scales, leading to time invariant patterns across temporal levels. For example, a particular work group may tend to utilize an escalation dynamic as a means of organizing. At microtemporal scales, this escalation dynamic may manifest itself as binges of creativity and/or escalating conflict during group discourse (Perry-Smith & Shalley, 2003), while at macrotemporal scales it may manifest itself as an escalating commitment of resources (Ross & Staw, 1993).

Second, macrolevel patterns may *constrain* finer-grained patterns through establishing temporal boundaries and subsequent "windows of opportunity." In our example the cycle of the semester created a natural constraint on the meso- and macropatterns within the SF, and perhaps on the microlevel interactions. In other ways, seasonal changes in work load or resource availability create natural, periodic forces that constrain the dynamics of microactivities to be periodic also. If dynamic patterns of leading are similar across time scales, then microlevel leadership behavior can be observed and used to predict what macrolevel behavior and outcomes will emerge. This improves a group's ability to self-monitor its performance in (near) real-time and take corrective action as necessary. For example, if conversational patterns were shown to scale to long-term patterns of group member satisfaction, then groups could be trained in how to create positive conversation patterns and monitor for dysfunctional patterns.

If similarities across time scales are not directly observed, it may be because more complex linkages across levels are operating (Van de Ven & Poole, 2005). Lack of temporal scaling would suggest that the observed leadership process is a relatively "high dimensional" phenomenon, meaning that an organization's dynamics emerge from the interaction of a large number of factors (Dooley & Van de Ven, 1999). In such circumstances, the leadership process must be characterized as highly idiosyncratic and contextual. In any actual leadership process, we would expect to observe elements of both: Along certain dimensions of leadership activity we may observe temporal scaling and strong, low-dimensional (simple) generative mechanisms, and along other dimensions we may observe more complex interactions indicative of high-dimensional behavior. Such differences may be due to the degree of influence from factors exogenous to the leadership process.

CONCLUSION

Complexity Leadership is offering a new theoretical framework for explaining the how leadership is enacted within the interactions of all organizational members, rather than by a specific person through their interactions only (Marion & Uhl-Bien, 2001; Uhl-Bien, 2006). This perspective may offer new insights into the emergence of innovation, the creation of order, and the dynamics of performance in twenty-first century networks and organizations (Lichtenstein, Uhl-Bien, et al., 2006).

The potential value of this effort is matched by its unique demands, namely the need to examine *how* leadership is expressed in the "space between" individuals, that is, in every day interactions (Bradbury & Lichtenstein, 2000). That is, in order to gain new insights into the dynamics of interaction we must go beyond—far beyond!—the traditional method of collecting data in one-time cross-sectional surveys. Specifically, capturing the subtle dynamics of leadership-within-interactions will require studies that are longitudinal and multi-level, collecting data that is rich and multi-faceted enough to capture the subtlety of the patterns in the system, and at the same time developing analyses which are abstract enough to see those patterns above the "trees" and branches and leaves and weeds of data (McKelvey, 2004; Lichtenstein, Dooley, et al., 2006). This chapter provides one pallet of possibilities for collecting data and framing analyses with these goals in mind.

Equally, this effort emphasizes an important direction in the application of complexity to management, and that is the use of real (nonsimulated) data from real (noncomputational) organizations. This direction, which runs counter to currently accepted norms in the emerging field of complexity, reflects a value on the richness and diversity of everyday organizational life, over and above the more commonly taken path of doing in-depth theory-creating simulations that are based on an unrealistically simple model of human behavior. Although there is room for simulation-based theory development (McKelvey, 1997, 1999), the quality of leadership in interactions is subtle and tacit, making it difficult to generate accurate computational models that reflect the degree of richness and (literally) complexity in behavior that a complexity theory of leadership is seeking to uncover.

The good news is there are an increasing number of non-simulation-based exemplars of complexity, each of which provides insights into the methods that can be used to uncover patterns of leadership interaction over time (e.g. Guastello, 1995; Chiles et al., 2004; Lichtenstein, Dooley, et al., 2006; Plowman, Baker, et al., 2007; Plowman, Solansky, et al., 2007). When combined with the right questions—many of which are represented in the papers that appear in the present volume—we will make strong headway in developing a new theory of leadership that goes beyond the myths of the hero or the scapegoat, and instead reflects the dynamic and emergent nature of leadership as it is enacted every day by supervisors, subordinates, and peers across all organizations.

REFERENCES

Abbott, A. (1992). From causes to events: Notes on narrative positivism. *Sociological Methods and Research, 20,* 428-455.

Balkundi, P., & Kilduff, M. (2006). The ties that lead: A social network approach to leadership. *The Leadership Quarterly, 17,* 419-439.

Boehm, B., & Turner, R. (2004). *Balancing agility and discipline.* Boston: Addison-Wesley.

Bono, J., & Anderson, M. (2005). The advice and influence networks of transformational leaders. *Journal of Applied Psychology, 90,* 1306-1314.

Bradbury, H., & Lichtenstein, B. M. (2000). Relationality in organizational research: Exploring the "space between." *Organization Science, 11,* 551-564.

Burkhardt, M. E., & Brass, D. J. (1990). Changing patterns of patterns of change: The effects of a change in technology on social network structure and power. *Administrative Science Quarterly, 35*(1), 104-127.

Carley, K. M., Lee, J. S., & Krackhardt, D. (2001). Destabilizing networks. *Connections, 24*(3), 31-34.

Chiles, T., Meyer, A., & Hench, T. (2004). Organizational emergence: The origin and transformation of Branson, Missouri's musical theaters. *Organization Science, 15,* 499-520.

Choudhury, T. (2004). *Sensing and modeling human networks.* Unpublished doctoral thesis, MIT.

Corman, S., Kuhn, T., McPhee, R., & Dooley, K. (2002). Studying complex discursive systems: Centering resonance analysis of organizational communication. *Human Communication Research, 28*(2), 157-206.

Denzin, N. K., & Lincoln, Y. S. (Eds.) (2000). *Handbook of qualitative research.* Thousand Oaks, CA: Sage.

Dooley, K., & Corman, S. (2002). *Arizona State University's Software Factory.* 2002 Decision Sciences Conference, San Diego, CA.

Dooley, K., Corman, S., McPhee, R., & Kuhn, T. (2003). Modeling high-resolution broadband discourse in complex adaptive systems. *Nonlinear Dynamics, Psychology, & Life Sciences, 7*(1), 61-86.

Dooley, K., Daneke, G., & Pathak, S. (2005, August). *Iridium's house of cards: The nature of entrepreneurial stages and stage transitions.* Academy of Management Conference, Honolulu.

Dooley, K. & Van de Ven, A. (1999). Explaining complex organizational dynamics. *Organization Science, 10,* 358-372.

Drath, W. (2001). *The deep blue sea: Rethinking the source of leadership.* San Francisco: Jossey-Bass & Center for Creative Leadership.

Freeman, L. C. (1979). Centrality in social networks: Conceptual clarification. *Social Networks, 1,* 215-239.

Guastello, S.J. (1995). Facilitative style, individual innovation, and emergent leadership in problem solving groups. *Journal of Creative Behavior, 29*(4), 225-39.

Guastello, S.J., Hyde, T., & Odak, M. (1998). Symbolic dynamic patterns of verbal exchange in a creative problem solving group. *Nonlinear Dynamics, Psychology, and Life Sciences, 2*(1), 35-58.

Gronn, P. (2002). Distributed leadership as a unit of analysis. *The Leadership Quarterly, 13,* 423-451.

Koehler, G. (2001). *A framework for visualizing the chronocomplexity.* Sacramento: California Research Bureau, and Time Structures.

Lichtenstein, B., Carter, N., Dooley, K., & Gartner, B. (in press). Complexity dynamics of nascent entrepreneurship. *Journal of Business Venturing.*

Lichtenstein, B., Dooley, K., & Lumpkin, T. (2006). Measuring emergence in the dynamics of new venture creation. *Journal of Business Venturing, 21,* 153-175.

Lichtenstein, B., Uhl-Bien, M., Marion, R., Seers, A., Orton, J. D. & Schreiber, C. (2006). Complexity leadership theory: An interactive perspective on leading in complex adaptive systems. *Emergence: Complexity and Organization, 8*(4), 2-12.

Marion, R., & Uhl-Bien, M. (2001). Leadership in complex organizations. *The Leadership Quarterly, 12,* 389-418.

McKelvey, B. (1997). Quasi-natural organization science. *Organization Science, 8,* 351-381.

McKelvey, B. (1999). Toward a Campbellian realist organization science. In J. Baum & B. McKelvey (Eds.), *Variations in organization science* (pp. 383-411). Thousand Oaks, CA: Sage.

McKelvey, B. (2004). Toward a complexity science of entrepreneurship. *Journal of Business Venturing, 19,* 313-342.

Mehra, A., Dixon, A., Brass, D., & Robertson, B. (2006). The social network ties of group leaders: Implications for group performance and leader reputation. *Organization Science, 17,* 64-79.

Meyer, A., Gaba, V., & Colwell, K., 2005. Organizing far from equilibrium: Nonlinear change in organizational fields. *Organization Science, 16,* 456-473.

Monge, P. R., & Contractor, N. (2003). *Theories of communication networks.* New York: Oxford University Press.

Nosek, J. (1998, March). The case for collaborative programming. *Communications of the ACM,* 105-108.

Pearce, C. L., & Conger, J.A. (2003). *Shared leadership: Reframing the hows and whys of leadership.* Thousand Oaks, CA: Sage.

Perry-Smith, J., & Shalley, C. (2003). The social side of creativity: A static and dynamic social network perspective. *Academy of Management Review, 28,* 89-106.

Plowman, D. E., Baker, L., Beck, T., Kulkarni, M., Solanksy, S., & Travis, D. (2007). Radical change accidentally: The emergence and amplification of small change. *Academy of Management Journal, 50*(3), 515-543.

Plowman, D. E., Solansky, S., Beck, T., Baker, L., Kulkarni, M., Travis, D. (2007). The role of leadership in emergent, self-organization. *The Leadership Quarterly* *18*(4), 341-356.

Poole, M., Van de Ven, A., Dooley, K., & Holmes, M. (2000). *Organizational change and innovation processes: Theory and methods for research.* Oxford, England: Oxford Press.

Ross, J., & Staw, B. (1993). Organizational escalation and exit: Lessons from the Shoreham nuclear power plant. *Academy of Management Journal, 36*, 701-732.

Schreiber, C., Singh, S., & Carley, K. (2004). *Construct: A multi-agent network model for the co-evolution of agents and socio-cultural environments.* Pittsburg, PA: Carnegie Mellon University, Institute for Software Research, International. Technical Report, CMU-ISRI-04-109.

Senge, P. (1990). *The fifth discipline.* New York: Doubleday.

Snijders, T. (2001). The statistical evaluation of social network dynamics. In M. Sobel, & M. Becker (Eds.), *Sociological Methodology dynamics* (pp. 361-395). Boston: Basil Blackwell.

Uhl-Bien, M. (2006). Relational leadership theory: Exploring the social processes of leadership and organizing. *The Leadership Quarterly, 17*(6), 654-676.

Van de Ven., A., & Engleman, R. (2004). Event- and outcome-driven explanations of entrepreneurship. *Journal of Business Venturing, 19*, 343-358.

Van de Ven, A. & Poole, M. S. (2005). Explaining development and change in organizations. *Academy of Management Review, 20*, 510-540.

Wasserman, S., & Faust, K. (1994). *Social network analysis: Methods and applications.* New York: Cambridge University Press.

Weick, K. E., & Roberts, K.H. (1993). Collective mind in organizations: Heedful interrelating on flight decks. *Administrative Science Quarterly, 38*(3), 357-381.

Weick, K.E., Sutcliffe, K., & Obstfeld, D. (2005). Organizing and the process of sensemaking. *Organization Science, 16*, 409-421.

CHAPTER 11

NETWORK LEADERSHIP

Leading for Learning and Adaptability

Craig Schreiber and Kathleen M. Carley

ABSTRACT

We introduce a dynamic network paradigm of leadership that focuses on organizational learning and adaptability. The concepts of our network leadership framework are presented and their relation to complexity theory concepts of leadership is discussed. The theoretical and methodological concerns of network leadership are subsequently identified. Dynamic network analysis is then described and used to analyze data from a real-world organization in terms of network leadership. Dynamic network analysis is a methodology that addresses both the theoretical and methodological concerns of network leadership. The analysis highlights key points that demonstrate the usefulness of the network leadership concept in real-world organizations. The results of the analysis also provide insight into the nature of network leadership, which forms the beginning foundations for a new theory of leadership.

Complexity Leadership, Part I: Conceptual Foundations
pp. 291–331

291

INTRODUCTION

Modern business and military organizations are facing highly volatile contexts that are much more dynamic, uncertain and knowledge-intensive than in the past. Many terms have been used in the literature to refer to this change in context. A partial listing of these terms includes the knowledge era (Uhl-Bien, Marion, & McKelvey, 2007), the information revolution (Arquilla & Ronfeldt, 2001), the information age (Stewart, 1997) and the new competitive landscape (Hitt, Keats, & DeMarie, 1998). For sake of clarity we refer to the new context throughout this chapter as the knowledge era. In the knowledge era, competitive advantage is gained by establishing organizational capabilities geared toward learning and adaptation (Bettis & Hitt, 1995). This is in stark contrast to the industrial era where the context was considered more stable and competitive advantage was established more through efficiency and control (Child & McGrath, 2001).

Traditional leadership theories were built upon organizational frameworks geared toward efficiency and control and thus have limited applicability for the knowledge era (Streatfield, 2001). As such, leadership theorists are now recognizing that a new paradigm and theory is needed (Uhl-Bien et al., 2007). This paper is devoted to advancing a new leadership paradigm. We take a recently developing framework for leadership, Complexity Leadership Theory (Uhl-Bien et al., 2007), as a basis and reconceptualize the tenets which are focused on learning and adaptability into a quantitative framework using dynamic network analysis. This reconceptualization results in what we term "network leadership." Network leadership is leadership of change and is comprised of two types of leadership—leadership of context and leadership in process. Together, these tightly intertwined types of leadership enable and enhance the emergent collective action that produces learning and adaptive outcomes.

In the following sections we present the network leadership concept and demonstrate with key points its usefulness in real-world organizations. First, we discuss complexity leadership theory and then reconceptualize the learning and adaptive tenets into a network leadership perspective. Next, we describe dynamic network analysis (DNA; Carley, 2003). DNA is an approach that provides both a theoretical framework and methodology for studying Network Leadership. As such it is an exciting and powerful lens for understanding the process of leadership. Then we demonstrate the use of DNA to model and analyze network leadership. We collected and analyzed data on a military organization specifically structured for learning and adaptability. Results of this effort inform us about the nature of network leadership and provide a foundation toward a theory of network leadership.

COMPLEXITY LEADERSHIP THEORY

Recently, several authors (Marion & Uhl-Bien, 2001; McKelvey, this volume; Uhl-Bien et al., 2007) have proposed a complexity theory approach to leadership called complexity leadership theory. In this approach, learning and adaptability are viewed as emergent outcomes that result from the collective action of agents[1] who are interdependently interacting at the nexus of diverse knowledge. In other words, complexity leadership theory views the organization as a complex adaptive system. There are several important aspects to this paradigm that we note below.

First, learning and adaptability are the result of what people do in an organization; they are the result of collective action. Collective action is necessary to achieving organizational purpose (Zaccaro & Klimoski, 2001). The knowledge era is a high-velocity environment ripe with change (Hitt et al., 1998) and achieving organizational purpose will depend on the organization's ability to learn and adaptively respond to change.

Second, the coevolution of human and social capital is at the heart of the collective action process. The combination of human capital and social capital is referred to as collective intelligence (McKelvey, this volume). Increases to collective intelligence occur when human capital and social capital coevolve within the organization (Carley & Hill, 2001; McKelvey, this volume). These increases then lead to learning and adaptive responses. This process is synonymous to multilevel learning (Carley & Gasser, 1999; Carley & Svoboda, 1996) where individual agents and teams learn as part of the process by which human capital, organizational structure, social capital, and culture change and evolve. A key factor to increasing collective intelligence is the existence of diverse knowledge. Diverse knowledge provides fertile input into the learning process. Conversely, learning is constrained without diverse knowledge.

Third, collective change agents are the competitive source of learning and adaptive responses. Tapping the collective intelligence of the organization's citizenry allows for a quicker response to change. This moves the paradigm away from the single "heroic" leader who has all the answers to one where the responsibility for learning and reasoning about change falls onto the collective organization.

Fourth, collective action needs to be stimulated, not controlled. Productive change occurs by way of interactions among an organization's citizenry (Bennis & Biederman, 1997). Top-down, command-and-control style leadership can stifle the development of collective intelligence by constraining interactions (Bennis, 1997; McKelvey, this volume). Constrained interactions limit the development of human and social capital (McKelvey, this volume). Quick, adaptive interaction patterns cannot be

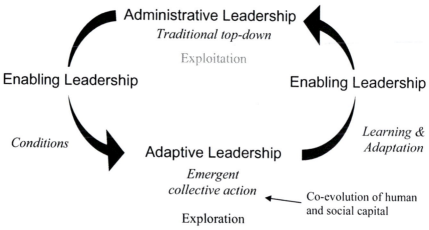

Figure 11.1.   Complexity leadership theory.

prescribed by fiat. They are stimulated by conditions such as decentralized decision making and strong learning cultures.

Last, while organizations need to stimulate emergent collective action they also have a bureaucratic nature and a need to control organizational outcomes efficiently for exploitation. This is known as the organizational design paradox (Child & McGrath, 2001). Therefore, Uhl-Bien et al. (2007) have proposed that knowledge era leadership is composed of three separate but entangled roles which accommodate the paradox: administrative leadership, adaptive leadership and enabling leadership (see Figure 11.1).

Administrative leadership is concerned with traditional top-down leadership. It is focused more on efficiency, control and the exploitation of responses. Adaptive and enabling leadership are concerned with emergent collective action. Emergent collective action is an exploration process for producing change in response to the dynamic challenges facing the organization. The adaptive and enabling leadership roles are focused on the production and dissemination of learning and adaptive responses. More specifically, adaptive leadership refers to the leadership that occurs within the interdependent interactions of emergent collective action. These leaders are the agents who advance the coevolution of human and social capital which in turn sparks collective intelligence.

Enabling leadership serves two functions. First, it creates conditions which stimulate emergent collective action and adaptive leadership. One way it does this is by limiting the top-down controls of traditional leadership that inhibit collective action (Powell, 1990) and stifle the coevolution of human and social capital (McKelvey, this volume). Second, it channels productive responses originating in the emergent collective action back up to administrative leadership for strategic planning and exploitation.

NETWORK LEADERSHIP

A network is a set of nodes and the relations among these nodes. Networks are conduits of change and network leadership is leadership of change. For instance, interactions among the nodes may diffuse knowledge which results in learning or relations may be adaptively restructured to combine resources and expertise which is needed in response to an emergent challenge. Leadership within the network facilitates change. Change—whether it is learning, adaptation or a combination of both—advances the coevolution of human and social capital. Knowledge era organizations are concerned about effective response to a changing environment. Therefore, network leadership is an important aspect of organizational functioning in this era.

We propose that the complexity theory approach to understanding leadership emphasizes two elements which are important to producing learning and adaptation: context and process. Context refers to the organizational conditions which not only allow for emergent interactions and collective action but also guide the system toward productive learning and adaptability through the use of internal (interdependency) and external tensions.[2] Process refers to the interdependent interactions between agents which lead to the diffusion and combination of knowledge that results in learning and adaptability.

Accordingly, network leadership entails two types of change leadership—leadership of context and leadership in process. Figure 11.2 shows how leadership of context and leadership in process relate to complexity leadership theory. *Leadership of context* enables organizational processes that allow for adaptable collective action responses to a changing environment. *Leadership in process* facilitates learning and adaptation through the emergent interactions and informal dynamics which form collective action.

In the Knowledge Era, organizational context must change in response to environmental volatility in order to support an adaptable learning environment. Changes in organizational context enable learning, which in turn enables change in the organizational context. The Knowledge Era is a learning era, and the process of learning and changes in organizational context are intimately intertwined.

Figure 11.2.   The relation of network leadership to complexity leadership theory.

Leadership of Context

One aim of the complexity science approach is to propose organizational contexts in which collective action can emerge in response to change. In other words, the aim is to inform the setting of conditions from which the system produces effective outcomes. Collective action is necessary to increase information processing speed and to learn at a faster rate. Faster learning is needed to sustain superior performance for knowledge era organizations (Child & McGrath, 2001). The organizational context referred to is the nature of the network within which informal dynamics occur. Therefore, the context from which collective action emerges is the informal structure, the sets of nodes and relationships, of the organization.

Contexts which promote learning will exhibit both internal and external tensions that foster interactions and introduce interdependence. The combination of interactions and interdependence enables learning; interactions induce knowledge flow and interdependence pressures people to act on knowledge. Examples of strategies that induce interactions are self-forming teams, deference to expertise and sensitivity to operations. Examples of strategies that induce interdependence are heterogeneous workgroups, role/expertise familiarity and decentralized problem solving.

Four key characteristics of organizational context which relate to interdependent interactions and the production of learning and adaptability are relational coupling (Kauffman, 1993), requisite variety (Ashby, 1960), network form (Powell, 1990) and stress (Marion & Uhl-Bien, 2001). Relational coupling, the degree of interdependent relations within a system, has been theorized as being relevant to productive outcomes (Kauffman, 1993) with moderate coupling considered the most conducive to producing learning and adaptive outcomes (Uhl-Bien et al., 2007). Low coupling does not generate enough interactive activity and high coupling can lead to information overload.

Requisite variety, the matching of internal complexity to environmental complexity, is associated with exploration (March, 1996) which involves the search for new knowledge (McGrath, 2001). Throughout this paper we will focus on a specific kind of requisite variety: knowledge diversity. Diverse knowledge, as previously described, is a necessary component in the process of learning (Hazy, 2004a) and adaptability in organizations. Without diverse knowledge, the organization lacks the impetus to produce significant gains.

Network form refers to the degree of status differentiation within the organization. Status differentiation can have an effect on the ability of the organization to produce emergent outcomes (Uhl-Bien et al., 2007). For instance, authority relations have a high degree of status differentiation. The top-down dynamics of authority relations can stifle collective action activity. Conversely, preference relations involve deference to expertise. These relations foster more bottom-up dynamics and collective action that produce emergent outcomes such as learning and adaptation.

Stress is an indicator of tension in the organization. Stress, or tension as it is often referred to, is a necessary component for production of emergent outcomes (McKelvey, this volume; Uhl-Bien et al., 2007) as it induces interactions and pressures agents to act. Such stress can be internal to the informal network as in task interdependencies among heterogeneous workgroups or external to it as in adversarial competition. Stress is needed for interactive complexity but overstressing can be counterproductive to the process.

Leadership in Process

Another aim of the complexity science approach is to propose leadership activities which improve collective intelligence. Learning occurs via interactions among agents in an organizational system. Interdependent interactions between agents lead to the diffusion and combination of knowledge and results in learning and adaptability. As agent interactions evolve in an organizational system, changes to both "what" an agent knows and "who" an agent interacts with will occur (Carley & Hill, 2001).

McKelvey (this volume) refers to this as the coevolution of human and social capital. This process is akin to neural network theory of how the brain functions and learns. Neural networks learn by neurons making dynamic connections to themselves through synaptic links. Organizations learn by human capital nodes making dynamic connections to themselves through social capital relations. Human capital appreciation accumulates energy in the form of knowledge. Energy flow in the informal network is knowledge flow through social interactions that are actuated by tensions originating in the organizational context. These social interactions are fluid and can change in response to changes in knowledge and tension. Change in social interactions can affect where, in the network, knowledge accumulates and builds upon itself and therefore where learning occurs. Analyzing the coevolution of human and social capital can give us insight into the effects that organizational contexts have on learning and adaptive outcomes.

Leadership in the learning process supports learning and adaptability through activities which foster knowledge flows, enhance interactions, advocate contextual change (structuration) and facilitate aggregation. Leaders in process, therefore, are those who shape communication structure. We propose that there are several forms of leadership in process that shape communication flows in various ways and that provide benefits toward productive outcomes. These leadership forms include: enhancing knowledge flows, creating interactions and interdependencies, maintaining relational coupling, increasing the speed of learning, and communicating new knowledge.

For instance, agents who are high in degree centrality (the number of others they are connected to) are influential in terms of knowledge flow within the network. The communication activities of degree central agents can have significant effects throughout the organization as they have the ability to enhance learning by accumulating knowledge and diffusing it to numerous others through their populous interactions.

Emergent leaders often enact network leadership by creating interactions and interdependencies. This happens when they direct others and coordinate their activities. Boundary spanners enact network leadership by providing connection and communicative flow to otherwise disparate parts of the organization. Agents who have close proximal reach, physical or social, can facilitate speed of information flow and provide network leadership by increasing the rate of learning. Agents who have new or different knowledge, such as organizational minorities, enact network leadership by sharing and diffusing diverse knowledge.

All of these leadership forms enable collective action and foster the production of emergent outcomes. These particular forms are not necessarily inclusive of all possible forms of leadership in process. Ongoing research into the formation of emergent collective action will most likely identify other forms of leadership in process.

In addition, the process of interfacing the informal and formal systems is also considered a part of leadership in process (see Figure 11.2). Uhl-Bien et al. (2007) describe such *entanglement* relative to the process of interactively interfacing the productive learning outcomes of collective action with the formal system. Recognizing that organizations are also bureaucratic or formal systems is important to the reality of organizing. Interfacing informal outcomes with formal channels allows organizations to diffuse learning outcomes through the formal system (Uhl-Bien et al., 2007) and to better exploit (March, 1996) learning and adaptation.

We agree with leadership complexity theorists that learning occurs through interactions among human agents but we also recognize that organizations in the knowledge era are sociotechnical systems and that learning can occur through interactions with technology. Technologies are often embedded with organizational knowledge (Argote & Ingram, 2000) such as the Xerox Eureka database (Brown & Deguid, 2000) which offers a substitute or complement to human agent interactions. Another example is a complex and risky technology, such as the space shuttle, which offers an occasion for experiential learning through investigation of anomalies (Vaughan, 1996). In addition, information technologies have spawned new ways for organizations to structure internal as well as external relationships (Nohria, 1992).

Two caveats to the process of learning are important to note. First is the cascading effect of change. Since the organizational system is a network, learning in a particular part of the structure can have cascading effects to other parts and eventually influence overall system behavior. Such cascading effects can be dramatic or trivial. Second is the subsystem rate of evolution. Human capital and social capital are interdependent but different subsystems. Although these subsystems coevolve, the respective rates of evolution can be different. Patterns of collective action, which generate learning and adaptability, are a function of these relative evolution rates.

Theoretical and Methodological Needs

The previous discussion focused on the "what" and "why" of network leadership. In short, network leadership is leadership of change which enables emergent collective action and promotes learning that fosters productive responses to volatility. Now we turn to the theoretical concerns of network leadership which are focused on understanding the *who, how* and *when*.

To understand *who* is a leader, including multiple *who's*, we need to examine the dynamic changes to the broad organizational context in which leadership is embedded. Dynamic network leaders are not necessarily those in appointed or authority positions. Leadership is embedded in context and network leaders emerge due to the need for learning and adaptation. Regardless of whether it is leadership of context or leadership in process, anyone could emerge as a leader. Identifying who is a leader becomes an important task which is non-trivial due to the complexity of the organizational context.

In addition, shifts in leadership make identifying leaders difficult. The dynamic landscape of the knowledge era results in changing needs for learning and adaptability. As the organization learns and adapts to the environmental changes, new leaders can emerge and previous leaders could be performing non-leadership roles (Ireland & Hitt, 1999). As the organizational context changes so can the leader.

Leadership is also not necessarily enacted by a single individual. Since the organizational context is a network, leadership may result from the activities of more than one person during a particular event or period in time. Leaders can be dispersed throughout the organization and these leaders can act and coordinate without centralized control (Ronfeldt & Arquilla, 2001). Leadership, therefore, can also be described as distributed (Gronn, 2002) and shared (Pierce & Conger, 2003).

To understand *how* and *when* leaders lead we need to understand both the natural evolutionary processes in organizations and the strategic intervention that leaders use to induce and guide change. Learning processes, such as the coevolution of human and social capital, are natural evolutionary processes which may result in the desired outcomes of learning and adaptability. But in order to get the desired outcomes, the organizational context has to not only be conducive for free-associated, interdependent interactions but also guide these interactions in productive directions. This is where *strategic interventions* come into play.

Network leaders use strategic interventions to foster productive collective action. For example, strategic interventions may be used to inject variety or change the evolutionary rate of learning. Such strategic interventions are intended to influence natural evolutionary processes; processes that cannot be controlled but can possibly be stimulated and guided. It is therefore necessary to understand the effects that strategic interventions have upon natural evolutionary processes. This will provide reasoning about *how* leaders lead. It is also necessary to understand natural evolutionary processes such as learning and the direction in which the organization is headed. As per the example above, when the system lacks diversity and learning is constrained, strategic intervention is needed. Understanding the natural evolutionary process will provide insight into *when* leaders should lead.

Methodologically, there is a clear need for longitudinal, multi-level analysis which permeates the theoretical concern for the *who, how* and *when* of network leadership. Complex interdependent interactions form aggregates or subgroups of agents (Holland, 1995). These subgroups can form larger subgroups among themselves and so on such that there are multiple levels of aggregation within the organizational context. As previously noted, learning can cause cascading effects throughout an organization and this includes effects across aggregate levels. Also, leadership can occur simultaneously and at multiple levels within an organization. There can be individuals leading as well as teams of people leading and who is leading an organization can dynamically shift over time (Schreiber, 2006). Longitudinal, multilevel analysis will offer insight into *who* is leading, *how* strategic interventions affect multiple levels of organizing and *when* strategic interventions need to be invoked.

Rapid change is a hallmark of the knowledge era and leadership of change is an important process within Knowledge Era organizations. When change occurs, it is not a static state - it is a dynamic state. To understand Network Leadership and develop theory, we need a methodology that analyzes both change of context and change in process at multiple levels of analysis.

RESEARCH AGENDA

In the remainder of this chapter, we demonstrate the usefulness of the network leadership concept in real-world organizations. We do so by using the dynamic network analysis methodology to highlight key points. In the first part of the analysis we show how dynamic network analysis relates to the concepts of network leadership. We use graph-level structural measures to characterize the organizational context. The characterizations are of the contextual categories previously described: relational coupling, variety, organizational form, and stress. Then we use node-level structural measures to characterize leadership in process. Leaders are identified within each leadership form: enhancing knowledge flows, maintaining relational coupling, increasing the speed of learning and communicating new knowledge.

In the second part we perform additional analysis to gain insights into the nature of network leadership. First, the following question was asked to gain an understanding of the impact that the different leaders in process have on the organization: "What would happen, immediately, were this leader not present?" Answering this question will provide an understanding of the benefit that each leader provided while enacting their leadership role during the situation at the time of data collection.

Then we run a virtual experiment to test two propositions about complexity leadership theory. Uhl-Bien et al. (2007) made specific propositions concerning what they called, enabling leadership. First, they proposed that enabling leadership fosters interactions among heterogeneous agents in the informal network. This enabling leadership spurs complex functioning that generates productive outcomes such as learning. Second, they proposed that enabling leadership provides a necessary interface between the informal and formal networks. This interface allows for effective dissemination of learning outcomes in the organization.

METHODS

In the methods section we first introduce dynamic network analysis and spend considerable space explaining it since it is central to the analysis. Then, we discuss how dynamic network analysis relates to network leadership. Next, we describe the empirical dataset that is used throughout the analysis. Last, we discuss each analysis that was performed.

Dynamic Network Analysis

Dynamic network analysis (Carley, 2003) is a new field of science which entails the theory and design of complex, dynamic networks and the study of emergent phenomena which are enabled and/or constrained by such networks. dynamic network analysis (DNA) extends the reasoning about social networks to large-scale, dynamic sociotechnical systems which have multiple coevolving networks. The coevolution of human and social capital is an example of the type of simultaneous analysis afforded by DNA (Carley & Hill, 2001). Applied to network leadership, DNA is a methodology and a theory for understanding changes of context and changes in process, both over time and at multiple levels of analysis.

DNA combines the methods of social network analysis and multiagent simulation. Social network analysis is used to analyze complex relational structure and multi-agent simulation is used to model and analyze longitudinal change dynamics. Three main components of DNA will be introduced in this chapter—MetaMatrix, ORA and Construct.[3] The MetaMatrix is a theoretical framework of network structure and change as well as a schema for storing data that is used for input to the other DNA tools. ORA is a statistical tool that is used to compute social network measures and perform statistical tests of static structure. Construct is a multi-agent network model that is used to reason about change dynamics and the coevolution of network structure.

Table 11.1.   Illustrative MetaMatrix

	People/ Agents	Knowledge/ Resources	Tasks/ Events	Groups/ Organizations
People/Agents	Social network	Knowledge/ resource network	Assignment network	Membership network
Knowledge/ Resources		Information/sub-stitutes network	Needs network	Core capabilities
Tasks/Events			Precedence ordering	Institutional relations
Groups/ Organizations				Interorganiza-tional network

The MetaMatrix

Organizations are composed of many overlapping networks. The MetaMatrix (Carley, 2002a; Krackhardt & Carley, 1998) is a theoretical framework for representing the various networks of an organization. See Table 11.1 for an illustrative MetaMatrix.

A plurality of node types (multimode) and relations (multiplex) are used to construct the various networks of the MetaMatrix. Typical node types include people, technologies, events, knowledge and organizations. Typical relations include friendship, advice, resource-access, task-assignment and participation. Each node type is represented by both the columns and rows of Table 11.3, thereby created a square MetaMatrix. It is represented this way because there can be relations within a particular node type, a people × people network is a social network, and there can be relations between node types, a people × task network is a task-assignment network. This representation captures the complex nexus of relationships that exist both within and between these node types. The various overlapping networks of the organization form the MetaMatrix, a complex meta-network.

These various networks are not independent of one another but are interdependent. For example, the social network (social capital) and knowledge network (human capital) coevolve in the following manner. Agents interact through their social relations and learn or create knowledge, thus updating their understanding which changes the knowledge network. This new updated understanding can subsequently influence who the agent interacts with in the future, thus changing the social network.

The MetaMatrix is an extensible framework where node types and relations are defined by the researcher according to the appropriate context of the organization and the research. Once collected, the MetaMatrix data is input into the other DNA tools for modeling and analysis.

ORA: Statistical Analysis of Social Networks

ORA (Tsvetovat, Reminga, & Carley, 2004) is a statistical network tool for analyzing complex networks. Statistical network analysis is used to characterize individuals, subgroups and organizations as well as identify influential nodes at any of the above levels of analysis. The characterizations and identifications are based on measures that are calculated on the various networks of the MetaMatrix. These measures range from traditional social network measures such as degree centrality, which are based on a single network to more complex measures such as cognitive demand,[4] which are based on several networks.

The complex measures capture more of the complex, interdependent realities of organizational life by taking into account the relations between networks. Ongoing research is being conducted for developing new measures which are appropriate for describing and contrasting networks. Although the development of complex measures is nascent to the field, our research has shown that such measures can provide useful insight. An example is cognitive demand which has been used to predict emergent leadership (Carley & Ren, 2001).

DNA Change Processes

A limitation of traditional social network analysis is that it does not represent agents as actively interacting and learning and thus altering their networks. Interpretations of behavior and potential outcomes are drawn from static network representations. In addition, forecasts of learning and adaptive outcomes across various levels of aggregation are extremely difficult as it requires the ability to think through the coevolution of networks in multiple complex dimensions.

Dynamic network analysis extends traditional social network analysis by modeling change that results from natural evolutionary and strategic intervention processes. In DNA, the process of change involves the addition and deletion of nodes and relations. Table 11.2 shows illustrative real-world change processes for nodes. This list is not intended to be inclusive of all change processes. Node types are listed at the top of the table and real-world examples that lead to node changes are listed underneath each type.

An example of node change from the table is turnover. Turnover involves the loss of people and possibly knowledge nodes. An organization has the potential of incurring negative effects due to turnover (Krackhardt & Porter, 1986). Another example of node change is innovation. Innovation involves the addition of knowledge and/or resource

Table 11.2.   Illustrative Real-World Change Processes for Notes

People/ Agents	Knowledge/ Resources	Tasks/ Events	Organizations
Promotion	Innovation	Goal Change	Organizational birth
Mobility	Discovery	Re-engineering	Organizational death
Recruitment	Redistribution	Development of new	New Markets
Downsizing	Training	technology	Alliances
Turnover	Forgetting	Stop usage of technol-	Mergers
	Consumption	ogy	Acquisitions
			Divestment
			Legislation of new entity

nodes. Innovation could lead to changes in other networks as research has shown that the adoption of innovation can be an occasion for the restructuring of social relations and roles (Barley, 1986).

Table 11.3 shows illustrative real-world change processes for relations. This table is a MetaMatrix where the columns and rows are node types. The cells are real-world examples that lead to relational changes between the nodes that make up a particular network. Again, this list in not intended to be inclusive of all possible change processes.

An example of relational change from the table is learning. Learning involves the addition of a relation between a person and knowledge (Carley & Hill, 2001). As previously described, learning can lead to subsequent changes in other networks such as the social network. Another example of relational change is task reassignment. Task reassignment involves the addition and deletion of relations between a person and various tasks. It should be generally noted that node changes which result in the deletion of a node also result in the deletion of all relations tied to that node.

Construct: A Multiagent Network Simulation of Interactions, Learning, and Adaptation

DNA simulation provides a means for reasoning about complex network changes as a result of both natural evolutionary processes and strategic interventions. DNA simulation models the organization(s) as a complex adaptive system (Carley & Gasser, 1999). Complex adaptive systems are a complexity theory approach to modeling organizational systems as it models the interactions among a heterogeneous set of agents. Learning and adaptation, or the lack thereof, are the products of agent interactions not the specific acts of agents.

Table 11.3.   Illustrative Real-World Change Processes for Relations

	People/ Agents	Knowledge/ Resources	Tasks/ Events	Organizations
People/ Agents	Motivating interactions Creating interdependency Boundary spanning Adaptation	Learning Innovation Enhancing knowledge flows	Creating interdependency Adaptation	Motivating interactions Creating interdependency Boundary spanning Adaptation
Knowledge/ Resources		Learning Innovation Enhancing knowledge flows	Learning Innovation	Learning Innovation Enhancing knowledge flows
Tasks/ Events			Creating interdependency	Creating interdependency Adaptation
Organizations				Motivating interactions Creating interdependency Boundary spanning Adaptation

For example, Construct is a DNA multiagent network simulation model for reasoning about dynamic network change (Carley, 1990, 1991, 1999; Carley & Hill, 2001; Schreiber & Carley, 2004a, 2004b; Schreiber & Carley, 2005; Schreiber, Singh, & Carley, 2004). Construct models both natural evolutionary processes and strategic interventions. Natural evolutionary processes such as learning and network coevolution are modeled using well-known theories and stylized facts. This includes theories of organizing such as the double interact (Weick, 1969) and structuration (Giddens, 1984); theories of cognition such as social information processing (Salancik & Pfeffer, 1978) and situated learning (Lave & Wenger, 1991); and stylized facts concerning human interactions such as the effects of homophily (Lazarsfeld & Merton, 1954) and proximity (Festinger, 1950).

Strategic interventions in the simulation are represented by purposeful change of the network. Such interventions could include the proximal placement of human agents as an attempt to infuse a hot group[5] or the addition of organizational capabilities as an attempt to integrate variety and spur learning and adaptation. Simulation allows for what-if scenarios of strategic interventions to forecast how these interventions affect the natural evolution of the network and emergent outcomes. Results of the simulation can also be used for theory creation.

Modeling natural evolutionary processes and strategic interventions allows for reasoning about how the organizational context supports learning and adaptability. This includes reasoning about when strategic interventions need to take place. Reasoning about organizational context and learning is a continual process as learning also changes the context of the organization—networks are constantly evolving and emerging. As noted previously, context and learning are intimately intertwined.

Hypothetical Use of DNA Tools

The following serves as a hypothetical example of using DNA when conducting research on network leadership. This example is intended to orient the reader as to the application of the tools just described. The hypothetical research project explores the coevolution of human and social capital for an organization. First, we will want to define the following networks from the MetaMatrix and collect data on them: social network, knowledge network and task network. The social network will capture relations among the agents (social capital), the knowledge network will capture the knowledge each agent knows (human capital) and the task network will capture the tasks assigned to each agent (assumed to influence agent relations and the application of knowledge).

Once the data are collected the networks can be input into the dynamic network analysis tools for analysis. For instance, ORA will produce measures that characterize the actual organization such as communication density, which is a measure of how many communication relations exist as compared to the total that could exist. This can provide feedback on the relational coupling and social capital structure of the organization. More ORA measures that relate to network leadership will be discussed later.

Then the networks can be input into construct, the multiagent simulation model, to forecast the diffusion of knowledge. The knowledge network (human capital) would initially define who knows what, the social network (social capital) would define who is talking to whom, and the task network could be used to weight the extent to which each agent talks to each other. For example, we can weight it so that agents who work on similar tasks will interact with each other more often than they do with agents who do not share similarity of tasks. During the simulation, agents will interact and exchange knowledge thereby diffusing it in the organization.

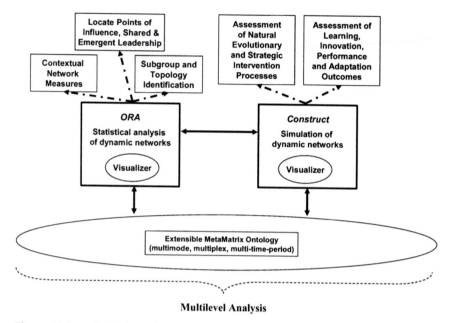

Figure 11.3.   CMU dynamic network analysis toolsuite for reasoning about complex sociotechnical systems.

How knowledge diffuses in the model depends on the interdependent interactions of the agents.

Both ORA and Construct are part of an interoperable tool chain for DNA developed at Carnegie Mellon University (Carley, Diesner, Reminga, & Tsvetovat, 2004). Figure 11.3 shows the tool chain and some illustrative analytic outcomes as related to network leadership.

Relating DNA to Network Leadership

Leadership of Context: Measures of Context
The following social network measures represent complexity science concepts relating to organizational context. The measures are broken down into categories relevant to the complexity science perspective: relational coupling, variety, organizational form and stress. The measures are computed at the graph or subgraph level of analysis depending on the organizational context boundaries being analyzed.

Complexity Context Category	Social Network Measure
Relational Coupling	Density
	Connectedness
	Average Speed
Variety	Learning Capacity
Organizational Form	Hierarchy
	Least Upper Boundedness
Stress	Cognitive Demand
	Knowledge Load

Relational Coupling

The social network measures of density, connectedness and average speed provide insight into the degree of interdependent relations in an organization.

Density (Wasserman & Faust, 1994) is a standard social network measure of the ratio of existing relations over all possible relations, ranging from 0 to 1. Unfortunately, density tends to go down as group size increases. Consequently, its main use is for comparing organizations that are similar in size. In general, for groups of relatively the same size, the group with the higher density is more tightly coupled. Of course, a midrange number would indicate the theoretically desired moderate coupling of complexity theory.

Connectedness (Krackhardt, 1994) is the degree to which each agent can reach every other agent in the network, ranging from 0 to 1 where 1 would indicate a fully connected graph. High connectedness is needed for dealing with complex and changing environments. Connectedness provides a structure—a relational coupling—that is at least essential for the collective to learn and adapt. One thing to note is that path length is not considered in this measure.

Average speed (Carley, 2002b) is the average of the inverse of all shortest paths among each pair of agents in the network, ranging from 0 to 1. Average speed is an indicator of communication speed and a 1 for this measure would be the fastest speed.

Requisite Variety

To assess requisite variety, we introduce a new measure into the MetaMatrix family of measures—learning capacity. Learning capacity is a transformative measure which assesses the potential increase for organizational learning. It is based on the existing knowledge network (human capital) and social network (social capital). Learning capacity is used as a measure of variety because leadership of variety is related to organizational learning and adaptation (Hazy, 2004b, 2007; Hazy & Tivnan, 2004). Learning capacity is calculated as follows. First, the maximum possible knowledge diffusion that could be achieved by the organization is obtained by multiplying the inverse of the reachability graph, obtained from the social network, with the knowledge network. The reachability graph takes into account the direction of ties in the social network which means that a full diffusion of knowledge may not result.[6] Next, the learning potential of the network is obtained by subtracting the original knowledge network from the maximum possible knowledge diffusion. This subtraction ensures that the original knowledge an agent possesses is not counted as potential learning. This step captures the highest level of learning that could occur in the organization given the current constraints of the networks. Next, the learning capacity is calculated as a ratio. This step divides the learning potential by the maximum possible knowledge diffusion. The measure ranges from 0 to <1 with a zero indicating there is no capacity for learning and a number close to one indicating there is a large capacity for learning.

Learning capacity is an indicator of complexity, more specifically to the amount of existing knowledge variety which could potentially be combined through existing relations. Changes to knowledge, people and relations would change the measure. It should be noted that this indicator gives us a sense of complexity and that full learning potential in a network, even if the measure is close to 1, would unlikely be reached.

Organizational Form

The social network measures of hierarchy and least upper boundedness provide insight about an organization's form.

Hierarchy (Krackhardt, 1994) is the degree of status differentiation as measured by the cycles present in the informal structure, ranging from 0 to 1. Cycles are an important characteristic of a network as they are indicators of information flow fluidity and rapid rework. Cycles can lead to quicker production of learning and adaptive outcomes. A value of 1 for this measure would indicate an absence of cycles.

Least upper boundedness (Krackhardt, 1994) is the degree to which agent pairs have a common deference agent, ranging from 0 to 1. A deference relation is measured by a directional tie from one agent to another. Note that a deference relation does not necessarily have to be to a formal superior and that agents can have several deference relations. Least upper boundedness is an indicator of conflict resolution whereas a common deference agent would be available to settle differences. A value of 0 for this measure would indicate that no pair of agents have a common deference.

Stress

Stress is an indicator of tension in a system. The social network measures of average cognitive demand and knowledge load provide insight
about the existing stress. These measures do not distinguish between
external or internal sources of stress. Rather, they are indicators of overall
stress. It should be noted that stress (tension) is needed to improve the
process of learning but that overstressing is counterproductive.

Average cognitive demand (Carley, 2002b) is the average amount of
effort all agents exert in the course of interacting and doing work in the
organization. This is a normalized value ranging from 0 to 1 whereas a 1
indicates a highly stressed organization.

Knowledge load (Carley, 2002b) is the average knowledge each agent
currently uses. This is a normalized value ranging from 0 to 1 where 1
indicates that all knowledge is used by every agent.

Leadership in Process: Identification of Influential Agents

The following leadership forms contribute to shaping communication
structure: creating interactions and interdependencies, enhancing knowledge flows, maintaining relational coupling, increasing the speed of
learning, and communicating new knowledge. Below we identify and
describe a social network measure that relates to each leadership form.
These measures are:

Measure	Leadership Form
Cognitive demand	Creating interactions and interdependencies
Degree centrality	Enhancing knowledge flows
Boundary spanner	Maintaining relational coupling
Closeness centrality	Increasing the speed of learning
Effective network size	Communicating new knowledge

Creating Interactions and Interdependencies

Cognitive demand is the amount of effort an agent exerts in the course
of interacting and doing work in the organization, ranging from 0 to 1.
This is the measure that was previously averaged to produce information
about organizational context and stress at the graph level. Agents high in
cognitive demand are likely to be emergent leaders (Carley & Ren, 2001).
The larger workload and sphere of interaction available to these agents
give them a better, more complex understanding of the situation. This
can push them into a position where they often need to direct others in
order to complete tasks. Agents high in cognitive demand will provide

interactive direction and establish interdependencies as they coordinate task assignments with others.

Enhancing Knowledge Flows

Degree centrality (Wasserman & Faust, 1994) is the normalized total number of relations for an agent, ranging from 0 to 1. This measure identifies agents who are likely to have the most interactions and who are therefore the most likely to learn the most knowledge. It is a powerful measure of influence. Agents high in degree centrality will facilitate knowledge flows through the network due to their accumulation of knowledge and high degree of interactions.

Maintaining Relational Coupling

Boundary spanner (Cormen, Leiserson, & Rivest, 2001) is the normalized component betweenness of an agent, ranging from 0 to 1. In effect, it measures agents as gatekeepers. Boundary spanner identifies agents who most likely connect otherwise disjoint groups in an organization. Boundary spanner agents will facilitate knowledge flows to parts of the organization that are normally hard to reach. These agents tend to overcome organizational barriers that prevent interactions and thus can play an important role in the complex functioning and dynamics of the informal network.

Increasing the Speed of Learning

Closeness centrality (Freeman, 1979) is the normalized average closeness in path length of an agent to all other agents in the organization, ranging from 0 to 1. This measure identifies agents who can most quickly communicate knowledge to the organization as a whole. These agents will provide speed of knowledge flow. This capability will be important for diffusing knowledge that is critical about the changing conditions in the environment. Closeness centrality agents can support faster learning and quicker adaptive response.

Communicating New Knowledge

Effective network size (Burt, 1992) is the number of nonredundant ties in an agent's ego network. In other words, it measures the structural hole that an agent fills. Effective network size identifies agents who are most likely to communicate new knowledge. These agents will interact with other agents who are largely not connected to one another and this facilitates the communication of nonredundant knowledge. Agents with large effective networks will increase the interactive complexity by channeling new knowledge through the network. This helps the organization learn, build knowledge, innovate and adapt.

Advantages for Leadership Theory

An obvious and prodigious advantage to using DNA is that its theoretical framework provides an understandable interface to the abstract nature of complexity theory. The categories of nodes and relations in DNA are based on organizational context. The researcher or practitioner is familiar with node types such as people, tasks, resources, and so on. Accordingly, it is easy to understand that people have relations to one another, that people are assigned to tasks, and so on. Also, the real-world change processes described above are enacted in DNA as the addition and deletion of nodes and ties. This representation of change within the theoretical framework is easily comprehensible.

In addition, at times, the networks can be visually depicted. The reasonableness of visual depiction depends on the size and complexity of the networks. Information is not easily conveyed when the networks are too large or too complex. But when networks either naturally lend themselves to depiction or are able to be reduced then this can expedite comprehension by illuminating contextual nature, change effects and possible strategic interventions.

Besides providing an understandable interface, DNA offers several other advantages to leadership theory because it is an integrated analytical framework spanning context and people. These advantages include:

- Representing organizations as multimode, multiplex entities with many networks captures more of the realistic nature and complexity of organizational life.
- Various categories of measures exist and provide insight for understanding the relational qualities of organizational context. Categories of measures include: relational coupling, variety, individual/shared/aggregate points of influence, emergent leadership, human capital and social capital (collective action), informal subgroup and topology identification.
- Various measures of leadership forms exist, thus enabling the user to capture leadership in process. These leadership forms include: creating interactions and interdependencies, enhancing knowledge flows, maintaining relational coupling, increasing the speed of learning, and communicating new knowledge.
- Identification, measurement and analysis of leadership events can be accomplished.
- Contextual changes and leadership events over time, both within and between organizations and events, can be compared and contrasted

- Using DNA tools the researcher or practitioner can analyze and reason about, in a systematic fashion, the complex interactive collective action process within a specified organizational context.
- Using DNA tools the researcher or practitioner can analyze and reason about organizational outcomes such as learning and adaptability.
- Multilevel analysis ranging from the individual agent level to market level can be done concurrently.

Data: Battle Command Group

To explore network leadership, we used DNA to analyze data collected from a real-world organization—a battle command group within the U.S. Army. This organization is comprised of decentralized, distributed and highly interdependent units. The distributed structure relies heavily on expertise, information flow and cross-functional collaboration. The battle command group is organized to operate in a network centric fashion[7] which is the military version of the network organization. It is intended to be a learning organization which can respond quickly to high-velocity changes. As such, the organizational structure can adapt to environmental conditions. In light of the focus on learning and adaptation, the battle command group is a good organization for studying Network Leadership.

Data were collected for the communication, task and knowledge networks of the organization. There were 165 people nodes, 51 task nodes and 51 knowledge (categories) nodes relating to the tasks. The data collection occurred during the beginning phases of a wargame exercise. People in the wargame were assigned functional roles such as commander or intelligence officer and the tasks that a person performed were related to the role they played.

Analysis

The data were analyzed using ORA and Construct. In this paper, we used ORA to analyze organizational context, identify influential individuals in the network leadership process and assess the nature of the leadership forms. Construct was used to reason about variations in context and how these variations enable complex functioning and learning outcomes.

Leadership of Context: Measures of Context

The MetaMatrix data were input into ORA and the graph level measures were computed. We provide an interpretation of each measure as it relates to the particular organizational context. The following is a recap of the measures for each contextual category.

Complexity Context Category	Social Network Measure
Relational Coupling	Density
	Connectedness
	Average Speed
Variety	Learning Capacity
Organizational Form	Hierarchy
	Least Upper Boundedness
Stress	Cognitive Demand
	Knowledge Load

Leadership in Process: Identification of Influential Agents

The MetaMatrix data were input into ORA and the individual level measures were computed to identify the top 5 leaders in process for each leadership form. We provide a discussion of leadership in process as it relates to the particular organizational context. The following is a recap of the measures for each leadership form.

Measure	Leadership Form
Cognitive demand	Creating interactions and interdependencies
Degree centrality	Enhancing knowledge flows
Boundary spanner	Maintaining relational coupling
Closeness centrality	Increasing the speed of learning
Effective network size	Communicating new knowledge

Reasoning About the Nature of Network Leadership: Leaders in Process

ORA was used to reason about the relative impact of different leaders in process. Each top leader for a leadership form, determined by the relevant measure, was separately taken out of the organization by isolating them in ORA using the Key Set Selector. Isolation deletes the agent node as well as all relations connected to that agent. New context measures were computed and compared to the original context measures. This happened five times, once for each leader. The comparison provided an assessment of each leader's impact on the organization by analyzing the changes to the network in their absence.

Leadership in Process: Reasoning About the Effects of Culture on Natural Evolution

Construct was used to reason about the two propositions by Uhl-Bien et al. (2007). To test these propositions, we simulated the organization under various cultural influences. These cultural influences were: a focus on interactions associated with formal role; a focus on informal interactions outside the formal role; and an integrated focus on both informal and formal interactions.[8] Agents in the battle command group played formal roles during the wargame and performed tasks associated with their formal role. As this is a modular organization, formal roles overlapped and agents performing similar formal roles also performed similar tasks.

Construct was initialized with the MetaMatrix data collected on the task and knowledge networks, thereby representing the organizational context and the formal roles of the agents. Then a virtual experiment was run in which each of the cultural conditions was sequentially varied. We collected the diffusion of knowledge that occurred under each cultural condition. The diffusion of knowledge represents the level of learning within the organization.[9] Each of the three conditions in the virtual experiment was replicated using Monte Carlo techniques 25 times and each run had 200 time periods.

We calculated error bars for the level of learning that was achieved at time period 200 in each of the conditions. Comparison of the results determined if there were significant differences in learning. If there is significant increase for the informal role condition, as compared to the formal role condition, then the proposition that complex functioning and learning outcomes are enhanced by enabling leadership will be supported. (Enabling leadership is concerned with informal interactions in the network.) If there is a significant increase for the integrated roles condition, as compared to both of the formal and informal roles conditions, then the proposition that the dissemination of learning outcomes through the organization is enhanced by enabling leadership which provides an interface between the formal and informal networks will be supported.

RESULTS AND DISCUSSION

Leadership of Context: Measures of Context

Table 11.4 shows the graph level measures which characterize the context of the battle command group. Note that the graph level is the organizational level for this analysis.

Table 11.4.   Measures of Organizational Context

Complexity Context Category	Measure	Value	Description
Relational coupling	Density	0.0286	The ratio of existing relations over all possible relations
	Connectedness	0.8164	The degree to which each agent can reach every other agent
	Average speed	0.2809	The average inverse of all pairs of shortest paths
Variety	Learning capacity	0.7721	The networks learning potential based on human and social cap.
Network form	Hierarchy	0.4156	The degree of pure hierarchical structure present in a network
	Upper boundedness	0.9957	The degree to which agent pairs have a common superior
Stress	Cognitive demand	0.0338	The average amount of effort for agents to complete tasks
	Knowledge load	1.9872	The average knowledge per agent

Relational Coupling

The 0.0286 density is not surprising for a group of this size. The 0.8164 connectedness means that this is a highly connected organization, although there are some isolates. This measure indicates that there is at least one path between almost all pairs of agents.

The 0.2809 average speed indicates that knowledge does not travel very quickly in this network. This means that although the organization has a relational coupling that connects mostly everyone, it is loosely coupled. Knowledge does not travel quickly because there are long paths between pairs of agents. Additional relations are needed to quicken the flow of knowledge and speed up the rate of learning. These additional relations, even though they may redundantly connect agent pairs, can provide shorter paths for knowledge flow.

Variety

The 0.7721 learning capacity indicates a large capacity for learning in this organization. Injecting non-redundant knowledge or adding nonredundant relations may increase the capacity. But given the current capacity, such strategic interventions may only be marginal or needed in the event of changing conditions. By virtue of the average speed measure above, the best strategic intervention may be adding redundant relations as this organization has a large capacity to learn but a slow rate of learning.

Organizational Form

The 0.4156 hierarchy measure indicates that the informal network has a moderate amount of cycles. The 0.9957 least upper boundedness also indicates that practically every node has a common superior for conflict resolution. This is not surprising as conflict resolution is an emphasis in military functioning.

These measures do not necessarily indicate that the organization will lack in learning or adaptability. Work on high-reliability organizations has shown that the structure of reliable organizations can change to fit the situation (Weick & Sutcliffe, 2001). This means that the level of cycles within the informal structure can fluctuate in response to the situation. These measures of organizational form indicate that the battle command group may also possess this ability whereas they have fewer cycles in normal operations but more cycles in rapidly changing and critical situations. In fact, given the stress analysis below this may be the case.

Stress

The 0.0338 cognitive demand indicates a very low amount of stress on the overall organization. Agents had a great deal of slack mental resource at the time measurements were taken. This makes sense as the data were collected at the beginning of the experiment when the battle lab exercise was just starting. The 0.0390 indicates a very low knowledge load as there are 51 knowledge categories in this organization. Again, agents are not stressed at this time and have slack cognitive resources.

These stress measures may account for the moderate amounts of cycles in the organization. From a complexity theory perspective the stress measures indicate the need for tension in the organization. As cognitive demand and knowledge load increase, interactions and knowledge flow should also increase as agents are working on complex tasks and trying to reduce the tension in the organization.

Leadership in Process: Identification of Influential Agents

Table 11.5 presents the influential agents of leadership in process by leadership form. The top five agents in each leadership form are listed.[10] An inspection of the table shows that, by and large, different agents per-

Table 11.5.   Leaders in Process

Measure	Agent	Value	Description
Cognitive Demand	Effects, HBCT1	0.0716	Agent who is most likely to emerge as a leader
	Fires & Effects, AVN	0.0716	
	Fires NCO, Fires BDE	0.0716	
	Plans, AVN	0.0716	
	Commander, HBCT3	0.0716	
Degree Centrality	FEC1, TAC CP1	0.0935	Agent who is most likely to have the most interactions and to learn more knowledge
	ACOFS G3, TAC CP1	0.0710	
	ACOFS G2, Uex Main	0.0710	
	Chief of Staff, Uex Main	0.0677	
	Effects, Fires BDE	0.0677	
Boundary Spanner	Plans, Maneuver	0.0295	Agent who most likely connects otherwise disjoint groups
	G3 COO, TAC CP2	0.0275	
	A2C2, TAC CP2	0.0241	
	MP, Maneuver	0.0234	
	Plans, AVN	0.0221	
Closeness Centrality	Comm. Officer, Maneuver	0.0397	Agent who can most quickly communicate to the organization at large
	TNC G6, Uey	0.0391	
	Network Eng., Uex Main	0.0388	
	C4/G6, TAC CP1	0.0373	
	Intel, Uey	0.0369	
	Coalition Center LNO, Uex Main	0.0369	
Effective Network Size	Effects NCO, HBCT1	11.0556	Agent who is most likely to communicate new knowledge
	G3 COO, TAC CP2	6.7000	
	Commander, Maneuver	6.5833	
	A2C2, TAC CP2	6.5714	
	Plans, Maneuver	6.3929	

form different forms of leadership. This finding lends support to the notion that collective change agents are the source of competitive advantage in the knowledge era. The collective intelligence of the organization's citizenry was being tapped in many ways by various leaders who were enacting diverse forms of leadership. Learning and adaptation were being developed through a collective dynamic.

These results also lend support to the notion of shared leadership within organizations. Obviously, leadership in the informal dynamic was

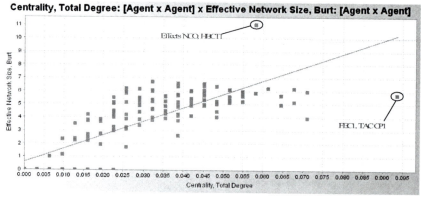

Figure 11.4.   Plot of the degree centrality and effective network size measures.

being performed by many agents. This means communication was being shaped by a collection of leaders. This shared leadership dynamic occurred across and within various leadership forms. For instance, the top leader in each form was different as leadership across forms was shared. In addition, there was clearly a shared leadership dynamic within forms which did not have a distinct top leader. An example is closeness centrality where the range among the top five was 0.0028.

These results also demonstrate that agents can enact multiple forms of leadership in process. For example, Plans, AVN provided leadership by creating interactions and interdependencies and by maintaining relational coupling.

There is also evidence of distinctive leadership as these leaders standout in comparison to everyone else. As an illustration, Figure 11.4 presents a plot of degree centrality against effective network size. Here we can see the distinctive leaders as they are outliers to the rest of the organization. The leaders shown are FEC1, TAC CP1, who enhances knowledge flow through his central position and Effects NCO, HBCT1, who communicates new knowledge through non-redundant relations.

The process of network leadership is itself a complex dynamic which is made up of a variety of leadership forms. Leadership can be distinctive and it can be shared, both within and between forms. Individual leaders can also enact leadership within multiple leadership forms. All this happens concurrently within the complex dynamic.

Reasoning About the Nature of Network Leadership

Two interesting results are highlighted from this analysis. The first result is the impact of each leader in process on the learning capacity

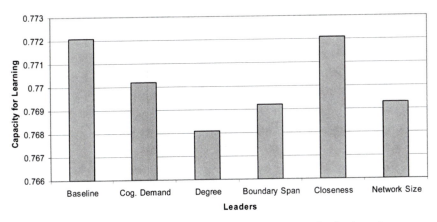

Figure 11.5.   The impact of leaders in process on the capacity for learning.

measure. Figure 11.5 presents a bar chart of these results. The baseline represents the condition where all leaders are present in the organization. Then there are the five separate analyses where one of the leaders is missing in the organization. Comparing each of these conditions to the baseline gives the resulting learning differential when the leader is missing and not enacting their structural role. These five separate analyses are shown together in Figure 11.5 for analytic clarity and comparison.

The degree centrality, boundary spanner and effective network size leaders all positively affect the organization's capacity for learning (i.e. with them missing the organizations learning capacity decreases). The degree centrality leader has the greatest impact. This result indicates that these leaders, especially degree centrality, are all important to the informal interdependent interactions of the collective. They all provide a type of benefit to the social capital structure that produces collective action and collective intelligence. Note: There is low average knowledge per agent in the Battle Command Group data and this is consistent across agents. This means that these results are due more to the structural role of the leader rather than the loss of knowledge in their absence.

The cognitive demand leader is also important but to a more moderate degree. In fairness, this analysis is during a time of nonstress in the organization and cognitive demand leaders emerge during times of stress. Therefore, these results may not be fully representative of the impact of cognitive demand leaders.

Another noticeable result is the lack of any impact on the capacity for learning by the closeness centrality leader. This is not all that surprising since the main benefit of closeness centrality leaders is speed of learning which the learning capacity measure does not capture.

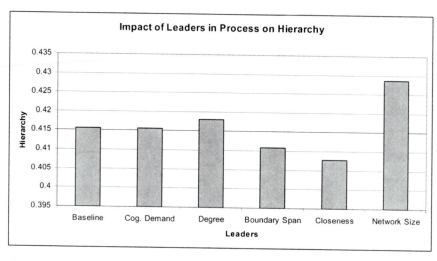

Figure 11.6.   The impact of leaders in process on hierarchy.

The second result is the impact of each leader in process on the level of hierarchy in the organization. Figure 11.6 presents a bar chart of these results. All five immediate impact analyses are shown together for analytic clarity and comparison.

The degree centrality and cognitive demand leader have very little impact. The equalizing effect on the hierarchy measure during the absence of the degree central leader suggests that this leader has ties to both formal leadership and the informal network. It also suggests that this leader is a natural interface between the informal dynamics and top management. The same can be said for the cognitive demand leader. But caution should be noted as this analysis may not represent the proper context in which cognitive demand leaders are important.

The boundary spanner and closeness centrality leaders provide some level of hierarchy in the organization as the level goes down in their absence. This is due to their ties to the chief of staff and theater top-level command group, respectively. These leaders are good candidates for interfacing the productive outcomes of the informal network with top management. But care should be taken with these leaders, along with the degree central leader, as they could also be conduits of top-down control.

Last, an interesting result occurs with the effective network size leader. This leader is very important to the informal interactions in the collective as the hierarchy measure increases considerably when he/she is not in the organization. This leader's ability to supply nonredundant ties to many people, as evidenced by the 11.0556 value for effective network size, has a definite impact on the emergent complex functioning within the organization. The effective network size leader provides critical social structure that promotes higher levels of cycles within the informal structure. This certainly can have a positive effect on the timely production of learning and adaptive responses.

Leadership in Process: Reasoning About the Effects of Culture on Natural Evolution

Figure 11.7 shows the results of the virtual experiment. There is a large increase in learning when there is a focus on informal network dynamics (219) as opposed to formal roles (172). The model suggests that free-associated interactions enable collective action and increased returns on learning outcomes. This provides support for the proposition that enabling leadership, which fosters interactions among diverse agents within the informal network, will generate productive learning outcomes (Uhl-Bien et al., 2007). In addition, there is also a small but significant increase in the integrated roles condition (221). The 95% confidence intervals for the formal, informal and integrated cultural conditions are respectively 171.83–172.40, 219.51–220.27, and 221.55–222.11. This suggests, as Uhl-Bien et al. (2007) have proposed, that integrating informal network learning outcomes into the formal channels provides additional gains. In the model, the gains are in terms of an increased rate of knowledge diffusion.

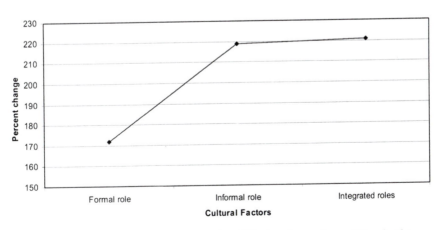

Figure 11.7.   Percent change in knowledge diffusion for each condition in the simulated organization.

The organization experienced increased gains through learning focused on the external environment and integrating this knowledge into the formal structure, that is, sharing what was learned with others performing the same task. This seems especially relevant to the battle command group under study as agents need to gather as much knowledge as possible to gain a situation awareness of the critically changing conditions of the battlefield. Such a process is facilitated by interacting and coordinating with others who have a different view of the space of operations. Also, the reports (tasks) that each agent produces are passed to the command level—the administrative leadership in Uhl-Bien et al.'s terms. Knowledge is then accumulated in a central structure which makes it easier to find in a large organization, such as the battle command group. This is analogous to the process of getting the innovative outcomes to the right places for strategic exploitation, especially when the collective as whole has access to the outcomes. In this process, productive outcomes generated in one part of the organization can more easily flow to other parts of the organization and generate additional learning and adaptability.

This result is also congruent with the writings of Ireland and Hitt (1999) where they argue that sustaining an effective organizational culture is a necessary component of twenty-first century leadership. According to these authors, organizational culture provides the context within which formulation and implementation of strategies occur. The increased learning as a result of certain cultures in this simulation underscores the effective culture argument. The results also relate to their claim of importance for establishing balanced controls by focusing both on gaining external information and on integrating that information with internal knowledge. In this simulation this is represented by disparate sets of knowledge about the environment where those working similar tasks have overlapping internal knowledge. Agents learned more about the external environment through informal channels, which connected them with others who had different knowledge concerning this environment. Integrating the new knowledge with internal knowledge via formal task roles produced an increased rate of learning within the organization. The emphasis in this simulation was on action not outcomes. It was concerned with the lower-level communication patterns that evolved and outcomes were emergent from these interactions.

CONCLUSION

Network leadership is a new paradigm for leading learning and adaptability in the rapidly changing and dynamic landscape of the knowledge era. This new paradigm is based in complexity theory and entails two types of change leadership: leadership of context and leadership in process. Leadership of context enables organizational processes that allow for productive collective action to emerge in response to a changing environment. Leadership in process facilitates learning and adaptation through the emergent interactions and informal dynamics which form collective action. This leadership type also channels the learning and adaptive responses to formal management for exploitation. In terms of theoretical concern, network leadership has needs for understanding *who* is leading, *how* they lead and *when* they lead. Methodologically, there is a need for multilevel and longitudinal analysis of the interdependent interactions and related outcomes of leadership in complex organizations.

We have introduced dynamic network analysis, a theory and methodology for analyzing and reasoning about complex adaptive systems. Through DNA, we can analyze issues regarding leadership of context and reason about leadership in process. DNA is an approach that addresses both the theoretical and methodological concerns of network leadership. It also provides an understandable interface to the abstract nature of complexity theory through the MetaMatrix theoretical framework. The practical application of DNA can also provide many useful normative assessments.

In this chapter, we demonstrated the use of DNA to study network leadership by analyzing data collected on a battle command group. We showed how measures of context relating to relational coupling, variety, organizational form and stress allow us to characterize the organization. From this characterization we can strategically assess the needs of the organization from a complexity theory perspective. For instance, the results indicated that the organization needed to speed their rate of learning, possibly by adding relational coupling through redundant ties. The amount of relational coupling has to be carefully addressed to avoid tight coupling which causes overload in the network and leads to non-productive outcomes. The results also indicated that tensions were needed in the organization as stress was low. This would help increase interdependent interactions and the flow of knowledge to spur more complex cognitive functioning and the development of collective intelligence. These analyses help to focus the efforts for leadership of context.

Then we described five forms of leadership in process that can be enacted by agents in a complex adaptive system. These forms and their respective measures include creating interactions and interdependencies, enhancing knowledge flows, maintaining relational coupling, increasing the speed of learning, and communicating new knowledge.

We identified the leaders enacting each form. The analysis showed that network leadership contains distinct leaders, leaders who enact multiple forms of leadership and shared leadership—both across and within forms of leadership. Network leadership is therefore a complex, interactive dynamic where many leaders are enacting several forms of leadership simultaneously. The simultaneous enactment of diverse leadership forms serves to shape the overall communications of the organization and to tap the collective intelligence of the organization's citizenry in many ways. Therefore, learning and adaptive responses are developed through a collective dynamic. Consequently, this analysis supports a paradigm shift for leadership where the impetus of change falls on the collective and is not the actions of a single "heroic" leader.

We then analyzed the impact of the top leaders within each form to gain an understanding of their influence in terms of leadership in process. This assessment indicated that, for the battle command group, the leaders high in degree centrality, boundary spanning and effective network size were particularly influential in the given context. Of course, under other contexts such as high tension and stress it is conceivable that other leaders, such as those high in cognitive demand, will play a much more influential role.

We also used simulation to reason about the effects of culture on the natural evolution of learning outcomes. The results of the simulation suggested that network leadership enables productive collective action through cultures which are focused on informal network dynamics and on integrating the informal outcomes with the formal system. These results also provided support for propositions about enabling leadership set forth by Uhl-Bien and colleagues (2007).

Through DNA we were able to address some of the theoretical concerns for the *who, how* and *when* of network leadership. We addressed *who* is leading by identifying leaders in process and assessing their related impacts on the organizational context. We addressed *how* leaders lead by analyzing the contextual character of the organization and discovering complexity needs which can help focus leadership of context activities. We also addressed *how* by running a virtual experiment which showed that organizational culture is an avenue for producing collective action and intelligence. We addressed *when* through the analysis of context to spot needs in complex functioning which require attention. In addition, results of the virtual experiment suggested that dynamic network leaders need to strategically intervene *when* the organizational culture is too focused on formal dynamics.

Dynamic network analysis is a novel approach to studying the complexities of network leadership. The benefits of the approach will certainly improve as more research goes into the methodology and theory of DNA. Because there are so many advantages to using DNA, not every analysis demonstrating its full use can be incorporated into one article. Other advantages besides the ones demonstrated in this paper include the identification and analysis of leadership events over time and the concurrent multilevel analysis of leadership within a complex organization. This paper has highlighted the kinds of leadership insights that can be gained from this approach and is a first step toward a theory of network leadership.

NOTES

1. We use the term agent throughout this paper to refer to a human agent, a person.
2. From a complexity theory perspective, collective action is not controlled in the traditional sense of top-down command and control, but in the sense of guiding the system toward productive outcomes. Guiding the system is needed when emergent behaviors emanating from systems of free association go off in directions that are nonproductive in terms of learning and adaptability (Uhl-Bien et al., 2007)
3. There are other components of DNA such as the text analysis tool Automap. This and other tools are not used for this particular analysis and, therefore, are not described.
4. Cognitive demand measures the effort an individual spends in performing their tasks and is based on the agent's various communication, knowledge, resource and task networks
5. A hot group is a small group of people who are dedicated to accomplishing a challenging task(s) usually performing well above normal standards.
6. A disconnected graph could also result in knowledge diffusion that is less than full.
7. Network centric refers to the robust ability to share information among nodes in a network. This provides an information advantage for increased effectiveness. The focus is on the network itself, and not on the top-leader which would be leader-centric.
8. The focus is equal for both informal and formal network interactions. The agents will focus 50% of the time on informal dynamics and 50% of their time on tasks associated with their formal roles.
9. The diffusion of knowledge measure in the construct model is used as a proxy for learning. Diffusion of knowledge measures the percent of total knowledge in the organization that the agents, on average across runs, have learned.
10. Closeness centrality lists six agents as the Intel and Coalition Center LNO had identical scores for the fifth ranking.

REFERENCES

Argote, L., & Ingram, P. (2000). Knowledge transfer: A basis for competitive advantage of firms. *Organizational Behavior and Human Decision Processes, 82,* 150-169.

Arquilla, J., & Ronfeldt, D. (2001). The advent of netwar (revisited). In J. Arquilla, & D. Ronfeldt (Eds.), *Networks and netwars: The future of terror, crime and militancy* (pp. 1-24). Santa Monica, CA: Rand.

Ashby, W. R. (1960). *Design for a brain* (2nd ed.). New York: Wiley.

Barley, S. R. (1986). Technology as an occasion for structuring: Evidence from observations of CT scanners and the social order of radiology departments. *Administrative Science Quarterly, 21,* 78-108.

Bennis, W. (1997). Cultivating creative genius. *Industry Week,* 84-88.

Bennis, W., & Biederman, P. W. (1997). *Organizing genius: The secrets of creative collaboration.* Reading, MA: Addison-Wesley.

Bettis, R. A., & Hitt, M. A. (1995). The new competitive landscape. *Strategic Management Journal,* 7(13), 7-19.

Brown, J. S., & Deguid, P. (2000). Balancing act: How to capture knowledge without killing it. *Harvard Business Review,* 78(3), 73-80.

Burt, R. S. (1992). *Structural holes.* Boston: Harvard University Press.

Carley, K. M. (1990). Group stability: A socio-cognitive approach. In E. Lawler, B. Markovsky, C. Ridgeway, & H. Walker (Eds.), *Advances in group processes: Theory & research* (Vol. VII, 1-44). Greenwhich, CT: JAI Press.

Carley, K. M. (1991). A theory of group stability. *American Sociological Review,* 56(3), 331-354.

Carley, K. M. (1999). On the evolution of social and organizational networks. In S. B. Andrews & D. Knoke (Eds.), *Special issue of research in the sociology of organizations on networks in and around organizations* (Vol. 16, pp. 3-30). Greenwhich, CT: JAI Press.

Carley, K. M. (2002a). Smart agents and organizations of the future. In L. Lievrouw & S. Livingstone (Eds.), *The handbook of new media* (pp. 206-220). Thousand Oaks, CA: Sage.

Carley, K. M. (2002b). *Summary of key network measures for characterizing organizational architectures:* Working paper, Carnegie Mellon University.

Carley, K. M. (2003). Dynamic network analysis. In R. Breiger, K. M. Carley, & P. Pattison (Eds.), *Dynamic social network analysis: Workshop summary and papers* (pp. 133-145). Washington, DC: The National Academies Press.

Carley, K. M., Diesner, J., Reminga, J., & Tsvetovat, M. (2004). *Interoperability of dynamic network analysis software.* CASOS Working Paper.

Carley, K. M., & Gasser, L. (1999). Computational organization theory. In G. Weiss (Ed.), *Multiagent systems: A modern approach to distributed artificial intelligence* (pp. 299-330). Cambridge, MA: The MIT Press.

Carley, K. M., & Hill, V. (2001). Structural change and learning within organizations. In A. Lomi & E. R. Larsen (Eds.), *Dynamics of organizations: Computational modeling and organization theories.* Menlo Park, CA: MIT Press/AAAI.

Carley, K. M., & Ren, Y. (2001). *Tradeoffs between performance and adaptability for C3I architectures.* Paper presented at the Command and Control Research and Technology Symposium, Annapolis, MD.

Carley, K. M., & Svoboda, D. M. (1996). Modeling organizational adaptation as a simulated annealing process. *Sociological Methods and Research,* 25(1), 138-168.

Child, J., & McGrath, R. G. (2001). Organizations unfettered: Organizational form in an information-intensive economy. *Academy of Management Journal*, 44(6), 1135-1148.

Cormen, T. H., Leiserson, C. E., & Rivest, R. L. (2001). *Introduction to algorithms* (2nd ed.). Cambridge, MA: MIT Press.

Festinger, L. (1950). Informal social communication. *Psychology Review*, 57, 271-282.

Freeman, L. C. (1979). Centrality in social networks: I. Conceptual clarification. *Social Networks*, 1, 215-223.

Giddens, A. (1984). *The constitution of society: Outline of the theory of structuration*. Berkeley: University of California Press.

Gronn, P. (2002). Distributed leadership as a unit of analysis. *Leadership Quarterly*, 13, 423-451.

Hazy, J. K. (2004a). *A leadership and capabilities framework for organizational change: Simulating the emergence of leadership as an organizational meta-capability*. Washington, DC: The George Washington University,

Hazy, J. K. (2004b). *A leadership and capabilities framework for organizational change: Simulating the emergence of leadership as an organizational meta-capability*. Unpublished dissertation, The George Washington University, Washington, DC.

Hazy, J. K. (2007). *Measuring leadership effectiveness in complex social systems*. Manuscript submitted for publication.

Hazy, J. K., & Tivnan, B. F. (2004). *On building an organizationally realistic agent-based model of local interaction and emergent network structure*. Paper presented at the 2004 Winter Simulation Conference, Washington, DC.

Hitt, M. A., Keats, B. W., & DeMarie, S. M. (1998). Navigating in the new competitive landscape: Building strategic flexibility and competitive advantage in the 21st century. *Academy of Management Executive*, 12(4), 22-42.

Holland, J. H. (1995). *Hidden order*. Reading, MA: Addison-Wesley.

Ireland, R. D., & Hitt, M. A. (1999.) Achieving and maintaining strategic competitiveness in the 21st century: The role of strategic leadership. *Academy of Management Executive*, 13(1), 43-57.

Kauffman, S. (1993). *The origins of order*. New York: Oxford University Press.

Krackhardt, D. (1994). Graph theoretical dimensions of informal organizations. In K. M. Carley & M. Prietula (Eds.), *Computational organizational theory* (pp. 89-111). Hillsdale, NJ: Erlbaum.

Krackhardt, D., & Carley, K. M. (1998). *A PCANS model of structure in organization*. Paper presented at the International symposium on command and control research and technology, Monterrey, CA.

Krackhardt, D., & Porter, L. W. (1986). The snowball effect: Turnover embedded in social networks. *Journal of Applied Psychology*, 71(1), 50-55.

Lave, J., & Wenger, E. (1991). *Situated learning: Legitimate peripheral participation*. Cambridge, England: Cambridge University Press.

Lazarsfeld, P., & Merton, R. (1954). Friendship as a social process: A substantive and methodological analysis. In M. Berger, T. Abel, & C. Page (Eds.), *Freedom and control in modern society*. New York: Octagon.

March, J. G. (1996). Exploration and exploitation in organizational learning. In M. D. Cohen & L. S. Sproull (Eds.), *Organizational learning*. Thousand Oaks, CA: Sage.

Marion, R., & Uhl-Bien, M. (2001). Leadership in complex organizations. *The Leadership Quarterly, 12*(4), 389-418.

McGrath, R. G. (2001). Exploratory learning, innovative capacity, and managerial oversight. *Academy of Management Journal, 44*(1), 118-131.

Nohria, N. (1992). Is a network perspective a useful way of studying organizations? In N. Nohria & R. G. Eccles (Eds.), *Networks and organizations: Structure, form and action* (pp. 1-22). Boston: Harvard Business School Press.

Pierce, C. L., & Conger, J. A. (Eds.). (2003). All those years ago: The historical underpinnings of shared leadership. In *Shared leadership: Reframing the hows and whys of leadership* (pp. 1-18). Thousand Oaks, CA: Sage.

Powell, W. W. (1990). Neither market nor hierarchy: Network forms of organization. In B. Staw & L. L. Cummings (Eds.), *Research in organizational behavior* (Vol. 12, pp. 295-336). Greenwich, CT: JAI Press.

Ronfeldt, D., & Arquilla, J. (2001). Networks, netwars and the fight for the future. *First Monday, 6*(10).

Salancik, G. R., & Pfeffer, J. (1978). A social information processing approach to job attitudes and task design. *Administrative Science Quarterly, 23,* 224-253.

Schreiber, C. (2006). *Human and organizational risk modeling: Critical personnel and leadership in network organizations*. Carnegie Mellon University, School of Computer Science, Institute for Software Research, International. Technical Report, CMU-ISRI-06-120.

Schreiber, C., & Carley, K. M. (2004a.) Going beyond the data: Empirical validation leading to grounded theory. *Computational and Mathematical Organization Theory, 10*(2), 155-164.

Schreiber, C., & Carley, K. M. (2004b). *Key personnel: Identification and assessment of turnover risk*. Paper presented at the 2004 NAACSOS conference proceedings, Pittsburgh, PA.

Schreiber, C., & Carley, K. M. (2005). *Ineffective organizational practices at NASA: A dynamic network analysis*. Carnegie Mellon University, School of Computer Science, Institute for Software Research, International. Technical Report, CMU-ISRI-05-135.

Schreiber, C., Singh, S., & Carley, K. M. (2004). *Construct—A multi-agent network model for the co-evolution of agents and socio-cultural environments*. Carnegie Mellon University, School of Computer Science, Institute for Software Research, International. Technical Report, CMU-ISRI-04-109.

Stewart, T. A. (1997). *Intellectual capital: The new wealth of organizations*. New York: Doubleday.

Streatfield, P. J. (2001). *The paradox of control in organizations*. London: Routledge.

Tsvetovat, M., Reminga, J., & Carley, K. M. (2004). *DyNetML: Interchange format for rich social network data*. Carnegie Mellon University, School of Computer Science, Institute for Software Research International, Technical Report CMU-ISRI-04-105.

Uhl-Bien, M., Marion, R., & McKelvey, B. (2007). Complexity leadership theory: Shifting leadership from the industrial age to the knowledge era. *The Leadership Quarterly, 18*(4), 298-318.

Vaughan, D. (1996). *The Challenger launch decision: Risky technology, culture and deviance at NASA*. Chicago: The University of Chicago Press.

Wasserman, S., & Faust, K. (1994). *Social network analysis: Methods and applications*. Cambridge, England: Cambridge University Press.

Weick, K. E. (1969). *The social psychology of organizing*. Reading, MA: Addison-Wesley.

Weick, K. E., & Sutcliffe, K. M. (2001). *Managing the unexpected: Assuring high performance in an age of complexity*. San Francisco: Jossey-Bass.

Zaccaro, S. J., & Klimoski, R. J. (Eds.). (2001). The nature of organizational leadership: An introduction. In *The nature of organizational leadership: Understanding the performance imperitives confronting today's leaders* (pp. 3-41). San Francisco: Jossey-Bass.

CHAPTER 12

A COMPLEXITY PERSPECTIVE ON LEADERSHIP DEVELOPMENT

Ellen Van Velsor

ABSTRACT

As the field of leadership moves toward being more informed by complexity and dynamic systems theories, our thinking about leadership development is shifting, as well, from an exclusive focus on the development of individuals in positions of authority, to a broader framework on the development of leadership (Day, 2000; Day & O'Connor, 2003; Van Velsor & McCauley, 2003). If, from a complexity perspective, leadership can be emergent from the interaction and correlation of individuals and groups, then developing leadership capacity might include enhancing interactive dynamics within organizations and developing organizational cultures and systems that recognize those dynamics as a key source of leadership (Drath, 2000). This chapter explores how complexity theory can inform the practice of leadership development so that an organization's capacity for emergent, collective leadership practices is enhanced. The leadership development methodology described here focuses on enhancing interactive system dynamics through facilitating the development of connections between individuals

Complexity Leadership, Part I: Conceptual Foundations
pp. 333–346
Copyright © 2008 by Information Age Publishing
All rights of reproduction in any form reserved.

and between collectives in an organization. Three key features of the approach are discussed and a case example is used to illustrate this practice.

In the past several years, complexity and dynamic systems perspectives have begun to inform thinking about leadership, expanding understanding of leadership as contextual and emergent from collective behavior and from group or organizational processes (Marion & Uhl-Bien, 2001; Osborn, Hunt, & Jauch, 2002; Uhl-Bien, Marion, & McKelvey, 2007). From a theoretical perspective, as individuals and collectives (e.g., groups or teams within organizations) interact and correlation occurs, emergent events or processes are created, one of which might be leadership. If one thinks of leadership as the accomplishment of a set of three tasks—setting direction, creating alignment, and building commitment (O'Connor & Quinn, 2003), then leadership can be a key outcome of both the behavior of individual agents and of the interaction of agents and of aggregates in the context of shared work (Day, Gronn & Salas, 2004).

As the field of leadership moves toward being more informed by complexity and dynamic systems theories, our thinking about leadership development is shifting, as well, from an exclusive focus on the development of individuals who are in, or preparing to be in, positions of authority, to a broader framework on the development of leadership (Day, 2000; Day & O'Connor, 2003; Van Velsor & McCauley, 2003). That is, if leadership, from a complexity perspective, can be emergent from the interaction and correlation of individuals and groups (in addition to having, as its source, an individual's behavior or an authority-based influence process), then developing leadership capacity might include working to enhance interactive dynamics within organizations and working to develop organizational cultures and systems that recognize those dynamics as a key source of leadership (Drath, 2000). From this point of view, leadership development has to do with the development of systemic processes, collective practices, and organizational cultures that facilitate the emergence of leadership as an outcome of interaction around shared work. The purpose of this chapter is to further explore how complexity theory can inform a practice of leadership development that works to enhance an organization's capacity for these emergent, collective processes and leadership practices.

ENHANCING INTERACTIVE DYNAMICS: LEADER AND LEADERSHIP DEVELOPMENT

Enhancing interactive dynamics is simultaneously an individual development task and a collective development task. At the individual level, the complexity leader's role has been described as one of facilitating interaction and correlation to enhance the probability of emergence of relatively unpredictable outcomes (Marion, 1999; Marion & Uhl-Bien, 2001; Uhl-Bien et. al, 2007). Behaviors that increase the likelihood of interaction and correlation may be behaviors such as those described by Heifetz (1994), including orchestrating conflict, managing the holding environment, or directing attention. Or, they may be some of those described by Marion and Uhl-Bien (2001), including managing and developing networks, or fostering and cultivating interdependencies. Some of these complexity leader behaviors might be learned through traditional individual leader development assessment, leader development coursework, and/or coaching. Other behaviors may be best learned by individuals while participating in a group or organization-focused development intervention, such as the ones described here. At the group level, learning to capitalize on interactive dynamics might mean bringing together teams having interdependent work, to learn the value and practice of working across boundaries within and external to their organization and to enhance information flow, knowledge resources and innovation. With increased group mastery at working across boundaries, this practice might eventually become a new organizational routine (Feldman, 2000; Pentland & Rueter, 1994) and/or a changed aspect of the organizational culture as a whole, thereby enhancing interactive dynamics across the system.

From an individual development perspective, one way we might typically think about enhancing interactive dynamics (correlation and emergence) would be to coach leaders (people having formal or informal authority) to shift their thinking about their leadership role from a control orientation (actually more of a management role) to a facilitation or catalytic role (e.g., orchestrating conflict or cultivating largely undirected interactions). This shift could involve a perspective change on the part of leaders (to reconceptualize their role), a self-awareness change (to understand their own need for the development of new skills), as well as skill development or behavior change (to be able to enact the new role). All of these leader development components (perspective and self-awareness change, skill development and behavior change) are probably required to enhance the likelihood that leaders in a particular organization will be comfortable and effective as catalysts of correlation and the emergence of unpredictable outcomes it can bring. And, as with many leader development initiatives, we might assume that once all "leaders" have benefited from these kinds of development (i.e., once they have become more effective complexity leaders), the behaviors, processes, and outcomes of groups and in the organization as a whole will change. But this is not necessarily the case. We know from traditional leader development evaluation research that the impact of individual development across large numbers of managers, while very valuable to the individuals and those who work around them, is not always productive of widespread change at an organizational level. To achieve change at a collective level, something more and different is often needed.

Another way to enhance the emergence of leadership in organizations might be through what is differentiated here as leadership development—that is the development of the organization's collective capacity for leadership emergence. According to complexity theory, emergence begins with the creation of aggregates—small groups of directly interacting individuals who have a common sense of shared identity. Of course, groups and teams with these characteristics abound in organizations. Complexity theory suggests further that aggregates interact with other aggregates to form meta-aggregates, which are essentially networks of aggregates, and that these dynamics are the result of the self-organizing properties of collectives (the idea of "order for free"). So, if leadership is a process that can emerge from the interaction of individuals and collectives in the context of shared work, there should be no limit to the leadership capacity available in organizations

Yet we know that a downside of the creation of aggregates, whether self-organized through bottom-up processes or organized by top down authority, is that, by definition, when an aggregate forms or is given an identity, a group boundary exists that has to be bridged for further interaction, correlation and emergence to happen. Whether networks of aggregates form in ways that promote the emergence of innovation, leadership, or other desired outcomes—that is, whether or not individuals and groups do connect regularly and unpredictably enough—is an empirical question, and is likely to be dependent on many factors having to do with organizational culture, systems, and processes. Connectivity can be, and often is blocked in a variety of ways.

It makes sense to say that to get different units across the same organization to interact within broad networks of interdependence based on emergent, distributed intelligence will not be reasonably accomplished through the development of individual leader skills alone.[1] While helping individual leaders to take on newer views of their organizational roles and develop the facilitative skills and behaviors necessary for "complex" leadership is certainly a critical piece of development work, to assume that this alone is sufficient is to assume that people in positions of formal authority (usually the "leaders" being developed) have full control over the processes, practices, and cultures in the organization—that creating change in "leaders" will by itself work to transform the collective. Rather, working directly with the organizational groups having those interdependencies—that is, doing leadership development—is what will be required. So, how might that be done?

A "CONNECTED LEADERSHIP" APPROACH

This paper describes some of the features of an approach to leadership development that includes the idea of leader development, but does not use individual development as a starting point. Instead the focus of this approach is on enhancing interactive dynamics in a system—that is, facilitating the development of connections between individuals and between groups in an organization. This approach can be understood as embodying many of the main constructs in complexity theory, in that it is focused on enhancing interaction and correlation across traditional organizational boundaries to facilitate the creation of new system dynamics and the emergence of both innovation and leadership from shared work. Three features of the approach that best illustrate this focus will be discussed here:

- The leadership development initiative is itself seen as a catalyst and a "practice field" for interdependent dynamics, creating a context for further connection and interaction across the organization
- Senior executives play a key role as sponsors and catalysts for change—acting as "social tags" to encourage interactive dynamics, model "complexity leader" behaviors, and create support for unpredictable outcomes
- An action-reflection engagement process that provides multiple opportunities for enhanced interaction between both individuals and groups, demonstrates the value of distributed intelligence, and provides support for learning as an orientation in a performance-oriented culture.

Leadership Development as Catalyst and "Practice Field"

While complexity theory suggests that the processes of interaction, correlation and emergence happen organically in all kinds of systems (i.e., the notion of order "for free"), a key goal of leadership development as understood here is to foster more interaction, correlation, and emergence in organizations across traditional boundaries of function, geography and the like. That this kind of leadership development initiative is seen as needed by key stakeholders in the organization means that these important system dynamics are not happening as much as is optimal. Some kind of catalyst is seen as needed to enhance complex system dynamics across organizational boundaries.

Complexity theory points to the vital role of catalysts or "tags" in changing or creating new interactive dynamics in a system. While it feels familiar to look to individual complexity leaders to play this role, the leadership development initiative itself can be a powerful catalyst for increased interaction, new connections, and new, emergent system dynamics, if the underlying design of the initiative reflects most of the "rules" of a complex system (e.g., interaction, interdependency, bottom-up dynamics, emergence of unpredictable outcomes). That is, a well-designed initiative can provide a "practice field" for interdependent action. A "practice field" can be a powerful metaphor for participants, in that during the initiative, new ways of engaging with each other are being tried out, less familiar leadership practices (ways of accomplishing direction, alignment, commitment) are emerging, and reflection (which is not a comfortable mode of being for most managers) is being put in balance with action (a very familiar mode for most managers).

Yet with any leadership development intervention, the time will come for it to end as a formal initiative. And while it can be provocative of new perspectives and the development of skills and practices, a "practice field" alone does not necessarily catalyze systems in the organization nor necessarily change minds or alter strong organizational cultures. Ways of interacting (or patterns of interactive dynamics) are deeply ingrained in organizations, so that changing or enhancing those most likely takes more than one kind of catalyst. Our approach includes the use of internal sponsors who serve as "social tags" and catalysts for emergence and change.

Senior Executives Sponsors as Social "Tags" and Catalysts for Emergence and Change

Senior executives within an organization can play a critical role in catalyzing social dynamics and emergence throughout the initiative and afterwards. When senior executives are aware of the need to facilitate complex interaction and are willing to become more comfortable with the idea of emergence of indeterminate states (rather than being most comfortable with control and coordination of determinate outcomes), the groundwork is at least partially laid for a successful complex (or "connected") leadership development initiative with the rest of the organization. This senior executive awareness may be present prior to the intervention and may have been the reason for its occurrence. Or, awareness may need to be cultivated or enhanced through specific development efforts aimed at senior execs and other stakeholders. If senior executives are sufficiently prepared to act as "complexity leaders" during the initiative and beyond, a more powerful leadership development initiative can be started, with more promise of good results. But as with any development initiative, if senior executives are not "on board," development needs to start with them for the effort to be successful in the long run (Pearce, 2004).

In the best of all possible circumstances, senior executives will be able to partner with the development initiative so that both can function as catalysts in what will be seen as a process of organizational change. The "practice field" is also "practice" for senior executive sponsors, in that it allows them the opportunity to model and become more comfortable supporting the emergence of unpredictable outcomes as a result of work on the action learning projects (more about these later). Because interacting across boundaries may be new or only partially tested for most participants, hearing senior executives tell stories about high-profile situations when dynamic, cross-boundary interaction led to positive organizational outcomes can be potent in its impact (Lissack & Roos, 2004; Palus & Horth, 2003). These stories tend to themselves become powerful "tags"— reference points that exemplify new ways of working together in the organization, and topics of much discussion among participants.

Yet for enhanced interactive dynamics to catch on in the organization beyond the intervention itself, more is needed than just good participation and support of senior executives during the initiative. That support needs to continue beyond the initiative, and become reinforced by way of new behavior and expectations on the part of senior executives. Organizational systems and processes need to be examined and redesigned so as to promote, rather than inhibit, interactive dynamics and inter-group connectivity. Somehow, the aforementioned "rules" of a complex system (interaction, interdependency, bottom-up dynamics, emergence of unpredictable outcomes) need to become part of the culture, systems and processes in the organization. We will turn to a discussion of this issue and the related complexity construct of "autocatalysis" a bit later in this chapter.

The Action-Reflection Engagement Process

A third feature of this approach is the use of an action-reflection engagement process. The design is comprised of basically three elements—action learning leadership teams, action learning team coaching, and plenary session "intensives" taking place over a period of about 6 months.

As the name suggests, action learning leadership teams are based on the principles of action learning—learning by directly tackling real organizational issues using tools and methodologies to prompt reflection and to enhance knowledge exchange. In particular, action learning leadership teams are focused on critical reflection about how leadership is being accomplished (how direction, alignment and commitment are being created, other than from an authority-based hierarchy) in the course of work on complex, shared projects. The reflection is facilitated over time by action learning coaches, trained to use a set of tools to help surface and question assumptions, foster collaborative and shared leadership, practice dialogue, and engage across internal and external boundaries, as needed.

The challenges posed to teams must be complex challenges, that is, challenges for which neither clear direction nor widely shared or easily implemented solutions exist. For example, one organization we worked with faced the complex challenge of finding ways to operate more nimbly and competitively in a highly unionized environment, characterized by a significant number of "work rules." One of the action learning teams in this initiative was given the following project charter:

- Identify the few problematic work rules that would give us the biggest impact if we changed them and explore the possible alternatives.

Questions they were asked to consider included:

- Why do the selected rules offer the maximum potential for impact?
- Which of these do we already have the ability to work with and change?

Their deliverable was to "Provide a plan for changing rules we now have the ability to change and provide recommendations on how we should proceed on the selected alternatives in those cases in which we do not now have the ability to change." Tackling this charter required the team to interact with many diverse groups, including union representatives, craft employees, supervisors and line managers, human resource professionals, and legal experts. It required that the team sort through volumes of data representing many divergent perspectives, and think through the long term implications of various kinds of change. It required them to change their individual assumptions and views on many issues over time, and to coordinate the opinions and needs of many different groups and constituencies in coming up with recommendations that most would see as feasible.

A second relevant feature of these action learning leadership teams has to do with the way they are constituted. Because a key design feature of this connected leadership development approach is to catalyze novel kinds of interaction between individuals and groups and to thus enhance social networks, the action learning leadership teams are made up of individuals from a variety of functions and diverse geographies. The teams will take on, by choice or assignment, issues that focus on functional or topic areas for which no team member has special expertise or management accountability. This requirement is designed to facilitate exploratory behavior and dynamic interaction among individuals within and outside the action learning leadership teams, between and across these teams, and across groups in the wider organization. We expect the outcome of these enhanced dynamics to be more and better distributed intelligence during the initiative, affording each group and every individual a more integrated understanding of the organization as a whole. We expect that in most organizations the complexity of the challenges, the lack of team experience with the problem posed by the project and the need to cross traditional boundaries to seek out information from dispersed sources all work together to enhance the probability that dynamic interaction will increase and that novel ideas and solutions will emerge. We also expect that these demands encourage participants to connect early on with the ultimate stakeholders for their project outcomes, a behavior related to successful implementation and integration of the team's work into organizational systems and processes.

In this connected leadership development approach, the action learning leadership teams are brought together twice in a six month period for larger scale "intensives," to ground and support their work on action learning projects. These intensives are sessions lasting from two to five days and serving several purposes. The first session is a kick off for the initiative, to communicate to all participants the purpose and design of the intervention, to form the action learning teams, and to have the teams choose their projects. This is the time at which the executive sponsors communicate to participants that the desired outcomes go beyond the deliverables of the projects to system wide positive turbulence, individual and organizational learning as critical and valued, cross-boundary interaction as a permanent new state, and emergence of unpredictable outcomes as "acceptable" and "safe."

The first large group session is also a time when senior executives interact with participants for purposes of storytelling to illustrate "complexity leader" capabilities, transmission of organization specific information, and networking. Both intensive sessions are settings in which action learning project teams can share knowledge and expertise across teams, build networks, and learn tools and techniques for reflection and idea-generation. During the second and closing "intensive" session, the teams present both the operational and the learning outcomes of their projects to the other teams and to the executive sponsor group. Going forward from this session, the executive sponsors are asked to work with the teams on implementation and hand off of the work, given that the sponsors are usually not the final "owner" of the team's work. Rather, that "owner" is an individual or group normally responsible for work in a particular domain.

So, with our previous example, if an action learning team had the project of coming up with "a plan for changing work rules they feel the organization has the ability to change and providing recommendations on how the company should proceed on the selected alternatives in those cases in which they do not now have the ability to change," sponsor support would be needed after the recommendations were presented, so as to get the required approvals for making the recommended changes and to begin implementation of those changes locally and/or nationwide. Certainly, the team will need to do some follow-up to help other individuals and stakeholder groups take on implementation of recommended rule and system changes. And in order for this "hand off" to be effective, those stakeholders likely had to have been involved in some way by the action learning team throughout the process. As can be seen in this example, an initiative like this one, employing a series of successful action learning projects, can potentially help individuals and groups see the value of enhanced interaction across existing "boundaries," also potentially bringing fresh perspectives to old problems, fostering innovation, and increasing comfort with the emergence of ideas and solutions from outside traditional areas of expertise and the emergence of leadership from across and outside of the traditional management hierarchy.

BUT WILL IT STICK?—AUTOCATALYSIS AND THE "TRANSFER OF TRAINING" ISSUE

Autocatalysis has been defined as "a state of organization in which different units interact within broad networks of interdependence based on emergent distributed intelligence and requiring no outside effort" (Marion & Uhl-Bien, 2001, p. 398). It seems safe to say that autocatalysis is, ideally, a central goal of the initiative being described here. It is what complexity leaders work to enable, what key stakeholders hope to achieve, and what would be productive of ongoing organizational leadership capacity as an outcome. So then, it seems that autocatalysis is what we might hope for in terms of the classic problem of "transfer of training." As a result of the catalyzing effects of both the initiative and the senior executive support, order (units interacting within broad networks of interdependence based on emergent distributed intelligence and requiring no outside effort) should ideally instantiate in the system and be self–perpetuating once the initiative comes to a formal end (i.e., once one of the initial two catalysts is withdrawn from the system). In this instance of autocatalysis (or "transfer"), as the formal leadership development initiative (that is, the large group intensives and action learning leadership teams/projects) ends, it would lose its social tag role and that role would ideally move from one shared by the leadership development initiative and senior executive sponsors to the participants themselves, with continuing support from senior executive sponsors. We would hope that the members of the action learning leadership teams would carry new "complexity leader" behaviors forward, that social networks might have expanded, and that group boundaries might have become more permeable as a result of increased interaction during the intervention. These shifts would be essential in moving the organizational learning and enhanced system dynamics beyond the groups who participated to other organizational members and groups. That is, action learning teams and team members would need to move back to their "home" bases as tags/catalysts for ongoing, continuous, and expanded interaction and correlation with other agents and aggregates. Yet this "stickiness" itself is emergent and unpredictable. It cannot be commanded or controlled but only facilitated and hopefully catalyzed.

So, what kinds of factors might facilitate this kind of "stickiness?" What factors might lead to catalyzing enhanced interactive system dynamics beyond the "practice field" provided by the initiative itself? Several possibilities come to mind, including the scope and scale of the initiative, the credibility of the perceived change in the organizational culture, and the degree to which the organization is successful in making learning and action equally strong attractors of attention and energy.

Scope and Scale of the Initiative

It seems reasonable to believe that an initiative that focuses on a very large group of participants over an extended period of time would have a greater probability of triggering autocatalysis (or "transfer") than one in which a very limited portion of organizational members participate. For example, if one were able to implement this kind of leadership development approach with most of the managers in an organization through a series of overlapping initiatives across several years, the desired outcomes may be more likely to "stick" than if a portion of managers went through a single initiative. That is because in the more extensive design, groups who participate at the start of the initiative would more likely continue to interact in an enhanced way due to the perturbation of ongoing action learning leadership teams in the environment over time. Over a period of perhaps 3 years, we might expect to see more permanently enhanced networks *as well as* new ways of working and of understanding how work and leadership best get accomplished in complex systems.

Credibility of Change in the Culture

It is not enough that senior executives communicate that expected and desired outcomes going forward include enhanced interaction across traditional boundaries and new leadership practices. Beyond communication, the desired outcomes (enhanced interaction across traditional boundaries, support for the emergence of unpredictable outcomes) should not be in tension with existing aspects of the culture, or if they are, that tension should be recognized as part of the difficulty of the change. In our work, we are seeing that changing organizational routines that have to do with minimizing surprise and unpredictability are hard to change. For example, at the end of the action learning project work and prior to the presentation of projects to senior executive sponsors in our second "intensive" whole group meeting, we see that action learning teams often do a "prepresentation" to their project sponsor, so that the sponsor is not surprised by any element of the work. And sponsors, wanting to be supportive of their teams' work, agree to this "dry run." This is an understandable and wise tactic from the point of view of many business cultures, but hardly supportive of the ideas of emergence and comfort with unpredictable outcomes. Comfort with some of the "rules" of complex systems can be hard to come by, even in complex organizations facing complex challenges and knowing they need to change.

For participants to go forward continuing to use new skills and more collective leadership practices, senior executives must continue to work to learn and use "complexity leader" skills to enhance interactive dynamics and foster the emergence of a new leadership culture. They must continue to support interdependent group work as a main source of organizational leadership and as an equal partner with other leadership practices (e.g., authority-based hierarchy as a source of leadership), so that participants in the process can gain trust that the use of those new ways will actually be supported going forward. The fact that the organization is investing in the initiative will not be enough. Participants must also come away from the "practice field" seeing and trusting that facilitating emergence, creating change and being comfortable with unpredictable outcomes will continue to be rewarded once the leadership development initiative comes to a formal close. As Arrow and her colleagues point out, aspects of a group's embedding context constitute a field of opportunities and constraints that make different courses of action more or less rewarding for a group (Arrow, McGrath, & Berdahl, 2000, p. 171), and as individual group members leave the "practice field" behind.

Action and Learning as Equally Strong Attractors

Most managers are action-oriented individuals, and the action learning projects they take on are a high visibility centerpiece of the initiative itself, representing key strategic challenges for the organization. So, the action learning projects tend to be very strong attractors for the participants. What is more problematic is enhancing the strength of reflection and learning as attractors of attention and energy—finding ways to ramp up the importance, credibility and visibility of the learning part of action learning. These aspects are, by far, weaker attractors among managers, if in fact they have any attraction power at all when work begins on the complex projects.

Enhancing reflection and learning as attractors is tricky when the performance stakes feel high on the projects themselves and/or when performance is more frequently and well-rewarded in a culture than is learning. Enhancing a learning orientation requires first of all, communication from the executive sponsors about the equal stature of learning outcomes. It requires that this communication be backed up by role modeling on the part of sponsors, making evident their own vulnerability and learning in the face of complex challenge, as part of storytelling and other interactions in their work with the teams. It requires that sponsors, in their ongoing work with action learning teams, continue to reinforce learning throughout the process. It is not enough that the action learning coaches play this role, as it is easy for them to be seen as "outsiders" doing their job, and participants can easily discount reflection and learning as external to the organization's "real" goals or as not a realistic fit with their organizational culture. If the power and credibility behind these learning-oriented activities does not counterbalance the action orientation of the organizational culture, the learning goals will be castoff by participants who will see those as features of the initiative and not permanent new aspects of their workplace environment. The stickiness of the work done during the initiative will be enhanced to the extent that action and learning outcomes can be balanced, with learning as a strong and equal attractor.

NOTE

1. Even "teambuilding" is not enough, as that strengthens relationships inside a team without often focusing on the level of interaction between teams across the organization.

REFERENCES

Arrow, H., McGrath, J., & Berdahl, J. (2000). *Small groups as complex systems.* Thousand Oaks, CA: Sage.

Day, D. V. (2000). Leadership development: A review in context. *The Leadership Quarterly, 11,* 581-613.

Day, D. V., Gronn, P., & Salas, E. (2004). Leadership capacity in teams. *The Leadership Quarterly Yearly Review of Leadership, 15*(6), 857-880.

Day, D. V., & O'Connor, P. M. G. (2003). Leadership development: Understanding the process. In S. E. Murphy & R. E. Riggio (Eds.), *The future of leadership development* (pp. 11-28). Mahwah, NJ: Erlbaum.

Drath, W. (2000). *The deep blue sea: Rethinking the sources of leadership.* San Francisco: Jossey-Bass.

Feldman, M. S. (2000). Organizational routines as a source of continuous change. *Organization Science, 11,* 611-629.

Heifetz, R. A. (1994). *Leadership without easy answers.* Cambridge, MA: Harvard University Press.

Lissack, M., & Roos, J. (2004). *The next common sense: Mastering corporate complexity through coherence.* London: Nicholas Brealey.

Marion, R. (1999). *The edge of organization: Chaos and complexity theories of formal social organizations.* Thousand Oaks, CA: Sage.

Marion, R., & Uhl-Bien, M. (2001). Leadership in complex organizations. *Leadership Quarterly Yearly Review of Leadership, 12*(4), 389-418.

O'Connor, P. M. G., & Quinn, L. (2003). Organizational capacity for leadership. In C. D. McCauley & E. Van Velsor (Eds.), *The Center for Creative Leadership handbook of leadership development* (2nd ed., pp. 417-437). San Francisco: Jossey-Bass.

Osborn, R., Hunt, J., & Jauch, L. (2002). Toward a contextual theory of leadership. *Leadership Quarterly, 13,* 797-837.

Palus, C., & Horth, D. (2003). Exploration for development. In C. McCauley & E. Van Velsor (Eds.), *The Center for Creative Leadership handbook of leadership development* (2nd ed., pp. 438-464). San Francisco: Jossey-Bass.

Pearce, C. L. (2004). The future of leadership: Combining vertical and shared leadership to transform knowledge work. *Academy of Management Executive, 18*(1), 47-57.

Pentland, B. T., & Rueter, H. H. (1994). Organizational routines as grammars of action. *Administrative Science Quarterly, 39,* 484-510.

Uhl-Bien, M., Marion, R., & McKelvey, B. (2007). Complexity leadership theory: Shifting leadership from the industrial age to the knowledge era. *The Leadership Quarterly, 18*(4), 298-318.

Van Velsor, E., & McCauley, C. (2003). Our view of leadership development. In C. McCauley & E. Van Velsor (Eds.), *The Center for Creative Leadership handbook of leadership development* (2nd ed., pp. 1-22). San Francisco: Jossey-Bass.

CHAPTER 13

LEADERSHIP OR LUCK?

The System Dynamics of Intel's Shift to Microprocessors in the 1970s and 1980s

James K. Hazy

ABSTRACT

In the 1970s and 1980s, the Intel Corporation transformed itself from a memory chip company into a microprocessor company. The case has been well documented and described in the context of corporate strategy and development. This paper examines the dynamics at work at Intel during this period as an example of how leadership, as considered in a complex systems context, and dynamic capabilities interact in organizations to enable adaptation independent of strategy making. The analysis uses complexity science concepts and system dynamics simulation techniques to shed light on Intel's successful transformation. The findings suggest that when complex systems leadership mechanisms are at work, successful transformation can occur provided certain structural antecedents are present as well. The findings also suggest that change cannot occur without certain leadership mechanisms. These leadership mechanisms—dynamic patterns of communication and action among individuals that produce effects not

Complexity Leadership, Part I: Conceptual Foundations
pp. 347–378

inherent in the individual acts—and the structural antecedents that enable change are described, and their implications are discussed.

Organizations as complex systems face dual challenges: surviving in the short term and adapting for the long term in the face of change. The Intel organization of the 1970s and 1980s was no exception. It was never a foregone conclusion that Intel would emerge at the end of the 1980s as the world's premier microprocessor company. Intel, like other organizations, had to balance a key tension: Managers had to execute the daily, weekly, and monthly tasks that maintained complex internal functioning while at the same time doing their best to adapt to changes in the environment. This tension has been characterized by March (1991) as the trade-off between exploitation and exploration. How important was Intel's leadership in navigating this tension?

It is arguable whether leadership was even a factor in Intel's transformation. Certainly, Intel was fortunate. As I describe in this paper, the microprocessor market was profitable from the beginning and grew quickly enough to counter Intel's eroding market position in memory chips. It was also fortuitous that the process technology they had developed for memory design and fabrication was quickly transferable to the microprocessor business reducing investment and stranded costs. Was Intel's management that good, or was the company just in the right place at the right time? Was their success due to leadership or to luck?

NEW APPROACHES TO LEADERSHIP RESEARCH

Late twentieth century leadership research, with its focus on individual behaviors and dyadic interaction, is inadequate in describing the complex dynamics that can lead to dramatic transformations like that at Intel. For this reason, recent research has recognized that leadership must be considered in a systems context, and suggests that complexity science might help enhance understanding of leadership in contemporary business contexts (Hazy, 2006c, 2007b; Lichtenstein, Uhl-Bien, Marion, Seers, Orton, & Schreiber, 2006; Marion & Uhl-Bien, 2001; McKelvey, this volume; Surie & Hazy, 2006; Uhl-Bien, Marion, & McKelvey, 2007). What has been called "adaptive leadership" (Lichtenstein et al., 2006; Schreiber & Carley, 2006; Uhl-Bien et al., 2007) acknowledges that in uncertain environments, collective direction—adaptation to change— emerges from interactions between team members, not just from formal leaders. The specific leadership activities that generate possible futures for the company and prepare it for adaptation have also been called "generative leadership" (Surie & Hazy, 2006), the term I will use here.[1]

This chapter describes a system dynamics model (Forrester, 1987; Sterman, 2000) of Intel that synthesizes theory associated with dynamic capabilities, leadership, and complexity science. The model is used to reconsider the case of Intel's transformation from a memory company to a microprocessor company in the 1970s and 1980s (Burgelman, 1994). Building upon a foundation of complexity science (Anderson, 1999) and the resource- and knowledge-based view of the firm (Barney, 1991; Makadok, 2001; Nelson & Winter, 1982), feedback loops are defined that enable the system to sustain itself through exploitation and to adapt to change through adaptive search or exploration (March, 1991). As Barnard (1938) said, leadership serves a purpose for the organization and its members (Goldstein & Hazy, 2006), as it did for Intel. In the model described here, that purpose is assumed to be survival and prosperity. This purpose is achieved by gathering resources from the environment and distributing them throughout the system and to its stakeholders.

A core premise of this chapter is that the nonlinear dynamics of exploitation and exploration occur continuously and simultaneously at all organizational levels. The system dynamics approach (Sterman, 2000) that is described in the next section will be used to show how the organizational dynamics at Intel in the 1970s and 1980s enabled the company to transform itself. The choice of words is purposeful. The system was able to "transform itself" in part through the workings of specialized system mechanisms—a term defined in the next paragraph—that together embody leadership across the organization. Individual leaders are involved, of course, but they do not operate *on* the organization, but rather *within* organizational processes, routines and cultural norms. For the employees at Intel, the behavior and decision signals associated with leadership came not from a single source, from "a leader" per se, but rather from their superiors, peers, and even subordinates who collectively led one another to catalyze and to reinforce decisions and actions that together constitute the leadership mechanisms that transformed Intel as a system.

To clarify terminology, a mechanism is "an assembly of elements producing an effect not inherent in any of them" (Hernes, 1998, p. 74). In this case, the mechanisms are dynamically assembled and reassembled as patterns of communication acts and influence relationships among interacting individuals producing particular system level effects. Leadership mechanisms are those that have the effect of navigating the system as an entity through a changing environment. They do this by catalyzing interactions and cooperation among individuals as they engage in exploitation and exploration projects, moving the system toward a purpose.

In later sections I describe three distinct leadership mechanisms that serve this purpose—each producing a distinctly different and yet necessary system level effect. Briefly, these mechanisms are as follows: The convergent leadership mechanism catalyzes agent interactions to improve the system's performance according to a purpose. The generative leadership mechanism catalyzes agent interactions to "generate" or create programs of action in response to the challenges and opportunities presented in the environment. Finally, the unifying leadership mechanism catalyzes agent interactions to define boundaries, establish a collective identity, and enable the system to act as a unity within the environment. I realize that thinking of leadership as a series of system mechanisms rather than as individual behaviors is a very different perspective. However, the case analysis that follows demonstrates the potential contribution of this approach.

The present analysis takes data from Burgelman's (1991, 1994) articles about Intel and reconsiders the case in the context of leadership mechanisms—system level elements composed of interactions among individuals within the system but with effects that are not inherent in any of them. It does so by utilizing the system dynamics techniques described in the next section. This new analysis of the case clearly demonstrates that under certain circumstances, top-down strategic intent—what Burgelman (2002) called "induced strategy" (p. 325)—is not always necessary in order for adaptation to occur. In the case of Intel's strategic shift, it was bottom-up, exploration-based "autonomous strategy" (Burgelman, 2002, p. 327) that led to Intel's wholesale transformation. But can what happened at Intel really be called "strategy" when top management was not involved in any meaningful way? Is "luck" a better term for that fortunate confluence of events that led to transformation at Intel? And what *was* the role of "leadership" in this transformation?

SYSTEM DYNAMICS AND EQUATION-BASED MODELING

Before describing the Intel case in detail, a brief discussion of the system dynamics modeling method is in order. The use of difference or ordinary differential equations (ODE) to model the dynamics of complex systems has a long history (Forrester, 1987; Sterman, 2000). In a recent review of computer models of leadership, Hazy (2007b) noted that system dynamics models have only recently been used in leadership research with promising results. The modeling process and key components of system dynamics models are described in this section.

System dynamics is a method for modeling variables and their rates of change in a system that exhibits nonlinearity in the relationships among variables over time. Level variables, or *stocks*, represent quantities that are relatively persistent over time, albeit with quantity changes. An example in the business context would be cash on hand, which fluctuates over time, but whose rate of change can be measured. Intangible quantities, like employee engagement, or organizational capabilities can also be represented as level variables. The profit and value creation indicators in a firm—such as revenue, earnings and cash flow—are level variables that are particularly relevant to the present analysis. As the firm operates in the environment, these variables accumulate as resources that are available to the system in the same way that water accumulates in a bathtub. Each resource level—like the water level in the bathtub—is represented in the model as a level variable, or a *stock level*.

Rates of change in variable levels, also called *flows*, and their interrelationships represent the nonlinear dynamics at work within the system. The stocks and how their levels change based upon their inward and outward flows—like water flowing from a spigot into the bathtub on the one hand, and out through the drain on the other—are adjusted by the system in pursuit of its purposes. All of these resource "stocks and flows"—the bathtubs, spigots and drains—together with the nonlinear relationships defining the overall system, are the essence of a system dynamics model. They represent the economic "plumbing" that supports and is supported by the firm. The accumulating stocks of available resources flow through the system—through various pipes into various bathtubs, if you will—for many different uses. Resources also flow from the system to stakeholders such as owners and employees.

Rates of change can be calculated as difference equations: that is, the difference in the value of a level variable after a period of time. These changes to the variable's value or level represent flows into or out of a variable. For example, at a semiconductor fabrication facility like Intel's, the silicon wafers from which microprocessors are made flow into a storage facility as deliveries arrive. They flow out of that storage facility as they are used to create the final product. The rates of change are flows. After a time period, a stock is equal to its initial value, minus outflows, plus inflows. This is a difference equation that describes a system's dynamics.

Different level variables across the system—stocks of different types of inventory, for example—can be related to one another through flows. When these relationships are all positive, such that an increase in one variable also increases the next, and when these relationships eventually feed back to the original variable—for example when increased finished goods inventory leads to greater profits that can be invested in more raw materials that can be converted to more work-in-progress inventory, and so forth—amplifying feedback loops can result. Without regulation from outside the loop, these amplifying feedback loops can become unstable, like feedback signals in an audio amplifier. If a negative relationship exists within the loop, however, such that an increase in one stock reduces the level of the next—increasing the water level in the tub triggers a valve that reduces the flow of water through the spigot into the tub, for example—a balancing feedback loop is created that regulates amplification and can stabilize the system. Further complicating the dynamics are the time delays that are often evident in feedback loops, particularly in human systems. It takes time to move silicon wafers from their point of manufacture to Intel's fabrication facility, for example. In these cases, level variables along a chain of causation do change, but they do so only after a time delay.

Also important to the equations are the parameters and auxiliary variables that specify and define the precise relationships at work in the equations. The values of these variables represent information flows and states within the system and the environment. They are used to tune the system dynamics in simulations. Often, however, empirical data are not available to support the specific values chosen for these variables. As such, these simulations are often only interpreted qualitatively, as is the case for the present analysis. Before going into the specifics of the Intel case, I describe the theoretical foundation underlying the model.

THEORETICAL BASIS DESCRIBING FIRM DYNAMICS

Research into the theory of the firm over the last quarter century has increasingly used an evolutionary perspective. Evolutionary economics (Nelson & Winter, 1982), organizational capabilities (Dosi, Nelson, & Winter, 2000), and dynamic capabilities (Teece, Pisano, & Shuen, 2000; Winter, 2000) have all been used to explain the dynamics of and tension between performance and adaptation in organizations. Over the last few years, however, these related views of the firm have begun to consolidate into a single theory. This synthesized approach focuses on dynamic capabilities (Helfat et al., 2006)—roughly defined as the ability of an organization to reconfigure itself in response to changes in its environment—and brings together the resource-based view (RBV) of the firm (Barney, 1986, 1991; Penrose, 1959; Peteraf, 1993), with its focus on differential access to critical resources, and the theory of the firm that is built upon the notion of organizational capabilities, competencies, routines and knowledge (Dosi, Nelson, & Winter, 2000; Hamel & Prahalad, 1994; Nelson & Winter, 1982; Teece, Pisano, & Shuen, 2000; Winter, 2000).

While dynamic capabilities represent the ability of organization to reconfigure itself, organizational capabilities are the routines and knowledge that together enable a collection of agents to perform organizational functions. In short, these are the building blocks that are reconfigured, repurposed or created by dynamic capabilities. Intel, for example, possessed process technology that enabled the fabrication of dynamic random access memory (DRAM) semiconductor chips, a capability that was its source of competitive advantage. As variations and improvements are tried, capabilities evolve, improve, and replicate themselves in the same way that organizational routines are said to replicate themselves (Nelson & Winter, 1982). For Intel, this process technology, and its adaptability, proved critical for its success in the emerging and lucrative microprocessor marketplace. Their process technology was repurposed to build new capabilities to address the microprocessor market. Dynamic capabilities come into play when existing capabilities are not enough and something new or different is required. Examples include innovation, the capacity to form strategic alliances and radical approaches to change, such as mergers and acquisitions (Helfat et al., 2006).

All of these perspectives consider continued access to excess profits as the basis for sustained competitive advantage and a key to the system's survival. Makadok (2001, 2002) presented a synthesized analysis of these perspectives in which he demonstrated the importance of profit-gathering potential and highlighted the tension between exploitation and exploration as popularized by March (1991). Although recognized in general terms, management and leadership mechanisms are typically not considered in this stream of research. By doing so explicitly, the present analysis contributes to theory. In later sections I describe how the leadership mechanisms at Intel interacted with its dynamic capabilities to enable transformation. Before describing the specific model used in the analysis, I provide background on the Intel case in the next section.

THE CASE OF INTEL

The well-known case describing Intel's strategic shift from memory chips to microprocessors (Burgelman, 1991, 1994) in the 1970s and 1980s can be usefully explored by thinking of Intel's transformation in the context of the company's dynamic organizational capabilities and as is described later, its leadership mechanisms—the system level patterns of communication, influence and action among individuals within the system that produce effects not inherent in any of the lower level activities. From its founding in 1968, Intel had focused on the development of process technology that enabled it to be successful in the dynamic random access memory (DRAM) semiconductor marketplace, a business line that was launched in scale during late 1970. One of Intel's customers, Busicom, had approached Intel in 1969 about developing a chip set for its new line of computers, and Intel assigned Marcian E. "Ted" Hoff Jr. to the project. As the project developed, the interactions and discussion about the opportunity among engineers from Busicom and Intel, and also within Intel, resulted in a different, more parsimonious single chip design—a more elegant solution to this customer's problem.

What resulted was a logic chip, the 4004 central procession unit (CPU) that eventually became the world's first microprocessor (Aspray, 1997). This scenario, comprised of resonant human interactions, opportunity identification, solution proposals, and the nurturing of the best ideas, is an example of the kind of leadership that was ultimately so important to Intel's success. As is described later, this particular type of leadership is called "generative" in that it highlights the importance of collaborative interactions across boundaries that generate new ideas and programs of action while at the same time managing the resulting complexity (Surie & Hazy, 2006). This was one of Intel's strengths during this period. As I describe later, it led directly to their success in the core product line of DRAMs as well as in microprocessors.

In this case, generative leadership paid off mightily as Intel continued to develop and sell the microprocessor product line with great success through the 1970s and early 1980s. But even then, microprocessor development was only seen as a side project, a distraction that was advocated and run by a group of midlevel engineers and managers. From these modest beginnings as a serendipitous exploration exercise, the sale of microprocessors eventually came to dominate Intel's sales as the company faced increasing competition in its efforts to exploit its traditional memory marketplace. Top management continued to think of Intel as a memory company during this period and did not recognize that a transformation was occurring. Although a top management decision to exit memory in favor of microprocessors was finally taken in 1985, it is clear from the Burgelman (1991) case data that, for Intel's business, the relative importance of microprocessors versus memory changed rather smoothly over a 13-year period, from 1972 to 1985. The cross over to dominance by microprocessors occurred in 1982—3 years *before* top management formalized the change.

This case illustrates the tension in management decision making between efforts aimed at exploiting known markets—top management was pushing the memory market at Intel—and those that explore the environment for new opportunities like the microprocessor. When significant opportunities are identified and nurtured in the organization, what Burgelman (2002) called an "autonomous strategic process" (p. 327), significant change can occur without, or even in direct conflict with, the efforts of the company's top managers. As shall be shown, the present analysis also highlights the significance of excess profits in particular their relative level and timing as well as the presence of appropriate leadership mechanisms across the organization.

THE SYSTEM DYNAMICS OF ORGANIZATIONAL CAPABILITIES

To study the impact of leadership on the Intel transformation, I used system dynamics modeling techniques to simulate the company during this period. When the interaction of Intel—or any company, for that matter—and the environment is reduced to mathematical equations in a system dynamics model, the logic goes like this:[2] As implied by the dynamic capabilities theory of the firm, the system is sustained as an economic entity by accumulating excess profits that derive from a privileged position in the environment. A firm that owns proprietary software, Microsoft, for example, demands—and gets—extra high prices and thus excess profit. More generally, patented technology, trade secrets, and unique access to scarce resources like oil or real estate can all lead to the excess profits.

The indicators of excess profits in the firm—revenue, earnings, and cash flow—accumulate as resources available to the system in the same way that water might accumulate in a bathtub for later use. Each resource level—like the water level in the tub—is represented in the model as a level variable, or a *stock* level. Resources with stock levels might be inventories, cash on hand, or other fungible assets, for example. These stocks and how their levels change based upon their inward and outward *flows*—like water flowing into and out from the tub—are adjusted as the firm pursues its purposes. All of the bathtubs in the organization, their spigots and their drains, in other words the "stocks and flows," together with the nonlinear relationships defining the overall system, represent the economic plumbing that is reconfigured by a firm's dynamic capabilities. The accumulating stocks of available resources flow through the system—through various pipes into various bathtubs, if you will—for many different uses. The stocks and flows at work at Intel and how they are affected by the firm's leadership mechanisms have been described in a specific system dynamics model called the *leadership and capabilities model (LCM)* (Hazy, 2004, 2006b). The LCM model as applied to Intel is described in the remaining sections of this chapter. First, however, it is useful to clarify the way leadership is considered in the LCM.

LEADERSHIP MECHANISMS VERSUS HEROIC LEADERSHIP

The information and resource flows described above are affected by the system's leadership mechanisms. In other words, patterns of communication, influence and action among interacting individuals within the system produce leadership effects for the system that influence the information and resource flows throughout the system's economic plumbing. Importantly, these effects are not inherent in any of the individual communications or actions that compose them, not even in the actions of a formal leader who might appear to some to be directing the action or to be in control.

This heroic, individual conception of leadership is inappropriate because the nonlinear, unpredictable nature of complex adaptive systems implies that the mechanisms of leadership must necessarily include the interdependent relationships among components of the system that determine system outcomes. The emergent dynamical patterns of reciprocal influence among individuals in groups and among interacting groups—in other words interactions among the system's components or capabilities—are the mechanisms that have the effect of orchestrating the flow of information and resources in the system. Individuals participate in these mechanisms of leadership, but they are not equivalent to them, not even the formal leader. Although these systemic patterns or mechanisms of influence in organizations have recently been studied theoretically (Panzar, Hazy, McKelvey, & Schwandt, 2007) and to some degree observed empirically (Hazy, this volume), they are not yet well understood. I will return to the particulars of these leadership mechanisms in a later section, but for now it is necessary to describe in more detail the flow of information and resources at Intel.

RESOURCE AND INFORMATION FLOW DYNAMICS AT INTEL

Taking as a foundation the assumptions of the dynamic capabilities theory or the firm described earlier, it follows that a firm's organizational capabilities enable it to garner excess profits. The capabilities that enable excess profits can be either existing or brand new. In the case of Intel, existing process technology and production capacity were key enablers of the firm's continued success in exploiting the memory market. On the other hand, brand new capabilities were being developed during Intel's exploration of the microprocessor market and these enabled continued success in that growing market as well. The dual processes of exploitation in current markets and exploration of new ones are described in this section.

As can be seen in Figure 13.1, a defining characteristic of the resource and information flow dynamics in a firm like Intel is the presence of two positive feedback loops (Hazy, 2006b). These loops emerge from the accumulating stock of resources within the firm that are fed by the gathering of excess profit. Resource allocation choices are made by agents based upon their own interests, but these are continually influenced by signals received from other agents, whether superiors, peers or subordinates, acting out the leadership mechanisms within the system (Hazy, 2006a). At Intel, these choices channeled resource flows to the continued exploitation of memory production capabilities on the one hand, and also to exploration and the building of new capabilities to serve the microprocessor market on the other. Both occurred simultaneously at Intel, to different degrees and at different times. Each of these positive feedback loops was continually balanced by negative feedback, both from the marketplace and from inside the system. These dynamics are described below.

The Exploitation Positive-Feedback Loops Gather Value for the System

As is shown in the lower-left positive loop in Figure 13.1 from the ODE (ordinary differential equations) simulation, as more of Intel's resources were allocated to the exploitation of memory fabrication capabilities, greater capacity came online. As a result of increases to scale, the rate at which excess profits were gathered into the system also increased. In the

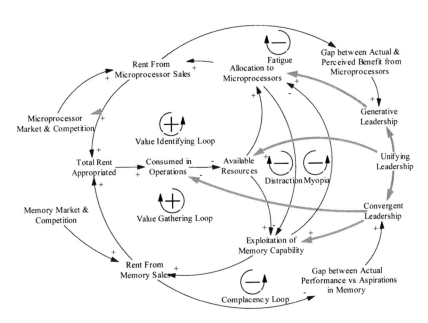

Figure 13.1.   A system dynamics representation of exploitation and exploration tension.

absence of moderating or balancing factors such as limits to market demand, competition, or loss of management focus, these nonlinear dynamics would have led to increasing profits at an increasing rate, a self-reinforcing value-gathering loop. Balancing factors were present, however. These are described next.

Balancing External Feedback Limits Exploitation in the System

Two external factors, limits to market size and competition, moderated this nonlinear positive feedback amplification effect at Intel. First, the market only demanded so many memory chips during a given time period. Limits to this market-carrying capacity at various points in time constrained the availability of excess profit to all of the players in the market. It was possible, therefore, to overbuild capacity and risk the cost of carrying underutilized assets if demand did not materialize. This was not the main constraint on Intel's growth during this period, however. A second constraint, competition, was a much more significant factor. For the most part, demand overall remained strong during this period. However, the presence of competitors interacted with overall market-carrying capacity to limit the availability of excess profits to Intel. During this period, Japanese manufacturers came online with superior scale economics. Not surprisingly, they increasingly won market share from Intel between 1972 and 1985. Ultimately, it was competition that caused Intel to exit the memory market (Burgelman, 1994).

Balancing Feedback From Within the System Can Limit Exploitation

Two internal dynamics also balanced the exploitation value-gathering loop at Intel. First, as management's aspirations with respect to market performance in the memory sector were achieved, complacency could have set in as the pressure to succeed attenuated with apparent success. To address this tendency in the face of continued competitive pressure, as is discussed in a later section in detail, agents acting out the leadership mechanisms at Intel periodically reset objectives and expectations, applying continual pressure on other agents to perform. Absent this pressure, available resources would have been absorbed in departmental nest-feathering activities like shorter work hours or skunk works—as unauthorized development projects are often called—that addressed the individual needs of influential agents rather than organizational ones (Nohria &

Gulati, 1996; Singh, 1986). With laissez-faire leadership like this, the system would self-regulate to an acceptable—but not maximum—level of performance. Even in laissez-faire environments, pressure from capital markets propagates through the system to demand at least a minimal level of acceptable performance to maintain access to capital markets.

A second internal balancing dynamic was the allocation of limited resources to exploration. This process is described in more detail below, but clearly, resources used for exploration were not available for exploitation. This was the case for the original microprocessor project at Intel. It was considered a promising and maybe lucrative "distraction," rather than a purposeful exploration (R. A. Burgelman, personal communication, January 11, 2006). In any case, it did consume resources that could have been used elsewhere. Explorations of this type were resource-consuming distractions from the continued exploitation of Intel's memory fabrication capabilities. These distractions consumed resources and could have reduced the level of profit gathered by the system. Importantly for Intel, although the flow of resources to microprocessors did indeed provide negative feedback to Intel's memory exploitation potential, for the system overall, profit actually increased when resources were allocated to microprocessors. From the beginning, margins for microprocessors were higher than those for memory.

The Exploration Positive Feedback Loops Identify Value

The upper-left positive loop in Figure 13.1 from the simulation reflects the dynamics inherent in the identification of opportunities and the marshalling of capabilities needed to benefit from them. As the loop implies, at Intel, flows of available resources were allocated to exploration—for example, the microprocessor project—as potential opportunities were explored and solutions were developed to address them. Part of this process was the generation of new capabilities to address the opportunities (Surie & Hazy, 2006). Eventually, after the appropriate capabilities are built up in the model, the excess profits derived from these new sources may increase (Christensen & Raynor, 2003)—as they did for the microprocessor project. As in exploitation, the exploration value identification loop is self-reinforcing once adequate profits are achieved.

In this case, however, long-time delays between exploration and appropriation of adequate profit can overwhelm the signal being amplified by positive feedback within the system dynamics. Considerable research has shown that for exploration to succeed, organizations must first increase their absorptive capacity (Cohen & Levinthal, 1990; Van den Bosch, Volberda, & Boer, 1999). That is, before they can develop new capabilities with a significant chance of success, they must first expend resources to learn and experiment. This introduces considerable time delay and in some cases makes a self-reinforcing exploration cycle difficult to sustain. As is described later, this effect was avoided at Intel because its process technology was readily transferable.

Balancing External Feedback Limits Exploration in the System

Like the exploitation loop, excess profit that results from exploration projects also depends upon two external factors: the demand of the new markets and the competitive dynamics in these new areas. In the case of new, developing markets, the dynamics and timing of market development are likely to be unpredictable and coevolutionary (Lewin & Volberda, 1999). They also emerge from interactions between potential customers and would-be suppliers (Surie & Hazy, 2006) and thus, to some degree, are enacted by the organization (Weick, 1979), its partners, and its competitors.

The search strategy implemented by the system limits the range of agent interaction with the environment. Thus, a strongly enforced strategy might serve to limit the firm's participation in some potentially fertile areas. Organizations simply do not have unlimited resources and therefore cannot do everything. Bounding the firm's search strategy in this way constitutes a balancing feedback loop that can limit the market possibilities identified through exploration. At Intel, the project that ultimately led to the invention of the microprocessor was identified serendipitously through generative leadership, as described earlier. It was not in any way a strategic exploration. To Intel's credit and ultimate good fortune, the project was not squelched by senior management as being nonstrategic. If it had been, Intel would have been limiting its search. As discussed below, when the system limits the scope of search, it also limits the number of new market possibilities that might provide resources to the system.

Balancing Loops Internal to the System

Because new markets can only benefit the organization if they are discovered through search, the value-identifying loop in Figure 13.1 is balanced internally by the aspirations inherent in the organization's perceived purpose and strategy. These in turn may limit the scope of search as described above. If aspirations are limited, or if they are mismatched with the opportunities that are emerging, the amplifying feedback loop that might nurture and grow a new opportunity—like the microprocessor market—is balanced by negative feedback that limits its development. The opportunities are simply never uncovered.

Alternatively, if results are long in coming, the perception that aspirations are not realistic may cause them to be lowered, and promising projects may be discontinued. This fatigue is often exacerbated by pressure on profits or by change of management regimes. In the face of limited success, sustaining investment in research and development and in business development projects may be difficult for management to stomach. In either case, without continued encouragement, the desired and current states converge, and the potential benefit of the exploration feedback loop is curtailed. These effects combine to make change efforts very difficult to maintain in the absence of sustained strategic initiatives and the leadership mechanisms that are needed to regulate these feedback systems.

An example of this internal limiting feedback mechanism was the case of Xerox Palo Alto Research Center (PARC) in the early 1970s. It was at PARC where the earliest version of the personal computer was developed. Unfortunately for Xerox, the developing opportunity was starved by management—in a limiting feedback loop—because its tremendous potential was not seen and nurtured (Smith & Alexander, 1988). During the analogous period at Intel, senior management did not squelch the microprocessor business, even though it was not considered strategic. One key difference: microprocessors were making money.

Intel was fortunate in that the microprocessor project was quite profitable from the beginning and continued to be profitable throughout. The project thereby avoided pressure to cut off funding due to exploration fatigue. Two factors contributed to this good fortune. First, from the start, microprocessors had higher margins than did the memory chips with which they were competing for resources. Second and equally important was the fact that Intel's process technology was easily transitioned from memory to microprocessors, so little start-up capital was needed to launch the microprocessor line. In short, a profitable consulting arrangement quickly became a profitable business.

Although the Intel case is unique, it is also instructive. The company managed to avoid both of exploration's limiting feedback mechanisms. It did so by fortunate circumstances rather than solid management practice, however. In other words, Intel was lucky. Resources were allocated to build microprocessor capabilities because the project was profitable from the beginning. In turn, the business gathered its own excess profit, which could be reinvested into additional capabilities over time as the virtuous feedback loop built its own momentum. External feedback was also not limiting. The market grew quickly, and Intel successfully beat back competition. These successes enabled Intel's management to "run with" the opportunity even though it was not perceived to be strategic. The successes did not challenge the identity of Intel's senior managers as the founders of a memory company because they were never forced to weigh difficult decisions about the new market's potential versus their fading fortunes in memory markets. Fortunately for Intel, as can be seen in Figure 13.2, microprocessors were taking off even as Intel's position in the memory market was eroding. Although luck was undoubtedly a factor in Intel's success, the importance of leadership cannot be overlooked. Just how leadership saved Intel is discussed in the next section.

LEADERSHIP AS AN INFLUENTIAL INCREMENT

As the environment changes it puts pressure on the organization to adapt. Forces internal to the organization likewise apply conflicting pressures tearing at the boundaries and making the problem of maintaining the system as an entity a never ending and ever changing challenge. Katz and Kahn (1978) argued that an "influential increment," otherwise known as organizational leadership, is required. In this analysis, *organizational leadership* is considered to be an organizational metacapability, just like other organizational capabilities. It is composed of a series of system mechanisms that bias the above-described dynamics at critical points to enable

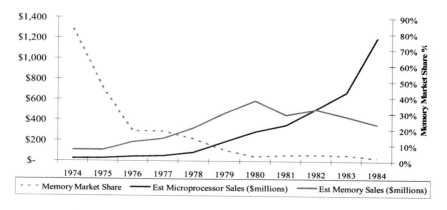

Note: Adapted from "Fading Memories: A Process Theory of Strategic Business Exit in Dynamic Environments," by R. A. Burgelman, 1994, *Administrative Science Quarterly, 39,* p. 37; and from Intel public filings.

Figure 13.2.   Estimated sales for microprocessor and memory (solid lines) and memory market share (dotted line on the right scale).

the organization to sustain itself as a system and to survive in a changing environment (Hazy, 2006b, 2007a). The posited mechanisms of organizational leadership are described below.

Convergent Leadership and Exploitation

The *convergent leadership* mechanism (Hazy, 2006c) is the influential increment that moves the system dynamically along a perceived convergence path. As components of the leadership metacapability, leadership mechanisms—dynamic patterns of communication and action among individuals within the system that produce effects not inherent in the individual acts—consist of collections of organizational routines, integrating knowledge and decision norms. These social structures engage agents as actors in an unfolding dynamic model of the system in interaction with the environment. The leadership model being enacted, once adopted by various agents, helps each to make sense of changing situations. It serves to orchestrate, at least to some degree, the seemingly autonomous decisions and actions of all who accept the model as their own, as simulations have shown (Hazy, 2007b). What without leadership would have been disparate, self-interested actions are woven into a delicately textured, coordinated, albeit often fragile whole. In this way, individual agents are coaxed into the service of a system of action by an emergent leadership mechanism.

To accomplish this orchestration, each agent develops or adopts from others a model of the organization, its purpose, and its desired performance. Activities that clarify roles, responsibilities, and accountabilities and then establish and enforce contingency between agent action and individual reward are orchestrated in accord with the model. Many of these actions will be recognized by readers as transactional leadership behaviors (Bass, 1985). This mechanism moves the actions of agents and presumably the system along a perceived path of convergence.

Intel's highly developed process technology and memory manufacturing capabilities are examples of outcomes when effective convergent leadership is in operation. At Intel, the production rule that led to success in microprocessors—that incremental spare capacity goes to the highest-margin product—was an artifact of the convergent leadership mechanism that catalyzed profit maximizing behavior in the organization. The production rule was enforced by all who bought into the profit maximizing model within the Intel system of action, and it enabled success in memory as well as in microprocessors. No individual or single set of individuals led the organizational adaptation toward microprocessors. The dynamical operations of the system itself did, in particular it was the action of Intel's convergent leadership mechanism.

Although convergent leadership is similar to "administrative leadership" as described in complexity leadership theory (Uhl-Bien et al., 2007), it differs in significant and important ways. First, convergent leadership implies that activities, objectives, and contingent rewards are specifically chosen and implemented to achieve a purpose (Barnard, 1938; Goldstein & Hazy, 2006)—towards which the system is converging. Second, the purpose is implied by the individual cognitive models in use by agents as they strive to predict the complex, nonlinear, and changing dynamics of the organization in the environment, a complex leader/follower interaction has been simulated computationally (Hubler & Pines, 1994). Third, convergent leadership implies more than the administration of the organization in its current state, the navigation of its bureaucratic systems; it implies direction and change over time toward some purpose. Convergent leadership involves catalytic action and decision within a dynamical system that is converging toward a structural attractor of some sort. In the case of Intel, the system was converging toward increasingly effective exploitation of the memory market using its process technology and manufacturing capabilities as a competitive differentiator.

At Intel, the actions and decisions of the managers and employees were organized to enable the system to converge toward a cost-competitive model of semiconductor fabrication. The convergent leadership mechanism, their management model, provided the organization's members, from the shop floor to senior management, with the cues they needed to take actions and make decisions that caused the system to converge toward their model of improved performance (Hazy, 2006a, 2006c). Convergent leadership signals came not from a single source, from "a leader" per se, but rather from superiors, peers, and even subordinates who collectively led one another to catalyze and to reinforce decisions and actions that moved the system toward its purpose (Hazy, 2006a). Traditional management practices that increased the exploitation of current capabilities to produce memory chips by improving efficiency and effectively handling process disruptions were included in the convergent leadership mechanism. Management practices that maintained the status quo in the face of change for individual rather than system purposes, such as acts like nest feathering and patronage activities as described in agency theory (Davis & Useem, 2002), were not included in the system's convergent leadership mechanism. Thus performance was improved by identifying gaps between aspiration and current performance and implementing specific programs to close the gaps. These activities "led the organization" as it converged toward an accepted model of operating excellence, albeit one that continually changed over time.

In the language of complexity science, convergent leadership enabled Intel to approach a dynamical system attractor, a state of relative stability that defined a local performance peak in memory chip fabrication. Further, by reducing internal complexity, the local peak was likely to exhibit a higher level of relative performance (Kauffman, 1995; Levinthal, 1997). Clarity within the operating environment reduced the need for interactions, led to unambiguous command and advice relationships, and established clear task and resource assignments. The approach was often directive, which reduced complexity and interdependency and therefore limited learning outside of the specific knowledge domain in use (Schreiber & Carley, 2006). It did, however, enable Intel to operate with greater relative stability within its market, memory chips.

The dynamics that emerge from reduced complexity can have the perverse effect of reducing learning and thereby limiting the organization's propensity to change (Carley & Ren, 2001; Carley & Svoboda, 1996; Levinthal & March, 1993; Schreiber & Carley, 2006). As an organization becomes more finely tuned to succeed within a given set of capabilities, a random long-jump adaptation to a different configuration becomes less and less likely to offer relative benefit. Levinthal and March (1993) called this "the myopia of learning" (p. 95). Burgelman (2002) observed this phenomenon at Intel in the epoch that followed the transformation chronicled here and called it "coevolutionary lock-in." Because of this phenomenon, sweeping change is difficult and unlikely, and yet transformation happened at Intel in the early 1980s. Coevolutionary lock-in is particularly prevalent with respect to exploration activities when there is a long time delay between the initial exploration and the realization of significant returns from the effort. To sustain exploration activity under these conditions requires a different kind of leadership. Intel escaped lock-in in the 1970s and 1980s, in part because it nurtured a generative leadership mechanism among some of its people. As described next, generative leadership by midlevel managers planted the seeds of transformation at Intel.

Generative Leadership and Exploration

The *generative leadership* mechanism in organizations is the influential increment that generates variety, diversity, and newness within the system. Activities that encourage boundary spanning, cross-functional teams, and open communication are examples of generative leadership (Surie & Hazy, 2006). Organizations that exhibit generative leadership identify and address potential opportunities by organizing interactions both internally, to improve effectiveness, and externally with customers, to open new markets. At Intel, the invention of the microprocessor was itself an example of the generative leadership mechanism in action, but there are many others. Burgelman (1991) told the story of Les Kohn, an enterprising technologist at Intel. Kohn bucked senior management and encouraged interactions that nurtured the development of a reduced instruction set computing (RISC) processor within Intel, even though it was against the company's explicit strategy. Kohn felt the opportunity was important for Intel and so worked with others to encourage the generative interactions that were needed to identify, develop, and nurture the project within the Intel organization, albeit somewhat surreptitiously.

Multiple examples imply that generative leadership within Intel was not coincidental but systematic. Burgelman (2002) called the situation at Intel an "ecology of strategy making" (p. 325). He referred to the bottom-up component epitomized by Kohn as an "autonomous strategic process" (p. 327) and used the above example to argue that an autonomous strategic process can be difficult to overcome. But how can bottom-up project initiation by individuals and groups be called strategic? It cannot. It is the system's generative leadership mechanism being acted out by the system's agents, not strategy as it is commonly defined. Furthermore, a stated strategy that waits for innovation to bubble up through the organization cannot work without an effective generative leadership mechanism.

What is persistent in organizations with a well-developed generative leadership mechanism is that they are constantly searching for opportunities, inside and outside the organization, learning about them through interactions, and then reforming the system itself to take maximum advantage of each one. A strategy induced by senior management is simply another obstacle for generative leadership to overcome. The renewal at Intel is better understood as a generative leadership success independent of any corporate strategy. That Intel's strategy ultimately embraced microprocessors is a demonstration of retrospective sense making (Weick, 1979), not strategy.

Generative leadership is focused on a specific purpose: the generation of options for the system in the face of change and uncertainty. It is more nuanced than the activities normally considered characteristic of transformational leadership, or of transactional leadership for that matter. The generative leadership mechanism establishes and clarifies an organization's adaptation plan (Holland, 1975), an aspect of its purpose, and by catalyzing interactions it develops opportunities for the organization (Surie & Hazy, 2006). These purposes may vary at different places in the organization as individual agents, on the shop floor, for example, develop their own vision of where the company should go, as Hoff and Kohn did for Intel (Burgelman, 1991). Projects throughout the organization may be implemented as skunk works or as authorized programs, but in either case, they need generative leadership to succeed. Generative leadership is the catalyst that releases internal energy key to sustaining exploration, experimentation, and nurturing of promising projects in light of ambiguity, uncertainty, and long time delays. Kohn was such a catalyst at Intel (Burgelman, 1991). He was a generative leader.

To identify and capitalize on opportunities, information is needed. To increase the flow of information from the market to the company and within the organization, generative leadership increases the complexity of influence, advice, task, and resource interactions within the organization. A more rugged performance landscape (Levinthal, 1997), at least locally, results. This ruggedness enables the system to shift future directions from one structural attractor to another (Dooley & Van de Ven, 1999). McKelvey (this volume) proposed that when the internal complexity of these interactions reaches a critical level, long-jump adaptation, or significant change, becomes more likely.

Unifying Leadership, Collective Identity, and Balance

The *unifying leadership* mechanism is the influential increment that maintains collective identity (Gioia, Schultz, & Corley, 2000) and balances the natural tensions from simultaneous exploitation and exploration. When acting as unifying leaders, individual agents develop, evolve, and share with one another a cognitive model of their group and the organization—including their boundaries, structure, and purpose. They catalyze activities that establish and enforce boundaries of inclusion or exclusion—for example, establishing and promoting "tags" like a company or team name, a dress code, or rites of membership that designate team membership and status; enforcing the responsibilities of membership by applying pressure on others to conform to relevant norms; or promoting and providing resources to overarching objectives with explicit task and reward interdependencies requiring unity of action among interacting agents.

Unifying leadership maintains the system as a unity within the environment, even in the face of change (Maturana & Varela, 1998). At the firm level, this unity is created and maintained by establishing the boundaries of the organization, its values and its norms; and by specifying what is and is not acceptable within the organization's identity, implicitly determining the mix of exploitation and exploration. For example, setting portfolio-pruning rules like the famous dictum established by Jack Welch at GE, namely, that each business unit had to be first or second in its industry or face being sold off (Slater, 2001), establishes the requirements of continued membership within the GE boundary.

At the firm level, Intel maintained its identity as a memory company long after it was a de facto microprocessor company. The retrospective recognition of this fact by Intel's founding team, the decision to exit the memory business, and the simultaneous elevation of Andy Grove—the first among them to recognize the new reality and the best positioned to move forward in this new reality—are two examples of the unifying leadership mechanism at Intel.

As former IBM CEO, Lou Gerstner (2002) pointed out regarding the transformation of IBM, for successful change to occur, an alternative must be available to the organization, one that is sufficiently robust such that comparable success is possible on a different platform. Only then can the organization's identity be changed to encompass the new reality. At Intel, for the reasons described, over time the microprocessor operation became a significant business in its own right—in fact by the early 1980s it was larger than the memory business. With such a robust platform available, successful transformation was possible at Intel. All that remained was for unifying leadership to change the company's overall identity. For the organization, it was a matter of retroactively acknowledging what was by then a reality and then deciding in 1985 to change the firm's boundary by exiting the memory business in favor of microprocessors. Undoubtedly, others in the organization had long before adopted a new microprocessor company identity at the group, team, and division levels. Unifying leadership is not confined to certain individuals on the top management team but operates at all levels across the organization. It answers the members' questions about who they are and why they are there wherever they are in the organization.

Not all firms are as fortunate as Intel and IBM. The existence of a robust alternative state is often complicated by long time delays. Opportunities must first be identified in external markets, absorptive capacity (Cohen & Levinthal, 1990) must be developed, and finally, capabilities to address the opportunities must be built. These things take time. Because the environment is largely unpredictable, even if generative leadership has nurtured a significant variety of potential opportunities for the organization, and even if unifying leadership has balanced exploration and exploitation through changes in boundaries and identity, there is still no guarantee that the organization will successfully migrate to a new structure. As the case of Intel shows, wholesale transformation requires that other factors fall into place as well.

INTEL'S TRANSFORMATION RECONSIDERED

As can be seen in Figure 13.3, the crossover to dominance of microprocessors at Intel occurred in 1982. Still, it was 3 years—not until 1985—before the decision to exit memory completed the transformation. The factors that contributed are explored in this section.

The process of transformation at Intel related directly to the exploitation of its core capabilities in process technology for fabricating memory chips (dynamic random access memory, or DRAM). Burgelman (1991) stated, "It was manufacturing prowess that made it possible for Intel to succeed in DRAM's where other memory start-ups ... had failed" (p. 243). In other words, it was the exploitation of Intel's current capabilities in process technology that sustained the firm. Intel had applied its capabilities against the developing market for memory chips and gained excess profit from the environment by selling its chips into the growing market.

The percentage of revenue derived from the sale of memory chips as simulated in the system dynamics mathematical model is shown in Figure 13.4. The memory sales percentages are shown in the top line on the left that gradually declines over time. Microprocessor mix is represented by the line that increases left to right. These simulated outcomes closely match the actual results at Intel during the same period, as shown in Figure 13.3. There similarity provides some confidence that by understanding the simulation, one can gain insights about what may have actually happened at Intel. Published data supports other simulation assumptions as well.

From Burgelman's (1994) data it also reasonable to infer that Intel's process technology was an organizational capability that transferred readily to microprocessors. Typically, one would expect a company like

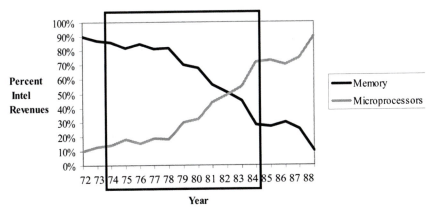

Notes: Adapted from data from Intel as cited in "Intraorganizational Ecology of Strategy Making and Organizational Adaptation: Theory and Field Research," by R. A. Burgelman, 1991, *Organization Science, 2*(3), p. 241.

Figure 13.3.   Actual product mix for memory chips and microprocessors for Intel; the period modeled in the simulation is indicated by the square.

Intel to endure a time delay as it develops absorptive capacity, the ability to understand and coevolve with the market (Cohen & Levinthal, 1990). Intel, however, found its existing process technology to be easily transferable to microprocessor fabrication. It lost no time, and absorbed minimal investment, in capitalizing on the opportunity offered by microprocessors.

For the present simulation, I inferred from these qualitative data that the parameter that determines the time delay between identifying an opportunity in the market and building the necessary capabilities to address it profitably were minimal. In other words, in the simulation I assumed there was no time delay associated with the building of absorptive capacity (Cohen & Levinthal, 1990) at Intel. The microprocessor business was immediately self-funding. Since the capital needs of the business did not conflict with those of the memory business, the microprocessor business was permitted to grow as the market grew, quite rapidly as it turned out.

Finally, opportunities in the market can be overlooked or missed if there is no generative leadership mechanism to identify, explore, and nurture them. As the story of Les Kohn illustrates, a generative leadership mechanism was clearly in place at Intel. The system dynamics simulation

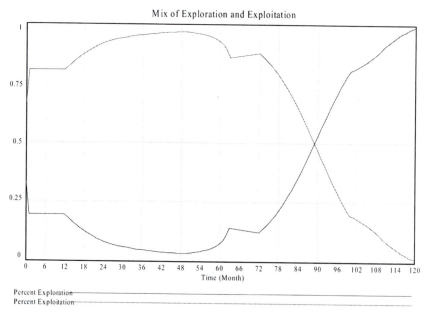

Figure 13.4.   System dynamics simulation of product mix model of Intel Corporation considering the impact of leadership as described in the text.

modeled this reality by assuming that resources were channeled to the exploration of the microprocessor opportunity and toward building the relevant capabilities, two observed effects of generative leadership.

Figure 13.4 shows the simulation of the Intel case when generative leadership is assumed to be active in the organization. The presence of generative leadership meant that new opportunities, in this case the microprocessor, were identified and nurtured with resources as the market required. Not shown in figure is the simulated outcome when generative leadership is not present. In that hypothetical case, the microprocessor is not invented, or if it is, it is not nurtured as a business—an error comparable to how Xerox starved the personal computer it had invented. Without generative leadership, memory continues to be Intel's main product line throughout the time period, but the decline in memory market share leads to the end of the firm as a profitable entity.

The Dynamics of Intel's Transformation

What actually enabled sweeping change at Intel? The exploitation value-gathering loop and its influential increment (Katz & Kahn, 1978), the convergent leadership mechanism, were sustaining the firm even as, unbeknownst to senior management, competitive pressures were beginning to limit the firm's future prospects in the memory industry. The unifying leadership mechanism maintained the identity of a memory company, but also encouraged a learning environment. A persistent generative leadership mechanism evolved to innovate and develop process technologies that could help the firm achieve its purpose as a memory company. With generative leadership, the microprocessor opportunity was identified and nurtured.

Although the original microprocessor project was a sanctioned diversion, an exploration activity in the value-identifying loop, it was not perceived by senior management to be strategic, although arguably other managers in the organization did perceive its strategic value. The project was, however, executed within the generative leadership mechanism within Intel as acted out by its champion. Senior management at Intel did not explicitly sanction the allocation of resources to continued exploration of microprocessor markets, however. Therefore, one can infer that Intel's exploration would not have been sustainable if it had come into conflict with the DRAM business in a way that would have reduced the resources available for its core business. In the case of microprocessors, however, margins were actually higher than those for memory, thus enabling continued exploration and ultimately the domination of the microprocessor feedback loop.

The simulation shows that if microprocessors were not more profitable than memory, resources would not have systematically flowed toward the building of microprocessor capabilities in the company without senior management involvement. If asked, they would most likely have refused, and as a result the transformation would not have occurred. Stated differently, the bottom-up transformation at Intel occurred in part because profits from exploration were immediate and sufficient to support a positive feedback loop. Intel's fabrication capabilities were immediately transferable to microprocessors, making absorptive capacity (Cohen & Levinthal, 1990) high enough to address the market immediately. Microprocessors were more profitable than memory from the start and so Intel's logical production rule—that excess capacity be allocated to the highest margin product—was the unimaginative routine that cinched the transformation. None of this would have mattered, of course, if generative leadership wasn't present to identify and nurture the microprocessor opportunity in the first place.

Importantly, at Intel there were no time delays associated with absorptive capacity or the rise in market demand. When the time delay between exploration and reward is such that exploration profits reinforce continued investment (i.e., the project pays for itself), as was the case at Intel, gradual transformation is possible. The system dynamics at Intel were such that positive feedback sustained the project, as long as internally initiated negative feedback did not dampen the momentum. During this period, Intel's exploitation/exploration dynamics never came into conflict with Intel senior management's stated aspiration to be a memory company, so management never moved to squelch the project. Equally important was the fact that from its earliest days the Intel culture had encouraged generative leadership throughout the organization, even without the explicit encouragement of top management. In sum, successful bottom-up transformations can succeed if: (1) the time delay between exploration and reward is such that embedded generative leadership activities, and the exploration that results, identify and nurture opportunities, (2) these opportunities are not in serious conflict with top-down induced strategy processes, and (3) market conditions favor the results of exploration.

DISCUSSION

An examination of the system dynamics of Intel's transformation implies that wholesale transformation can occur absent a senior management change initiative—as it did at Intel—if at least five conditions are present.

First, convergent leadership must gain excess profit from its existing capabilities, like memory fabrication at Intel, so that resources remain available to the organization to support exploration. Second, generative leadership (Surie & Hazy, 2006) must create the conditions in which new opportunities are identified and nurtured. The invention of the original microprocessor and the subsequent invention of a RISC processor are just two examples of a healthy generative leadership mechanism at Intel. Studies of successful product launches have demonstrated the importance of creating conditions where innovation can flourish (Lynn & Reilly, 2002).

Third, in the absence of induced strategy (Burgelman, 2002) to sustain funding of slowly developing loss-making initiatives, projects must be self-funding early in their development cycle. Self-funding helps to mitigate the risk of early termination due to exploration fatigue. The Intel microprocessor is a prime example of this idea, which is also consistent with studies that have described successful innovation projects (Christensen & Raynor, 2003; Davila, Epstein, & Shelton, 2006).

Fourth, conditions must exist, as they did at Intel with the production rule, such that resources are allocated to the new capabilities commensurate with the market opportunity. If either too many or too few resources are allocated, management decisions can doom a project. On the one hand, over funding creates unachievable expectations. On the other, under funding starves a project just when learning is most critical. As was shown with the Xerox example (Smith & Alexander, 1988) and many others, this is not always easily achieved in organizational settings. In Burgelman's (2002) continuing longitudinal study of Intel's fortunes, he described the Andy Grove epoch at Intel—from 1987 to 1998—which occurred after the period modeled in this article. It was characterized, he wrote, by an "induced strategy process" rather than autonomous strategy. Burgelman identified a phenomenon he calls "coevolutionary lock-in," where a supplier's close reciprocal link with its customers and its markets precludes the pursuit of autonomous strategy. A similar phenomenon was described by Christensen (1997). Breaking from this state, it seems, is extraordinarily difficult. Perhaps the approach described in this article is a way to gain additional insights into the dynamics surrounding these difficult practical challenges.

Fifth and finally, unifying leadership must maintain identity, or else change it, as was the case when Intel "officially" changed into a microprocessor company in 1985. New boundaries were identified and new membership rules were established as the last vestiges of a memory culture were pruned away. In the end, this analysis implies that both leadership and luck guided Intel's successful transformation.

A contribution of the present analysis is a demonstration of how system dynamics techniques can be used to examine the Intel case more closely in order to illuminate not only its strategy-making ecology (Burgelman, 2002) but also the role of dynamic capabilities and the very nature of leadership in organizations. Further research over different epochs at Intel and at other companies will make it possible to discern the complex dynamics at work in organizational systems. As firms face accelerating technologic and geopolitical changes related to globalization, understanding these dynamics is more critical than ever. By taking a close look at a single case, this article highlights the usefulness of the complex systems paradigm as a way of reasoning about the complex problems facing organizations today. It is also a demonstration of the power of system dynamics as a technique to explore the many nonlinear relationships at work in organizations and their markets.

ACKNOWLEDGMENT

This chapter benefited from the comments of Robert A. Burgelman, David R. Schwandt and the editors of this volume. However, any errors or omissions are the author's alone.

NOTES

1. This term is preferred in this chapter because it reflects the specific purpose of these leadership actions and decisions—to generate alternatives or options for the system. The term "adaptive" implies success in an uncertain and contingent world. In practice, ex ante, actions and decisions cannot be called "adaptive" since environmental contingencies are unknown and success cannot be assumed. In contrast, the term "generative" does not assume successful adaptation but instead refers specifically to the generation of variations and recombinations among capabilities. These experiments may provide adaptation potential; but due to uncertainty, they may or may not prove successful in the long run. For this reason, *generative leadership* better describes the leadership that led to successful transformation at Intel. The company's invention of the microprocessor was an idea that addressed an opportunity and eventually grew into a business line. That it was adaptive for Intel as a whole was serendipitous. Adaptation of the company required, in addition to the rapid growth of the microprocessor market, other structural factors that are described later in the article. In the

case of Intel, many observers would call the confluence of these conditions just plain luck rather than effective leadership.

2. The detailed description and mathematical treatment of the conceptual framework and system dynamics model used in this article was developed and described by Hazy (2004) elsewhere.

REFERENCES

Anderson, P. (1999). Complexity theory and organization science. *Organization Science, 10*(3), 216-232.

Aspray, W. (1997). The Intel 4004: What constituted invention? *IEEE Annals of the History of Computing, 19*(3), 4-15.

Barnard, C. (1938). *The functions of the executive*. Cambridge, MA: Harvard Press.

Barney, J. B. (1986). Strategic factor markets: Expectations, luck and business strategy. *Management Science, 32*(10), 1231-1241.

Barney, J. B. (1991). Firm resources and sustained competitive advantage. *Journal of Management, 17*(1), 99-120.

Bass, B. M. (1985). *Leadership and performance beyond expectations*. New York: The Free Press.

Burgelman, R. A. (1991). Intraorganizational ecology of strategy making and organizational adaptation: Theory and field research. *Organization Science, 2*(3), 239-262.

Burgelman, R. A. (1994). Fading memories: A process theory of strategic business exit in dynamic environments. *Administrative Science Quarterly, 39*, 24-56.

Burgelman, R. A. (2002). Strategy as vector and the inertia of coevolutionary lock-in. *Administrative Science Quarterly, 47*(2), 325-357.

Carley, K. M., & Ren, Y. (2001, June). *Tradeoffs between performance and adaptability for C3I architectures*. Paper presented at the Command and Control Research and Technology Symposium, Annapolis, MD.

Carley, K. M., & Svoboda, D. M. (1996). Modeling organizational adaptation as a simulated annealing process. *Sociological Methods & Research, 25*(1), 138-168.

Christensen, C. M. (1997). *The innovator's dilemma*. New York: HarperBusiness.

Christensen, C. M., & Raynor, M. E. (2003). *The innovator's solution*. Boston: Harvard Business School Press.

Cohen, W. M., & Levinthal, D. A. (1990). Absorptive capacity: A new perspective on learning and innovation. *Administrative Science Quarterly, 35*, 128-152.

Davila, T., Epstein, M. J., & Shelton, R. (2006). *Making innovation work: How to manage it, measure it, and profit from it*. Upper Saddle River, NJ: Wharton School Publishing.

Davis, G. F., & Useem, M. (2002). Top management, company directors, and corporate control. In A. Pettigrew, H. Thomas, & R. Whittington (Eds.), *Handbook of strategy and management* (pp. 233-259). London: Sage.

Dooley, K. J., & Van de Ven, A. H. (1999). Explaining complex organizational dynamics. *Organization Science, 10*(3), 358-375.

Dosi, G., Nelson, R. R., & Winter, S. G. (Eds.). (2000). *The nature and dynamics of organizational capabilities*. Oxford, England: Oxford University Press.

Forrester, J. W. (1987). Nonlinearity in high-order models of social systems. *European Journal of Operational Research, 30*(2), 104-109.

Gerstner, L. V. (2002). *Who says elephants can't dance: Inside IBM's historic turnaround*. New York: HarperBusiness.

Gioia, D. A., Schultz, M., & Corley, K. G. (2000). Organizational identity, image, and adaptive instability. *Academy of Management Review, 25*(1), 63-81.

Goldstein, J. & Hazy, J. K. (2006). Introduction to: *The functions of the executive* chapter 2 - The individual and organization *Emergence: Complexity and Organization, 8*(4).

Hamel, G., & Prahalad, C. K. (1994). *Competing for the future*. Boston: Harvard Business School Press.

Hazy, J. K. (2004). *A leadership and capabilities framework for organizational change: Simulating the emergence of leadership as an organizational meta-capability*. Unpublished dissertation, The George Washington University, Washington, DC.

Hazy, J. K. (2006a, June). *Emergent signaling networks in complex socio-technical systems: How cooperative interactions among agents contribute to system sustainability*. Paper presented at the North American Association of Computational Social and Organization Science, University of Notre Dame, South Bend, IN.

Hazy, J. K. (2006b, August). *Leadership as an organizational meta-capability: A system dynamics simulation showing the role of leadership in organizational sustainability*. Paper presented at the Academy of Management, Atlanta, GA.

Hazy, J. K. (2006c). Measuring leadership effectiveness in complex socio-technical systems. *Emergence: Complexity and Organization, 8* (3), 58-77.

Hazy, J. K. (2007a, August). *Parsing the "influential increment" in the language of complexity: Uncovering the systemic mechanisms of leadership influence*. Paper to be presented at the Academy of Management Annual Meeting, Philadelphia.

Hazy, J. K. (2007b). Computer models of leadership: Foundation for a new discipline or meaningless diversion? *The Leadership Quarterly, 18*(4), 391-410.

Helfat, C. E., Finkelstein, S., Mitchell, W., Peteraf, M. A., Singh, H., Teece, D. J., et al. (2006). *Dynamic capabilities: Understanding strategic change in organizations* (1st ed.). New York: Blackwell.

Hernes, G. (1998). Real virtuality. In P. Hedström & R. Swedberg (Eds.), *Social mechanisms: An analytical approach to social theory* (pp. 74-101). Cambridge, England: Cambridge University Press.

Holland, J. H. (1975). *Adaptation in natural and artificial systems*. Cambridge, MA: The MIT Press.

Hubler, A., & Pines, D. (1994). Prediction and adaptation in an evolving chaotic environment. In G. Cowan, D. Pines & D. Meltzer (Eds.), *Complexity: Metaphors, Models and Reality* (Vol. Proceedings Volume XIX, pp. 343-382). Reading, MA: Addison-Wesley.

Katz, D., & Kahn, R. L. (1978). *The social psychology of organizations* (2nd ed.). New York: John Wiley.

Kauffman, S. A. (1995). *At home in the universe: The search for the laws of self-organization and complexity*. New York: Oxford University Press.

Levinthal, D. A. (1997). Adaptation on rugged landscapes. *Management Science, 43*(7), 934-950.

Levinthal, D. A., & March, J. G. (1993). The myopia of learning. *Strategic Management Journal, 14*, 95-112.

Lewin, A. Y., & Volberda, H. W. (1999). Prolegomena on coevolution: A framework for research on strategy and new organizational forms. *Organization Science, 10*(5), 519-534.

Lichtenstein, B. B., Uhl-Bien, M., Marion, R., Seers, A., Orton, J. D., & Schreiber, C. (2006). Complexity leadership theory: An interactive process on leading in complex adaptive systems. *Emergence: Complexity and Organization, 8*(4), 2-12.

Lynn, G. S., & Reilly, R. R. (2002). *Blockbusters: The five keys to developing great new products.* New York: HarperBusiness.

Makadok, R. (2001). Toward a synthesis of the resource-based and dynamic-capability views of rent creation. *Strategic Management Journal, 22*, 387-401.

Makadok, R. (2002). Research notes and commentary: A rational-expectations revision of Makadok's resource/capability synthesis. *Strategic Management Journal, 23*(11), 1051.

March, J. G. (1991). Exploration and exploitation in organizational learning. *Organization Science, 2*(1), 71-87.

Marion, R., & Uhl-Bien, M. (2001). Leadership in complex organizations. *Leadership Quarterly, 12*(4), 389.

Maturana, H. R., & Varela, F. J. (1998). *The tree of knowledge: The biological roots of human understanding* (R. Paolucci, Trans.). Boston: Shambhala.

Nelson, R. R., & Winter, S. G. (1982). *An evolutionary theory of economic change.* Cambridge, MA: The Belknap Press of Harvard University Press.

Nohria, N., & Gulati, R. (1996). Is slack good or bad for innovation? *Academy of Management Journal, 39*(5), 1245-1264.

Panzar, C., Hazy, J. K., McKelvey, B., & Schwandt, D. R. (in press). The paradox of complex organizations: Leadership as multiplexed influence. In J. K. Hazy, J. Goldstein, & B. B. Lichtenstein (Eds.), *Complex systems leadership theory* (pp. 299-320). Mansfield, MA: ISCE.

Penrose, E. T. (1959). *The theory of the growth of the firm.* New York: Wiley.

Peteraf, M. A. (1993). The cornerstones of competitive advantage: A resource-based view. *Strategic Management Journal, 14*(3), 179-191.

Schreiber, C., & Carley, K. M. (2006). Leadership style as an enabler of complex functioning and innovation in a network organization. *Emergence: Complexity and Organization, 8*(4), 61-76.

Singh, J. (1986). Performance, slack, and risk taking in organizational decision making. *Academy of Management Journal, 29*(3), 562-585.

Slater, R. (2001). *Get better or get beaten: 29 secrets of GE's Jack Welch* (2nd ed.). New York: McGraw Hill.

Smith, D. K., & Alexander, R. C. (1988). *Fumbling the future: How Xerox invented, the ignored, the first personal computer.* New York: William Morrow.

Sterman, J. D. (2000). *Business dynamics: Systems thinking and modeling for a complex world.* Boston: Irwin: McGraw-Hill.

Surie, G., & Hazy, J. K. (2006). Generative leadership: Nurturing innovation in complex systems. *Emergence: Complexity and Organization, 8*(4), 13-27.

Teece, D. J., Pisano, G., & Shuen, A. (2000). Dynamic capabilities and strategic management. In G. Dosi, R. R. Nelson, & S. G. Winter (Eds.), *The nature and dynamics of organizational capabilities* (pp. 334-362). Oxford, England: Oxford University Press.

Uhl-Bien, M., Marion, R., & McKelvey, B. (2007). Complexity leadership theory: Shifting leadership from the industrial age to the knowledge era. *The Leadership Quarterly, 18*(4), 298-318.

Van den Bosch, F. A. J., Volberda, H. W., & Boer, M. D. (1999). Coevolution of firm absorptive capacity and knowledge environment: Organizational forms and combinative capabilities. *Organization Science, 10*(5), 551-568.

Weick, K. (1979). *The social psychology of organizing* (2nd ed.). New York: McGraw-Hill.

Winter, S. J. (2000). The satisficing principle in capability learning. *Strategic Management Journal, 21*, 981-996.

CHAPTER 14

PATTERNS OF LEADERSHIP

A Case Study of Influence Signaling in an Entrepreneurial Firm

James K. Hazy

ABSTRACT

The article describes a case study of leadership within an expansion stage, venture capital backed company over a fourteen month period. The study is unique in that it assumed a complex adaptive systems definition of leadership—as an influence signaling network that organizes cooperative interactions and decisions among autonomous agents—rather than a traditional perspective where leadership is embodied in selected individuals. A mixed-method is used that combines qualitative and quantitative techniques to describe in detail the changing state of the organizational system. The study covers a critical period of change for the organization and ends when the CEO steps down. Leadership trends and critical concerns are identified; potential causes are described. The usefulness of the approach for both research and practice is discussed.

Complexity Leadership, Part I: Conceptual Foundations
pp. 379–415

In early September 2006, the CEO of a growing software company stepped down just as this research study with them was completed. Although the firm's business results were on target, something else was wrong. The mood among the company's employees had soured; discontent was spreading. The Board of Directors (BOD) decided to take action. This study illuminates the situation that led to this important event in the life of the company. It examines the state of leadership throughout the company during the period that preceded the crisis, and in particular, it explores the broader context in which the BOD decision was taken.

The circumstances in this company provide a useful environment to test recent assertions in complexity leadership theory. Complexity science researchers have begun to argue against the long held belief that leadership is embodied in a single "leader." Instead they assert that leadership is better defined as an emergent systemic phenomenon that can only be understood in the context of individual and collective interactions in a complex adaptive system context.

If leadership is to be understood as a phenomenon that emerges from within the events and the interactions of agents (Lichtenstein et al., 2006; Marion & Uhl-Bien, 2001; McKelvey, 2003; McKelvey, this volume), then a theory is needed that includes, among other things, the specific nature of "system-level services" or functions (what Katz & Kahn, 1978, called "the influential increment" above and beyond normal routine directives) that support certain specific demands of the organization as a complex adaptive system (Holland, 1995). In particular, one would need an approach that enables researchers to observe and measure the leadership influential increment (Katz & Kahn, 1978) as it dynamically influences system processes critical to performance and adaptation.

Given that the complex adaptive systems of interest are made up of autonomous agents, for a leadership theory to be useful it would need to include the specific mechanisms that determine, amplify, and distribute signals or cues among agents across the system. To understand what this means, some definitions are needed. Signals were defined by Holland (1975) as "stimuli" (p. 22) that the system is able to receive and interpret. With multiple agents within a system, these signals must be distributed among the agents and interpreted in ways that improve the system's survival potential. Presumably, system level mechanisms are needed to do this. Hernes (1998) defined a system mechanism as an "assembly of elements producing an effect not inherent in any of them" (p. 74). In this case, the mechanisms that distribute and interpret signals from the environment are patterns of communication acts and the influence relationships among interacting individuals that taken together produce the system level effects that are experienced by agents in the system as leadership (Panzer, Hazy, McKelvey, & Schwandt, 2007).

The signaling system would also need to coordinate the actions of agents across time and space (Holland, 2001) to enable a state of mutual cooperation as each individual pursues its own self interest (Nowak, 2006). As such, the signals would serve to bias and enforce the local rules of interaction governing individual decisions and actions. The theory would need to explain how these signals are distributed, how they are received and implemented, how they came to exist, and how they subsequently evolved to effectively organize diverse cooperative activities across a complex system.

The challenge for researchers is to frame a description of this signaling in terms of the functional demands of the system so that mechanisms of leadership can be defined and studied in real-world organizations. An important step in this formulation is the development of indexes that measure the levels of various types of leadership signaling (experienced as behavior and decision "cues" by the organization's members) at work across the organization (Hazy, 2006b). The presence of these signals, one could assume, would be reported by the organization's members as a received biasing signal that influences their perceptions of the operational local rules of interaction—their work rules, polices and norms—that govern their daily activities. The idea would be to measure and track these biasing signals over time and to catalog the patterns that consistently emerge in well-specified situations, following a competitive pricing action, for example. Instrumentation must be developed to monitor and visualize an organization's "leadership state" as it encounters environmental and internal structural challenges. With the proper instrumentation, one could classify various organizational states under well-specified conditions. This approach is analogous to a knowledge base of human brain scans where cognitive states are measured, cataloged and related to experiential situations.

An approach for this kind of research has been proposed by Hazy (2006b). For the present analysis, Hazy's method was used to develop a measurement instrument. That instrument was used to see if signals of this type could be detected and interpreted within a subject company, in this case a 50 person, venture capital backed online learning company. In the end, the posited signals were detected and a visualization scheme was developed to map the changing patterns of leadership signaling activity. The period of observation begins approximately 1 year after the company was purchased from its founders by professional investors and ends with a change in CEO 14 months later.

First, I provide a brief background on the case. This is followed by a discussion of the conceptual framework, measurement instrument, and the data collection methods used. Next, the case analysis itself is presented and discussed. This is followed by concluding comments about the contributions of this study.

BACKGROUND ON THE CASE

Over a 16 month period from June 2005 through September 2006 an expansion stage, venture capital backed company located in suburban Philadelphia, Pennsylvania in the United States was studied in detail. The research was conducted to determine the nature of influence signaling within the organization and was based upon a conceptual framework proposed by Hazy (2006a, 2006b). As is described in the Methods section, the researcher had complete access to documentation, the opportunity to poll all employees on three separate occasions, and the chance to hold private interviews with all senior executives as well as follow-up meetings with employee groups to clarify concerns and issues.

Background of the Company

The focal company, located in suburban Philadelphia, Pennsylvania, develops and sells training software and media to multinational companies who use the products to train their employees cost effectively. The company was not yet profitable during the study period but had plans to get there, had sales of roughly $7 million for fiscal 2006, and was experiencing year over year growth of about 80%.[1] Up until the final weeks of the project and after all of the data had been gathered, all signs indicated that the owners were satisfied with the company's business trajectory.

The firm was primarily housed in a single location in a suburban office complex. Approximately 30 of the 45 to 50 people in the company were located there. These were primarily the people responsible for technology, media production, and instructional design, the group called, "Production" in the study. The culture was open and informal. An observer, upon entering the office itself, might be struck by the quiet and darkness of the physical facility. The lights were dimmed to minimize screen glare, and the office was always very quiet and usually seemed empty. Besides the main office, the sales and global service groups resided in regional offices (mostly in their homes) around the country. One sales manager was located in Europe. The three top managers, the CEO, COO, and VP Sales, all resided remotely. Most weeks, the COO, to whom the production group reported, spent 3 days at the suburban office; the CEO was there less often, and the VP of sales was almost always in the field.

The company had been in existence for over 10 years when in May 2004 it was purchased by an investor group. The change of control marked a significant event for the company and its employees. Prior to the change of control, the company was managed by the owners, a husband and wife, for its cash flow to support their lifestyle. Most of the work in the company was the customized development of course materials. This customized approach implied that only 5 to 10 projects were sold and completed in a given year. Projects were managed in cross functional teams, and there was considerable direct contact with the clients by all involved. Projects were sold by the owners and then implemented by the team so there was little need for a specialized sales and marketing staff.

In May of 2004, the company was purchased by its current owners, three venture capital firms and its management team. The plan was to transform the organization into a growth company by implementing two changes: (1) staffing and training a sales organization to accelerate revenue growth, and (2) refocusing the production group toward the development of off-the-shelf products rather than the customized development that had been the company's mainstay. The leadership challenges faced by the company during this period of change are the focus of this study. Deep dive observations were made in June 2005, after the first year of new ownership, in December 2005, and in August 2006. With this as background, I now return to the case and describe the results of these observations. First, however, I describe the conceptual framework and methods used in the study.

OBSERVING ORGANIZATIONAL LEADERSHIP

It is common experience that in the human resources and leadership development fields, soft skills have traditionally been measured using survey instruments. Business results, in contrast, typically have been measured with firm or department level financial or operating outcomes. Neither measurement scheme, however, provides insight into the *mechanisms* that enable the achievement of business results. In particular, they do not recognize that results are achieved through dynamic interactions among people, and presumably, therefore, through the dynamic signaling mechanisms that are experienced as leadership. Unless people know what is expected of them as actors in a system and how they must act to achieve these ends, there will be no positive results. The field needs a direct measure of the process whereby individual agents receive and interpret the behavioral and decision making cues or signals that organize their local interactions and decisions and form them into a coordinated system of cooperating agents. Along the way the agents create value for themselves, other participants and for the organization.

Defining "Leadership Signaling in Complex Systems"

To address the need for organization level metrics of leadership influence, human organizations are assumed to exhibit characteristics that can be modeled using complex adaptive systems' (CAS) methods and tools—that is, they can be studied as non-linear dynamical systems composed of autonomous agents and exhibiting self-organizing and emergent properties (Holland, 1995; McKelvey, 2001; McKelvey, 2003; Prigogine & Stengers, 1984; Stacey, 1996; Thietart & Forgues, 1995). One of the properties of a CAS is the propensity to change from within, to reinvent itself through variation and recombination of its component parts. This property leads to coevolution at multiple levels—coevolution of the system with its environment on the one hand, and coevolution among the system's components, cooperating groups and/or individual agents on the other (Lewin, Long, & Carroll, 1999; Lichtenstein, 1995; McKelvey, 1999). The changing characteristics of individual agents impact the evolution of higher levels of functioning within the system, while the expressed characteristics of the system in totality impact the evolution of each of the smaller entities down the chain all the way to the individual agents.

Some have proposed that for an organization to be effective, its agents must be bound together through a complex signaling network among and between the agents making up the system (Hazy, 2006a; Holland, 2001). Signaling networks provide information about the system and its state within the environment. By sharing a common signaling network, individual agents receive a similar set of signals to cue aspects of their decision making and behavior, and in so doing, they experience a common system-level collective perspective; they experience being part of a whole. The signals received operate locally to cue, direct, and enforce cooperative behavior and to coordinate action and decision toward some purpose. The signaling network is bidirectional and multiplexed. It is bidirectional in that influence among agents is mutual, for the most part, although there are exceptions, like for example, some military commands. It is multiplexed in that the network incorporates and combines many disparate signals originating from multiples sources and transmits them to multiple destinations (Panzer et al., 2007).

An example of this signaling process has been described as "shared leadership" (Panzer et al., 2007), a special case of what is more commonly know as "peer pressure." Computer simulations have shown that when a parameter that measures peer pressure crosses a certain threshold value, cooperation toward a purpose can emerge among disinterested agents even when only a single agent's self interest is served by cooperation (Phelps & Hubler, 2006). Thus, on the receiving end of these signals, each agent processes the signal along with other information that is available. When leadership is strong, the agent is influenced or biased by these ambient signals as it determines its individual choices for action and decision. The specific signals and their strength may vary, but this leadership signaling process occurs regardless of the agent's position in the network or the agent's formal role.

Self-organizing forces *at the system level* that are perceived by an observer from outside the system, and leadership activities *at the individual level* that are perceived by the organization's members from inside the system, are merely two sides of the same coin. The organizing activities that occur to influence the behavior of agents are received by them as norms, goals, procedures and rewards and are interpreted by the organization's members as *leadership*. Agents follow leaders only in the context of this signaling network. The process is temporal and relates to influences operating on each agent's set of rules that govern its local interactions. If an agent's local interactions are being governed, the agent is being led. If an agent is influencing the rules of others, it is leading. These signals, if detected and measured by an observer could offer a picture of leadership patterns as organizations face and respond to various situations. Recording and understanding these patterns may help define variations in organizational leadership as the environment changes. More importantly, a better understanding of these patterns may eventually provide hints about which patterns are associated with success and which predict failure.

Leadership Signals Organize Complex Adaptive System

If one is to understand the influence of leadership on organizational outcomes, one must first understand in what activities the organization is engaged as a complex adaptive system. Hazy (2004) described an organization as a resource and information processing system of cooperating agents. Building on the idea of dynamic capabilities within organizations, Hazy described a framework, called the *leadership and capabilities model* (LCM), where resources and information are processed to sustain the organization and its members. Dynamic capability is defined to be "the capacity of an organization to purposely create, extend, or modify its resource base" (Helfat et al., 2006, p. 4); this concept has grown increasingly prevalent over the last 25 years as a theory of organizations (Dosi,

Nelson, & Winter, 2000; Nelson & Winter, 1982; Teece, Pisano, & Shuen, 1997; Barney, 1991; Hazy, 2004b; Peteraf, 1993).

Following March (1991) and others (Levinthal & March, 1981, 1993), Hazy (2005) argues that, due to the potential for change and uncertainties about the future, systems that explore the environment in search of new sources of energy or resources (i.e., new markets) increase the alternatives available to them and therefore tend to survive (Hazy, 2004a). By focusing attention and resources on potential opportunities, the system—or the agents within it—may have time to catalyze agent cooperation and the recombination of existing capabilities in anticipation of opportunities that could develop in the future (Phelps & Hubler, 2006). In this way, the system reinvents itself as it struggles to gain continued access to necessary resources. It processes information about itself and its environment in an effort to match its internal variety with the variety of environmental resources (e.g., markets) (Ashby, 1962). If it succeeds, it has adapted. During this process, the system redistributes resources to balance exploitation and exploration (March, 1991). By influencing payoffs to agents and biasing cooperation strategies, the agents in the system actively alter the direction in which the system is heading and may even change the system's basin of attraction—the dynamical state toward which the system tends over time (Dooley & Van de Ven, 1999; McKelvey, 2003).

As has been well described in the organization science literature (Barnard, 1938; Cyert & March, 1963; Simon, 1955), all of the above must be done through the cooperation of agents engaged in coordinated activities across time and space (Barnard, 1938). Complexity science tells us that these activities are organized through a bottom-up process wherein local rules govern these interactions. At the same time, because the interactions must be coordinated across time and space, a sophisticated signaling—a behavior cueing process—must exist (Holland, 1995). These local rules and the leadership signals that bias them over time are described in the next section.

Leadership and Capabilities Model (LCM)

A conceptual version of the leadership and capabilities model (LCM) is shown in Figure 14.1. For a system of human interactions to be a complex adaptive system, it must have two aspects: First, autonomous agents must interact in some form of coordinated action. Second, the agents and the sociotechnical arrangements of agents, resources, tasks, and knowledge must change, and to the extent they improve the system's ability to make use of the environment (Holland, 1995), these changes must be differentially selected and retained by the system in response to changes in the environment. The LCM posits that leadership is central to this process of change, variation, selection, and retention.

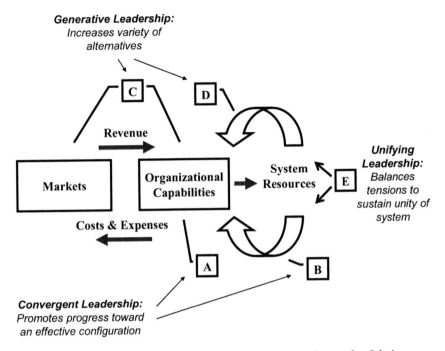

Figure 14.1.   Complex adaptive human systems support the needs of their members by building and maintaining capabilities that appropriate resources from the environment and store excess as system resources. Leadership mechanisms influence this process at five points of leverage, as indicated by A, B, C, D, and E, that are described in the text.

As the Figure 14.1 illustrates, Hazy (2006a) argues that when organizations act as complex adaptive systems, the influential increment of Katz and Kahn (1978) can be modeled as three distinct leadership mechanisms that collectively bias systems dynamics. They do this by exerting influence at five leverage points shown in the figure as A, B, C, D and E. The first two, A and B, support the convergence of the system toward an attractor that represents an effective configuration in light of known sources of resources. This is convergent leadership. The following two points, C and D, generate variety in the system and increase possibilities available within the system in the event environmental forces require adaptation. This is generative leadership. The final leverage point, E, balances tension within the system and performs activities that maintain the sense of unity and purpose for the system and its members as internal tensions ebb and flow. This is unifying leadership.

Convergent Leadership

Leadership operates to catalyze convergence within the system toward what is perceived by the actors to be a state that is more beneficial to them, one that represents a more deeply formed structural attractor basin in phase space. Cooperation like this dominates individual opportunism when the agents see their benefit to cost ratio as sufficiently large to overcome the cost of bringing along the other cooperating agents that may or may not add value (Nowak, 2006). In other words, leadership emerges to help members of the organization improve their cooperative effectiveness and to marshal the resources that are needed to achieve a purpose. The leadership mechanism does this by transmitting and reinforcing signals sent from some agents and received by others. Their effect is achieved at two leverage points in the system.

At the first point, "A" in Figure 14.1, leadership activities encourage members to expend their individual energy for the system's purpose rather than for their own (Barnard, 1938). They do this by creating the perception that the benefits of cooperation outweigh the costs. Recent research has identified the evolutionary mechanisms whereby cooperation emerges naturally in systems of autonomous agents such as cells, organisms, or societies (Nowak, 2006). In a recent computer model (Phelps & Hubler, 2006), it was shown that a bifurcation—what amounts to a phase shift—can occur in a social interaction dynamical system as agent activity changes from individual self-interested behaviors to a cooperating social structure. This occurs when peer pressure interacts with the self-interested action of even a single agent. When unspecified leadership activities were assumed to increase the "peer pressure parameter" gradually, a rapid shift in social structure occurred after a time delay. Effective leadership accelerates the system dynamics of this phase shift from individual to cooperative action.

This mechanism is what is implied by convergent leadership pressure point A in Figure 14.1. By co-opting additional agent energy in this way, as leadership pressure is increased, efficiency is likewise increased. Overall, production costs to the system are reduced, and the flow of resources from the system into its environment—for example, to the members in the form additional wages—is reduced. With coordinated action the system converges toward more efficient cooperative operation, as Barnard (1938) described, and ultimately with greater efficiency comes more resources available for the system's use. This is only true, of course, provided individual agents do not co-opt the resources for their own exclusive use.

At the second point of leverage, shown as "B" in Figure 14.1, leadership activities bias the flow of resources within the system to increase or improve the system's current capabilities. This involves attracting resources, such as investment in technology, human and intellectual capital, and other assets that increase the system's capacity and effectiveness at appropriating known resources and processing them for the system's benefit.

A recent laboratory experiment and computational model (Dal Forno & Merlone, 2006) demonstrated that differences in the specific leadership approach used to organize a group's activities were related to that group's differential success at accumulating resources, in particular, recruiting followers and resources to a project. System dynamics modeling has been used to demonstrate how a perceived "direction" or "vision" can become a catalyst to attract resources (Jacobsen & House, 2001) and how activities in support of an idea or a vision may be routinized over time into accepted cooperative practices that define human social capital to improve effectiveness (Davis, 2005). Thus, as the system converges toward an ever deepening attractor basin in a stable market, there is an increase in the level of resources available to the system. This remains true, of course, provided the system remains matched to the environment (Ashby, 1962) and available resources are not co-opted by opportunistic agents (Williamson, 1985) for their own account.

Generative Leadership

Leadership also operates to catalyze processes that continually renew the organization in the face of change. It does this by increasing the variety of alternatives available to the system, experimenting with new internal configurations of capabilities and exploring the environment for new resources (Surie & Hazy, 2006). By increasing the interaction complexity among these various parts of the system, generative leadership activities also tend to flatten or reduce the steepness of the system's perceived attractor basins (Dooley & Van deVen, 1999). This can also reduce the perceived benefit to agents and thus the basin of attraction associated with the various cooperation strategies available to them (Nowak, 2006). This flattening may enable a large scale change in the system's overall orientation, a "long jump" adaptation, as the system and its agents shift from one basin of attraction on the landscape to another. This capability is important particularly if the environment or the internal structural situation in the organization require it. Generative leadership creates the potential for change by exercising influence at two leverage points in the system.

At point C, shown in Figure 14.1, leadership can increase the flow of information within and across the organization's boundary. By encouraging individual agents to span boundaries and interact in new ways, leadership encourages learning, sharing of knowledge and experimentation. As long as the benefit to cost ratio remains greater than the number of other agents that are carried along in the event of success, this cooperation strategy forms a basin of attraction for its agents (Nowak, 2006). As the number of other agents increases, however, greater benefit is needed to maintain a relative basin of attraction and sustain the strategy (Nowak, 2006). On the other hand, computational modeling has shown that in turbulent environments organizations with boundaries that are more permeable to information may well be more adaptive than others (Hazy & Tivnan, 2003). As more information about the environment is imported into the system, the system has more possibilities for appropriating resources. As long as a basin of attraction for the cooperative strategy can be maintained through generative leadership, these models imply that when knowledge is changing rapidly, permeable boundaries enhance an organization's potential for survival.

At the fourth point, shown as "D" in Figure 14.1, leadership can bias the flow of the organization's resources toward nurturing opportunities that were identified in the learning and experimentation process. Generative leadership encourages cooperative strategies among agents that build new capabilities and address previously unknown opportunities. When new capabilities are built up over time, new sources of resources can be harvested in the environment, a critical component of adaptation. Computer modeling has shown that different communication styles by a single agent in a formal leadership role can have a lasting effect on the information flows in the system (Schreiber & Carley, 2006). A participative style (versus a directive style) increased information flow in all directions, distributes the demands of leadership among multiple agents and presumably increases collaboration and innovation as has been shown in case studies (Surie & Hazy, 2006). Closely matching the variety within the system to the variety of opportunity in its environment has the effect of increasing the adaptation possibilities for the system (Ashby, 1962).

Unifying Leadership

Finally, leadership operates to unify the system and to balance centralized control versus distributed control throughout the system (Solow & Szmerekovsky, 2006). In doing this, it balances the system's convergence and generative mechanisms. On the one hand, in relatively stable and predictable local environments—like functional groups deep within the organization, for example—agents within the system are organized by cooperative strategies that are converging toward a model of effective performance. This approach is often more easily coordinated within a centralized control structure.

On the other hand, in unpredictable and rapidly changing local environments, agents are drawn into a variety of different cooperative strategies, each with a relatively shallow basin of attraction. Flexibility is a key characteristic because the environment may change quickly and in unpredictable ways. This approach is more likely to be maintained with distributed, localized control that absorbs complexity from the environment and matches internal capabilities with emerging opportunities (Surie & Hazy, 2006).

As conditions in the environment are observed and interpreted by the system (Daft & Weick, 1984) the problem of balancing convergent and generative leadership patterns and of disambiguating potential outcomes becomes one of building and maintaining unity in a system with so much diversity. Unity and identity must be maintained both as it is perceived by its members and in reality. Such a system is increasingly stressed by distributed structural tension between efficient operations on the one hand and the need to change strategies in order to adapt on the other. For the system as a whole to test approaches and gather feedback from the environment, system level decisions which disambiguate multiple possible futures (that is make choices such as selling off business units or instituting new initiatives) are taken and feedback on success or failure is processed.

The unifying leadership mechanism does this balancing by exercising influence at a point, shown as "E" in Figure 14.1, in the system. For an organization to operate as a unity, agents operating within the unifying leadership mechanism must be able to take a system perspective to balance the points of tension inherent in the other four points of leverage described. These distributed leadership mechanisms respond to system level effects and manage the storage, distribution and use of system resources for the long and short term benefit of the system and its stakeholders.

During Intel's transformation from a memory company to a microprocessor company in the 1980s, senior management only recognized the change retrospectively and changed the company's espoused strategy. But the unifying leadership mechanism was working all along. This change in strategy was accompanied by a change in the company' senior management team, a reflection of the company's changing identity (Hazy, this volume). These changes reflect the operation of the unifying leadership mechanism even to the point of changing the company's CEO along with its identity. Computational modeling has been used to explore situations that favor centralized control by management versus the distributed control that so impacted Intel during that period (Solow & Szmerekovsky, 2006). Additionally, determining and changing boundaries, for example exiting the memory business in the case of Intel, are influenced by the biasing signals of the unifying leadership mechanism.

Recapitulating the Leadership Mechanisms

Together, the three leadership types acting on these five leverage points (and perhaps others) distribute multiplexed signals through the system to enable the leadership influential increment to guide the system as an entity with a unity of purpose. Under the influence of many multiplexed leadership signals the agents in the system are able to appropriate resources from the environment, support its member agents and other coevolving entities such as its customers and suppliers, and at the same time generate internal variety and possibilities. In this way, agent cooperation strategies and the system's internal capabilities adapt and coevolve with the environment.

For this study, leadership is defined to be, not a person or persons, but a multiplexed signaling network that promotes and regulates reciprocal cooperation strategies among autonomous agents. The present study demonstrates that these signals can be detected through even the crude instrumentation described in the next section. It also demonstrates qualitatively that the strength of several of the signals relate directly to observed effects in the organization.

METHODS

The present research involved a case study where a detailed analysis of an expansion stage, venture capital backed company was performed to identify and measure the leadership signals received by agents and to gauge their impact on local practices. The above described leadership mechanisms were assessed in the instrumentation. The intent was to understand how leadership signals are received at various points in the organization and how these signals change over time. To explore this issue, the case study design included three distinct deep dive phases at six month intervals. The data collected during these stages and the timeframe when it was gathered is summarized in Table 14.1. The various information sources are described below.

Interviews

At each stage of the study executives at the company were interviewed before surveys were administered to determine the mood of the organization and the perceptions of senior management. Over the project, executives and employees spent over 125 hours in interviews and discussion groups. The meetings with senior management provided a general sense of the organization, clarified issues and demonstrated for the researcher

Table 14.1.   Summary of Data Gathered

Subject	June 2005	December 2005	August 2006
CEO	Interview and survey	Interview, survey and team meeting	Interview and survey
COO	Interview and survey	Survey and team meeting	Interview and survey
CTO	Interview and survey	Survey and team meeting	Survey and group interview
VP Sales	Survey	Survey and team meeting	Interview and survey
CFO	Interview and survey	Survey and team meeting	Interview and survey
Middle Management	Survey	Survey and team meeting	Survey and group interview
Development and Production	Survey	Survey and team meeting	Survey and group interview
Sales, Marketing and Customer Support	Survey	Survey and team meeting	Survey
Other			Archival Document Review May 2005 through Sept 2006

the limits to understanding that members of senior management were forced to accept in the normal course of business. This was an important context for determining the incremental value of the information provided by the survey instrument.

Surveys

A survey was created specifically for this study based upon the leadership signaling framework proposed by Hazy (2006b) and summarized in a prior section. The survey was based upon the twenty cells Hazy suggested that are shown in Table 14.1. The survey and its administration are described below.

The survey was designed and developed to measure the strength of received signals without regard to a particular individual's position in the organization.[2] All employees, including executives, were surveyed three times at 6 month intervals. In effect, everyone, regardless of position, was considered to be a follower of an evolving leadership mechanism. The surveys were administered online by an independent consulting firm. Only aggregate results were shared with the company to preserve anonymity. For all three surveys, the response rate exceeded 90%. Other pertinent details are provided in the results section.

Before being used for the study, the survey was piloted with a panel of 45 human resource professionals, business professionals, and students. Comments were gathered and suggested clarifications were incorporated into the survey instrument. The final survey was loaded into a Web-based online service to be administered. As this was a study to test the potential usefulness of the Hazy (2006b) framework and not the instrument per se, no addition effort beyond the pilot was made to validate the instrument.

The survey was used to gather perceptions from all individuals at various locations within the organization. The questions were aimed at measuring leadership signals received by employees without specifying whether the signals were received from the CEO, executive management, middle management, peers or subordinates (see Table 14.2). In other words, what was detected was the ambient strength of a generic leadership signal field that was perceived to be influencing local decisions and interaction rules, without regard to its origin.

Because a high response rate was critical, the survey itself was designed to minimize the time it took to respond. In addition to a few demographic and general questions, 20 questions, one for each cell in the 5 x 4 matrix suggested by Hazy (2006b) and shown in Table 14.2, were asked. In particular, the five value levers and four cultural cornerstones described by Hazy provided a convenient way to systematically identify how effectively the leadership cues were being distributed throughout the organization and to what effect. Measuring the signal level in each of these 20 cells constitutes the measurable social effects of the embedded leadership metacapability of the organization.

Finally, for each question, survey respondents had the opportunity to offer additional comments or to expound on their response. General comments were possible as well. All comments were complied and analyzed along with the quantitative data.

Group Meetings and Discussions

At the midway point in the study, in January 2006, an all-employee meeting was held and the survey results were shared and discussed. Little in the way of follow-up initiatives resulted. As a final stage in data gathering, in August and September 2006, small group meetings were held with middle management and with the entire production group to clarify concerns and to better understand the survey results. Each of these meetings included 9 to 15 employees and lasted about 3 hours.

Table 14.2. Metrics to Monitor Leadership Cues Distributed Throughout the Organization

| | Cultural Aspects | | | |
Value Creating Levers	Common Understanding of Strategy and Roadmap	Member Engagement and Commitment to Participate	Decision Quality and Timeliness	Execution Norms That Match Capabilities to the Environment
Agents work for collective benefit, not their own	Does leadership make the expectations for each individual clear and provide a roadmap to meet them?	Has leadership engaged people mentally and emotionally to be committed to the organization's goals?	Does leadership make and require timely, quality decision making?	Does leadership enable thoughtful execution that includes adjusting to change while still meeting objectives?
Improve process effectiveness and teamwork	Does leadership clearly describe what is expected of each work group and how this fits into the organization's overall efforts?	Are members engaged in their teams/work groups and committed to improving their processes?	Are team members empowered by an effective decision-making context in and around their teams?	Do team members operate within an effective execution environment that adjust to change but meets commitments?
Learn and share information	Where appropriate, does leadership make learning and knowledge sharing expectations clear?	As appropriate, are members intellectually engaged in learning and sharing ideas?	Does learning and sharing of knowledge inform the decision-making process in the organization?	Do learning and sharing of knowledge about the environment and about internal capabilities come together during execution?
Nurture new ideas such as variations or recombinations of capabilities	Where appropriate, does leadership clearly support and set customer-oriented objectives for some potentially risky ideas that have promise, and *stop* others?	As appropriate, are team members personally engaged side by side with senior management to nurture ideas to launch?	Do team members feel that decision making on new idea initiatives is culturally fast-paced, fact-based, and appropriate for the situation?	Do team members feel that execution on new idea initiatives is culturally customer needs focused, iterative, and flexible as appropriate for the situation?
Balance resource allocation and risk	Do members feel there are clear and consistent strategies and objectives to provide context cues when weighing performance and risk?	As appropriate, are members personally engaged in risk assessment, performance analysis, and forecasting when allocating resources?	Do team members feel that decision making is timely and fair and based upon consistent objective indicators?	Do team members feel that execution plans systematically eliminate risks and appropriately allocate resources?

Document Review

In addition to primary data gathered from the management and the employees, the researcher had access to financial results and plans, board of directors presentations, and all other information that was requested and was available. This was important in understanding the underlying business context under which leadership was being conducted.

RESULTS AND ANALYSIS

The results of this data collection and qualitative analysis are described below. Because this study was intended to detect leadership signaling and interpret the results qualitatively, statistical analysis of the survey results was not performed.

General Observations

One important general inference from the interview process was that the baseline data clearly showed that even though the organization was apparently of a manageable size, particularly compared with much larger organizations—it ranged from 44 to 50 people at different times during the study—in general, senior management's perceptions contained little detail about how well their leadership efforts were getting through to the employees. In addition, senior management possessed little information that was specific enough to be actionable. Senior managers sensed the mood, some more correctly than others, but had little idea of what it meant with regard to business results or how they might proactively address the situation. For example, early in the study there was a generalized sense that things were going well, and the survey confirmed that they were. By the time the last survey was conducted, there was a sense that things were no longer going smoothly. There was even disagreement at the senior level about administering this survey for the third time—they did not really want to risk opening up a flood of discontent. Not all members of senior management were aware of this situation.

Interestingly, however, when the organizational climate grew worse—a perceived change verified by the survey results for the final period—rather than looking for and diagnosing systemic failings that could be corrected, the COO identified individuals in the production group as problem employees and labeled them "bad apples." There was a similar reaction by both the CEO and the COO to a negative turn in mood within the five person global services group, the group that worked closely with

customers on installation and support. In this case, however, the identified "bad apple" resigned soon after the survey and took one of her direct
reports with her. As is described in more detail below, an analysis of the
data does provide some support for the in situ management interpretation that "a few bad apples poisoned the barrel." There are some indications in the data that changes in the signaling network may have resulted
from the resonances in others that came about from the actions of the
"bad apples." Of course, these perturbations could also be considered
"bottom-up leadership" or perhaps "counter-leadership" actions that
contributed, perhaps positively, to a change in the formal leadership
structure. But causality is not established. Therefore, neither the interpretation of management nor the inference of intranetwork resonance is con-
clusive.

The Company as an Enterprise

Figure 14.2 shows the mean scores from the survey for the entire company at three points in time, June 2005, December 2005 and August
2006. This figure also shows how the survey data are graphically represented. The lighter the shading, the higher the signal level detected.
More directly, lighter shading means that respondents answered more
positively to the relevant survey question. Dark shading implies survey
responses where employees disagreed that the particular leadership signal was present and influencing their local interactions.

The inner ring of triangles represents the level of engagement felt by
the employees. Bright white implies a fully engaged employee along that
dimension, whereas a dark triangle identifies a disconnected employee
who is likely to act on his or her own account. The second innermost ring
represents the perceived quality of the decision environment. White
shading implies clear decision authority is perceived and timely and fact
based decision making is the norm. The darker the ring, the more
problematic decision making is perceived to be. The third ring from the
center represents confidence in operational execution within the
company, while the outermost ring reflects the clarity of the road map
that the employee believes he or she is to follow. White shading implies
absolute clarity of purpose and direction along the particular dimension.
As shading darkens there is increasing confusion and uncertainty. The
leadership mechanisms and levers of influence described in the prior
section are represented along the perimeter of the pentagon as shown in
the figure.

The data shown here are also available for each employee, for work
groups and for divisions in the company. That is, the strength of

leadership cues was measured for each agent and each component entity as well as the overall system. Eventually, the individual level of analysis will be used in studies of this kind. With the crude instrumentation currently in use, however, the signal to noise ratio is low at the individual level. For this reason, except for the illustrative individual level analysis described in the next section, qualitative inferences are made using only aggregate data for this study.

As can be seen from Figure 14.2, there was decline in the overall state of leadership over the study period. By looking at the dynamics of subgroups, the underlying drivers become apparent. Focusing on the Production group highlights the key issues confronted by the company.

The Production Group

Figure 14.3 shows the mean scores from the survey for the production group. The same data are also available for each employee, as is described

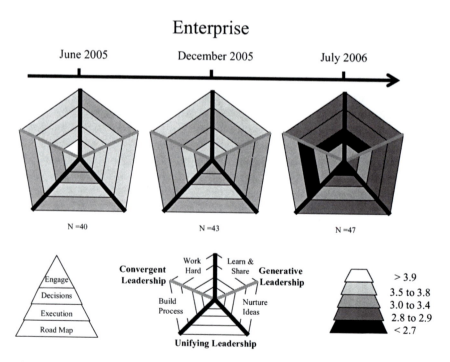

Figure 14.2.   Graphical representation of the decline in the strength of the leadership signaling mechanism over 13 months.

Production

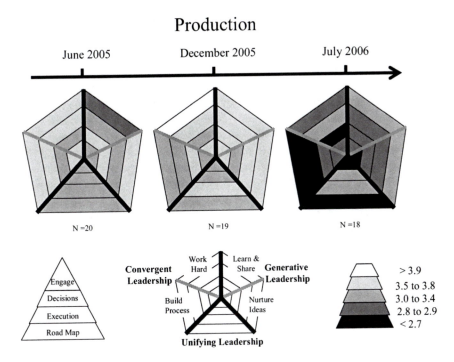

Figure 14.3. The decline in the leadership state perceived in the production group seems to indicate concerns about convergent leadership, perhaps related to the elimination of bonuses.

later using two examples. The figure shows three "snapshots" taken 6 months apart. As can be seen in the figure, in the first snapshot, June 2005, the most lightly shaded cells (implying high signal levels) are on the left side of the pentagon indicating that this group was receiving strong convergent leadership cues. The employees were thus encouraged to work hard for the firm and act to improve process effectiveness. Presumably, included in these high signal levels was the implicit belief that individual and team effort would be rewarded.

There was a concern for this group, however. In the June 2005 timeframe, there was a relatively low signal level cueing action and communications to enable learning and knowledge sharing among team members. In the figure, the darker shading on the right of the pentagon indicates a weakness in generative leadership signals. In a postsurvey interview, the COO interpreted this decline as a response to reduced customer interaction that resulted from the company's change in strategy. As the company moved from custom to off-the-shelf products, a change the organization called "fix the mix," developers were less involved in the creative, highly interactive aspects of product design. Perhaps, the COO reasoned, this sense of loss was reflected in the survey results.

The management of the company saw these results in July 2005. As such, they may have implicitly initiated programs to address this issue, although this was not indicated. In any case, modest improvement in these areas can be observed in the December, 2005 profile also shown in Figure 14.3. The cells just to the right of center under the heading "learn and share," in the figure, were mostly lightly shaded at that point. This change indicates that by December the employees reported receiving higher signal levels cueing behaviors that promoted learning and knowledge sharing.

The overall situation deteriorated by August of 2006. In an interview to explore the reasons behind the downturn, the COO indicated that annual performance bonuses were not distributed this year due to a "push to profitability." Although the lack of bonuses was communicated much earlier, as early as May 2005, the actual event occurred between the second and third survey. Giving bonuses or rewards tied to performance is a behavior associated with contingent reward leadership, a type of transactional leadership (Bass, 1985; Judge & Piccolo, 2004). As described earlier, these behaviors are a key aspect of all leadership, but in particular, of convergent leadership, which is represented on the left side of the August 2006 figure. The disillusionment with respect to contingent rewards can be seen as a significant darkening in the cells on the left side of the pentagon. By August 2006, it appeared that employees no longer trusted that rewards would follow engaged participation.

For illustration purposes, Figure 14.4 shows the data for two employees who were identified retrospectively by management as thought leaders; one was perceived to be a problem, the other a role model. The first was identified by the COO as a "bad apple" who joined the company after the first survey. The second individual in Figure 14.4 was identified as an informal leader who had been with the company for years and was considered a positive influence, a "role model" for the employees. As can be seen from these individual profiles, the signals that other agents reported were not "heard" by these two influential agents in the same way. The "bad apple" did not hear the leadership signals well at all, while the "role model" was much more positive than the mean.

The Sales Group

One of the anecdotal complaints among the employees was the emergence and persistence of functional silos between the production

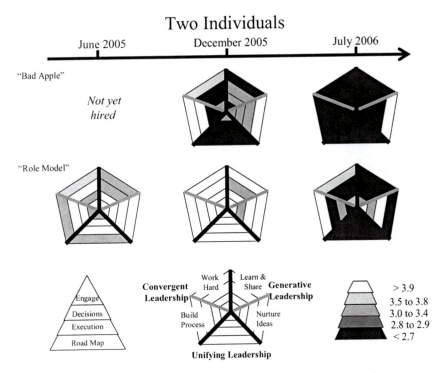

Figure 14.4.   The changing perceptions of two individuals' perceived by senior management to be influential; one "bad apple" identified retrospectively by management as a cause of the problem; the second a "role model" perceived by management to be an informal leader.

and sales groups. As can be seen in Figure 14.5, the divide is also evident in the data. The sales group remained positive throughout the study period although a moderate reduction in signal strength was observed in the final period.[3] Significantly, sales personnel were always paid on commission and therefore were not affected by the decision to discontinue bonuses. This may explain the continued high signal levels in the convergent leadership cells for the sales group.

Specific inferences can also be made from the data. Notable, for example, is the disproportional change in the decision making and execution signals received on the left side of the pentagon in the figure, that is, within the convergent leadership mechanism Perhaps, this represents the reduction in horizontal convergent leadership signal strength emanating from across the organization in the production group. Rather more extreme is the decline in perceived innovation leadership signals from the generative leadership mechanism, a phenomenon not nearly as apparent

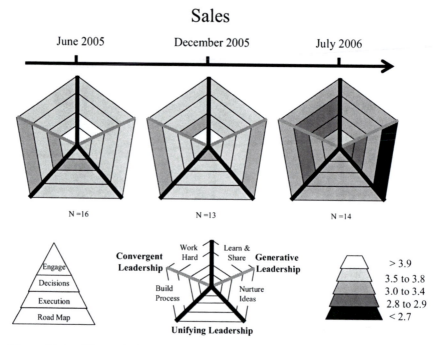

Figure 14.5.   The evolution of the sales organization indicates decline direction regarding the innovation aspects of generative leadership.

in the production group All of these effects, it could be argued, are observed resonances within the nonlinear signaling network that arise from the weakened signals within the production group. To the extent leadership mechanisms within production are observed to be fragmenting, Sales likewise experiences weakening or confusion in the multiplexed leadership signals they are receiving

Executive Team

The progression of leadership perception in the executive team is perhaps most telling, and it turns out, also perhaps predictive. As can be seen, the six person executive team began experiencing weakened signals in December 2005, before the same was observed more broadly in August of 2006. Although this was observed and communicated to the CEO and COO in December, it was discounted by them as reflective of impatience and frustration rather than an indication of trouble ahead.

These negative indicators are particularly telling in three areas: the execution dimensions of convergent leadership, the roadmap dimension of unifying leadership, and the innovation component of generative leadership. All of these showed a marked decline from June 2005 to December 2005, anticipating, and perhaps even predicting, similar declines across the broader firm 6 months later.

Post Script: Change of Leadership

After of the data for this study were gathered, but before all of the follow-up meetings were completed, the board of directors (BOD) and the CEO agreed it was best for all involved if the CEO would step down. The story given in explanation was that the absentee nature of management was perceived to be a growing problem, and because the CEO was not willing to relocate to the area, a replacement was needed.

The VP of sales and marketing, who along with the CEO was an investor in the business along side the venture capitalists, was temporarily given the title of president while a search for a new CEO was initiated.

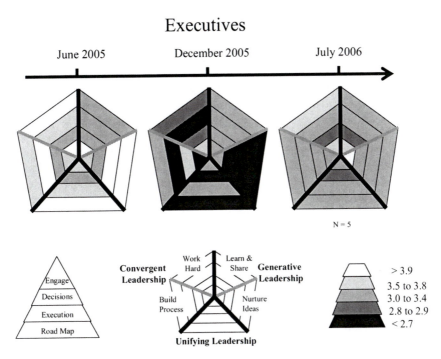

Figure 14.6. The executive perceptions of leadership state anticipated a decline in all three leadership mechanisms; subsequently Executives seem anticipate a turn around or are in denial.

The new president agreed to move to the area temporarily and to spend more time with the production group at the office location.

DISCUSSION

The case study described here chronicles the leadership story of a successful entrepreneurial company during a critical period. It follows the perceptions of employees for a period that begins at a point approximately one year after the company was purchased by a venture capital group and continues until the point when the CEO stepped down 14 months later. The data and analysis provide support for the usefulness of this approach to organization study. When leadership influence is measured as the multiplexed signaling network that promotes and regulates reciprocal cooperation strategies among autonomous agents, the effects of leadership can be detected and interpreted to useful effect. A result of this approach is a richness and clarity in the underlying dynamics of leadership influence that would otherwise be obscured by perceptual filters and individual judgment. By extension this analysis supports a research agenda that explores this approach further in an effort to refine and extend it.

Even with the primitive instrumentation used in the study new insights were gained that illuminate the actions of management and the board of directors. When the positive leadership pattern in the organization took a downturn between December 2005 and August 2006, the COO made two explanatory observations. First, that a few bad apples spoiled the barrel. Second, that the decision not to provide annual bonuses to the production employees (sales employees were always on commission rather than bonus plans) caused the mood change. The board, by their action to remove the CEO, seemed to believe that it was absentee management that led to the downturn. The data gathered and analyzed in this case study offer additional insights and alternative diagnoses and prescriptions.

Individual Versus Systemic Causes

The explanatory assertion of the COO—that unrest began with a few individuals and spread through the organization—may describe the pattern of diffusion observed in the data. There is insufficient evidence in the data to conclude one way or another with any confidence. However, one would expect that a pattern that begins with a few unhappy individuals and then spreads outward to include many others, would be observed in any case, although perhaps with different individuals as the first movers. How else would a new and potentially controversial interpretation of the environment diffuse and take hold within a group, particularly when it is contrary to the prior dominant one? As network theorists argue, a new consensus has to start somewhere and then diffuse through the network (Krackhardt, 2001). This pattern does not imply that the early adopting individuals are "the problem." If it was not them, then other agents would have defected from the dominant cooperation strategy.

Systemic failings may still be at the root. There are other indications that what happened at this company was indeed a systemic failing, facts that could not be explained by the "bad apple" theory. For example, as described earlier, the mood of the executive team turned negative at the same time the bad apples soured. And, the "role model," who was perceived to be a positive influence was actually a follower—at least with respect to the organization's mood—rather than a leader as management believed. If senior management was looking to him as a measure of the organization's mood, they were behind the curve rather than ahead of it. An alternative interpretation of events is that by assigning blame, senior management was using a management heuristic to act in the face of complexity and ambiguity. From a practical perspective, the tendency in humans to diagnose problems by assigning blame to individuals, to assign accountability, enables what is perceived to be decisive action in the face of apparent yet indeterminate failure. By assigning blame, actionable alternatives become clear. Personnel action of one kind or another can be implemented to "fix" the problem, at least *appear to* deal with the situation.

Another attractive explanation for the downturn was the decision to discontinue annual performance bonuses. Like the tendency to blame individuals, this explanation is incomplete. Indeed, it is common sense that if one's reward is not clearly contingent upon one's actions, motivation and the desire to cooperate would suffer. If no compensating changes in reward structures were made to counter balance the elimination of bonuses, one would expect a decline in leadership metrics, at least those elements associated with the contingent reward style of transactional leadership (Bass, 1985; Judge & Piccolo, 2004). This effect is most visible in the production group data. It can be seen as a darkening of convergent leadership signals on the left side of the pentagon between December 2005 and August 2006.

Observing this effect is not the same as saying nothing short of reinstating bonuses can be done to stem the decline, however. Complementary programs could have been initiated to amplify other aspects of the leadership signals that were weakened by the bonus decision. The data analysis described here offers a clear prescription for corrective action independent of a costly decision to reinstate the bonuses. Improving work conditions, for example providing additional flexibility in work rules, would reduce the perceived cost of cooperating and thus offset the perceived reduction in benefit. More directly, other forms of reward—such as peer recognition or compensatory time off for overtime—are other examples of compensating policies. Interestingly, according to management, these policies were already in place at the company. However, these very programs were suggested in the small group discussions as ways to compensate for the elimination of bonuses. It was clear from the discussions that flexible work arrangements were considered desirable as substitutes for lost bonuses, but although they were theoretically already in place, they were not perceived to be operating in practice.

The tendency to assign blame to individuals escalated rapidly culminating in the extraordinary step of changing CEOs. It seems that in these situations, the preferred solution to a difficult problem is to give the problem a face, "If you can't or won't solve the problem, I'll find someone who will." Although providing the appearance of clear accountability, this approach can also lead to a highly politicized environment where problems are denied rather than addressed and where success is "claimed" rather than actually achieved. Where individuals are blamed for systemic failings, the temptation is to assume a defensive posture to avoid blame and potentially the loss of position or status. Transparency into systemic problems like is provided in this study can provide a buffer against a culture that encourages such behavior. Additional insights can also be gained by looking more deeply into each leadership mechanism.

Convergent Leadership

As the organization shifted from a custom development shop to an off-the-shelf product development organization, there is an implied focus on convergent leadership as individual actions are redirected toward a new business model. Leadership's focus on convergence to this new model can be observed in the data. As shown in Figures 14.2, 14.3 and 14.5, before the downward trend in 2006, convergent leadership—as represented by the cells on the left side of each figure—was strongly felt by the organization's members in each of the subgroups surveyed.

For the production group, the primary leadership signals recognized— the lightly shaded cells—were those of convergent leadership. These signals were intended to catalyze the convergence of employee interactions and cooperation toward the off-the-shelf production model. This was particularly clear in December 2005 when the highest signal level reported implied that there was a clear roadmap for individual action. This timeframe corresponded to the official roll-out of the "fix the mix" program, which apparently provided a crystal clear roadmap for individual action.

At the same time, however, as the slight darkening of the build process cells in the profile reflects, there was less clarity—darker cells—around how the "fix the mix" initiative would impact work processes within the production group. The difference identified here is an example of the complex interactions among multiplexed leadership signals that must be considered in organizations. Changes to the roadmap can potentially create confusion about the definition of effective process, as seen here. By August 2006, the realization that bonuses would not be given was further evidence to the employees that leadership signals to catalyze process improvement were weak, as can be seen in the dark cells. Rewards of any kind were not believed to be tied to process improvements. As such, leadership toward process improvement was difficult for the employees to discern.

The sales group was being built up over the period under study. Their responses indicated a consistent high level of convergent leadership signals, although these too declined a bit in August 2006. Perhaps this change reflected confusion, or "noise," in the leadership signals coming from horizontal diffusion effects due to changes occurring in the production and global services groups.

The executive profile is perhaps the most telling. By virtue of the high status roles of executives, they occupy unique positions in the signaling network. First of all, the signals they initiate would most likely have higher initial signal strength than the signals of others. But perhaps more importantly in this case, executive managers also act as "repeaters" in the signaling network, amplifying the signals they receive while reducing ambient noise and crosstalk—transmission confusion caused by overflow among independent multiplexed signals—wherever possible. As can be seen in Figure 14.6, the convergent leadership signals that reinforce execution norms are dark in December 2005 as reported by the executive group. It is reasonable to suggest that the "repeater" function of executive management was not in force during this period. It is also a reasonable hypothesis that it is this weakness in the network—the lack of signal clarification and reinforcement by the top managers in the company—that is the root cause of the decline. As can be seen, by August 2006 the executive group was either attempting to rectify the problem, or they were in denial about the state of the system. In any case, they were severely disconnected from the mood of the company.

Generative Leadership

The generative leadership signals within the company catalyze activities that generate and nurture learning and new ideas. These went through a series of changes during the study period. Although there was a decline in responses from the production group, it was considerably less than the decline on the convergent leadership side. The most significant change in the perceived level of generative leadership signaling was on the sales side.

For the sales group, while convergent leadership was strong, declining a bit in August 2006, as a newly formed group, they were in a learning mode during this period. Generative leadership signals that encouraged interactions and identified new opportunities (Surie & Hazy, 2006) were also strong through December 2006. As can be seen, the clarity of the roadmap began blurring in December and by August 2006 was dark. From the sales group point of view, leadership was providing very little signaling as to how the sales employees were expected to build the innovation pipeline. This also affected their engagement in collectively building an innovation culture. Importantly, the decline in generative leadership signal levels was not simply a result of the overall decline in their mood at the company. The production group's view of innovation remained reasonably strong during this period. Something else was going on.

As described earlier, the executive group showed perceived signal weakness across the board in December 2005. The weakness in signals with respect to nurturing innovation is the most significant, being very dark in all areas except signals that lead to employee engagement. This same pattern had surfaced in sales by August 2006. There is a smaller affect in production. This implies that there are different dynamics at work within the two groups. Where in August 2006 the production group was not receiving convergent leadership signals, the sales group was not hearing generative leadership signals. Both of these situations were presaged by weak signals received by the executive team six months earlier.

Unifying Leadership

During the period under study, the company in question was changing its identity, changing its boundaries by adding and staffing a sales group, and changing its strategy to support the growth objectives of its new owners. These changes represent significant leadership challenges. Tugs and pulls on the collective identity of a group, changing boundaries, or changing rights and privileges of membership within an organization, all evident here, are dynamically organized by the unifying leadership mechanism.

For almost a decade the company had been family owned. In interviews, the long time employees fondly remembered how the owner and his wife ran the company as an extension of their family. The purpose of the enterprise was maintaining the owners' lifestyle, and the employees benefited from a nurturing environment. When the company was sold to professional investors, the firm's identity was bound to change. Its primary goal was now growth and shareholder value creation. After the transaction, the founder and prior owner stayed on for about a year to help smooth the transition. He had just left the company when this study began in June 2005. The organization's struggle with a change in identity was surfaced in the debriefing meetings as a part of the morale problem at the company.

The present analysis helps the observer to understand this assertion. At first glance it would appear that the employees' assertion was not valid. After all, the reported perceptions of unifying leadership signals remained positive, albeit only slightly so, through December 2005, several months after the founder left. Further, the two individual profiles shown in Figure 14.4 show that it was the new employee not the long-time employee who reported weak unifying leadership signals. At least in the Production group, it seemed as though the unifying leadership signals were coming through stronger for the long-time employees than for the new ones. Further, in the sales group, where all of the employees were new, the perception of unifying leadership was also positive, indicating a generally positive outlook among new employees as well. An alternative interpretation of these facts, however, is that the marginally positive responses resulted from halo effects from other causes. For sales, for example, new hires would be expected to remain positive for a honeymoon period, and for production, the results may reflect residual goodwill left over from the prior leadership regime. Indeed, a close review of the employee comments reveals that the employees did not feel involved in these things. There were few signals of this type present. They indicated that their positive answers reflected trust in management. They wanted to express support.

By December, however, little unifying leadership signaling was reported at the executive team level. By August 2006 this effect was visible across the company. The lack of executive commitment and the absence of proactive signaling to rebuild a new collective identity ultimately dampened any residual affects, any echoes from the past. This led to the meltdown in August 2006. Specific changes can also be seen in the data.

One major initiative of the new regime involved building a professional sales organization essentially from scratch. This was new to the company, and there were complaints among employees that silos were developing between sales and production. This concern can be understood as a boundary change for the organization. In the old regime, sales had always been managed safely from within the rest of the company, mostly by the founder. Members of the production group had been included in many discussions, deliberations, and other interactions with customers. The sales process had been informal, collegial, and collaborative. Now, with a professional sales organization, internal boundaries were established, and the external boundaries, that had previously only gently separated the developers from their customers, were hardened as production was relegated to the low profile back office. Boundaries between the firm and its customers were now less permeable (Hazy et al., 2004) to members of the production group. This change, as it became more obvious after December 2005, was not well understood and led to declines in the unifying leadership signals that were perceived.

In this short period, the organization's purpose had changed from the custom development of a few projects to support the owner's lifestyle to the development of off-the-shelf products that were sold by a professional sales team to fuel growth and create shareholder value for investors. This change of purpose was actualized as a change in strategy. Because of this change, unifying leadership should have been an important component of the leadership metacapability, but as the data show, in this case unifying leadership was not effective. This gap ultimately led to the crisis of confidence that culminated in a change in CEO. The analysis described here helps observers understand the underlying dynamics at work in companies like this one and suggests solutions to related problems that might arise in other organizations.

Future Research Directions

This case study demonstrates how useful a complex systems approach to leadership can be in both research and practice. By gathering and interpreting leadership signaling data researchers and practitioners alike can better understand the complex interactions at work within human organizations. Contrary to what is implied by the accountability heuristic applied by the Board at the CEO level, leadership is not simply a matter of what's happening at the top. The thoughtful observer seeks to understand how leadership signals are received, used, amplified, modified, and interpreted throughout the organization. Only with the proper diagnosis can targeted correctives be implemented.

As useful as this case analysis was, however, the analysis underlying this study is only a tentative beginning. Because the underlying dynamics that were uncovered are nonlinear and newly identified, it was not always clear to the researcher, or to the participants for that matter, what to make of the analysis, how to interpret the results, and what actions were indicated.

As was described, the participants reacted in much the same way they would have anyway, without the data: They blamed individuals for the organization's problems. Sharper resolution in instrumentation and more convincing arguments in the analysis are needed if this approach is to change the way accountable parties deal with complex organizational challenges.

To sharpen analysis of this type in the future, the constructs defined and the survey instrument itself should be further developed and validated. More importantly, however, researchers must develop better ways to analyze and interpret the data and compelling arguments for action that are based upon rigorous empirical results. One potentially fruitful avenue for this research strategy is to explore the "blame game" in the context of leadership signaling in organizational settings. When, if ever, is blame a useful heuristic? When is it potentially destructive?

Computational modeling could be a useful approach to more fully define and explore relevant variables and the interactions among them. A rigorously developed computational model could be used to dynamically predict various aspects of organizational performance. This work would enable researchers to clarify the nature of the dynamic processes at work, to determine methods to gather data and to form hypotheses to be tested in field experiments. Computer models could be fully specified in richly defined and documented case studies, wherein actual data would be used to populate the model. Alternative choices could be simulated computationally and the results validated in the actual organization. This would enable researchers to more completely specify the leadership/operations interfaces (for example, decision making) and the dynamics underlying their interactions. These critical interactions could then be further explored in enhanced agent models, wherein local interaction dynamics, within and external to the organization, could be more fully explored.

Field research is also needed to further develop this theoretical framework. Empirical studies could offer empirical support for the relationships encoded in computer models and used to support the analysis. Detailed case studies that focus on specific metrics and their interactions would be very useful. Survey instruments could be developed to measure the subfactors that make up the leadership signaling metrics described here. Results of this type would be useful in further field studies and would also potentially provide canonical inputs into ever more sophisticated computer models of organizational dynamics. Metrics could then be used in quantitative studies to determine the predictive power of the leadership and capabilities model (LCM) and other models in real world organizations. Most importantly, both of these methods could be combined, so that a model-based cumulative science of organizational leadership could become a reality.

NOTES

1. The specific characteristics of the company are altered in this description to maintain anonymity but these changes do not alter the substance of the observations in any way.
2. Respondents answered questions on a scale ranging from 1, indicating that the respondent strongly disagreed with a statement indicating that the signal was present, to 5 indicating that he or she strongly agreed with the statement. The complete survey is available from the author.
3. This figure does not include the five person global service group which had a profile closer to the production group.

REFERENCES

Ashby, W. R. (1962). Principles of the self-organizing system. In H. V. Foerster & G. W. Zoph (Eds.), *Principles of self-organization* (pp. 255-278). New York: Pergamon.

Barnard, C. (1938). *The functions of the executive*. Cambridge, MA: Harvard Press.

Barney, J. B. (1991). Firm resources and sustained competitive advantage. *Journal of Management, 17*(1), 99-120.

Bass, B. M. (1985). *Leadership and performance beyond expectations*. New York: The Free Press.

Cyert, R., & March, J. (1963). *A behavioral theory of the firm*. Englewood Cliffs, NJ: Prentice-Hall.

Daft, R. A., & Weick, K. E. (1984). Toward a model of organizations as interpretation systems. *Academy of Management Review, 9*(2), 284-295.

Dal Forno, A., & Merlone, U. (2006). The emergence of effective leaders: A experimental and computational approach. *Emergence: Complexity and Organization, 8*(4), 36-51.

Davis, J. N. (2005). *How is charisma routinized? A new look at an old question*. Unpublished dissertation, Texas Tech University, Lubbock.

Dooley, K. J., & Van de Ven, A. H. (1999). Explaining complex organizational dynamics. *Organization Science, 10*(3), 358-375.

Dosi, G., Nelson, R. R., & Winter, S. G. (Eds.). (2000). *The nature and dynamics of organizational capabilities*. Oxford: Oxford University Press.

Hazy, J. K. (2004a). *A leadership and capabilities framework for organizational change: Simulating the emergence of leadership as an organizational meta-capability*. Unpublished Dissertation, The George Washington University, Washington, DC.

Hazy, J. K. (2004b, June). *Leadership in complex systems: A meta-level information processing capabilities that bias exploration and exploitation*. Paper presented at conference of the North American Association of Computational Social and Organization Science, Carnegie Mellon University, Pittsburg, PA.

Hazy, J. K. (2006a, June). *Emergent signaling networks in complex socio-technical systems: How cooperative interactions among agents contribute to system sustainability.* Paper presented at the North American Association of Computational Social and Organization Science, University of Notre Dame, South Bend, Indiana.

Hazy, J. K. (2006b). Measuring leadership effectiveness in complex socio-technical systems. *Emergence: Complexity and Organization (E:CO), 8*(3), 58-77.

Hazy, J., & Tivnan, B. F. (2003, December). Simulating agent intelligence as local network dynamics and emergent organizational outcomes. In S. Chick, P. J. Sanchez, D. Ferrin, & D. J. Morrice (Eds.), *Proceedings of 2003 Winter Simulation Conference* (pp. 1774-1778). New Orleans, LA: INFORMS College of Simulation.

Hazy, J., Tivnan, B. F., & Schwandt, D. R. (2004). Permeable boundaries in organizational learning: Computational modeling explorations. *InterJournal Complex Systems, 1063,* 1-8.

Helfat, C. E., Finkelstein, S., Mitchell, W., Peteraf, M. A., Singh, H., Teece, D. J., et al. (2006). *Dynamic capabilities: Understanding strategic change in organizations* (1st ed.). New York: Blackwell.

Hernes, G. (1998). Real virtuality. In P. Hedström & R. Swedberg (Eds.), *Social mechanisms: An analytical approach to social theory* (pp. 74-101). Cambridge, England: Cambridge University Press.

Holland, J. H. (1975). *Adaptation in natural and artificial systems.* Cambridge, MA: The MIT Press.

Holland, J. H. (1995). *Hidden order: How adaptation builds complexity.* Reading, MA: Addison-Wesley.

Holland, J. H. (2001). *Exploring the evolution of complexity in signaling networks.* Retrieved August 22, 2002, 2002, from http://www.santafe.edu/sfi/publications/wplist/2001

Jacobsen, C., & House, R. J. (2001). Dynamics of charismatic leadership: A process theory, simulation model, and tests. *The Leadership Quarterly, 12*(1), 75-112.

Judge, T. A., & Piccolo, R. F. (2004). Transformational and transactional leadership: A meta-analytic test of their relative validity. *Journal of Applied Psychology, 89*(5), 755-768.

Katz, D., & Kahn, R. L. (1978). *The social psychology of organizations* (2nd ed.). New York: Wiley.

Krackhardt, D. (2001). Chapter 8: Viscosity models and the diffusion of controversial adaptations. In A. Lomi & E. R. Larsen (Eds.), *Dynamics of organizations: Computational modeling and organizational theories* (pp. 243-269). Menlo Park, CA: AAAI Press/MIT press.

Levinthal, D. A., & March, J. G. (1981). A model of adaptive search. *Journal of Economic Behavior and Organization, 2,* 307-333.

Levinthal, D. A., & March, J. G. (1993). The myopia of learning. *Strategic Management Journal, 14,* 95-112.

Lewin, A. Y., Long, C. P., & Carroll, T. N. (1999). The coevolution of new organization forms. *Organization Science, 10*(5), 535-550.

Lichtenstein, B. B., Uhl-Bien, M., Marion, R., Seers, A., Orton, J. D., & Schreiber, C. (2006). Complexity leadership theory: An interactive process on leading in complex adaptive systems. *Emergence: Complexity and Organization (E:CO)*, *8*(4), 2-12.

Lichtenstein, B. W. (1995). Evolution or transformation: A critique and alternative to punctuated equilibrium. *Academy of Management Journal, Best Papers Proceedings*, 291-300.

March, J. G. (1991). Exploration and exploitation in organizational learning. *Organization Science, 2*(1), 71-87.

Marion, R., & Uhl-Bien, M. (2001). Leadership in complex organizations. *Leadership Quarterly, 12*(4), 389.

McKelvey, B. (1999). Avoiding complexity catastrophe in coevolutionary pockets: Strategies for rugged landscapes. *Organization Science, 10*(3), 294-321.

McKelvey, B. (2001). What is complexity science: It is really order-creation science. *Emergence, 3*(1), 137-157.

McKelvey, B. (2003). Emergent order in firms: Complexity science vs. the entanglement trap. In E. Mitleton-Kelly (Ed.), *Complex Systems and evolutionary perspectives of organizations: Applications of complexity theory to organizations*. Oxford: Pergamon.

Nelson, R. R., & Winter, S. G. (1982). *An evolutionary theory of economic change*. Cambridge, MA: The Belknap Press of Harvard University Press.

Nowak, M. A. (2006). Five rules for the evolution of cooperation. *Science, 314*, 1560-1563.

Panzer, C., Hazy, J. K., McKelvey, B., & Schwandt, D. R. (2007). The paradox of complex organizations: Leadership as integrated influence. In J. K. Hazy, J. Goldstein, & B. B. Lichtenstein (Eds.), *Complex systems leadership theory* (pp. 299-320). Mansfield, MA: ISCE.

Peteraf, M. A. (1993). The cornerstones of competitive advantage. *Strategic Management Journal, 14*(3), 179-191.

Phelps, K. C., & Hubler, A. W. (2006). Towards an understanding of membership and leadership in youth organizations: Sudden changes in average participation due to the behavior of one individual. *Emergence: Complexity and Organization, 8*(4), 28-35.

Prigogine, I., & Stengers, I. (1984). *Order out of chaos: Man's new dialogue with nature*. New York: Bantam Books.

Schreiber, C., & Carley, K. M. (2006). Leadership style as an enabler of organizational complex functioning. *Emergence: Complexity and Organization, 8*(4), 61-76.

Solow, D., & Szmerekovsky, J. G. (2006). The role of leadership: What management science can give back to the study of complex systems. *Emergence: Complexity and Organization, 8*(4), 52-60.

Surie, G., & Hazy, J. K. (2006). Generative leadership: Nurturing innovation in complex systems. *Emergence: Complexity and Organization (E:CO), 8*(4), 13-26.

Simon, H. A. (1955). A behavioral model of rational choice. *Quarterly Journal of Economics, 69*(1), 99-118.

Stacey, R. (1996). Management and the science of complexity: If organizational life is nonlinear, can business strategies prevail? *Research Technology Management, 39*(3), 8-10.

Teece, D. J., Pisano, G., & Shuen, A. (1997). Dynamic capabilities and strategic management. *Strategic Management Journal, 18*(7), 509-533.

Thietart, R. A., & Forgues, B. (1995). Chaos theory and organization. *Organizational Science, 6*(1), 19-31.

Williamson, O. E. (1985). *The economic institutions of capitalism.* New York: The Free Press.

ABOUT THE AUTHORS

Kathleen M. Carley, professor of computer science, Institute for Software Research, Carnegie Mellon University (kathleen.carley@cs.cmu.edu). Kathleen received her PhD from Harvard in mathematical sociology. Her research combines computer science and social science techniques to address problems in social and dynamic networks, organizational change, team design, counterterrorism and bioterrorism. She has developed a number of technologies including ORA, a statistical toolkit for analyzing and visualizing multidimensional networks, and AutoMap, a text-mining system for extracting semantic networks from texts and then extracting the social networks from those. In addition she had developed multiple large-scale multiagent network models including BioWar, a city-scale dynamic-network agent-based model for understanding the spread of disease and illness due to natural epidemics, chemical spills, and weaponized biological attacks and Construct a model of information diffusion and network evolution.

Craig Crossland, PhD candidate, Management & Organization Department, Smeal College of Business, Pennsylvania State University (crc198@psu.edu). Craig is a doctoral candidate in strategic management at Pennsylvania State University. His research interests lie in the areas of managerial discretion, institutional theory, and social networks. Craig is quietly hopeful that this paper heralds the start of a long and productive academic career.

Kevin J. Dooley, professor, Department of Supply Chain Management, W.P. Carey School of Business, Arizona State University (kevin.dooley

417

@asu.edu). Dr. Dooley is a world-known expert in the application of complexity science to organizations. He has published over 100 research articles and coauthored an award winning book, *Organizational Change and Innovation Processes*. He has coauthored two patents concerning Centering Resonance Analysis, a novel form of network text analysis, and is cofounder and CEO of Crawdad Technologies, LLC. Crawdad provides text mining software and services for applications in market research. He has a PhD in mechanical engineering from the University of Illinois.

Dennis Duchon (dduchon@utk.edu) is a distinguished professor of management at The University of Tennessee. He received his PhD from the University of Houston. His publications have appeared in *Journal of Applied Psychology, Organizational Behavior and Human Decision Processes, Journal of Management, MIS Quarterly, Journal of Management Studies, The Leadership Quarterly*, among others. His research interests include decision making in organizations, work motivation, leadership, and complexity science.

Jeffrey Goldstein, professor in the Department of Management, Marketing, and Decision Sciences, Adelphi University (goldstei@adelphi.edu). He is also an Associate clinical professor at the Derner Institute for Advanced Psychological Studies at Adelphi. Dr. Goldstein is director of research for the School of Business and in 2000 was a visiting professor at the NATO Advanced Studies Institute on Nonlinear Dynamics held in Moscow, Russia. Dr. Goldstein is coeditor-in-chief of the journal *Emergence: Complexity and Organization*, a board member of the journal *Nonlinear Dynamics, Psychology, and Life Sciences*, and is on the science advisory board of the Plexus Institute. Jeff is the author of numerous scholarly publications and has made presentations and led workshops throughout the world at leading businesses, universities, and other institutions.

James K. Hazy, associate professor of management, marketing and decision science, Adelphi University School of Business (hazy@adelphi.edu). Dr. Hazy has over 25 years of executive experience at AT&T, Ernst & Young and start-up businesses with roles such as EVP of business operations, CFO, vice president financial planning and analysis and director of M&A. At Leadership Science, LLC he advised firms like Eastman Chemical, American Electric Power and numerous entrepreneurial businesses. He teaches entrepreneurship and management to undergraduate, graduate and executive students. His doctorate is with distinguished honors from George Washington University and his MBA in finance with distinction from the Wharton School. He has published numerous journal articles and chapters and is coediting two books on complexity and leadership.

Martin Kilduff, Kleberg/King Ranch Centennial Professor of Management at the University of Texas at Austin McCombs School of Business (mjkilduff@gmail.com). Dr. Kilduff received his PhD at Cornell and currently serves as editor of *Academy of Management Review*. His work focuses on social networks including the book (coauthor Wenpin Tsai) *Social Networks and Organizations* (Sage, 2003); and the recent coauthored articles "A paradigm too far? A dynamic stability reconsideration of the social network research program" *AMR*, 2006 (with Wenpin Tsai and Ralph Hanke); "Deconstructing diffusion: An ethnostatistical examination of *Medical Diffusion* network data reanalyses" *Organizational Research Methods*, 2007 (with Hongseok Oh); and "Emotion helpers: The role of high positive affectivity and high self-monitoring managers," *Personnel Psychology*, forthcoming (with Ginka Toegel and Narasimhan Anand).

Benyamin B. Lichtenstein, assistant professor of management and entrepreneurship in the Management/Marketing department at the University of Massachusetts in Boston (B.Lichtenstein@umb.edu). His research utilizes insights from complexity science to explore the dynamics of entrepreneurship, leadership, and organizational change. In addition he is exploring how organizational learning can catalyze successful interorganizational collaborations for sustainability. Since receiving his PhD from Boston College, Benyamin has published over 40 journal articles, proceedings, and book chapters, including articles in *Organization Science, Journal of Business Venturing*, and *Academy of Management Executive*, where he received the "Article of the Year" award in 2000.

Robert G. Lord, distinguished professor, Department of Psychology, University of Akron (rlord@uakron.edu). Dr. Lord earned his BA in economics from the University of Michigan and his PhD in industrial/organizational psychology from Carnegie Mellon University. His research has focused on complexity theory, neural networks and information processing, implicit leadership theories, leadership categorization theory, the role of follower identities in the leadership process, leadership and emotions, self-regulation and motivation, and the development of leadership skills. He has published widely in the leadership field and has coauthored books on *Leadership and Information Processing* (with Karen Maher) and *Leadership Processes and Follower Self-Identity* (with Doug Brown).

Russ Marion, professor in Department of Educational Leadership, Clemson University (marion2@clemson.edu). Dr. Marion is author of a number of books and articles on leadership and complexity theory, including *The Edge of Organization, Leadership in Education*, and "Leadership in Complex Organizations" (*The Leadership Quarterly*). He recently coedited a special issue of complexity leadership for *The Leadership Quarterly* and serves on the editorial board of that journal. He coorganized two workshops on complexity leadership at the Center for Creative Leadership and George Washington University in 2005. Russ has presented on complexity leadership at the India Institute of Technology, the Institute for Management Development in Switzerland, and in workshops on destructing complex movements at the U.S. Department of Defense.

Bill McKelvey, professor of strategic organizing and complexity science, Department of Human Complex Systems and Computational Social Science, UCLA Anderson School of Management (mckelvey@anderson .ucla.edu). Dr. McKelvey (PhD, MIT, 1967) is a leading scholar in the area of complexity and organization. His book, *Organizational Systematics* (1982) remains a definitive treatment of organizational taxonomy and evolution. He chaired the building committee that produced the $110,000,000 Anderson Complex. He directed over 170 field study teams on strategic improvements to client firms. In 1997 he initiated activities leading to the founding of UCLA's Center for Human Complex Systems & Computational Social Science. Dr. McKelvey has coedited *Variations in Organization Science* (1999) and special issues of *Emergence* (now *E:CO*) and *JIT*. He has 55 papers on complexity science applied to organizations and management.

Andrzej Nowak is professor of psychology and director of the Center for Complex Systems, Institute for Social Systems, at the University of Warsaw (andrzej.nowak@psych.uw.edu.pl). He holds appointments in the Department of Psychology at Florida Atlantic University and the Department of Social Psychology on Internet Technology and Communication at the Warsaw School of Social Psychology. He has written four books and numerous articles on psychology, and is a leading expert in the area of dynamical social psychology.

Donde Ashmos Plowman (dplowman@utk.edu) is a distinguished professor of management at The University of Tennessee. She received her PhD from The University of Texas at Austin. Her publications have appeared in *Academy of Management Journal, Academy of Management Review, The Leadership Quarterly, Decision Sciences, Journal of Management Studies, Health Services Research*, among others. Her current research interests include organizational change, leadership, decision making, interpretation, and participation in complex adaptive systems.

Craig Schreiber, (craigschreiber.acad@gmail.com) research associate, National Research Council. Craig recently received his PhD in computation, organizations and society from Carnegie Mellon University and was a member of the Center for Computational Analysis of Social and Organizational Systems. He is currently a NRC research associate working for the Army Research Laboratory in the field of dynamic network analysis. His current research is focused on network leadership and organizational adaptation.

David R. Schwandt, professor of organizational studies, The George Washington University Graduate School of Education and Human Development, Department of Counseling and Human and Organizational Studies (schwandt@gwu.edu). Dr. Schwandt is the former director of the Executive Leadership Doctoral Program and the Center for the Study of Learning. His current research involves organizational issues that relate to collective cognition, complex adaptive systems, and organization development. Specific areas of inquiry include organizational learning, strategy development and implementation, collective sensemaking and organizational change. Before joining the faculty, he served as the director of organizational development at the United States General Accounting Office. He is the author of several articles, book chapters, and a book related to the sociological aspects of organizational learning, strategy formulation, and managerial cognition.

Wenpin Tsai, associate professor of management, Department of Management and Organization, The Pennsylvania State University (wtsai@psu.edu). Dr. Tsai received his PhD in strategic and international management at the London Business School. His current research interests include social capital, knowledge transfer, network evolution, and cooperative and competitive interactions inside and across organizations. He has published a book on social networks (coauthor Martin Kilduff) and several articles on social capital and knowledge transfer in *Academy of Management Journal*, *Academy of Management Review*, *Strategic Management Journal*, and *Organization Science*. He was also a guest editor for a Special Research Forum on "Building Effective Networks" in *Academy of Management Journal*.

Mary Uhl-Bien, professor in Department of Management, Howard Hawks Chair in Business Ethics and Leadership, and associate director of the Gallup Leadership Institute, University of Nebraska-Lincoln (mbien2@unl.edu). Dr. Uhl-Bien has published articles on leadership (e.g., relational leadership theory, leader-member exchange, followership, and complexity leadership) in leading national and international journals, including *Academy of Management Journal, Journal of Applied Psychology, Journal of Management, Human Relations,* and *The Leadership Quarterly.* She is senior editor of the Leadership Horizons Series published by Information Age Publishing, and serves on the editorial boards of the *Leadership Quarterly* and the *Academy of Management Journal.* She has consulted with organizations, including State Farm Insurance, Walt Disney World, the U.S. Fish & Wildlife Service, British Petroleum, and the General Accounting Office.

Robin R. Vallacher, professor of psychology, Department of Psychology, Florida Atlantic University and Research Affiliate, Center for Complex Systems, Warsaw University, Poland (vallacher@fau.edu). Dr. Vallacher has research interests in a wide variety of topics in social psychology, from basic principles of social cognition, action identification, and self-concept to issues in social justice and social change. In recent years, his work has centered on identifying the invariant properties underlying these otherwise diverse phenomena. He and his colleagues are investigating the dynamism and complexity associated with such phenomena as self-regulation, social judgment, close relations, intergroup conflict, and the emergence of personality from social interaction. Dr. Vallacher has published five books, including two with Andrzej Nowak, that develop the implications of dynamical systems for social psychology.

Ellen Van Velsor is group director and senior fellow at the Center for Creative Leadership, Greensboro, North Carolina. She is coeditor of the *Handbook of Leadership Development* (1998, 2003), and coauthor of *Breaking the Glass Ceiling: Can Women Reach the Top of America's Largest Corporations?* (1987, 1991). Dr. Van Velsor has authored numerous book chapters and articles, including "Leadership Development as a Support to Ethical Action in Organisations" (*Journal of Management Development,* 2007), "Developing Organizational Capacity for Leadership" (Hooijberg, Hunt, Boal, & Antonakis, 2007), and "Constructive-Developmental Coaching" (Ting & Scisco, 2006). Her current research focuses on practices related to successful execution of CSR.